D0367735

The Dog Lover's Companion to Boston

**4TH
EDITION**

JoAnna Downey & Christian J. Lau

AVALON
TRAVEL

THE DOG LOVER'S COMPANION TO BOSTON
THE INSIDE SCOOP ON WHERE TO TAKE YOUR DOG

JoAnna Downey & Christian J. Lau

Published by
Avalon Travel Publishing
1400 65th Street, Suite 250
Emeryville, CA 94608, USA

Printing History
1st edition—1999
Fourth edition—January, 2007
5 4 3 2 1

Text © 2007 by JoAnna Downey & Christian J. Lau
All rights reserved.
Illustrations © 2007 by Phil Frank.
Maps © 2007 by Avalon Travel Publishing, Inc.
All rights reserved.
Illustrations are used by permission and are the property of the original copyright owner.

ISBN: 1-56691-972-X
ISSN: 1089-2737

Editor: Shari Husain
Series Manager: Kevin McLain
Copy Editor: Donna Leverenz
Graphics: Tabitha Lahr
Production: Elizabeth Jang
Map Editor: Kevin Anglin
Cartography: Kat Bennett
Index: Greg Jewett

Cover and Interior Illustrations: Phil Frank

Distributed by Publishers Group West

Printed in the United States by Malloy Inc.

All rights reserved. No part of this book may be translated or reproduced in any form, except brief extracts by a reviewer for the purpose of a review, without written permission of the copyright owner.

Although every effort was made to ensure that the information was correct at the time of going to press, the author and publisher do not assume and hereby disclaim any liability to any party for any loss or damage caused by errors, omissions, or any potential travel disruption due to labor or financial difficulty, whether such errors or omissions result from negligence, accident, or any other cause.

ABOUT THE AUTHORS

JoAnna and Chris have been friends ever since their dogs George and Inu introduced them in the Common years ago. In addition to this book, they are also the authors of *The Dog Lover's Companion to New England* and *The Dog Lover's Companion to New York City*, both published by Avalon Travel Publishing.

George and Inu passed away shortly after the production of this book. They will be missed and remembered very fondly. George was a mix of bearded collie, Tibetan terrier, puli, and Portuguese water dog—in other words, a "cannardly." While residing at Buddy Dog, an animal shelter, he picked JoAnna out of the multitudes and hitched a ride home. When he wasn't out sniffing trails and conducting research for his newspaper column, George loved to chase squirrels and bark at people.

Inu was proud of his heritage and carried his golden retriever lineage with style. Although an enormously social animal, Inu also loved the solitude of the Great Outdoors—a taste he developed while living in the Berkshires for the first three years of his life. Needing a home and deciding city life would provide the attention he so dearly loved, he traveled to Boston, adopted Chris Lau, and happily called Beacon Hill his own. When not out swimming or riding the surf, Inu could be found in the Boston Common working the crowd, looking for free pats, food, and adulation.

When JoAnna and Chris aren't exploring New England or discussing baseball in general, and the Red Sox in particular, JoAnna is a freelance writer and contributing editor to *Dog Fancy Magazine* and Chris works in the financial industry and is a full-time dad to his son Connor.

to George and Inu

CONTENTS

BOSTON

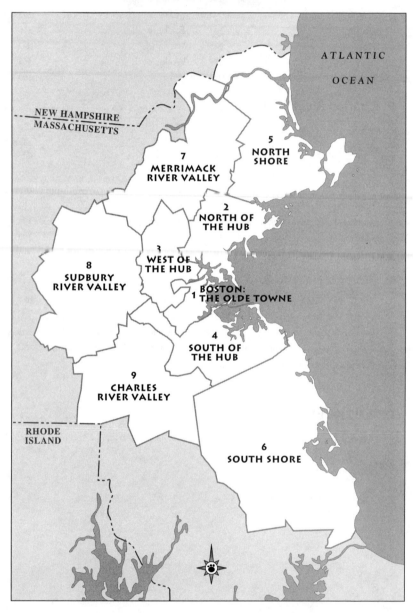

ATLANTIC

OCEAN

NEW HAMPSHIRE
MASSACHUSETTS

7
**MERRIMACK
RIVER VALLEY**

5
**NORTH
SHORE**

2
**NORTH OF
THE HUB**

3
**WEST OF
THE HUB**

8
**SUDBURY
RIVER VALLEY**

**1 BOSTON:
THE OLDE TOWNE**

4
**SOUTH OF
THE HUB**

9
**CHARLES
RIVER VALLEY**

RHODE
ISLAND

6
SOUTH SHORE

MAPS

Introduction

"Now, Charley is a mind-reading dog. There have been many trips in his lifetime, and often he has to be left at home. He knows we are going long before the suitcases come out, and he paces and worries and whines and goes into a state of mild hysteria, old as he is."

—From *Travels with Charley*, by John Steinbeck

There was a time when dogs could go just about anywhere they pleased. Well-dressed dogs with embarrassing names attended afternoon teas, while their less-kempt counterparts sauntered into taverns without anyone blinking an eye.

No one thought it strange to see a pug-nosed little dog snuggled on his mistress's lap on a long train journey. Equally accepted were dogs prancing through fine hotels, dogs at restaurants, and dogs in almost any park they cared to visit.

But as the world gets more crowded and patience grows thinner, fewer and fewer places permit dogs. As deep as the human-dog bond goes, people seem to feel increasing pressure to leave their dogs behind when they take to the open road.

The guilt that stabs at you as you push your dog's struggling body back inside the house and tug the door shut can be so painful that sometimes you just can't look back. Even a trip to the grocery store can become a heart-wrenching tale of woe.

John Steinbeck's blue poodle, Charley, was a master of powerful pleas that were carefully designed to allow him to accompany his people on trips. Eventually his hard work paid off, and he won himself a seat in Steinbeck's brand-new truck/house on their epic trip across America. They sought and found the heart of this country on their journey across 34 states.

The pleas whipped up by our dogs, George and Inu, aren't always as masterful as Charley's, but they can be devastatingly effective. When George, a shaggy, 30-pound bearded collie-terrier mix, gets the bad news that he has to stay at home, he tortures JoAnna by hiding behind the potted plant in the front hall. He slinks into the corner right by the front door, looking oh-so-pitiful, but refusing to disappear into the bedroom, thereby forcing JoAnna to pass him on her way out. And there he sits, peering pathetically between the scrawny branches, ears down and eyes mournful, silently pleading with her to change her mind. Inu, a golden retriever, uses a different tactic. He curls into a tight little ball and sinks way down onto the floor so that only his and puppy-dog eyes can be seen. The message is clear: How can you go out and have all that fun without me?

To avoid this doggy guilt, we've adapted our lifestyles to include our dogs whenever possible. We tend to rent videos instead of going to the movies. We take our dogs to the post office, the grocery store, the hardware store, and wherever else we can get away with it. We set out to learn which places in our neighborhood are dog friendly, and with this book we've taken things even further.

For *The Dog Lover's Companion to Boston*, we've tried to discover the best of everything you can do with your dog in the Greater Boston area. Along the way, we've met people and dogs we never would have known, talked to folks in jobs we never knew existed, discovered trails and towns that were once only names on a map, and best of all, allowed our dogs to lead us, instead of the other way around. George and Inu always seemed to know that out on the trail it was their job to teach us the hidden joys a particular park had to offer. We would never have experienced these places in the same way without them.

We found that although Boston and its environs are densely populated, there are many parks and conservation lands just outside the city that provide a slice of doggy bliss. And you'll find dozens of diversions where your canine pal can join you. Your dog can go on a harbor cruise, catch an outdoor movie, march in a pets-only parade, and make a lot of new friends, all with you tagging along. You can explore the little-known parks tucked away in each town and travel in style at the many hotels, restaurants, and outdoor cafés that welcome you and your dog. Our hope is that after reading this book, you'll find it even harder to close your door on that lovable little mug of hers; we also expect your dog's tail will be wagging on a regular basis. And we hope you'll learn things about Boston you never knew. We certainly did!

The Paws Scale

At some point we've got to face the facts: Humans and dogs have different tastes. We like eating oranges and smelling lilacs and covering our bodies with soft clothes. They like eating roadkill and smelling each other's unmentionables and covering their bodies with horse manure.

The parks, beaches, and recreation areas in this book are rated with a dog in mind. Maybe your favorite park has lush gardens, a duck pond, a few acres of perfectly manicured lawns, and sweeping views of a nearby skyline. But unless your dog can run leash free, swim in the pond, and roll in the grass, that park doesn't deserve a very high rating.

The very lowest rating you'll come across in this book is the fire hydrant symbol 🐾. When you see it, that means the park is merely "worth a squat." Visit one of these parks only if your dog just can't hold it any longer. These parks have virtually no other redeeming qualities for canines.

Beyond that, the paws scale starts at one paw 🐾 and goes up to four paws 🐾🐾🐾🐾. A one-paw park isn't a dog's idea of a great time. Maybe it's a tiny park with few trees and too many kids running around. Or perhaps it's a magnificent-for-people park that bans dogs from every inch of land except paved roads and a few campsites.

Four-paw parks, on the other hand, are places your dog will drag you to visit. Some of these areas come as close to dog heaven as you can get on this planet. Many have water for swimming or zillions of acres for hiking. Some four-paw parks give you the option of letting your dog off leash. Others have restrictions, which we'll detail in the descriptions.

You will also notice a foot symbol 👣 every so often. The foot means the park offers something extra special for humans in the crowd. You deserve something for being such a good chauffeur.

This book is not a comprehensive guide to all of the parks in the Greater Boston area. We've tried to find the best, largest, and most convenient parks. Some areas have so many wonderful parks that we found ourselves getting jaded. What would have been a four-paw park in one area looked like a mere two- or three-paw place after seeing so many great spots in another area. Other cities had such a limited supply of parks that for the sake of dogs living and visiting there, we ended up listing parks that wouldn't be worth mentioning otherwise.

Since street signs and signposts are often confusing in Massachusetts, we've given specific directions to all the parks. When you ask a Bostonian how to get somewhere, you'll most often get a look that says, "If you have to ask, you shouldn't be going there." Or you'll get scrambled and vague directions that result in your becoming hopelessly lost. Although we've tried to make it as easy as possible for you, we highly recommend picking up a detailed street map before you and your dog set out on your adventures.

To Leash or Not to Leash...

That is not a question that plagues dogs' minds. Ask just about any normal, red-blooded American dog if she'd prefer to visit a park and be on leash or off, and she'll say, "Arf!" (Translation: "Is this a trick question?") No doubt about it, most dogs would give their canine teeth to be able to frolic without that dreaded leash.

When you see the running dog symbol 🐕 in this book, you'll know that under certain circumstances your dog can run around in leash-free bliss. The rest of the parks demand leashes. We wish we could write about the places where dogs get away with being scofflaws, but those would be the first parks the animal-control patrols would hit. We can't advocate breaking the law, but if you're going to, please follow your conscience and use common sense.

And just because dogs are permitted off leash in certain areas, that doesn't necessarily mean you should let your dog run free. In state forests and large tracts of land, unless you're sure your dog will come back to you when you call or will never stray more than a few yards from your side, you should keep her leashed. A deer or rabbit that crosses your path could mean hours of searching for your stray dog. And an otherwise docile homebody can turn into a savage hunter if the right prey is near. In pursuit of a strange scent, your dog could easily get lost in an unfamiliar area.

Be careful out there. If your dog really needs leash-free exercise but can't be trusted in remote areas, she'll be happy to know that several beaches permit well-behaved, leashless pooches, as do a growing number of beautiful,

fenced-in dog exercise areas. Boston is a little behind other parts of the country in providing spaces where our four-footed friends can play unfettered, but it seems to be catching up.

There's No Business Like Dog Business

There's nothing appealing about bending down with a plastic bag or a piece of newspaper on a chilly morning and grabbing the steaming remnants of what your dog ate for dinner the night before. It's disgusting. Worse yet, you have to hang on to it until you can find a trash can. And how about when the newspaper doesn't endure before you're able to dispose of it? Yuk! It's enough to make you wish your dog were a cat.

But as gross as it can be to scoop the poop, it's even worse to step in it. It's *really* bad if a child falls in it, or—gasp!—starts eating it. And have you ever walked into a park where few people clean up after their dog? The stench could make a hog want to hibernate.

Unscooped poop is one of a dog's worst enemies. Public policies banning dogs from parks are enacted because of it. At present a few good Boston parks and beaches that permit dogs are in danger of closing their gates to all canines because of the negligent behavior of a few owners. A worst-case scenario is already in place in several communities—dogs are banned from all parks. Their only exercise is a leashed sidewalk stroll. That's no way to live.

If we had a nickel for every dog constable that listed violations of the pooper-scooper laws as the thing that made their job most difficult, let's just say we could quit our day jobs. Almost everyone we spoke to named unscooped poop as their number-one headache—and the thing most likely to make their towns ban dogs from public parks. Several town leaders told us the biggest pressure they have right now is what to do about the "dog problem" complaints they receive from local residents.

Just be responsible and clean up after your dog everywhere you go. Stuff plastic bags in your jackets, your purse, your car, your pants pockets—anywhere you might be able to pull one out when needed. Or if plastic isn't your bag, newspapers do the trick. If it makes it more palatable, bring along a paper bag, too, and put the used newspaper or plastic bag in it. That way you don't have to walk around with dripping paper or a plastic bag whose contents are visible to the world.

If you don't enjoy the squishy sensation, try one of those cardboard or plastic bag pooper-scoopers sold at pet stores. If you don't feel like bending down, buy a long-handled scooper. There's a scooper for every taste.

We've tried not to lecture about scooping throughout the book, but it does tend to be JoAnna's pet peeve. To help keep parks alive, we should harp on it in every park description, but that would take another 100 pages, and you'd start to ignore it anyway. And if we mentioned it in some parks and not others, it might convey that you don't have to clean up after your dog in the descriptions where it's not mentioned. Trust us. *Every* park has a pooper-scooper law!

Etiquette Rex: The Well-Mannered Mutt

While cleaning up after your dog is your responsibility, a dog in a public place has his own responsibilities. Of course, it really boils down to your responsibility again, but the burden of action is on your dog.

Etiquette for restaurants and hotels is covered in other sections of the introduction. What follows is some very basic dog etiquette. We'll go through it quickly, but if your dog's a slow reader, he can go over it again: No vicious dogs; no jumping on people; no incessant barking; dogs should come when they're called; dogs should stay on command; no leglifts on backpacks, human legs, or any other personal objects you'll find hanging around beaches and parks.

Everyone, including dogs, makes mistakes, but you should do your best to remedy any consistent problems. It takes patience, and it's not always easy. For instance, George considers it his doggy duty to bark at weird people—at least those he thinks are weird (and we hate to say it, but he's usually right). But that's no excuse. Strange folk or not, your dog shouldn't be allowed to bark at others unless they're threatening you or breaking into your house.

And Inu has this selective hearing problem. He only pays attention to commands when the wind is blowing a certain way (at least that's his explanation). Tell him to come one day, and he's right there. But when the breeze is blowing toward a certain great smell… well, it seems to cloud his usual good hearing. But "under voice control" means all the time. If your dog won't obey

you, fix the problem or put him on a leash. There are certain public behaviors that should not be tolerated in a dog. George and Inu are constantly learning their boundaries the hard way, and we're constantly learning to avoid situations that might make our sweet dogs look like canine delinquents. There's a limit to the "dogs will be dogs" adage.

Safety First

A few essentials will keep your traveling dog happy and healthy. When planning a trip with your dog, know his limitations. Some dogs are perfectly fine in a car; others get motion sickness. Some dogs happily hop in their traveling crates for airline flights; others are traumatized for hours. Only you know your dog's temperament. Here are some guidelines to consider before you hit the road:

Heat: If you must leave your dog alone in the car for a few minutes, do so only if it's cool out and if you can park in the shade. Never, ever, *ever* leave a dog in a car with the windows rolled up all the way. Even if it seems cool, the sun's heat passing through the window can kill a dog in minutes. Roll down the window just enough for your dog to get air, but so there's no danger of him getting out or someone breaking in. Make sure he has plenty of water.

You also have to watch out for heat exposure when your car is in motion. Certain cars, such as hatchbacks, can make a dog in the backseat extra hot, even while you feel okay in the driver's seat.

Try to take your vacation so you don't visit a place when it's extremely warm. Dogs and heat don't get along, especially if the dog isn't used to heat. The opposite is also true. If a dog lives in a hot climate and you take him to a freezing place, it may not be a healthy shift. Check with your vet if you have any doubts. Spring and fall are usually the best times to travel.

Water: Water your dog frequently. Dogs on the road may drink even more than they do at home. Take regular water breaks, or bring a heavy bowl (the thick clay ones do nicely) and set it on the floor so your dog always has access to water. When hiking, be sure to carry enough for yourself and a thirsty dog.

Rest stops: Stop and unwater your dog. There's nothing more miserable than being stuck in a car when you can't find a rest stop. No matter how tightly you cross your legs and try to think of the desert, you're certain you'll burst within the next minute. But think of how a dog feels when the urge strikes, and he can't tell you the problem. There are plenty of places listed in our book for you to allow your dog to relieve herself.

How frequently you stop depends on your dog's bladder. If your dog is constantly running out the doggy door at home to relieve himself, you may want to stop every hour. Others can go for significantly longer without being uncomfortable. Watch for any signs of restlessness and gauge it for yourself.

Car safety: Even the experts differ about how a dog should travel in a car.

Some suggest doggy safety belts, available at pet supply stores. Others firmly believe in keeping a dog kenneled. They say it's safer for the dog if there's an accident, and it's safer for the driver because there's no dog underfoot. Still others say you should just let your dog hang out without straps and boxes. They believe that if there's an accident, at least the dog isn't trapped in a cage. They say that dogs enjoy this more anyway.

We tend to agree with the latter school of thought. Inu and George travel very politely in the backseat and occasionally love sticking their snouts out of the windows to smell the world go by. The danger is that if the car kicks up a pebble or annoys a bee, their noses and eyes could be injured. So we usually open the window just enough so our dogs can't stick out much snout.

Whatever way you choose, your pet will be more comfortable if he has his own blanket with him. A veterinarian acquaintance uses a faux-sheepskin blanket for his dogs. At night in the hotel, the sheepskin doubles as the dog's bed.

Planes: Air travel is even more controversial. Many people feel it's tantamount to cruel and unusual punishment to force a dog to fly in the cargo hold like a piece of luggage. And there are dangers to flying that are somewhat beyond your control, such as runway delays—the cabin is not pressurized when on the ground—and connecting flights that tempt the wrong-way fates.

JoAnna and George have racked up some serious frequent flyer miles in George's 14 years of life, without ever having a problem until recently. But problem-free flying is getting more difficult. After September 2001, the airlines dramatically changed their rules and made canine travel virtually impossible in the summer months. Airlines are also required to make public the number of dogs that have died, been lost, or injured while on their airline. The result is many airlines have just decided to forego animal travel during the hot season. George and JoAnna have been left stranded twice in the summer when the airlines decided to change their blackout periods without notifying them—even after they had made specific reservations. Bottom line? Make sure you check your airlines' pet record before considering to fly with that airline. And more and more pet services are springing up to help harried travelers handle the changes. A good source for finding travel services in your area is the website www.PetsOnTheGo.com. You'll find a complete listing of transport companies and airline regulations.

If you must fly, however, don't leave anything to chance. There are some very specific rules you can follow to ensure your dog's safety. For example, always book nonstop flights. Don't take the chance that your dog could be misdirected while changing planes. And always inform the flight crew you are traveling with your pet. That way they can inform you when your dog has boarded the plane safely and will take extra precautions when on the runway. Also, make sure you schedule takeoff and arrival times when the temperature is below 80° F and above 35° F. And don't forget to consult the airline about its regulations and required certificates. Most airlines will ask you to show a health certificate and possibly proof of a rabies vaccination. Finally, call the airline the day before your departure to be sure your dog is booked and allowed to travel.

The question of tranquilizing a dog for a plane journey is difficult. Some vets think it's insane to give a dog a sedative before flying. They say a dog will be calmer and less fearful without taking a disorienting drug. Others think it's crazy not to afford your dog the little relaxation he might not otherwise get without a tranquilizer. We suggest discussing the tranquilizer issue with your vet, who will take the trip's length and your dog's personality into account.

On their first flight together, JoAnna gave George a very mild sedative. He was very dehydrated afterward, so on the return leg he went without the drug. He was just fine and has not been sedated since. Flying is not his favorite activity, but it's better than being left at home, so he trusts JoAnna to make sure he's treated okay.

The Ultimate Doggy Bag

Your dog can't pack her own bags, and even if she could, she'd probably fill them with dog biscuits and chew toys. It's important to stash some of those in your dog's vacation kit, but here are some other items to bring along: bowls, bedding, brush, towels (for those muddy days), first-aid kit, pooper-scoopers, water, food, prescription drugs, tags, treats, toys, and, of course, this book.

Be sure your dog wears her license, identification tag, and rabies tag. On a long trip, you may even want to bring along your dog's rabies certificate. Some parks and campgrounds require rabies and licensing information. You never know how picky they'll be.

It's a good idea to snap one of those barrel-type IDs on your dog's collar, too, showing the name, address, and phone number of where you'll be vacationing. That way if she should get lost, at least the finder won't be calling your empty house. Carrying a picture of your dog, in case the two of you become separated, is also not a bad idea.

Some people think dogs should drink only water brought from home so their bodies don't have to get used to too many new things. We've never had a problem feeding our dogs tap water from other parts of the state, nor has anyone else we know. Most vets think your dog will be fine drinking tap water in most U.S. cities.

Bone Appétit

In Europe, dogs enter restaurants and dine alongside their folks as if they were people, too. (Or at least they sit and watch and drool while their people dine.) Not so in America. Rightly or wrongly, dogs are considered a health threat. But many health inspectors will say they see no reason why clean, well-behaved dogs shouldn't be permitted inside a restaurant.

Ernest Hemingway made an expatriate of his dog, Black Dog (a.k.a. Blackie), partly because of America's restrictive views on dogs in dining establishments. In "The Christmas Gift," a story published in *Look* magazine in 1954, he describes how he made the decision to take Black Dog to Cuba, rather than leave him behind in Ketchum, Idaho:

> This was a town where a man was once not regarded as respectable unless he was accompanied by his dog. But a reform movement had set in, led by several local religionists, and gambling had been abolished and there was even a movement on foot to forbid a dog from entering a public eating place with his master. Blackie had always tugged me by the trouser leg as we passed a combination gambling and eating place called the Alpine where they served the finest sizzling steak in the West. Blackie wanted me to order the giant sizzling steak and it was difficult to pass the Alpine .... We decided to make a command decision and take Blackie to Cuba.

Fortunately, you don't have to take your dog to a foreign country in order to eat together at a restaurant. Boston has many restaurants with outdoor tables, and these establishments welcome dogs to join their people for an alfresco experience.

The law on patio-dining dogs is somewhat vague, and you'll discover different versions of it. But in general, as long as your dog doesn't go inside

a restaurant (even to get to outdoor tables in the back) and isn't near the food preparation areas, it's probably legal. The decision is then up to the restaurant proprietor.

The restaurants listed in this book have given us permission to tout them as dog-friendly eateries. But keep in mind that rules can change and restaurants can close, so we highly recommend phoning before you get your stomach set on a particular kind of cuisine. Also, even if they are listed here as allowing dogs, as a courtesy you should politely ask the manager if your dog may join you on that particular day. Remember, it's the restaurant owner, not you, who will be in trouble if someone complains.

Some basic restaurant etiquette: Dogs shouldn't beg from other diners, no matter how delicious that steak looks. They should not attempt to get their snouts (or their entire bodies) up on the table. They should be clean, quiet, and as unobtrusive as possible. If your dog leaves a good impression with the management and other customers, it will help pave the way for all the other dogs who want to dine alongside their best friends in the future.

A Room at the Inn

Good dogs make great hotel guests. They don't steal towels, and they don't get drunk and keep the neighbors up all night. This book lists dog-friendly accommodations of all types, from motels to bed-and-breakfast inns to elegant hotels. But the basic dog etiquette rules are the same.

Dogs should never be left alone in your room. Leaving a dog alone in a strange place is inviting serious trouble. Scared, nervous dogs can tear apart drapes, carpeting, and furniture, or injure themselves. They can also bark nonstop and scare the daylights out of the housekeeper. Just don't do it.

Only bring a house-trained and de-fleaed dog to a lodging. The former is a no-brainer. And with the advent of so many excellent topical flea treatments, such as Program, Frontline, and Advantage, the latter shouldn't be a problem either. Many of the pet fees charged at hotels go towards de-fleaing your room after a pet's visit, but we suggest not leaving any tiny hitchhikers behind for the kind innkeeper to clean up. That's the fastest way to lose guest privileges at top hotels.

It helps if you bring your dog's bed or his blanket. He'll feel more at home and won't be tempted to jump on the bed. If your dog sleeps on the bed with you at home, bring a sheet and put it on top of the bed so the hotel's bedspread won't get furry or dirty.

After a few days in a hotel, some dogs come to think of it as home. They get territorial. When another hotel guest walks by, it's "*Bark! Bark!*" When the housekeeper knocks, it's "*Bark! Snarl! Bark! Gnash!*" Keep your dog quiet, or you'll both find yourselves looking for a new home away from home.

For some strange reason, many lodgings prefer small dogs as guests. All we can say is, "Yip! Yap!" It's really ridiculous. Large dogs are often much calmer and quieter than their tiny, high-energy cousins. (Some hotel managers must think small dogs are more like cats. *Wrong*.) If you're in a location where you can't find a hotel that will accept you and your big brute, it's time to try a sell job. Let the manager know how good and quiet your dog is (if he is). Promise he won't eat the bathtub or run around and shake the hotel. Offer a deposit or sign a waiver, even if they're not required for small dogs. It helps if your sweet, soppy-eyed dog is at your side to convince the decision-maker.

You could always sneak dogs into hotels, but we don't recommend that you attempt to do so. The lodging might have a good reason for its rules. Besides, you'll always feel as if you're going to be caught and thrown out. You race in and out of your room with your dog as if ducking sniper fire. It's better to avoid feeling like a criminal and move on to a more dog-friendly location. For a sure bet, try a Motel 6, a Red Roof Inn, the Kimpton Hotels, or Starwood Resorts. Most of these establishments allow you to bring your dog with you. Some have more lenient pet rules than others.

The lodgings described in this book are for dogs who obey all the rules. Rates listed are for double rooms unless otherwise noted.

Natural Troubles

Chances are that your adventuring will go without a hitch, but you should always be prepared to deal with trouble. Make sure you know the basics of animal first aid before you embark on a long journey with your dog.

The more common woes—ticks, burrs, poison ivy, and skunks—can make life with a traveling dog a somewhat trying experience.

Ticks are hard to avoid in Massachusetts. They can carry Lyme disease, so you should always check yourself and your dog thoroughly after a day in tick country. In fact, it's a good idea to keep checking for a day or two after you've been out. Ticks are crafty little critters, and it's not unusual to find ticks on your dog two, three, and four days after your walk in the woods. Don't forget to check ears and between the toes.

If you find a tick that is unattached, you can remove it from your dog with your hands, but tweezers are best. If you find an attached tick (it's usually swollen and looks like a dark corn kernel), use tweezers to grasp it as close to your dog's skin as possible and pull it straight out. If you are unable to grasp the tick close to the skin, try twisting it counterclockwise, "unscrewing" the tick's head. Frequently they will let go. Avoid leaving any tick mouthparts embedded under your dog's skin. Disinfect the area before and after removing the pest.

The tiny deer ticks that carry Lyme disease are difficult to find. Consult your veterinarian if your dog is lethargic for a few days, has a fever, loses her appetite, or becomes lame. These symptoms could indicate Lyme disease. If you spend a lot of time in any of the woodlands we recommend, we suggest you have your dog vaccinated.

Burrs—those round pieces of dry grass that attach to your socks, your sweater, and your dog—are an everyday annoyance. But in certain cases, they can be lethal. They can stick in your dog's eyes, nose, ears, or mouth and work their way in. Check every nook and cranny of your dog after a walk if you've been anywhere near dry grass. Be vigilant.

Poison ivy is also a common menace. Dogs don't react to poison ivy, but they can easily pass its oils on to people. If you think your dog has made contact with poison ivy, avoid petting her until you can get home and bathe her (preferably while wearing rubber gloves). If you do pet her before washing her, make sure you don't touch your eyes and wash your hands immediately.

If your dog loses a contest with a skunk (and she always will), rinse her eyes first with plain warm water, then bathe her with dog shampoo. Towel her off, then apply tomato juice. If you can't get tomato juice, you can also use a solution of one pint of vinegar per gallon of water to cut through the stink.

He, She, It

In this book, whether neutered, spayed, or *au naturel,* dogs are never referred to as "it." They are either "he" or "she." We alternate pronouns so no dog reading this book will feel left out.

A Dog in Need

If you don't currently have a dog but could provide a good home for one, we'd like to make a plea on behalf of all the unwanted dogs who will be euthanized tomorrow and the day after that and the day after that. JoAnna adopted George from an animal shelter and Chris saved Inu from inattention at the hands of his previous owners. We believe in and support all efforts to control the existing dog population (spay or neuter your dogs!) and to assist the ones who currently and desperately need homes. Animal shelters and humane organizations are overflowing with dogs who would devote their lives to being your best buddy, your faithful traveling companion, and a dedicated listener to all your tales of bliss and woe.

For information, contact your local shelter or the National Humane Education Society (521-A East Market Street, Leesburg, VA 20176; website: www.nhes.org), a nonprofit organization that teaches people about the importance of being kind to animals and maintains the Peace Plantation Animal Sanctuary for dogs and cats.

Need a nudge? Remember the oft-quoted words of Samuel Butler: "The great pleasure of a dog is that you may make a fool of yourself with him and not only will he not scold you, but he will make a fool of himself, too."

14

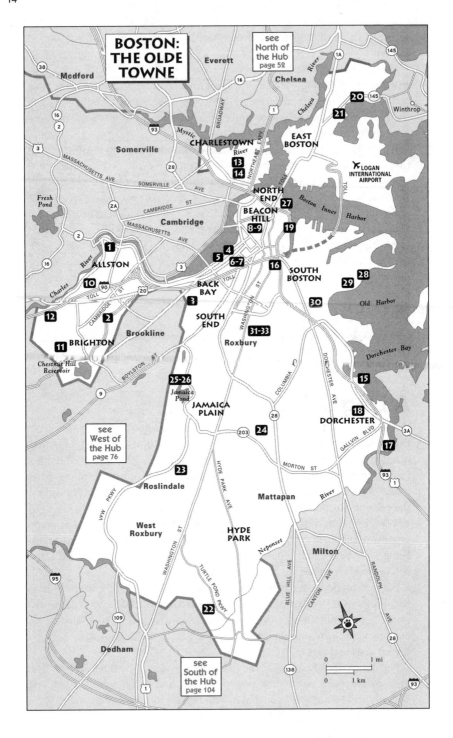

BOSTON: THE OLDE TOWNE

see North of the Hub page 52

Everett

Chelsea

Medford

38

145

16

Winthrop

20 145

21

Somerville

93

16

2

3

MASSACHUSETTS AVE

SOMERVILLE AVE

Mystic River

BROADWAY

NORTHEAST EXPWY

CHARLESTOWN

13

14

EAST BOSTON

✈ LOGAN INTERNATIONAL AIRPORT

28

2A

CAMBRIDGE ST

Cambridge

NORTH END

27

BEACON HILL

8-9

19

Boston Inner Harbor

TOLL

TOLL

Fresh Pond

2

MASSACHUSETTS AVE

Charles River

ALLSTON

1

5 4

6-7

16

SOUTH BOSTON

28

29

16

10

90

20

CAMBRIDGE ST

BACK BAY

TOLL

WASHINGTON ST

30

Old Harbor

12

2

SOUTH END

Brookline

3

ROXBURY

31-33

15

11 BRIGHTON

Chestnut Hill Reservoir

BOYLSTON ST

Dorchester Bay

9

25-26

Jamaica Pond

JAMAICA PLAIN

COLUMBIA

DORCHESTER AVE

18 DORCHESTER

see West of the Hub page 76

28

24

203

17

3A

GALLVIN BLVD

93

23 Roslindale

MORTON ST

HYDE PARK AVE

Mattapan

River

1

VFW PKWY

West Roxbury

WASHINGTON ST

HYDE PARK

Neponset

Milton

95

TURTLE POND PKWY

BLUE HILL AVE

CANTON AVE

RANDOLPH AVE

109

22

138

28

Dedham

1

see South of the Hub page 104

93

0   1 mi

0   1 km

CHAPTER 1

Boston:
The Olde Towne

Historically and culturally rich, Boston is a big little city or a little big city, depending on whether you put the emphasis on its population or acreage. Every section is unlike any other. For easy reference, we've arranged the city by its neighborhoods, which is how Bostonians think of themselves anyway. Unlike most dogs, who really couldn't care less whether they're labeled a poodle, a retriever, or a mutt, Boston natives take their cultural heritage very seriously, and their neighborhoods reflect their ethnic and civic pride. Explore these areas and their parks in the spirit of multiculturalism, and you'll find each place you visit different from the last. Dogs and their owners will discover, unfortunately, that all Boston parks have one thing in common: leash laws.

The Emerald Necklace: In 1893, Boston parks founder Charles Eliot joined forces with renowned Central Park landscape architect Frederick Law Olmsted to create the first planned park system in the United States. Their first project was the famous Emerald Necklace. This series of beautiful parks

PICK OF THE LITTER—OLDE TOWNE

BEST PLACE TO EAT TOGETHER
Café Esplanade, Back Bay (page 24)

BEST PLACE TO SEE AND BE SEEN
Frog Pond Jazz Café, Beacon Hill (page 29)

BEST CITY PLACE TO STAY
Nine Zero Hotel, Beacon Hill (page 30)

BEST DOGGIE TREATS
Polka Dog Bakery, South End (page 51)

BEST SOUTHIE EVENT
That Doggone Walk, South Boston (page 48)

BEST FUNDRAISER
Walk for the Animals, Back Bay (page 21)

encompasses the Arnold Arboretum, Back Bay Fens, Boston Common, Commonwealth Avenue Mall, Franklin Park, Jamaica Pond, Olmsted Park, Riverway, and what many consider to be the crowning jewel of the necklace, the Public Garden. Extending from downtown Boston out to Jamaica Plain, the Necklace forms a continuous chain of greenery weaving within Boston's man-made structures. As in all Boston parks, dogs must be leashed. The parks are open every day, 6 A.M.–11:30 P.M. For more information, contact the Boston Parks and Recreation Department at 617/635-4505.

Department of Conservation and Recreation's Division of Urban Parks and Recreation (DCR): Formerly known as the Department of Conservation, this organization manages the Metropolitan Parks System in the Boston metro area. The DCR administers recreation areas in 34 towns and cities in the Greater Boston area, including many parks in this chapter. For more information on its history and holdings, see the Resources section.

Riding the T: We expect that you'll be traveling to most of these locations by car, and our directions reflect this assumption, but many parks can be reached by mass transportation. Most conveniently, you may take your pup on the Massachusetts Bay Transportation Authority (MBTA) subway system. We've taken our dogs on the T many times, and it's a terrific way to get around.

There are some restrictions: Your dog must be leashed at all times. If your pooch is small enough to fit in a lap carrier, you may bring her along for the ride at any time. Otherwise, during weekdays your dog may not ride from 7 A.M.–9 A.M. or from 4 P.M.–7 P.M. During off-peak weekday hours and throughout the weekend, however, Rover is free to ride the rails.

The first time Chris took Inu on the T, he was just waiting for someone to eject them from the train. Yes, he had checked with the Transportation Authority in advance, but still he thought the information had to be wrong. So he hauled Inu on a trip out to Longwood, just to prove that the guy on the phone had to be joking.

The trip out was uneventful. No one so much as even looked their way. Presumably a golden retriever is preferable to some of the other odd sorts who typically share the cars. No one kicked them off; in fact, no one even cared.

On the way back, however, things didn't go quite as smoothly. During the time between when they departed the train and reboarded, it had poured. That meant Inu was a very wet dog on the way back into the city. Wet dogs smell like, well, wet dogs. And this time, a soggy golden retriever *wasn't* preferable to some of the odd types who may climb on board. They survived the trip, but had to endure cold, silent stares, and disapproving harrumphs. Hmm. When you think about it, it was just an ordinary day on the T....

For more information, contact the Massachusetts Bay Transportation Authority at 617/222-3200; website: www.mbta.com.

Allston

PARKS, BEACHES, AND RECREATION AREAS

❶ Charles River Reservation
(See Boston: The Olde Towne map on page 14)

The Charles River Reservation encompasses many sections across four cities. For the sake of convenience, we've divided it into segments, using the bridges along the river as boundaries. Dogs must be leashed. Managed by the Department of Conservation, all sections of the reservation are open 6 A.M.–11:30 P.M. 617/727-9547.

Western Avenue Bridge to Larz Anderson Bridge Section
🐾🐾

This is the only walk-worthy stretch of the reservation in Allston. Other segments constitute little more than thin stretches of paved path along Storrow Drive. But in this part, you'll discover two wide, green lawns divided by the path along the river's edge. The John Weeks, Jr. Bridge bisects the open areas. Looping gracefully over the river, this elegant stone footbridge is one of the loveliest sites along the Charles. It will take you over to Cambridge and

Memorial Drive if you choose, or just provide a pleasant view over the water. You and your leashed dog can sun or play on the grassy areas, but expect to rub shoulders with lots of other folks on spring and summer days.

❷ Ringer Park

🐾 (See Boston: The Olde Towne map on page 14)

If you live near Ringer Park, your leashed dog probably exercises you here. For out-of-towners, no parking is available, and the park just isn't alluring enough to merit a trip. With a ball field, a playground, and enough surrounding woods to excite your dog, this should be a pleasant neighborhood park. We're happy to report that since our first edition the small woods surrounding the park have been cleaned up, so you won't have to be a tenderfoot when you walk here.

From Cambridge Street, take either Gordon Street or Allston Street south. Parking is for Allston-Brighton residents only. Open 6 A.M.–11:30 P.M. 617/635-4505.

Back Bay

Home of the new Victorians and the nouveau riche in the late 1800s, Back Bay is known for its wide boulevards and graceful mansions. Built on landfill over the Charles River marshes in the mid 19th century, the neighborhood served as the innovative upstart challenging the "old money" of its cousin, Beacon Hill. The bowfront windows of the brownstones here are distinctly non-Colonial and today attract the young professionals and students who flock to Boston each year. Trendy Newbury Street makes for great browsing, and the stately Commonwealth Avenue Mall is unarguably one of the most elegant streets in New England. Dogs abound here, and many merchants love them, judging from the treats they hand out to their four-footed patrons.

PARKS, BEACHES, AND RECREATION AREAS

❸ The Back Bay Fens

🐾🐾 (See Boston: The Olde Towne map on page 14)

While Fido can't escort you into venerable Fenway Park to catch the Red Sox in action, both of you can play ball in this large park beyond the bleachers. The Fens runs more than two miles along Hemenway Avenue, all the way from the ballpark, past the Museum of Fine Arts, to the Isabella Gardner Museum. You'll get in a good walk or run here, roll in the grass, or just kick up your heels. Bridges and benches await you, and your happy dog will find plenty of room to romp on leash.

Unfortunately the section near Fenway Park is the least desirable in the Fens. Trash and swampy ponds make it unsafe for dogs; the ungroomed shrubbery

makes the going difficult for people. A few minutes in this area should get you both humming "Take Me Away From the Ballgame."

You'll encounter more inviting terrain in the central section, by the Museum of Fine Arts, where walkways and trails wind through open lawns and fields. Ponds, however, run the gamut from murky to downright slimy, so your dog will want to think twice before jumping in. The ducks seem to like it, but "ducky" is not the highest endorsement we can give to a swimming hole.

The southwestern portion runs from the Brookline town line to the Gardner Museum. It's almost a mile long and two city blocks wide. A path through the center of the park offers the best walking in the Fens. The inner walkway is bordered by a mix of grass, shrubs, trees, and, once again, mucky ponds. Sorry, water dogs. If you plan to use the outer walkways, be especially careful on Park Drive and Fenway Drive; both are busy routes.

Parking can be tough here. You'll find some metered parking along Park Avenue, Hemenway Avenue, and Boylston Avenue, but most spots are residential. Open 6 A.M.–11:30 P.M., but not recommended after dark. 617/635-4505.

4 Charlesgate Dog Run

🐾🐾🦴 (See Boston: The Olde Towne map on page 14)

Boston's first official dog run, opened in September 1998, was a step in the right direction. But only a very small step. No matter what city officials tell you, merely building it does not mean the dogs will come. Call us ungrateful, but this small 55-by-80-foot rectangle isn't exactly the most enticing place for dogs and their owners. First, there's the location. Nestled between busy Massachusetts Avenue and Storrow Drive, a visit here will make you feel like you're playing on the track of the Indy 500. And that is if you can find it. To reach the run, you have to cross busy Massachusetts Avenue and find the stairway that takes you down below the road, and when you get there, more than likely, there won't be any other dogs waiting to play with you.

Managed by the Back Bay Neighborhood Association and the Department of Conservation, the park has a bench, two trees, some grass, and a view of the Charles River. Okay, so it's off leash, but location is still everything. The entrance is located off the western side of the Massachusetts Avenue Bridge. Open 6 A.M.–11:30 P.M. 617/727-5114, ext. 538.

🖪 Charles River Reservation

(See Boston: The Olde Towne map on page 14)

We've divided this long riverside expanse into sections. All segments are managed by the Department of Conservation; Dogs must be leashed. Open 6 A.M.–11:30 P.M. 617/727-9547.

The Esplanade
😃😃😃😃 🐾

Bike, jog, picnic, in-line skate, stroll, swim. No matter what activity you and your canine pal like, you'll find no roomier or more scenic spot in the city to enjoy it.

Nestled along the Charles River and stretching from the Museum of Science to Massachusetts Avenue, the Esplanade spans many of the neighborhoods in this chapter. From Back Bay, access is via the Dartmouth Street, Hereford Street, or Massachusetts Avenue Bridges. From Beacon Hill, you can reach the park by crossing Storrow Drive at the Charles Street Bridge or the Arthur Fiedler Bridge at Arlington Street.

The walk from the Museum of Science to the Massachusetts Avenue Bridge covers about 3.5 miles. Water borders the path on both sides, with the Charles to the west and river estuaries to the east. The water in the estuaries tends to be cleaner and more shallow than the river; if your dog is a swimmer, she should dip her paws here.

The expanse between the Fiedler Bridge (named for Arthur Fiedler, the longtime conductor of the Boston Pops) and the Hereford Street Bridge is the best area for exercising your dog. A statue of Arthur Fiedler graces the grassy knoll beside the Hatch Shell amphitheater. Generous swaths of grass, well separated from busy bike paths, provide plenty of room for stretching your legs. Most Back Bay dog owners use this space, and both you and your pooch can meet up with neighborhood regulars for a friendly hello. The two-mile loop from one end to the other takes about 40 minutes, give or take a few breaks for socializing.

DOG-EAR YOUR CALENDAR—OCTOBER

Head of the Charles Regatta: It wouldn't be October in New England without a trip to the Head of the Charles Regatta. This is the largest single-day collegiate rowing event in the country. Rowers travel from all over the world to participate, but you can see it in your own backyard for free. The race runs along the Charles River; arrive early for a ringside seat. Our dogs love the commotion. They assume that everyone has shown up to give them a pat and a scratch. The regatta occurs every year, rain or shine, on the third Sunday in October, 8 A.M.–4:30 P.M.; 617/864-8415.

DOG-EAR YOUR CALENDAR—SEPTEMBER

Walk a mile (or two) in my shoes: What dog doesn't love going for a walk? And dog owners love it, too, especially when the walk counts for something besides a breath of fresh air and a good sniff. On the third Sunday in September, the Massachusetts Society for the Prevention of Cruelty to Animals (MSPCA) hosts its annual **Walk for the Animals,** a fund-raiser for its animal shelters held at the Boston Common. Take a stroll and then participate in an amateur dog show. If your pooch boasts a hidden talent beyond the usual "roll over" or "shake" tricks, sign her up! Stupid pet tricks are encouraged. Call the MSPCA for current details at 617/522-7400; website: www.walkforanimals.com.

Stay to the inner edge along the river for full-out running and playing with your dog. This will help you avoid the cyclists who are *supposed* to stay on the outer edge along Storrow Drive—a good idea that's often poorly executed. Keep your dog on leash, as in all DCR parks.

If you venture along the walkway next to Storrow Drive, you'll find the Lotta Crabtree Dog Fountain, donated to the city in 1937 by a New York actress who retired to Boston at the turn of the century. Never married, Crabtree lived and traveled with her huskies throughout her career. The memorial (a statue of one of her beloved dogs) features a drinking fountain for thirsty canines.

On Sunday, parking is allowed on Storrow Drive between the Longfellow Bridge and the Esplanade's western end.

Harvard Bridge to Boston University Bridge Section

The span southwest of the Esplanade, between Massachusetts Avenue and the Boston University Bridge, is much narrower and less attractive than its northerly neighbor. Although it offers a decent walk, some parts narrow to a single-lane path along Storrow Drive where you may have to dodge cyclists and joggers. Every spring when the cyclists appear, a few accidents occur because dogs, their owners, or riders aren't paying attention to others around them, so stay on your toes. Aerobics-loving dogs will find a small fitness course at the widest spot, but even that won't give them much of a workout.

6 Commonwealth Avenue Mall

 (See Boston: The Olde Towne map on page 14)

Boston's dignified equivalent to Hollywood's Walk of Fame, this boulevard park extends for seven blocks down the center of Commonwealth Avenue,

DOG-EAR YOUR CALENDAR—APRIL

March of Dimes Walk America Walk-A-Thon: This annual fund-raising event provides an afternoon of fun while doing something good for others. Each year on the last Sunday in April, the 10K walk starts at noon at the Hatch Shell on the Esplanade. Participants wind their way along the Charles River and back again for charity. At the end of the road, you'll find food and a free concert (one year the House of Blues sponsored the event). For additional information, call the March of Dimes at 800/BIG-WALK (800/244-9255); website: www.walkamerica.org.

from Arlington Street near the Public Garden to Hereford Street. Bordered by Victorian brownstones and lined with gas lamps, this is one of Boston's most beautiful streets. Each block has a large green space divided by a wide walkway with shady elm trees, wrought-iron benches, and statues commemorating notables from Boston's past. Stroll along the mall, and you'll believe you've gone back in time—to an age when dogs were born with silver bowls to feed from and chased horse-drawn carriages down the avenue. It's still a great place to walk your leashed dog and it's well maintained, but cars speed by on both sides, so Fido must be a little streetwise. No fence prevents dogs from running out into the street.

At the end of the mall at Hereford Avenue, you'll discover an enclosed area where you can train puppies, teach older dogs to observe the street boundaries, or just socialize with other dog owners.

The Back Bay Neighborhood Association has been fighting the good fight on behalf of dog owners and their canine pals here. To answer complaints about pooper-scooper offenders, the group has placed mutt mitt dispensers between the blocks of Exeter and Fairfield Streets, and the blocks of Clarendon and Dartmouth Streets, but it's a chore to keep them replenished, so do your part in picking up after your pooch. The group is also gathering funds to build dog fountains on the blocks between Dartmouth and Clarendon Streets and between Fairfield and Gloucester Streets. To contribute or for information on the group's activities, call Luanne Pryor at 617/247-2366.

The mall is open for strolling 24 hours a day. It's well lit and amply populated in the evening hours. 617/635-4505.

7 Copley Square

 (See Boston: The Olde Towne map on page 14)

Set in the heart of the Back Bay beside historic Trinity Church, this spot hustles and bustles with the best of them in any season. But on a warm summer

DOG-EAR YOUR CALENDAR—JULY

Boston Pops Fourth of July Concert: No one makes a bigger deal out of Independence Day than Bostonians. The annual Boston Pops Fourth of July Concert and fireworks demonstration attracts more than 250,000 people, so get there early if you want a good spot. The seats around the Hatch Shell (for the Pops concert) are usually gone the day before, but if you bring your blanket, Frisbee, picnic basket, and plenty of water, you won't mind staking out your territory along the banks of the Charles sometime during the day. The concert starts at 8 P.M. and is piped in all along the Esplanade for the 245,000 folks who can't get close to the live action. Fireworks begin at 9:30 P.M. This is a special day in Boston, and your patriotic pooch will be thrilled to be included (unless he's afraid of loud explosions). Our dogs love being out all day and usually sleep for two days following the event. 617/266-1492.

evening, it's a great place to watch people go by. From the cafés on Boylston Street, you can gaze at passersby in the square and admire Trinity Church's reflection in the glass facade of the John Hancock Building.

Within the square, you'll find a refreshing fountain surrounded by grass and seats for outdoor concerts. Nearby is a charming bronze statue of Aesop's "Tortoise and the Hare" commemorating the Boston Marathon which ends at Copley Square. Our dogs have been startled many times by the bunny which is twice as big as they are. The park is well maintained with shrubs and plants, but there are no fences or barriers to protect your dog from the busy intersections. During the dog days of July and August, food festivals often occupy the

square, filling the park with all manner of sights, sounds, smells, and tastes to delight and distract you and your canine; if your dog is a "chow hound" (the eating kind, not the breed), be forewarned! The square is between Boylston Street, Dartmouth Street, and St. James Avenue. Open 24 hours, with lots of foot traffic. 617/635-4505.

PLACES TO EAT

Au Bon Pain: Yes, they serve great croissants and café au lait. But their true French colors can be found in their attitude toward our four-footed friends. Just like at a real French brasserie, you may bring your dog into the outdoor area and happily sip your cappuccino with her tucked contentedly under your chair. Share a bit of your baguette, and she'll cry *merci*. 431 Boylston Street; 617/859-2858.

Café Esplanade: Alongside the Hatch Shell on the Esplanade, this outdoor restaurant overlooks a peaceful estuary. It also offers a wide variety of soups, sandwiches, and unusual beverages, and a great patio for you and your dog to enjoy them on. After ordering our mango iced tea, we asked for a bowl of water for our dogs. Happily, the owners had already anticipated their furry customers' needs. At the back of the café is a dog bowl filled with fresh water. It's a perfect spot to take Spot after a jog or long walk along the Charles River. Open seasonally April–October and on special-event weekends. On Storrow Drive at the Hatch Shell; no phone.

Finagle-A-Bagel: For us, there are 15 kinds of bagels and 11 kinds of cream cheese (along with sandwiches and such). For Inu, George, and other canines, there's a welcome place to sit and munch on any scraps they can finagle. 535 Boylston Street; 617/266-2500 or 800/862-4081.

Starbucks: Normally we don't list chain restaurants in this book, but this coffeehouse has one of the best patios and people-watching locations on Newbury Street—we had to include it. Located between Exeter and Dartmouth Streets, you'll find a spacious patio where you and your dog can waste the day watching the beautiful people roam by. You'll also meet up with plenty of other canines playing hooky. 165 Newbury Street; 617/536-5282.

Stephanie's On Newbury: Hip dogs, and those who just want to be hip, hang out at this outdoor café and pick up some new tail-wagging moves while dining on a delicious selection of continental cuisine. Just be prepared to wait for one of the outdoor tables on warm summer evenings. 190 Newbury Street; 617/236-0990.

Tealuxe: This latest alternative to the coffee invasion, Tealuxe offers tea, sandwiches, pastries, and other civilized food for British Cockers and Brittany spaniels. Actually all breeds (and their people) are welcome at this cozy teahouse located on busy Newbury Street. Take a break from window-shopping with some scones and clotted cream. Your pup can join you on the patio overlooking the street. Cheerio! 108 Newbury Street; 617/927-0400.

Travis Restaurant: Really a diner in fancy surroundings, this is one of the best places in Boston to get an old-fashioned breakfast; or, in the words of a great philosopher: good food, cheap. Best of all, you get outdoor tables on the most fashionable street in Boston. Your dog will love licking the scraps of your hash browns, and you'll enjoy both a full stomach and having change in your pocket. Open for breakfast and lunch only. 135 Newbury Street; 617/267-6388.

Vox Populi: Formerly the Back Bay Brewing Company, this Boston restaurant may have changed their beer emphasis to a seafood-and-steak combo, but the important part is still intact—their ample outside seating area. The food is a combination of hip and trendy nouvelle cuisine, but the best part of a visit here is the great street scene. Try the salmon or the shrimp appetizer and when in doubt, go with the burger and steak fries. Dogs are allowed outside but be prepared to fight for a table. People can be such animals! 755 Boylston Street; 617/424-8300.

PLACES TO STAY

The Colonnade Hotel: This Back Bay hotel really rolls out the red carpet for Rover. There are no size restrictions or extra fees, but they do ask that you let them know your pet will be accompanying you. They will also provide extra dog bowls, leashes, and biscuits if you forget to bring them along. Rates are $185–290; 120 Huntington Avenue, Boston, MA 02116; 617/424-7000; website: www.colannadehotel.com.

Hotel Commonwealth: This European-style boutique hotel is a convenient alternative to the bigger hotels in the Boston area. Located along beautiful Commonwealth Avenue in a mostly residential section, it is a skip away from the Green line on the Boston subway system. They have rooms that look out over Fenway Park or face tree-lined Commonwealth Avenue. Smaller dogs preferred, but the hotel is willing to negotiate on size restrictions on a dog-by-dog basis. Dog beds are available at check-in, and a "pet turn down" service (including water bowl and pet treat) is provided. Rates are $250–400 plus a $25 pet fee per stay. 500 Commonwealth Avenue, Boston, MA 02115; 617/933-5000 or 866-784-4000; website: www.hotelcommonwealth.com.

Eliot Suite Hotel: This elegant suite-style hotel is located in the heart of Back Bay—just a block from trendy Newbury Street and within easy walking distance of the Esplanade and Storrow Drive dog run. All suites have a kitchen area and living room. Dogs are welcome, and dog-walking services are available on request. Rooms are $255–415 per night. 370 Commonwealth Avenue, Boston, MA 02116; 617/267-1607; website: www.eliothotel.com.

Four Seasons Hotel: Boston's only five-diamond hotel goes out of its way for dogs—and well it should for the rates it charges! When you check in, your pet receives a welcome package that includes a pet menu, feeding bowl, dog bones, and a treat. Special bottled water and dog beds are available on request.

Now that's doggone hospitable. The staff will even arrange for a dog walker if you need to leave your pup for a few hours. Rates are $325–850 per night. 200 Boylston Street, Boston, MA 02116; 617/338-4400; website: www.fshr.com.

Hilton Back Bay: This conveniently located hotel is close to all the Back Bay hot spots. There are great city views from the top floors and rooms big enough to feel right at home. Best of all, they welcome well-behaved dogs! Please let the management know you will be traveling with your pet, as special rooms will be set aside for you. Rates are $189–375 per night. 40 Dalton Street, Boston, MA 02115; 617/236-1100 or 800/445-8667; website: www.hilton.com.

Ritz-Carlton: This elegant European-style hotel has always been one of the most highly regarded in Boston. After a renovation in 2002, this hotel is even more beautiful than ever. Fortunately, dogs under 40 pounds are welcome to share a room with their owners here. Conveniently located overlooking the Public Garden at Newbury Street, you'll be close to parks, restaurants, and plenty of shopping. The rooms feature marble bathrooms, French furnishings, plush down comforters and pillows, and those fluffy bathrobes that, in this case, are not for your own Fluffy. There is a $30 pet fee per night, and you must sign a damage waiver on check in. Rooms are $295–1,500 per night. 15 Arlington Street, Boston, MA 02116; 617/536-5700; website: www.ritzcarlton.com.

Sheraton at the Prudential Center: You'll find this hotel, located between Back Bay and the South End, a good city bet. The management asks you to notify them well in advance that you'll be accompanied by your dog. Rates are $149–389. 39 Dalton Street, Boston, MA 02199; 617/236-2000; website: www.sheraton.com.

The Westin at Copley Place: This deluxe hotel in the Copley Place shopping mall provides easy access to shopping and many nearby parks. Dogs under 40 pounds are allowed, and please tell the management that you'll be traveling with your dog when you make your reservation. Your pal, of course, must be leashed at all times and isn't allowed in the mall. Rates range from $194–425. 10 Huntington Avenue, Boston, MA 02116; 617/262-9600; website: www.westin.com.

Beacon Hill

One of Boston's oldest communities, Beacon Hill is home to the state legislature and many of the city's most illustrious citizens—both past and present. John, Abigail, and Henry Adams, Louisa May Alcott, Henry David Thoreau, Ralph Waldo Emerson, John F. Kennedy, and current Senator John Kerry are just a few of the notables who have made their homes here. Fiercely protected by its historical preservation societies, Beacon Hill maintains a direct link to a bygone era with cobblestone streets, gas lamps, and brick brownstones. More dogs live here per square foot than in any other neighborhood in Boston, and locals love the social bonhomie that their canines bring to life on "the Hill."

PARKS, BEACHES, AND RECREATION AREAS

🐾 Boston Common

🐾🐾🐾 (See Boston: The Olde Towne map on page 14)

Created in 1640 as an ordinary cow pasture, the Common lays claim to being the oldest public space in the country. If you live in Boston, this park is the most common spot to take your leashed dog on a daily basis. Located along historic Beacon Hill and the State House, the Common has been a gathering place for people and their animals for more than 300 years. Although it's small for a city park and often shows the wear and tear of continual use, it has managed to preserve the warmth of a small-town square.

Our favorite area is the west side of the Common, where Beacon Street and Charles Street meet. Renovated in 1998, it tends to be the best hangout for canines. Above the underground parking area is a large open grassy area that's great for throwing balls and Frisbees; it's here that most of the dogs get their exercise. Farther up the hill are shade trees and more terrain for those who want to sit and watch their dogs play. On any morning, you'll find a group of dogs playing and chasing each other on the open grassy areas adjacent to the Public Garden. Walk by again in the early evening, and you'll think they've been there all day. A mutt mitt dispenser is provided near the entrance of the park at Spruce and Beacon Streets.

Near the State House, you'll find another hilly expanse where dogs can run and play. This area is close to the Park Street T Station, so it gets a little more foot traffic. But there's plenty of room for all if you just respect the suits going to and from work each day. And we are happy to note that the east side of the Common is much more inviting these days due to continued park improvements, the addition of the new Ritz-Carlton on Tremont Street, and the disappearance of Boston's nearby red-light district, the Combat Zone.

Before the Common was renovated in 1998, the open space by the Charles Street entrance was still mostly a joyous leash-free haven for dogs. The dog owners and the rangers worked together to regulate this little bit of doggy heaven. But alas, times changed, and the Common became a battleground between dog lovers and city officials. Rangers started routinely ticketing dog owners who turned a deaf ear to the city leash laws. One dog owner we know was actually followed home by an over-zealous animal control officer after refusing to give his name to the official. Fortunately, through the efforts of Beacon Hill D.O.G., the city agreed to a pilot leash-free program in 2002. We are happy to report the pilot was a success, and in 2005, the "Pilot" was lifted and off-leash hours are here to stay. Currently dogs are allowed off leash 6:30 A.M.–8 A.M. and 5 P.M.–7 P.M.

The Department of Conservation and the Boston Parks and Recreation Department jointly manage the Common. Until more off-leash hours are allocated, your dog must be leashed, except in the early morning hours. And as tempting as it is during hot summer days, dogs are not allowed in the children's swimming pool, known as the Frog Pond.

The Boston Common is between Charles Street, Beacon Street, Park Street, and Tremont Street. Open 6 A.M.–11:30 P.M. 617/634-4505.

◻ Public Garden

😺 😺 ◀● (See Boston: The Olde Towne map on page 14)

Walk across Charles Street from the Boston Common, and you'll find yourself in the Public Garden. This beautiful and elegant park is the jewel of the Emerald Necklace, which makes up the Boston city parks. Set aside in 1867, this park, with its graceful willows, duck pond, famous Swan Boats, and lush green grass, is arguably the most gorgeous park in the city of Boston. And as in all city parks, your dog must admire it on a leash.

This is not a park for frolicking in, but it's a great place to sit and watch the world pass by. If your dog can enjoy sitting quietly beside you, enjoy by all means! But if he needs a lot of exercise or is overly rambunctious and wants to chase every squirrel in sight (and many make their home here), then this is probably not the park for you.

When JoAnna and George first moved to Boston, they were delighted to find themselves living so near the Public Garden. Soon they learned, however, that the park is also a place to get in trouble. You see, its big pond (the same one of the legendary Swan Boats and the children's story *Make Way for Ducklings*) draws like a doggy magnet. It's got that perfect mix of duck gunk and city algae that seems to be enormously appealing to every dog (and especially George) on a hot summer day.

On their first visit, JoAnna didn't see any signs or warnings, so she thought, "Heck, why not let the poor guy go in for a quick dip?" The kids in the park were delighted as he swam after sticks, and they all begged to be the next to throw the ball for him. The rangers were not so amused, as a stern hand on JoAnna's criminal shoulder soon made apparent.

DOG-EAR YOUR CALENDAR—APRIL

Canines Curing Cancer: Join your canine cronies at the annual **American Cancer Society's Dogswalk Against Cancer,** held the last weekend in April across the country. Boston's event includes a .75-mile parade around the Boston Common followed by contests, raffles, and giveaways. Walkers are asked to support the fight against human and animal cancers with pledges or a $20 registration fee. For exact date and information, contact the American Cancer Society at 617/635-7400.

DIVERSION

Black Heritage Trail: This historic tour through Beacon Hill commemorates the many contributions African-Americans have made to the growth of Beacon Hill, Boston, and the United States. The tour's highlight is the celebrated Saint Gaudens bas-relief memorial to Robert Gould Shaw and his 54th Regiment, whose story was depicted in the movie *Glory*. The route also includes the African Meeting House—the oldest black church in America—and the many majestic homes of Beacon Hill.

Although Fido is not allowed inside the African Meeting House, the rest of the tour is outdoors, and he will certainly enjoy the many fire hydrants, lampposts, and other stops in this dog-friendly neighborhood. You can both bone up on a little history and get some exercise while you're at it.

Rangers lead tours on this National Park System trail three times a day on weekends and holidays. Obtain maps and brochures for self-guided walks, and additional information about ranger-led tours, at the Boston National Historic Visitor Center, 15 State Street. The visitor center is open daily, 9 A.M.–5 P.M.; 617/742-5415.

George was hauled out of the drink, cuffed and paw printed, and unceremoniously placed on the "bad dog" list (really a "bad owner" list) for "flagrant felonious acts of swimming" (our term, not theirs). JoAnna, of course, was also sternly reprimanded. Both slunk away into the night, never to venture into the garden again by the light of day. Melodrama aside, the list is true, the ban on swimming is real, and you'll be ticketed if your dog's name appears on that list more than once. If you want to spare your dog the life of a wanted outlaw, take heed: No swimming in the Garden. Except after dark.

A mutt mitt dispenser is located at the Charles Street and Beacon Street entrance. The Public Garden is between Arlington, Beacon, Charles, and Boylston Streets. Open 6 A.M.–11:30 P.M. 617/635-4505.

PLACES TO EAT

Café Vanille: Tasty tarts and truffles top the menu of this tantalizing pastry shop. The outdoor seating makes it a perfect stop for you and your trusty terrier when you are out antiquing on Beacon Hill's famous Charles Street. Other menu treats include espresso, ice cream, and delicious breakfast choices. 70 Charles Street; 617/559-9799.

Frog Pond Jazz Café: When the jazz gets too hot here, the band can literally step off stage to cool off. The makeshift stage sits in the Frog Pond and is a pleasant addition to an already tasty Americana menu of pasta, salads, and chicken dishes at this outdoor café. You and Fido can indulge your tastes on the outdoor patio while enjoying the pondside setting. Boston Common; 617/635-2121.

PLACES TO STAY

Nine Zero Hotel: This latest entry into the boutique hotel market in Boston has been a big hit. Located on the east side of the Common near the theater district, you'll be close to Downtown Crossing, Back Bay, and the Freedom Trail. You might not want to leave your room, however, since this dog-friendly

DIVERSIONS

Clang, clang, clang goes the trolley: Take your dog on a city tour of Boston. **City View Trolley Tours** offers a trip through Beantown that covers the Freedom Trail, the Boston Tea Party ship, the Quincy Market, the North End, Beacon Hill, Back Bay, Bunker Hill, and the New England Aquarium among others. Tickets can be purchased in person at the Boston Common Visitor Information Kiosk at the Park Street Station or outside the Long Wharf Marriott Hotel near the New England Aquarium. To order tickets by phone, call 617/363-7899. An all-day ticket includes unlimited reboarding stops. The full tour is narrated by a guide and takes one hour. All dogs must be leashed and be able to sit at your feet or on your lap. Hours of operation are daily from 9 A.M. City View, P.O. Box 267, Boston, MA 02132; website: www.cityviewtrolleys.com.

Explore Beantown by foot: A nifty nonprofit organization called **Boston by Foot** offers several walking tours through selected areas of the city. They encourage you to bring your leashed dog along, and they take special care to make sure your four-footed friend is comfortable. Choose between Freedom Trail tours, walks around historic Beacon Hill, an unusual walk along the Waterfront, or their popular Boston Underground tour which features the many engineering feats in Boston's history. There's even a Boston by Little Feet tour especially for children. Dogs welcome on all tours. For information, call 617/367-2345; website: www.bostonbyfoot.com.

Fine dough for Fido: When your dog gets a craving for sweets, stop by **Fi-Dough,** a bakery just for dogs! Featuring dreamy "desserts" and gourmet dog treats and biscuits, this specialty store has the goods to satisfy any sweet tooth. They also sell cool pet accessories and sponsor occasional seminars for the health of your pet. 103 Charles Street, Boston, MA 02114; 617/723-3266; website: www.fidough.com.

DIVERSION

Tip a canoe, and Fido, too: Your dog may never want to set paw on dry land again after a day of **canoeing the Charles River.** May–October you can rent a canoe at the boathouse in Christian Herter Park. The river bend around Allston-Brighton is especially popular with paddlers because of its many hidden coves and smooth-flowing water. Daily and hourly rentals are available. Turn into the Christian Herter Park parking area and follow signs to the Charles River Canoe and Kayak Center. In the Charles River Reservation, off Soldiers Field Road; 617/965-5110.

hotel provides cozy dog beds, treats from Polka Dog Bakery, and chicken broth lollipops to all their canine guests. Ask for the "In the Doghouse" package. Oh yes, people love the accommodations, too! Rates range from $175–325 per night. No extra fee for pets. 90 Tremont Street, Boston, MA 02111; 617/772-5800; website: www.ninezero.com

Ritz-Carlton Boston Common: This latest addition to the Boston hotel scene is a welcome one. Not only is this 200-room hotel gorgeous, but they welcome dogs up to 40 pounds. (And we've seen larger, so be sure you sit up and beg nicely.) Overlooking the Boston Common, a stay here puts you close to the historic downtown, and you won't have to go far to find a place to walk your dog. You and your pup will be treated to lovely modern rooms with all the amenities. There is a $30 pet fee per night in addition to the room rates, which are around $395–1,500 per night. 10 Avery Street, Boston, MA 02111; 617/524-7100; website: www.ritzcarlton.com.

Brighton

PARKS, BEACHES, AND RECREATION AREAS

🔟 Charles River Reservation

(See Boston: The Olde Towne map on page 14)

Brighton claims three sections of the reservation on the Charles River area. All are run by the Department of Conservation and have leash laws. Open 6 A.M.–11:30 P.M. 617/635-4505.

Christian Herter Park Section

The best section in Brighton, this roomy spot is a fine alternative to the often crowded Esplanade downtown and the busy stretches along Harvard

University. The Publick Theatre unfurls its plays here, and you'll find canoe rentals, ample parking, long walkways (popular with runners, joggers, and in-line skaters), and easy swimming access to the Charles River.

Soldier's Field, home of Harvard Stadium and the famous Harvard-Yale football game, is just across the street from Christian Herter Park. Even though your pooch isn't welcome in the stadium, he can reenact his own Big Game on the green outside. And, yes, Inu, we know: real wide receivers don't have to wear leashes. The section runs from the Eliot Street Bridge to the Arsenal Street Bridge, along Soldier's Field Road.

🐾🐾 Gallagher Memorial Park

 (See Boston: The Olde Towne map on page 14)

Water dogs will thank their stars that this neighborhood park encircles Chandler Pond, where swimming is allowed. And the water is fairly clean (by canine standards). For a pleasant, half-mile morning or afternoon stroll with your leashed dog, you can walk around three-quarters of the pond, but stay off the north side, which is private property. Street parking is allowed along Lake Shore Road, except on Boston College game days.

From Commonwealth Avenue, take Lake Street heading north. Turn right on Lake Shore Road and continue to the park. Open 6 A.M.–11:30 P.M. 617/635-4505.

🐾 Rogers Park

 (See Boston: The Olde Towne map on page 14)

Live in the neighborhood? Then this small local park should suffice for a quick stop or a run. It's well maintained, but during summer, Galvin Field is overrun by local baseball players. Visitors can park on Foster Street directly in front of the entrance steps. Dogs must be leashed.

From Commonwealth Avenue, take Foster Street north. Open 6 A.M.–11:30 P.M. 617/635-4505.

Charlestown

PARKS, BEACHES, AND RECREATION AREAS

🐾 Bunker Hill Monument

🐾 🐾 (See Boston: The Olde Towne map on page 14)

On June 17, 1775, British and colonial troops fought the first major battle of the Revolutionary War on Bunker Hill. Today the monument commemorating the event is the local dog hangout of choice in Charlestown. Only two city blocks square, it's not a big park, but it's the only centrally located green space in the area. A cast-iron fence surrounds the acre-square knoll, protecting your dog from the traffic speeding by. Since there's a strict leash law here, you

DOG-EAR YOUR CALENDAR—JUNE

Doggie Day: The annual St. John's Church Doggie Day is held every June in Paul Revere Park. The day's events include pet contests, pet ownership education, health seminars, and safety workshops. Refreshments and food are available, and vendor booths are open for all your pet's needs (or wants!). The event runs from 10 A.M.–1 P.M.. For more information, contact St. John's Church at 617/242-1272.

shouldn't have to worry about Muttley making a beeline for historic Warren Tavern for a few beers with Paul Revere.

The monument is between Hill Street, Concord Street, Lexington Street, and Tremont Street. Open 24 hours. 617/242-5669.

14 Paul Revere Park

🐾🐾 (See Boston: The Olde Towne map on page 14)

If you have trouble explaining the benefits of the $15 billion Big Dig Project that has been snarling Boston roadways for over 10 years, look no further than the first park built on reclaimed land. That's right, this recently created park has the distinction of occupying land along the Charles River Dam where the elevated Northeast Expressway once connected to the Tobin Bridge. Now that the highway is underground, dogs and people can enjoy five scenic, grassy acres overlooking the Charles River; more open space is planned. Dogs must be leashed here. The park is part of the Boston Harbor Walk and is managed by the Department of Conservation.

The park is located along the Charles River between the Charles River Dam and North Washington Street/Charlestown Bridge. Open 6 A.M.–11:30 P.M. 617/626-1250.

Dorchester

PARKS, BEACHES, AND RECREATION AREAS

15 Dorchester Shores Reservation

🐾🐾🐾 (See Boston: The Olde Towne map on page 14)

When it came to rating this new park, scattered along the shores of Dorchester Bay and the mouth of the Neponset River, we invoked the "Summer in the City" rule. There really isn't much here, and what exists is partial landfill broken up into sections with the Southeast Expressway as a backdrop. It doesn't sound very attractive until the first summer day comes and your dog is desperate for a refreshing swim. Then it becomes a real hot spot. It's amazing what a little water access can do for your ratings.

The park is divided into three sections: Malibu Beach, Tenean Beach, and Victory Road Park. Victory Road Park is the most attractive. This little-known, half-mile long, man-made island will offer your dog plenty of swimming opportunities, and you will enjoy a pleasant walk on a grassy loop trail.

The Malibu and Tenean Beach sections have better beaches, but that means they attract the summer sunbathers and are a little too crowded when you need them most.

The entire reservation is part of the Department of Conservation system which requires dogs to be leashed at all times. Dogs are not permitted in the designated swimming areas from late June until early September.

To get to Victory Road Park from the Southeast Expressway, take Exit 13 (northbound side only) to Victory Road. The park, a small parking area, and a footbridge are on your immediate right.

To get to Tenean Beach from the Southeast Expressway, take Exit 12 to the Neposet Circle and Tenean Street. Turn left onto Conley Street. The park and parking is on your right.

Malibu Beach is off Morrissey Boulevard just north of the Southeast Expressway at Exit 14. Open dawn–dusk. 617/727-6034.

16 Peters Park Dog Run

🐾🐾🐾 🐕 (See Boston: The Olde Towne map on page 14)

Go dog, go! Big dogs, little dogs, black dogs, white dogs—all are happy campers in this latest addition to the soon-to-be-growing list (we hope!) of dog runs in the city. The run itself is an ample area with a few amenities, namely, a bench, a tree or two, and some trash cans. But the dogs don't seem to mind. We suggest you bring your own water in the summer months, as the grass is long gone and it can get pretty dry and dusty. The park at large is managed by the Boston Parks and Recreation Department; dogs must be leashed everywhere except the run and are not allowed on the ball fields or playgrounds.

The park is located between Washington Street and Shawmut Avenue near East Berkeley Street. Open 6 A.M.–11:30 P.M. 617/635-4000.

🐾 Pope John Paul II Park

🐾🐾🐾 (See Boston: The Olde Towne map on page 14)

This project from the Department of Conservation is a good one. Over two years in the making, the park opened in 2001 on reclaimed land at the mouth of the Neponset River. Its western border is the Southeast Expressway. That may not sound like a must-see, but the DCR deserves a nice round of applause for Pope John Paul II Park. Boasting restored wetlands, acres of rolling grass-covered hills, two miles of bike paths, playgrounds, parking, and even some limited river access, it is already a popular destination for many Dorchester residents. The spacious lawns, easily viewable from the Expressway, cause motorists trapped in traffic to look longingly for one of those signs saying, "If You Lived Here, You'd Be Home Now." Fortunately, the only ones lucky enough to live here are the ducks and geese, but the rest of us are welcome to visit.

Dogs need to be leashed and should be careful at the water's edge where glass and other debris is abundant.

To get to the north entrance from the Southeast Expressway, take Exit 12 to Gallivan Boulevard. The park is on the right just before Neponset Circle.

To get to the south entrance from the Southeast Expressway, take Exit 11B to Granite Avenue. Make the first right onto Hilltop Street and the first right onto Hallet Davis Street into the park. Open dawn–dusk. 617/727-6034.

🐾 Ronan Park

🔥 (See Boston: The Olde Towne map on page 14)

This park has a great view of Dorchester Bay, but that's about the only thing to recommend it unless your dog is in need of a quick outdoor pit stop. The panorama of the bay is terrific, but your dog probably won't give two sniffs about that. The tiny park is less than an acre. Dogs must be leashed.

Between Adams Street, Mount Ida Road, and Robinson Street. Open 6 A.M.–11:30 P.M. 617/635-4000.

Downtown Boston/Financial District

PARKS, BEACHES, AND RECREATION AREAS

🐾 Post Office Square

🐾 (See Boston: The Olde Towne map on page 14)

Post Office Square is a great example of what government and business can accomplish when they get their heads on straight. What was once a parking garage and major eyesore in the heart of the Financial District is now one of the most popular lunchtime destinations in the city. The park came to life when the surrounding business community financed the demolition of the

DIVERSIONS

Freedom Trail: Both you and your Yankee Doodle dog can discover the roots of the American Revolution on this great free walk. The 2.5-mile self-guided stroll leads you through Boston's oldest neighborhoods. Top billing goes to the State Capitol, the Old State House (not to be confused with the new State House along the Boston Common), the Old North Church, and Paul Revere's House. Along the way, you'll also encounter the Granary Burial Yard, Copp's Hill Burying Ground, and the Bunker Hill Monument. The entire route is marked with a painted red line on the sidewalks and streets of Boston.

Chow hound alert! The many aromas of Quincy Market and the Italian restaurants in the North End are sure to entice both human and canine nostrils. Steer clear until mealtime, or we won't be held responsible for any digestive trouble you may incur.

The Freedom Trail starts at the visitor center in the Boston Common located near the intersection of Park and Tremont Streets. The booth is open daily, 9 A.M.–5 P.M. For a 90-minute guided tour, call 617/242-5642 or 617/242-5689.

Harborwalk: Always a work in progress, the Harborwalk continues to make strides as a great way to explore and enjoy Boston's waterfront. Depending on the latest extent of the Big Dig construction, the trail winds along the hidden and tranquil walkways of the harbor piers: Long and Rowes Wharfs. The current version of the brick and cobblestone trail runs along the Freedom Trail in the North End, to Christopher Columbus Waterfront Park, on to the pedestrian-only Northern Avenue Bridge over the Fort Point Channel, and finally to the Esplanade. The trail north into Charlestown and South Boston continues. Grassy spots are limited. 617/536-4100; website: www.bostonharborwalk.com.

garage, rebuilt it underground, and topped it off with a beautiful park of lush grass, a bubbling spray fountain, ivy-covered trellises, and a sidewalk café. The park is only a block in size, but very popular, especially at noontime with brown baggers and people watchers. We won't declare it a daily destination for your dog, but it certainly is a refreshing oasis if you are in this part of the concrete city. The square is managed by the Friends of Post Office Square. Dogs must be leashed.

The park is bordered by Congress, Franklin, Milk, and Pearl Streets. Open 24 hours a day. 617/423-1500.

PLACES TO EAT

Ames Plow Tavern: In the summer, when there is outdoor seating among the cobblestones, this watering hole is a good stop for a true taste or drink of old Boston. The pub is always filled with a mix of locals and tourists. The beer list is long, and the pub menu includes chowder, fish and chips, and burgers. Your dog will need to sit outside on the patio area. 9 Commercial Street; 617/523-8928.

Faneuil Hall Marketplace/Quincy Market: Gastronomic grazers will discover more than 25 restaurants and food shops in this open-air marketplace. You're welcome to order a hearty sampling of wares at the inner food court and take it out to the many benches and curbstones to enjoy with your dog. There are also plenty of outdoor restaurants that line the cobblestone marketplace which welcome you and your pup. Just tell 'em Inu and George sent you. 617/523-1300; website: www.faneuilhallmarketplace.com.

Hood Milk Bottle: Not only is the giant Hood Milk Bottle one of the most recognizable features along the Fort Point Channel, it is also a quick and refreshing stop for a snack or lunch. It is located right on the boardwalk in front of the Children's Museum, where there is plenty of outdoor seating and views along the Channel. The fast-food menu always includes ice cream but constantly varies according to the latest concessionaire in place. Located at the Children's Museum on Congress Street. No phone.

Milk Street Café: Not only does this café have location, location, location, but the food is pretty good too. Right in Post Office Square, the Milk Street Café serves up tasty bagels, muffins, coffee, sandwiches, salads, and rollups for breakfast and lunch. The café has its own outdoor tables in the square, or you can just get it to go and sit anywhere within the park. Post Office Square; 617/350-7275.

Sel de la Terre: Not only is this one of the best French restaurants in Boston, but you can get your gourmet cuisine to go. During the summer, Sel de la Terre prepares specialty picnic boxes of delicious sandwiches, pâtés, and cheeses that are perfect for packing when dining along the nearby waterfront. 255 State Street; 617/720-1300.

DIVERSION

Pass the Milk Bone, matey: Hungry pups and their owners should check out the **Boston Harbor Lunch Cruises.** Each tour takes only 45 minutes; bring along your lunch and your leashed dog. The cruises to nowhere offer a break from the office, a little boating pleasure, and some fresh air for the both of you. They run twice a day, at noon and 1 P.M., Monday–Friday in July and August. 617/227-4321.

PLACES TO STAY

Hyatt Regency: Located near all the major city parks and historic Downtown Crossing, this modern hotel is happy to accommodate your pet with advance notice. No size limit, but there is a $50 pet fee per stay, and dogs are allowed in smoking rooms only. Rates are $225–350. 1 Avenue de Lafayette, Boston, MA 02111; 617/451-2600; website: www.hyatt.com.

Langham Hotel: You and your pup will be treated in style at this beautiful hotel located in the heart of the financial district. The rooms are spacious and luxurious, and a free continental breakfast is included each morning. Close to Fanueil Hall, Post Office Square Park, and the waterfront, this makes for a great weekend getaway. Rates range from $250–450 plus a $50 pet fee per stay. 250 Franklin Street, Boston, MA 02110; 617/451-1900; website: www.langhamhotels.com.

Onyx Hotel: Readers Iain and Jane Montgomery wrote to tell us how much they and their black lab, Tess, enjoyed staying at this hotel. They aren't alone. This recent entry into the Boston hotel market goes all out for their canine guests. Located a short walk from Downtown Crossing and Fanueil Hall Marketplace, Onyx Hotel is a great jumping-off spot to explore Boston. The pet package offers amenities like gourmet biscuits upon check-in, pooper-scooper bags, a dog-walking and pet-sitting service, and dog bed upon request. Rates range from $180–390 per night. 155 Portland Street, Boston, MA 02114; 617/557-9955 or 866/660-6699; website: www.onyxhotel.com.

Seaport Hotel: This new 426-room hotel is conveniently located across from the World Trade Center overlooking Boston Harbor. With contemporary facilities, full amenities, and comfortable rooms, you and your dog can stay in style and still be within walking distance of historic Boston. They welcome dogs up to 50 pounds. Rates are $189–225 per night. 1 Seaport Lane, Boston, MA 02210; 617/385-4000; website: www.seaportboston.com.

East Boston

PARKS, BEACHES, AND RECREATION AREAS

20 Belle Isle Marsh Reservation

🐾🐾🐾 (See Boston: The Olde Towne map on page 14)

If you're looking for something a little different, but not too far out of the way, hop on the T and visit Boston's last remaining saltwater wetlands. The 152 acres of Belle Isle Marsh are part of the Department of Conservation park system and provide a unique environment for a short walk with your leashed pup.

The well-maintained, mile-long path of crushed stone loops through tall reeds and open grassy expanses where the marsh has been mowed. Along the way, you'll find a short boardwalk and observation tower offering excellent views of the Boston skyline and Belle Isle Inlet. Although you might not think it possible given the color of the water here, there is an abundance of wildlife that thrives in this mixture of salt water and grass. Look for crabs, herons, and blackbirds.

The best part is that all of this is available to you via public transportation. Take the Blue Line to Suffolk Downs Station and exit onto Bennington Street. The park is right across the street on your left.

If you choose to drive, take Route 1A to Bennington Street/Route 145 east 1.5 miles. The park is on the right. Open 9 A.M.–dusk. 617/727-5330.

21 Constitution Beach

🐾🐾 (See Boston: The Olde Towne map on page 14)

This flat and sandy beach stretches for three-quarters of a mile, and the water is calm and clean—for Boston Harbor. Off the beach you'll find some grassy areas, picnic tables, and plenty of parking. Planes fly overhead, scooting in and out of Logan Airport just across the small bay, so the thought of civilization is never too far away. No one would travel here from the coast of Maine just to go for a dip, but it's a decent swimming spot if you live in town. As with all Department of Conservation beaches, dogs are not allowed on the beach from May 1 through September 30; at other times, dogs must be leashed.

From Route 1A, take Bennington Street/Route 145 east. Turn right on Saratoga Street (following Route 145). Turn right immediately on Barnes Avenue. Open dawn–dusk. 617/727-9547.

PLACES TO STAY

Hilton Hotel: Whether you and your dog are heading into or out of town, this airport location is perfect for those times when you and your pup are too tuckered out to travel any farther. No extra charge for Fido or size restrictions. Rates are $149–290. One Hotel Drive, Boston, MA 02128; 617/568-6700; website: www.hilton.com.

Hyde Park

PARKS, BEACHES, AND RECREATION AREAS

22 Stony Brook Reservation

🐾🐾🐾 (See Boston: The Olde Towne map on page 14)

Although it's only a stone's throw from Boston, this preserve has a true countryside feel. There are 464 acres of woods to sniff and explore and 10 miles of easy-to-find trails to hike. Stony Brook is a well-kept secret, and you'll probably find yourself on a solitary walk. But the park is well maintained, so the silence will be welcome rather than eerie.

DIVERSION

Canine Strolls: Join the pack for a group hike led by a DCR Park Ranger. Every other Sunday from June–August, you and your dog are invited for a nature hike at Stony Brook Reservation in Hyde Park. The canine strolls begin at 10 A.M. and last about an hour. What a great way to get some exercise and meet new dogs and their owners. For dates and information, call 617/333-7404; website: www.mass.gov/dcr/events/bhhikes.pdf.

Although you'll discover many trails off the beaten path, the most accessible and well-beaten one is just off Enneking Parkway. Beginning to the right of the parking lot, the trail takes you past Stony Brook (yes, there actually is one), which flows through the center of the reservation and into Turtle Pond. It joins the Charles River farther downstream. Dogs who like to swim should head to Turtle Pond in the reservation's western portion. The pond is just off the trail, about a quarter of a mile from the parking lot at Enneking Parkway.

If you want to make the full two-mile loop, walk past the pond on the bridle path and cut through the woodsy trail leading toward the George Wright Municipal Golf Course. The east trail returns you to the trailhead and your car. The whole loop takes about 40 minutes to complete. Dogs must be leashed.

The park is bordered by the Enneking Parkway, Turtle Pond Parkway, and Washington Street. Open 6:30 A.M.–11 P.M. 617/361-6161.

Jamaica Plain

PARKS, BEACHES, AND RECREATION AREAS

23 Arnold Arboretum

🐾🐾🐾 🐾 (See Boston: The Olde Towne map on page 14)

A glittering gemstone in the Emerald Necklace, this 265-acre park is owned by the city of Boston, which leased it to Harvard University in 1872 for 999 years at the whopping cost of $1. The university got quite a deal. If you're fond of fronds, you'll encounter more than 5,000 varieties of plant life from around the world here, including many rare botanical specimens. If you're in need of the kind of outdoor therapy that only a nature walk can provide, the arboretum is a must to visit. It's cultivated nature at its finest.

To fully explore the park takes about two hours, but you can pick your favorite sections and head right there. An excellent map by the front office can help you choose your destination. Or you can follow your pup as he follows his nose.

The terrain unfolds in a series of gentle grassy slopes with woods in and around the perimeter. You'll discover the most inviting forested areas in the park's back end, in South Woods or Peter's Hill Woods, which you can easily access via the Poplar Gate off South Street. Here you can roam among oaks, poplars, conifers, and pear and crabapple trees. On Peter's Hill, the highest point in the park at 285 feet, you'll get a great view of downtown Boston and all the greenery in between.

Flowering trees and plants occupy the front section of the arboretum, near the main gate. In spring, their spectacular blooms will really knock you out. Huge linden and chestnut trees shade aromatic lilacs, azaleas, and silverbells, among many other species. All trees and plants are clearly marked, and there are plenty of grassy areas, so you don't have to fear your dog tramping about in the plants. The highest point in this section is Bussey Hill, but the tree cover is too thick to allow a view.

If you want to find an area where your dog has a little room to exercise her legs, we recommend the Central Woods, which can be reached from the Centre Street Gate. A stretch of forest surrounding a long and gentle slope, this section provides more open space than anywhere else in the arboretum.

Locals tend to walk their dogs near the main entrance and gather near the main gates in the evenings for a little doggy socializing. Dogs must be leashed; respect the rare and beautiful plants here by observing all signs telling you where you can and cannot go. Only authorized vehicles are allowed in the park, so you needn't worry about cars speeding through.

The folks at the arboretum are friendly and helpful. Stop by the main entrance to ask questions, pick up a map of the park, or inquire about the park-sponsored nature walks and other events throughout the year on which your dog can accompany you. Admission and maps are free; generous souls will find donation boxes for their contributions.

Parking is not available in the arboretum, but you can park along the Arborway in designated areas.

To get there using public transportation, take the Orange Line to the Forest Hills stop and walk a block up Centre Street.

By car from Route 128, take Route 9 east to Jamaicaway south. At the Arborway rotary, take the Arborway and follow signs to the Arnold Arboretum and Franklin Zoo. The main entrance is a short block up from the rotary on your right. Open sunrise–sunset. 617/524-1718.

24 Franklin Park

 (See Boston: The Olde Towne map on page 14)

Really an expansive ring of woods surrounding the Franklin Park Golf Course, this park is fine for locals looking for a spot to stretch their legs with their dogs. Otherwise, the woods are a bit unkempt and scattered with broken glass, so we can't really recommend making a special trip out here.

To reach the park, follow the directions given for the Arnold Arboretum; continue one mile past the arboretum on the Arborway, and you'll see signs directing you to the park. Park across from the Franklin Zoo. Open 8 A.M.–11:30 P.M. 617/635-4505.

25 Jamaica Pond

(See Boston: The Olde Towne map on page 14)

Directly next to Olmsted Park is its twin, Jamaica Pond, which was established a year after Olmsted Park. The two have similar terrain, but Jamaica Pond is on a larger piece of land. At the park's southern tip near Parkman Boulevard, a shore section offers easy access to the clear, deep water where your dog can take a dip. Trails and walkways around the pond provide great strolls. Picnic facilities and benches are spread throughout the park, and plenty of sparse woods surround-

DIVERSION

Walk, don't run: On any given weekend in any given town, joggers can usually scare up a 5K race to participate in. Many races now include a two-mile fun walk after the road race. Jamaica Plain's annual Franklin Park Walk/Run features both events, and your dog is welcome to join in. While we don't encourage taking your dog on the run, the walks are a fine way to enjoy the same experience. This event benefits the Boston Parks and Recreation Department, the organization that maintains many of the parks listed in this chapter. The race starts at 9:30 A.M. on Thanksgiving day. You pay $10 to participate; there's no charge for your dog. For more information, call 617/635-4505.

ing the main walkway offer sniffing opportunities. Bicycles and in-line skaters are not allowed, so you won't have to dodge traffic. Walkers and joggers do use the park quite frequently, however, so allow passing room on the paths.

Dogs must be leashed. Parking is scarce, but you can leave your car along Perkins Street if you're lucky enough to find a spot.

From Route 9, take the Jamaicaway south. Turn right on Perkins Street. Open dawn–11:30 P.M. 617/635-4505.

26 Olmsted Park

🐾🐾 (See Boston: The Olde Towne map on page 14)

Established in 1891 as a link in Boston's Emerald Necklace, this park provides a quiet respite from the furious pace of the Jamaicaway zipping by just feet away. Named for Frederick Law Olmsted, the primary landscape architect for the Boston park system, it offers a woodsy, meandering, mile-long stroll around Leverett Pond. The path is far enough away from the busy street to make you think you're out in the woods. With all of the forest's excellent sniffing and squirrel-chasing options, your dog should be quite happy here. The pond, while not crystal clear, is clean enough for water hounds, and the grounds are well maintained. Although most of the street parking is for residents, you can park along Pond Road or Willow Pond Road. As in all Boston parks, dogs must be leashed.

From Route 9, turn south on the Jamaicaway or Pond Street; you can enter the park from either side. Open dawn–11:30 P.M. 617/635-4505.

North End

Boston's oldest community, home of Paul Revere and many other tradesmen in colonial times, this wonderfully cramped little neighborhood is a hidden delight. Today's North Enders tend to be young urban professionals and old-world Italians. The streets twist and turn, and driving here can be a nightmare, but if you and your dog want a real taste of Italy's charms, wander through the nooks and crannies of this fascinating area.

PARKS, BEACHES, AND RECREATION AREAS

27 Christopher Columbus Waterfront Park

🐾🐾 (See Boston: The Olde Towne map on page 14)

North End dog lovers bring their four-legged friends here to hang out and socialize. A lovely park along the water with some grassy areas, the main attraction is its lively canine social scene. Enclosed and geometrically designed gardens give the park a secret-hideaway feel. Many small steps lead among the diverse sections, some hidden by vines running up columns, others divided by wrought-iron fences. Even though the park itself is fairly small,

DIVERSION

North End saints' feasts: From late July through the end of September each year, the North End celebrates its Catholic patron saints by holding feasts and street festivals in their honor. The locations and saints honored vary, but not the fun. The biggest event is the **Fisherman's Feast** in mid-July. Some events feature fireworks, so stay away if your dog is skittish. 617/391-7715.

the layout allows you to constantly discover new nooks and crannies that you hadn't noticed before.

A beautiful waterfront pavilion runs along the water, offering shade and benches for resting or a sidewalk for walking. Keep a close eye on your dog here; the seawall edge from the walkway is not very high, but the drop-off is steep, so it would be hard to fetch your dog out of the drink if he went in. Dogs must be leashed. It's safe in the evening because of the park's proximity to hotels and the New England Aquarium.

The park is located off Commercial Avenue, between Commercial Wharf and Long Wharf. Open 24 hours. 617/635-4505.

PLACES TO EAT

In the space-starved North End, there are few restaurants that have enough outdoor seating for you and your dog to sit comfortably. There are many restaurants, however, that have benches outside where you can eat your cannoli, slurp on your Italian ice, or share a pizza to go. We suggest you just start wandering, and it won't be long before your nose will show you the way.

Joe's American Grill: This North End hangout overlooks the Boston Harbor and Christopher Columbus Park. A great place to stop after walking your dog, you and your pup are welcome to dine along the outer perimeter of the patio. Offering a varied menu of Mexican, American, and Asian cuisines, there's a little something here for everyone. 100 Atlantic Avenue; 617/367-8700.

PLACES TO STAY

Boston Harbor Hotel: Wander out the front door of this harborfront establishment, and you and your dog can stroll out along the Harborwalk to Christopher Columbus Waterfront Park. This is a fabulous, but pricey, four-star hotel offering top dog accommodations for guests' four-footed friends, too. Ask for the special Luxe Pup package—a portion of your room charge benefits the MSPCA. Rates are $200–450. 70 Rowes Wharf, Boston, MA 02110; 617/439-7000; website: www.bhh.com.

DIVERSIONS

Be a pinup pup: Is your dog worried that her wish list of chew toys won't make it to the North Pole in time for Christmas? Well, she can give Santa the list in person at the **Massachusetts Society for the Prevention of Cruelty to Animals' Annual Santa Photo Days** at the Colonnade Hotel in Boston. The small fee for the photo benefits the MSPCA's animal protection and humane education programs. Call the MSPCA for exact dates and time in December. 350 Huntington Avenue; 617/522-7400; website: www.mspca.org.

Be an angel for Angell: Be part of the spirit of Christmas at the **Angell Memorial Annual Tree Lighting Ceremony.** Folks are encouraged to bring their dogs to this traditional event benefitting the Pet Assistance Fund for pets and their owners who can't afford medical treatment. If you make a donation before the end of November, the MSPCA will put your pet's photo on a special ornament and hang it on the tree. To receive information and the ornament request form, call 617/522-7400 or download the material at www.mspca.org.

South Boston

PARKS, BEACHES, AND RECREATION AREAS

28 Castle Island Recreation Area

(See Boston: The Olde Towne map on page 14)

The entire Castle Island Recreation Area runs just under three miles along Day Boulevard from Fort Independence to Carson Beach. This park has it all: sand, sea, grass, fresh air, birds, squirrels, room to romp, and a beautiful view of the harbor. Castle Island offers so much that we've broken it down into smaller sections, which we've listed and rated below. It's quite a find, and well worth the trip if you haven't had the pleasure of visiting before. Come in winter, spring, or fall, and you'll have the place mostly to yourself. You can park in a lot at the end of Day Boulevard near the fort; street parking is also allowed as indicated. Dogs must be leashed.

Getting here can be a little tricky. If you're driving from downtown, take the Southeast Expressway to the JFK Library exit (Exit 15) and follow signs to Day Boulevard. Or in South Boston, take Dorchester Avenue to East Broadway and continue to the beach. Open dawn–dusk. 617/727-5250.

Carson Beach

This long beach extends 1.8 miles, wrapping around Day Boulevard before ending at the old gazebo at the far edge of the recreation area. Our dogs have enjoyed running after the shorebirds and chasing balls on the hard, flat sand here. The beach is protected by the harbor, so it's a safe place to swim. But the best recommendation comes from the dogs: heading back, they always sleep soundly all the way home and into the evening.

Columbus Park

Across the street from Carson Beach is a ball field and an open expanse for the dogs to run freely. They'll probably want to be on the beach, but on a hot summer day, when the beach is swarming with people and off-limits, the park is a decent alternative.

Fort Independence

This park hugs the fortified walls of Fort Independence, extending from Pleasure Bay out to the harbor and back around. Here's its history: Built in 1634, the stronghold was originally dubbed Castle William by the British, after King William III. During the Revolutionary War, it served as a British garrison until 1776. It kept its name until 1799, when President John Adams rededicated it as Fort Independence. Of course, your pup won't care a lick about the history lesson with all the sweet and salty sea air to inhale as you hike.

You can stroll for just under a mile along the path around the fort, or walk up the hill to the grassy area directly below the walls. The outer path has a

seawall, but it's very close to the deep water. Keep an eye on your dog if you think he may take a dive. George couldn't care less about the water's edge, but Inu, always captivated by the sirens, ventures a little too close to the rocky rim for our comfort.

Another hiking option is to follow the path out to the jetty that rings Pleasure Bay. This is a 2.1-mile walk, if you take the entire loop around. The path extends so far out into the harbor that you'll need your sea legs. It's cold and blustery in winter, but during the rest of the year, you'll find the walk quite invigorating and a solid workout for you and your dog. You can see Thompson Island off to your right in the middle of the harbor. Whale-watching tours may pass you on their way to Stillwagon Bank. A great day trip, the fort makes an extra-special weekend walk with your dog.

M Street Beach

From the entrance, continue west on Day Boulevard and you'll reach M Street Beach. It's a thin strip of sand, but the water's fine for swimming. The old women's bathhouse and gym, built in 1931, are located on this beach and still used today. Inside you'll find steam rooms, changing rooms, and exercise areas, making you believe you've traveled back to the age of flappers. We kept expecting to see Charlie Chaplin doing cartwheels in the sand. But if Charlie's a no-show, you can go ahead and try a few yourself. Leashed dogs are allowed on the beach but can't go into the bathhouse.

Marine Park

Alongside Day Boulevard, overlooking Pleasure Bay, this section lies at the entrance to Castle Island and provides a picnic area and an open green for running. Our dogs are always eager to explore the bushes and benches, but in no time we notice them gazing longingly at Pleasure Bay Beach across the street. Since the park isn't fenced off from the busy traffic on Day Boulevard, you should make sure your dog doesn't bolt for the sand. The park's a decent option on hot summer days when the beach gets crowded with sunbathers.

Pleasure Bay Beach

A smallish beach, it has one clear virtue: dogs are allowed to swim in the water. It's also got a great sandy stretch for running. In the summer months, dogs are only permitted after 6 P.M., but during the off-season they're welcome any time. The water is protected from the open seas, so if your dog doesn't like waves, he should be comfortable here. A seawall provides a barrier between the beach and the street, protecting those frisky dogs who tend to roam just a little too far.

DIVERSION

Take a paws: Join the legion of two- and four-footed friends for this 2.5-mile walk around Castle Island on the first weekend of May. **That Doggone Walk,** a fund-raising event for the Animal Rescue League, got off to a great start in 1998 and is now an annual event. You are encouraged to walk with your pets or in memory of pets that have departed. The event starts at 9 A.M. and goes on all day with various activities that include the Blessing of the Animals--administered by a nondenominational minister--pet education, pet vendors, races, contests, and good food for all! 617/426-9170; website: www.arlboston.org.

29 South Boston Vietnam Memorial Park

 (See Boston: The Olde Towne map on page 14)

Centered around a 1989 monument to local men and women who died in the Vietnam War, this park is set in the heart of South Boston along East Broadway. The Southie dogs that Inu and George meet here have just enough Irish savvy to give them a run for their money. They like to show our city slicker dogs the way things work in South Boston.

Well-situated among residences and retail shops, the park overlooks the Lee Playground and the Reserved Channel. With open lawns and sidewalks on a large city block, it's a popular local neighborhood park. Dogs must be leashed.

The park is located between East Broadway, M Street, and N Street. Open 6 A.M.–11:30 P.M. 617/635-4505.

30 Thomas Park

(See Boston: The Olde Towne map on page 14)

This park, the recipient of a major face-lift in 1997, is part of the Boston National Historic Park system, an organization dedicated to preserving and commemorating important American Revolution sites in the city. On March 4, 1776, General John Thomas and his men placed an American artillery on this hill that finally forced the British to evacuate Boston on March 17, 1776. Dorchester Heights gave General Thomas a commanding view of the city and harbor, and you and your dog will experience the same exhilaration when you visit here. This isn't a big park, but it is the most popular hangout for dogs in South Boston, so you'll find plenty of canine companionship here. Dogs must be leashed.

At Sixth Avenue and G Street. Open 6 A.M.–11:30 P.M. 617/635-4505.

South End

PARKS, BEACHES, AND RECREATION AREAS

🐾 Blackstone Square/Franklin Square

🐾 🐾 (See Boston: The Olde Towne map on page 14)

Established in 1849 and separated by Washington Street, these twin parks are among the top places to go for South Enders. Each is a city block long. Fences protect your dog from the busy traffic on Washington Street.

As with any twins, similarities abound. Both squares are spacious and well maintained. Both feature large central fountains with clean, free-flowing water in which dogs are welcome to take a cooling dip. And both require that pooches be leashed, even when they're splashing in the drink.

The only significant difference between the parks is tree coverage. Blackstone Square has several large oak trees that provide plenty of shade on hot August days. Franklin Square has few trees and allows plenty of sunshine to warm walkers on chilly December days.

The parks are located between Shawmut Street, St. George Street, Brookline Avenue, and Newton Avenue. Open 6 A.M.–11:30 P.M. 617/635-4505.

🐾 Southwest Corridor

🐾 🐾 (See Boston: The Olde Towne map on page 14)

No matter what the weather, this lengthy greenbelt along the border of Back Bay and the South End promises an enjoyable, protected stroll. (The corridor also stretches through Jamaica Plain, Roslindale, Hyde Park, and beyond, but we can only recommend the South End section for a visit.) A long sidewalk runs through the middle, bordered by grass and gardens on both sides. The many garden beds are cared for by local residents; in spring the blooms make a walk here really special.

DIVERSION

Be a Daytripper: For a twist on the whole doggie daycare scene, sign your dog up for a Doggie Daytripper excursion. Outings include hikes in off-leash beaches, woods, and parks for well-behaved pups. The trips are chosen with your dog's age, temperament, and physical fitness in mind. It's the next best thing to being there yourself! For details, rates, and excursions, call 617/306-1863; website: www.doggiedaytrippers.com.

DIVERSION

Fetch Fido, please: Don't have a car? Need help transporting your pup to the vet? To a grooming appointment? Maybe you just need to drop her off at a friend's home or need some errands run. That's where Fetch Four-Legged Limo comes to the rescue. This full-service taxi service will fetch Fido and ferry him wherever he wants to go. They'll even arrange for air transportation and do all the paperwork for you. Rates range from $25 for a round-trip within the city to $100 for air transportation. Sit. Come. Fetch...please! 617/480-6900; website: www.fetchlimo.com.

Lots of dogs and strollers frequent the corridor; as in all Boston parks, dogs must be leashed. A small access road winds through here, so be on the lookout for the occasional car. You'll find a small enclosed area near Massachusetts Avenue that can be used for puppy training or off-leash practice; it's not big enough to serve as a dog run.

The park is between Huntington Avenue and Columbus Avenue, extending from Yarmouth Avenue to Massachusetts Avenue. The main entrance is just across from the Back Bay T Station. Open 6 A.M.–10 P.M 617/727-0057.

33 Titus Sparrow Park

🐾🐾 (See Boston: The Olde Towne map on page 14)

This 1.5-acre park, part of the Southwest Corridor, is another popular gathering place for South End dog owners. It features a modest-sized hilly and grassy area where your leashed dog can romp with other canines. The small but well-maintained park is centrally located for most South End residents.

The park is on West Newton Avenue, off Columbus Avenue. Open 6 A.M.–11:30 P.M. 617/727-0057.

PLACES TO EAT

Tremont 647: Join the pupparazzi for Saturday afternoon happy hour on the patio at this local restaurant. Every Saturday up to five dogs are welcome to mix and mingle courtesy of the management and Polka Dog Bakery, who supplies the doggie hors d' oeuvres. How does lamb on a stick or pizza-flavored treats sound? Woof! 647 Tremont; 617/266-4600.

DIVERSIONS

Bless your pooch: The first week of May is **National Be Kind to Animals Week.** The Boston Animal Rescue League holds open houses all week, and on the first Sunday in May, a priest is on hand to administer a blessing upon you and your dog. This annual event is now held as part of **That Doggone Walk** at Castle Island. We don't know about you, but we could always use a little divine intervention. 617/426-9170.

Say cheese with Santa: Pose your pooch with Santa for a memorable holiday snapshot. Pet photos with St. Nick are an annual event at **Boston's Animal Rescue League.** Get your dog's picture taken with the Jolly One on the first Saturday in December. The flashbulbs are popping, 10 A.M.–2 P.M. at 10 Chandler Street; 617/426-9170.

Mark the Spot for Spot: If your dog likes cookies (and what dog doesn't like cookies?) then this latest Boston doggie bakery, will hit Spot's spot. **Polka Dog Bakery** provides fantastic doggie treats for many Boston hotels, restaurants and everywhere your dog wants to be. Located in the South End, your dog can choose from a myriad of flavored treats, special occasion cakes and high-end pet products such as collars, leashes and beds. 256 Shawmut Avenue; 617/338-5155; website: polkadogbakery.com.

PLACES TO STAY

Chandler Inn: This comfortable hotel features 56 rooms, an easy walk to Copley Plaza and Boston's Back Bay and, best of all, rooms at the inn for your pup. Small dogs preferred, but the management is somewhat flexible for well-behaved pooches. Rates are $99–169 per night. A refundable deposit is required for your pup. 26 Chandler Street, Boston, MA 02116; 617/482-3450 or 800/842-3450; website: www.chandlerinn.com.

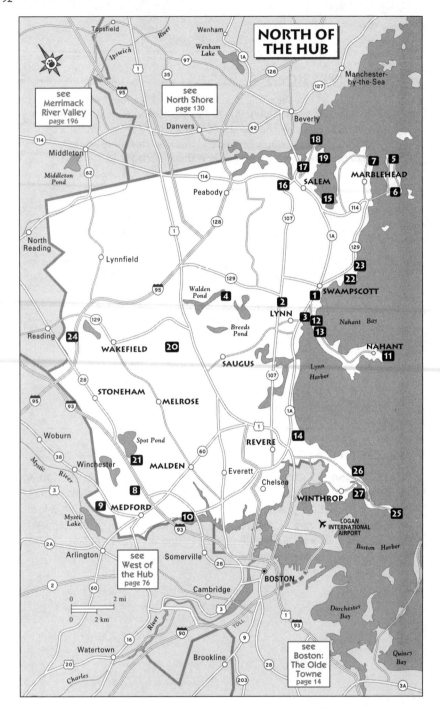

NORTH OF THE HUB

see Merrimack River Valley page 196

see North Shore page 130

Topsfield

Wenham

Wenham Lake

Ipswich River

Manchester-by-the-Sea

Beverly

Danvers

Middleton

Middleton Pond

Peabody

North Reading

Lynnfield

Walden Pond

Breeds Pond

SALEM

MARBLEHEAD

18
17 **19**
16 **7** **5**
15 **6**

SWAMPSCOTT

23
22
1
2
LYNN
3 **12**
13

Nahant Bay

NAHANT
11

Lynn Harbor

4

Reading

24

WAKEFIELD **20**

SAUGUS

STONEHAM

MELROSE

Spot Pond

Woburn

Winchester **21**

MALDEN

Everett

Chelsea

REVERE

14

WINTHROP
26
27
25

LOGAN INTERNATIONAL AIRPORT

Boston Harbor

8

9 MEDFORD

Mystic Lake

Mystic River

10

Arlington

see West of the Hub page 76

Somerville

Cambridge

BOSTON

Dorchester Bay

Watertown

Charles River

Brookline

see Boston: The Olde Towne page 14

Quincy Bay

0   2 mi
0   2 km

CHAPTER 2

North of the Hub

The folks and their dogs in the cities just north of Boston are a hard-working breed. Seafarers and international traders first settled coastal towns such as Salem and Marblehead. At one time, Salem ranked among the top seaports in the world, serving as a center for trading routes to the Far East.

Today the area is as bustling as ever. And you'll find some great wild places to explore, including rugged, rocky coasts and flat, sandy beaches. Although all beaches are off-limits during the summer months, dogs can play along many coastal areas in the off-season and after regular park hours.

Inland, Breakheart Woods, Lynn Woods, and Middlesex Fells Reservations are excellent hiking spots for dogs and people alike. Long ago the Department of Conservation and its founder, Charles Eliot, set about preserving these precious woodlands for the enjoyment of future generations. Thanks to them, folks and their dogs can experience the New England woods as our ancestors once did. So when the dog-eat-dog world of big-city life gets you down, head north, young pup! North of the Hub, that is.

PICK OF THE LITTER—NORTH OF THE HUB

BEST BEACH ACCESS
King's Beach, Lynn (page 54)

BEST WOODSY PARK
Lynn Woods Reservation, Lynn (page 55)

BEST PLACE TO RUFF IT
Middlesex Fells Reservation, Medford (page 60)

BEST PLACE TO STAY IN A HISTORIC DISTRICT
Diamond District Bed & Breakfast Inn, Lynn (page 57)

BEST SEASIDE RESORT
Seagull Inn, Marblehead (page 60)

The Department of Conservation and Recreation's Division of Urban Parks and Recreation (DCR): Formerly the Metropolitan Parks System, the DCR administers recreation areas in 34 towns and cities in the Greater Boston area, including many parks in this chapter. Dogs must be leashed in all DCR areas. For more information on its history and holdings, see the Resources section.

The Trustees of Reservations: This preservation organization manages more than 75 parks and reservations on nearly 18,000 acres throughout the Commonwealth, including lands in this chapter. Dogs must be leashed on Trustees properties. For more information on the group, see the Resources section.

Lynn

PARKS, BEACHES, AND RECREATION AREAS

1 King's Beach/Lynn Beach

🐾🐾🐾 (See North of the Hub map on page 52)

These two connecting beaches make up the entire eastern Lynn oceanfront. Together with adjacent Long Beach and Nahant Beach, they form 2.5 miles of waterfront for you and your dog to explore and enjoy. Although they adjoin the flat, sandy beaches on the Nahant Peninsula, King's and Lynn Beaches are rugged cliffs that drop sharply into the sea.

If it's not too cold, go for a dip at Nahant Beach and then dry your leashed pup off with a walk along the cliffs here. Follow the popular Lynn Shore Drive walkway/bike path for your stroll. It runs the length of all four beaches, offering pleasant views of Nahant Bay. On most days, you and your dog will have the place to yourself. George and Inu like to take a break at Red Rock Peninsula, which separates King's and Lynn Beaches. The grassy area offers a fine place to shake off that last bit of beach sand.

From Route 1A, take the Lynnway to Lynn Shore Drive. There is plenty of free nonresident parking, or street parking is available on Lynn Shore Drive. Hours are dawn–11 P.M. in the summer and dawn–dusk in the winter. 781/662-8370.

2 Lynn Common

🐾 (See North of the Hub map on page 52)

Lynn is just the place to find the common touch. Set in the center of town, Lynn Common serves as the local hub of activity, and with good reason. It's a lovely, well-kept park with grass, trees, benches, band shells, and gazebos. A half-mile-long narrow stretch between busy North Common and South Common Streets, it's not the ideal place for your leashed dog to get an aerobic workout. But you'll find it's perfect for a Sunday jaunt to get out and meet your neighbors.

From Route 1A, head west on Central Avenue to North Common Street. Park along the street around Lynn Common. Open dawn–dusk. 781/598-4000.

3 Lynn Heritage State Park

🐾 (See North of the Hub map on page 52)

Overlooking Lynn Harbor, this small park features five acres of green lawn and a modest boardwalk where you can stroll and take in some fresh air. George wishes there were a little more room for ball chasing, but Inu, always the good sport, makes the best of the situation by climbing down the rocky seawall and taking a dip.

The park's Heritage Museum, off Washington and Union Streets, preserves examples of Lynn's industrial heyday as a shoemaking hub. It's off-limits to dogs, but since they don't wear shoes, they probably wouldn't be too interested anyway. Dogs must be leashed in the park.

From Route 1A, take the Lynnway and follow signs to the parking lot. Open dawn–dusk. 781/598-1974.

4 Lynn Woods Reservation

🐾🐾🐾🐾 (See North of the Hub map on page 52)

It's easy to find open spaces and woods when you're far from Boston, but there's something special about finding that great escape close to the city limits. Lynn Woods is a terrific example of such a getaway. Lynn ranks as the

10th most densely populated city in Greater Boston, but right in its backyard is Lynn Woods: a spacious, 1,800-acre forest wonderland dotted with ponds. Encompassing a quarter of Lynn itself, the pristine reservation will give you a good idea of what a New England forest looked like more than 300 years ago. Unfortunately, dogs used to be able to explore this woodsy wonderland sans leash. But due to some unruly dogs and a refusal by some owners to pick up after their pets, well, you know the whole sad song. It's being played out in open areas across the country. No more leash-free freedom. Now dogs visiting Lynn Woods must wear their leashes. It's enough to make you want to pull out your fur!

You can enter the reservation through two major access points. To the east is the Great Woods Road entrance, and to the south is the Penny Brook Road entrance. The dirt roads were long ago closed to vehicle traffic, but there is plenty of parking at both gates.

From Great Woods Road, you can easily reach the eastern arm of Walden Pond, which stretches almost to the parking lot. A half mile down the road you'll find a waterside picnic area. Walden Pond and its tree-lined shore provides a wonderful setting for whiling away a day. We've spent many an afternoon here picnicking, and the dogs love to swim in the sparkling lake. No, this isn't the same pond that Henry David Thoreau wrote about in his classic *Walden*. You'll find that one in Concord, in Walden Pond State Reservation, but it doesn't allow dogs.

Hikers can choose from more than five miles of forest trails. Branching off Great Woods Road before the picnic area are Burrill and Loop Roads. Both lead to lovely vistas over Lynn Woods, Boston, and New Hampshire. Loop Road heads a quarter mile to the peak of 272-foot Mount Gilead. At 285 feet, Burrill Hill is the highest point in Lynn, and the one-mile hike here is a bit steep in places. At the top you'll find Stone Tower, an abandoned observation lookout; although you're welcome to examine it, numerous missing or broken steps make climbing unsafe.

The other forest lane in this area is Dungeon Road. Running one mile from Great Woods Road to Burrill Road, it leads to Dungeon Rock and Breed's Pond. Both destinations show why this is poor farming country—you have to be part mountain goat to navigate your way. The shoreline of beautiful Breed's Pond is made up entirely of boulders and cliffs; if your dog's sure of foot, he'll love it. Dungeon Rock is a big, house-sized rock with plenty of nooks and crannies for your canine pal to explore.

If your dog likes to dig, this is one place where his skills might come in handy. According to legend, Captain Veal, a renowned pirate, buried his treasure at Dungeon Rock but lost it and probably his life in a landslide. Your dog won't be the first to try to find the treasure chest; you'll see many signs of past excavation attempts among the rocks. But no one's found the loot yet, so there's a chance your pooch may finally earn his keep.

From the Penny Brook Road entrance at the park's southern end, you can follow the forest road 1.5 miles north to connect with Dungeon and Great Woods Roads. Along the way, you'll cross some minor trails that access the remote side of Birch Pond to the west. Lovely Birch Pond is about a mile long, and like the other ponds here, it's a perfect spot for swimming and fishing.

You can reach the Great Woods Road entrance from Route 128 by taking Exit 44 to Lynnfield Street/Route 129. Drive three miles and then turn right on Great Woods Road.

To get to the Penny Brook Road entrance from Route 1, take the Walnut Street/Lynn exit and go two miles. Turn right on Penny Brook Road. Open dawn–dusk. 781/593-7773.

PLACES TO EAT

Superior Roast Beef: Before heading into the Lynn Woods, pick up some last-minute subs here. Try to guess which is their specialty. On the corner of Lynnfield Street/Route 129 and Great Woods Road; 781/599-3223.

PLACES TO STAY

Diamond District Bed & Breakfast Inn: Built in the 19th century, this bed-and-breakfast is only a half block from Lynn Beach and within easy access of the heart of town. Charming and luxurious, it offers 11 rooms, all decorated differently; dogs are allowed in only two of the rooms, so be sure to call ahead. A full breakfast is served each morning on the spacious verandah. Dogs are welcome with advance approval. Rates are $145–260. 142 Ocean Street, Lynn, MA 01902; 781/599-5122 or 800/666-3076; website: www.diamonddistrictinn.com.

Malden

PARKS, BEACHES, AND RECREATION AREAS

Middlesex Fells Reservation

See Middlesex Fells Reservation, Eastern Section, in the Stoneham section in this chapter.

Marblehead

One of the most picturesque harbor towns in all of New England, Marblehead is a must-see. A major harbor since colonial days, this town served as both a center of the whaling industry in the 18th century and of the merchant trade in the 19th century. Today the homes of wealthy merchants and leaders of American independence are yours to explore, and the area's harbor views and natural beauty ensure that you and your dog love every single minute of your visit.

PARKS, BEACHES, AND RECREATION AREAS

5 Chandler Hovey Park

😸 (See North of the Hub map on page 52)

Nobody seems to recall who Chandler Hovey was, including the folks at the town hall, but he got this park named for him. Here you'll discover Marblehead Lighthouse, one of the more untraditional lighthouses in New England. An iron structure rather than a quaint, painted-wood building, it looks a bit like an oil rig. The view from the top is spectacular, spanning the rocky tip of Marblehead Neck. Across the harbor is Fort Sewall (see listing below), and beyond that you can glimpse the northern coast up to Gloucester. There's parking and a small grassy field. You also get high winds, plenty of jagged cliffs, and big waves, so watch your step and your leashed dog's paws, too.

From Route 1A, take Route 114 east into Pleasant Street. Turn right on Ocean Harbor Avenue. Continue across the Marblehead Causeway and another mile to the park at the road's end. Open dawn–dusk. 781/631-3350.

6 Devereux Beach

😸😸😸 (See North of the Hub map on page 52)

Who needs a boogie board when you can bodysurf like George and Inu? They're still, like, planning to catch the awesome waves at Maui, dude, but until then, Devereux Beach is the place to be.

This small beach on the Marblehead Causeway is a great spot to ride the waves or just relax along the shore. It's only about a half mile long and, thanks to a profusion of seaweed, doesn't attract big summer crowds. That means there will be more dogs here than people—which makes it way cool in our book, dude.

Here's our dilemma in telling you about this place: it's got a big "No Dogs" sign. But we've been coming to this beach for years (before we could read, obviously) and are always joined by other local dogs. So what's the scoop?

Parks Supervisor Tom Hammond assured us that we can, indeed, use this beach any time from October 1– May 1. The "No Dogs" sign pertains to summer months only. But canines must be leashed at all times, and you must pick up after your dog. Although

DIVERSION

Marblehead Historic District Walking Tour: Explore Marblehead's rich maritime history on either a one- or two-mile tour through downtown and along the harbor. In its early years, Marblehead served as one of the principal ports of the New World, and the walk leads you to the 18th-century homes of its many artisans and craftspeople. It also passes landmarks of the American Revolution. The stroll ends at Marblehead's picturesque harbor, where you can grab a bite to eat or shop till you drop. Pick up a map at the Chamber of Commerce (52 Pleasant Street) or at the Visitor Center on the corner of Pleasant and Essex Streets; 781/631-2868.

this is still the official policy, there are plenty of folks in Marblehead who want to ban dogs all together. The main reason? People don't pick up after 'em. So, please, if you use this beach, bring along a shovel and use it for more than building sand castles.

From Route 1A, take Route 114 east into Pleasant Street. Turn right on Ocean Harbor Avenue. The beach entrance is on the right at the start of the Marblehead Causeway. Open dawn–dusk. 781/631-3350.

7 Fort Sewall

 (See North of the Hub map on page 52)

Fort Sewall, on the cliffs of Gales' Head, was built in 1742 to protect Marblehead Harbor. It may not be the most spacious spot for a dog, but he'll love the fresh sea air and the small, grassy lawns. Squint and you can even picture your pooch manning—er, dogging—the cannons during the American Revolution and the War of 1812.

Well, okay, your dog probably prefers a chew toy to a musket. But you'll still enjoy the spectacular views from the walkway and park benches over the harbor, Marblehead Neck and Lighthouse, and the outer islands. Not to mention the hundreds of boats you can see sailing the choppy waters.

The rocky cliffs that meet the pounding surf around the fort make it difficult to go swimming. If your dog would like to go for a dip, there's plenty of room by Front Street among the colorful dinghies and lobster traps. The fort has restrooms and a leash requirement.

From Route 1A, take Route 114 east into Pleasant Street north. Turn right on State Street and then left on Front Street. Park along Front Street or in the small parking lot on Front Street just past Franklin Street. Fort Sewall is a quarter-mile walk up Front Street. Open dawn–dusk. 781/631-3350.

PLACES TO EAT

Flynnies at the Beach: After a dunk and a splash at Devereux Beach, stroll to this café and get a quick lunch to go. You can choose between seafood plates or something from the grill. They prefer to keep the outdoor patio for two-legged customers, but you're welcome to eat at any of the nearby public picnic tables along the beach. It's open April 1–October 1. Devereux Beach; 781/639-3035.

The Landing: Dogs aren't allowed inside or on the porch at this restaurant for fine seafood, but that's okay. Just ask for the corner table on the patio, along the railing, and your dog can sit right next to you. From here, both of you can count the sails of the many sailboats in the harbor. And as for the meal, you may be willing to pass him a piece of your roasted Marblehead scrod, but it's doubtful you'll want to share the garlic mashed potatoes. 81 Front Street; 781/631-1878.

The Muffin Shop: All you get is a cute little bench out front for you and your dog. Still, the gourmet coffee and the pumpkin muffins hit the spot after roaming through historic Marblehead. 126 Washington Street; 781/631-8223.

PLACES TO STAY

Seagull Inn: Who couldn't love a place called Seagull Inn? Fortunately the name isn't even the best thing about it. This quaint bed-and-breakfast inn, located on Marblehead Neck, affords a harbor or ocean view from every window. There are three suites to choose from, and all include small kitchen facilities, fireplaces, a deck, and antique furnishings. But we think the best thing about this charming inn is that dogs are welcome with management approval. Rooms range from $125–250 per night. 106 Harbor Avenue, Marblehead, MA 01945; 781/631-1893; website: www.seagullinn.com.

Medford

PARKS, BEACHES, AND RECREATION AREAS

🐾 Middlesex Fells Reservation, Western Section

🐾🐾🐾🐾 (See North of the Hub map on page 52)

It's hard to believe that you could get lost in the woods so close to Boston. And although we can never remember it happening to us, it does happen to many of the visitors to the Middlesex Fells Reservation. Eventually, we, er, they, find the highway that runs through the middle of the park and find the way out. But with 2,060 acres and 50 miles of trails and carriage paths, things can get confusing.

The park is so big that it spreads across five towns: Malden, Medford, Melrose, Stoneham, and Winchester. The Northwest Expressway/I-93 divides it down the middle, creating eastern and western sections (see also Stoneham,

Middlesex Fells Reservation, Eastern Section, in this chapter). Before you head out on a hike, pick up a trail map from park headquarters in Stoneham. The map costs $4, is expertly made, and definitely comes in handy on the trail.

The western section is the larger, less developed, and more popular half of the reservation. Here long trails wind through rich woods and rugged terrain, providing just the kind of leg stretch that your dog needs on a Saturday afternoon. Don't come expecting a quick 10-minute walk—a visit to the Fells means you're going hiking.

Access the reservation either from the centrally located Sheepfold parking area or the Long Pond/Bellevue Pond parking lots on the western side. The Sheepfold, a popular gathering place for dogs and owners, is a 10-acre open meadow where you can picnic, toss balls, or just soak up some sunshine. Two trails leave from here. The 5.2-mile Reservoir Trail loops around the North, Middle, and South Reservoirs. Although they look inviting, the ponds are off-limits to dogs and people. The Skyline Trail, 6.9 miles long, also circles the reservoirs but in a wider arc. It covers the entire western section of the Middlesex Fells Reservation and at points rises above the tree line to offer fine views of the surrounding wilderness.

Both trails can be reached from Bellevue and Long Ponds. From here, take the third major trail, Cross Fells Trail. It runs 4.5 miles from east to west across the entire park, forming the only connection between the eastern and western sections at the Fellsway West Bridge. When crossing, be careful of traffic on the Northeast Expressway. Throughout the area, your dog will find a number of small brooks and marshes to cool herself on a summer afternoon, but on day hikes, be sure to carry extra water as well. Dogs must be leashed.

To reach the park headquarters from the Northwest Expressway, take Exit 33 to the Roosevelt Circle rotary. Follow the Fellsway West/Route 28 north. Turn right on Elm Street and then head left on Woodland Road at Molyneaux Circle. The park office is on your right, just past Ravine Road, at the intersection with Pond Street.

To get to the eastern trailheads from the Northwest Expressway, take Exit 33 to the Roosevelt Circle rotary. Follow the Fellsway West/Route 28 north. The Sheepfold parking lot is on your left after crossing the expressway.

Or to reach the western trailheads from the Northwest Expressway, take Exit 33 to South Border Road at the Roosevelt Circle rotary. After a quarter mile, you'll find the Bellevue Pond and Long Pond parking lots on the right. If they're full, there are several pullouts along the road. Open dawn–dusk. 781/322-2851.

9 Mystic River Reservation, Mystic Lakes Section

🐾 (See North of the Hub map on page 52)

Along the eastern shores of the Upper and Lower Mystic Lakes, you and your dog can enjoy a scenic, one-mile hike over rolling green terrain through a narrow woodland. The lakes, each about a half mile long, form the headwaters of the Mystic River, which flows into Boston Harbor. Although in places the traffic on the Mystic Valley Parkway skirts the trail, it's still worth a visit, especially in the summer, when cool breezes off the water keep your leashed dog from overheating.

From High Street/Route 60, take the Mystic Valley Parkway north. After a quarter mile, parking areas are available on the left. Open dawn–dusk. 781/662-5230.

🔟 Mystic River Reservation, Torbert McDonald Park Section

🐾🐾 (See North of the Hub map on page 52)

Cattails and marsh grasses grow tall along the Mystic River in Torbert McDonald Park, covering the entire shoreline. If your dog manages to push his way into the river here, he's earned his swim. But instead of wading through cattails, you can try walking on the paved bike path that runs alongside the river. It's about two miles long and takes you through most of the park.

The park's western section has several ball fields where dogs are not permitted, but they're welcome on the path and lawns. This section is divided from the rest of the park by the Mystic Valley Parkway. Use the bike path to pass under the road.

The central and best portion of Torbert McDonald Park is an open grassy area of low, rolling hills that overlook the easy-flowing Mystic. It's popular with sunbathers, picnickers, dog walkers, and everyday parkgoers. You'll find plenty of room to romp with your leashed dog.

Exceptionally tall marsh grasses (some over six feet high) grow in the park's eastern portion. Assorted trails crisscross their way through the high grass, creating a maze. It's a strange, wild place, where all you see and hear are the swaying cattails. Although the trails are great, the area is frequently used for hidden trysts. Make sure you make plenty of noise coming through the grass.

The Mystic River Reservation is managed by the Department of Conservation.

From the Northwest Expressway/I-93 in Somerville, take Exit 29 heading north or Exit 28 heading south to the Fellsway/Route 28 north. Just after crossing the Mystic River, take the Mystic Valley Parkway/Route 16 west. The parking lot is on the left. Open dawn–dusk. 781/662-5230.

PLACES TO STAY

AmeriSuites: This comfortable corporate hotel offers 158 rooms in a suite-style setting. All rooms include a full breakfast each morning. Dogs are welcome with prior approval. Rooms are $149–189 per night. 116 Riverside Avenue, Medford, MA 02155; 781/395-8500; website: www.amerisuites.com.

Melrose

PARKS, BEACHES, AND RECREATION AREAS

Middlesex Fells Reservation

See Stoneham, Middlesex Fells Reservation, Eastern Section, in this chapter.

Nahant

PARKS, BEACHES, AND RECREATION AREAS

11 Lodge Memorial Park

🐾🐾🐾🐾 (residents) 🐾 (nonresidents)

(See North of the Hub map on page 52)

Nahant, occupying the entire Nahant Peninsula in Massachusetts Bay, is a lovely, quiet New England coastal town, and that's the way residents want to keep it. That means they don't need the likes of you and your big-footed dog coming around, messing things up. At least that's the less-than-warm message we got.

The tip of the peninsula, East Point, is home to Northeastern University's Marine Science Center and Lodge Memorial Park. Although the park is open to visitors and leashed dogs, the small parking area only welcomes residents, and street parking is prohibited. This is true for most of Nahant, and the fine is steep, $35, as we painfully discovered. If you're a nonresident, skip to the next park. If you happen to be a resident or know someone who is, you're in luck.

The high cliffs of beautiful East Point signal the beginning of the rocky coastline for which northern New England is famous. From here, some three miles into the bay, you get great views of seabirds, the coast, lighthouses, and passing ships. Explore some of the short, unmarked trails along the cliffs, or just grab a seat on the benches or rocks and take in the refreshing sea breezes.

From Route 1A in Lynn, take the Lynnway east. At the rotary, take Nahant Road across the Causeway into Nahant. Follow the road to the end of the peninsula and the park. Open dawn–dusk. 781/595-5597.

12 Long Beach/Nahant Beach

🐾🐾🐾 (See North of the Hub map on page 52)

The Department of Conservation doesn't allow dogs on the beach from May 1–September 30, but the two of you can enjoy strolling along the sands during the off-season. The only exception to this rule is "Doggy Beach," a small strip of beach next to the old Fireman's House on the right side as you cross the Causeway. Due to local outcry, the city has made this single exception to the no-dogs moratorium. Mutt mitts are conveniently located at the entrance to the sandy beach for cleanup. You know the drill.

The arm of Nahant helps to shelter the beaches from most of the cold coastal winds that strike New England, so it can be a fine late-fall and early-spring playground. You'll have no trouble finding parking—there's space for more than 1,300 cars here. At one time, there were plans to have a ferry dock for North Shore commuters here. Although the ferry never materialized, the parking lot did. At least you won't be wondering where you're going to "paahk the caah."

During low tide, you'll also find plenty of room on the beach. Connected with King's Beach and Lynn Beach in neighboring Lynn (see the listing in this chapter), the sand runs more than 2.5 miles. And it's clean, due to the gentle rolling action of the waves off Nahant Bay.

Legend has it that the Nahant Monster lurks within the waters just off the coast. Over the years, locals have reported many sightings of the sea serpent. It is said to be twice the size of the Loch Ness Monster, have hideous green and red scales, and to come ashore to feed on just about anything. Hmm—did Inu swim through a clump of seaweed again? Dogs must be leashed.

From Route 1A in Lynn, take the Lynnway east. At the rotary, take Nahant Road across the Causeway into Nahant; extensive beach parking is on the left. Open dawn–dusk. 781/662-5230.

13 Short Beach

🐾🐾 (See North of the Hub map on page 52)

Just a little farther up the road from Long Beach is the well-hidden but equally invigorating Short Beach. And you guessed right, it's much shorter than Long Beach. (The city must have been hard-pressed for creative names here.) Out-

of-towners haven't discovered it because there is no parking, but you can still get there. Simply park at Long Beach and walk the bike path south along Nahant Road for a half mile. Leashed dogs are allowed September 30–May 1. Open dawn–dusk. 781/662-5230.

PLACES TO EAT

Tides Restaurant & Pub: Although the menu isn't terribly original—it consists of the usual burgers, fish and chips, and ice-cream choices—the location makes up for everything. Order right from the service window and stroll over to adjacent Long Beach for a beachfront dinner—the sand adds just the right extra spice. 2 Wilson Road; 781/593-7500.

Revere

PARKS, BEACHES, AND RECREATION AREAS

🐾 Revere Beach

🐾🐾 (See North of the Hub map on page 52)

A roomy paved path separates this narrow, three-mile-long beach from Revere Beach Boulevard. Even though dogs aren't allowed on the beach from May 1–September 30, you and your canine companion can do some summertime people-watching from one of the shaded pavilions along the paved walkway.

In the off-season, the calm waters and flat, relatively clean seashore make for a decent outing. It gets rather cold in winter, but in fall and spring, you'll find the sea breezes refreshing. The beach is managed by the Department of Conservation, so dogs must be leashed.

From Route 1A, take Beach Street to Revere Beach Boulevard. Parking is available right along the beach. Open dawn–dusk. 781/727-8856.

PLACES TO EAT

Kelly's: A trip to Revere wouldn't be complete without a stop at Kelly's, which is world famous for its roast beef sandwiches and lobster rolls. Expect anything you order from one of the to-go windows to bring out your dog's "I'm-so-hungry" eyes. Across the street is Revere Beach, where you'll find plenty of seating along the beach pavilions. 410 Revere Beach Boulevard; 781/233-5000.

Kell's Kreme: Yes, the name is a take-off on nearby Kelly's, but the soft serve here is no copycat. We think it's the best on the North Shore and our dogs agree! 437 Revere Boulevard; 781/289-2892.

PLACES TO STAY

Comfort Inn & Suites: This new hotel is only a few miles from Boston's Logan Airport, so travelers on their way into or out of town may find this a convenient place to stay. Offering standard rooms and king-size suites with full amenities and a free continental breakfast each morning, you may think this is as good as it gets. You'd be wrong. It gets better, because dogs are welcome. Rates are $149–209 per night, but there is an additional $100 charge per stay for your pet. 85 American Legion Highway, Revere, MA 02151; 781/485-3600; website: www.comfortinn.com.

Salem

It's hard to resist calling this town bewitching. We're referring, of course, to the infamous Witch Trials of 1692, which shall forever be associated with Salem's name. However, Salem has managed to make a virtue of this dark moment in its history. Reminders of the witch hunt lure visitors to its Witch Museum, and while in town, folks discover traces of its less notorious but illustrious past as a maritime power. From the time of the Revolutionary War through the mid-1800s, Salem played a major role in the Far East spice and silk trade. Today its harbor still thrives. Other must-see attractions include the House of the Seven Gables and the Peabody Essex Museum.

PARKS, BEACHES, AND RECREATION AREAS

15 Forest River Park

 (See North of the Hub map on page 52)

This pleasant little local park on Salem Harbor draws lots of strollers and picnickers. A paved walkway circles the shady trees and lawn, and beaches that bookend the park provide swimming access. Head for the park's western side so you don't have to view the Salem power plant across the harbor. Dogs must be leashed.

From the intersection of Routes 1A and 114 in the center of town, take West Street east. The park is at the end of West Street. Parking is available; during summer nonresidents must pay a fee. Open dawn–dusk. 978/744-0171, ext. 21.

16 Ledge Hill Park

 (See North of the Hub map on page 52)

Take a steep, quarter-mile climb to the top of Ledge Hill for a view over the town, or simply take advantage of the big grassy fields to run around and stretch your legs. The park itself is poorly maintained. Your dog must be leashed.

From the intersection of Routes 107 and 114 in the center of town, follow North Street/Route 114 west. Turn left on Mason Street. A small parking lot is on the right. Open dawn–dusk. 978/744-0171, ext. 21.

17 Salem Common

 (See North of the Hub map on page 52)

A big, open, well-maintained park in the heart of town, Salem Common is a perfect spot for doggy socializing, ball throwing, or just a leisurely sniff.

DIVERSION

Salem Heritage Trail: To take this 1.7-mile, self-guided walking tour of historic Salem, follow the painted red line along the city's sidewalks. Stroll past the House of the Seven Gables (immortalized in Nathaniel Hawthorne's novel of the same name), Pickering Wharf, and other notable wharves and maritime buildings. You'll also wander by the Salem Common and many wickedly fascinating sites of the Salem Witch Trials. Dogs are not allowed inside any of the museums. Pick up a free map at the National Park Service Visitor Center at 2 Liberty Street; 978/744-0004.

Protected from the traffic on Washington Square by a wrought-iron fence, this space offers plenty of room for you and your pooch to stretch your legs and meet the neighbors. Across the street from the Salem Witch Museum, it's in walking distance from many historical points of interest. If you live here, you probably use the park daily. If you're just passing through, we recommend it as a stop on your way in or out of town. Dogs must be leashed.

From the center of town at the intersection of Routes 114 and 1A, follow Derby Street east. Turn left on Hawthorne Boulevard. The common is at the intersection of Washington Square. Open dawn–dusk. 978/744-0171, ext. 21.

Willows Park

 (See North of the Hub map on page 52)

White willow trees, imported decades ago from Europe, give this scenic and well-designed park at the end of Salem Neck its name. Beneath a canopy of shady willows, a walkway meanders past a yacht club, pier, amphitheater, and gazebo. Along the way, you can admire views over Beverly Harbor and Collins Cove. Although it's not a very large area and your dog must be leashed, you'll both enjoy visiting the small beach on the northern tip and then walking up to the cliffs across the park lawn.

From the center of town at the intersection of Routes 114 and 1A, follow Derby Street east to Fort Avenue. The park is at the end of the road on the Salem Neck Peninsula; street parking is available. Open dawn–dusk. 978/744-0171, ext. 21.

Winter Island Memorial Park

 (See North of the Hub map on page 52)

Fort Pickering, located on the tip of Winter Island, is the gateway to Salem Harbor. You and your dog can wander along what remains of the fort on the short cliffs of the island or explore the small beach area. A stroll through some

DOG-EAR YOUR CALENDAR—MAY

Salem Seaport Festival: On Memorial Day weekend each year, Salem launches its summer season with this annual fair held in the Salem Common. You and your pup can mix and mingle with other folks while enjoying the food stands, arts and crafts, and entertainment. On every subsequent summer weekend, you'll find a festival--some big, some small--happening on the common. Most are suitable for your dog to attend. For specific information on each weekend's events, call the Chamber of Commerce at 978/744-0004.

of the interior fields takes about 15 minutes. This park won't dazzle you, but you can catch a view of the Atlantic Ocean here that just might wash away the winter cobwebs. Dogs must be leashed on this property.

From the center of town at the intersection of Routes 114 and 1A, follow Derby Street east into Fort Avenue. Turn right on Winter Island Road. Street parking is available. Open dawn–dusk. 978/744-0171, ext. 21.

PLACES TO EAT

Derby Fish and Lobster Company. Whenever Inu and Chris meet for lunch in Salem, they do it here, right in the heart of town. The railed outdoor patio is a perfect place to hang out. A busy guy like Inu always arrives late, so Chris usually orders some chowder while he's waiting. Once Inu shows up, they order a full meal. The menu features grilled swordfish, seafood kabobs, bouillabaisse, and the best cornbread this side of the Mason-Dixon line. 215 Derby Street; 978/745-2064.

PLACES TO STAY

Hawthorne Hotel: With 89 charming rooms, this beautiful and stately hotel in the heart of Salem is an upscale lodging where you and your pooch can bunk down in style. Right next to the Salem Common, it's a stone's throw from the Salem Witch Museum, restaurants, and shopping. The management prefers smallish dogs; call ahead and discuss your dog's needs with them first. Rates are $105–309 per night. Dogs are $7.50 per night. 18 West Washington Square, Salem, MA 01970; 978/744-4080 or 800/SAY-STAY (800/729-7829); website: www.hawthornehotel.com.

Salem Inn: A little gem of a bed-and-breakfast, this inn was built in 1834 by Captain Nathaniel West. It has 31 surprisingly spacious rooms, all with private baths. Continental breakfast will be served to you in the morning, but you'll have to bring the food for Fido. It's just a few blocks from the center of

DOG-EAR YOUR CALENDAR—OCTOBER

Haunted Happenings: The month of October belongs to Salem and anyone who wants to celebrate Halloween in true "witchly" fashion. Ongoing throughout the month, the site of the Salem Witch Trials provides the perfect backdrop for a Halloween parade, historic walking tours, and an art festival, as well as plenty of tricks and treats. Many retail stores decorate the sidewalks with jack-o-lanterns and will treat your dog to biscuits and water. For a full schedule of activities and events, call 978/744-3663; website: www.hauntedhappenings.org.

town on a rather busy thoroughfare, but for the charm and the price—$119–189 a night—it's a good bet for an enjoyable weekend. Dogs are an additional $15 per stay. 7 Summer Street, Salem, MA 01970; 978/741-0680 or 800/446-2995; website: www.saleminnma.com.

Stephen Daniels House: This historic bed-and-breakfast is within easy walking distance of all of Salem's haunts. It's small, only eight rooms, but very quaint and cheerful. You may bring your dog with you, but let the proprietors know you plan to do so when reserving your room. Small dogs are preferred, but large dogs won't be excluded necessarily. Rates are $115–125 per night. 1 Daniels Street, Salem, MA 01970; 978/744-5709; website: www.salemweb.com.

Saugus

PARKS, BEACHES, AND RECREATION AREAS

20 Breakheart Reservation

🐾🐾🐾 🐾 (See North of the Hub map on page 52)

The first thing you'll notice about Breakheart Reservation is that a paved road loops through the middle of it. This need not break your heart. One-mile Pine Tops Road, a single-lane, one-way route, is closed to auto traffic most of the year. Bikers, walkers, runners, and stroller pushers who don't want to rough it on the hiking trails are the only traffic it sees.

From Memorial Day–Labor Day, Pine Tops Road is open to cars. The loop makes for a pleasant ride, mostly because it retains the feel of a country lane weaving its way through forest groves. Many oak and pine branches reach down right over the road. The four of us drove the road, but Inu and George didn't appreciate the scenery as much as we did. The delicious woodland scents wafting into the car made them eager to bolt for the forest. When we finally stopped driving and flung open the doors, all we saw were two four-footed figures bounding off into the horizon.

The centerpieces of the reservation are Silver and Pearce Lakes. Surrounded by swaying pines, both clean, clear lakes sparkle in the sunshine. Pearce Lake has a public beach for swimming and a large parking lot. Dogs can swim in either lake, but they're not welcome on the beach. It's no great loss, however, as the Pearce Lake beach tends to get crowded. Silver Lake is smaller and more secluded—and a better bet for you and your dog.

Both areas have scenic shoreline trails that circle the water and enough side trails to ensure a good workout. The path around Pearce Lake stretches about 1.5 miles, and the hike to Silver Lake is a country mile. If your pup is up for more exercise, try the unmarked routes that venture into the woods on the west side of the lakes.

The rest of the reservation's trail system is well worth exploring because of the varied landscape. You can hike under the rich forest canopy or climb up to clearings on the rocky peaks for splendid views of the North Shore. Try the two-mile Ridge Trail, which runs along the western border and crosses some of the park's more rugged terrain.

Breakheart Reservation requires that visiting dogs be on a leash. The reservation's 640 acres are managed by the Department of Conservation. Pick up a free trail map at the ranger station located at the main entrance.

From Route 1, take the Lynn Fells Parkway west for .1 mile. Turn right on Forest Street. Parking is available at the reservation entrance and during the summer at the two lakes. Open 10 A.M.–6 P.M. The entrance gate closes at 5 P.M. 781/233-0834.

PLACES TO STAY

Colonial Traveler Motor Court: This 24-room motel isn't what we call luxurious, but it's clean and comfortable. Best of all, dogs are allowed in select rooms. Continental breakfast is served each morning. Rates are $69–99 per night with an additional $10 charge for Rover. 1753 Broadway, Saugus, MA 01906; 781/233-6700; website: www.colonialtraveler.com.

DIVERSION

Saugus Iron Works National Historic Site: With your pooch by your side, you can tour reconstructed ironworks and smelting furnaces and see for yourself why Saugus is considered the birthplace of the American iron and steel industry. Operated from 1646 to the 1670s, this was one of the first industrial sites in the New World. Most exhibits are outside or inside the blast furnace barn and power mill; your leashed dog is more than welcome to view them with you. The site is open 9 A.M.–5 P.M. (until 4 P.M. November–March), except on major holidays. Admission is free. 244 Central Street; 781/233-0050.

Stoneham

PARKS, BEACHES, AND RECREATION AREAS

21 Middlesex Fells Reservation, Eastern Section

🐾🐾🐾🐾 (See North of the Hub map on page 52)

Almost entirely encompassing an area known as the Virginia Wood, the eastern part of the Middlesex Fells Reservation is the smaller of the park's two sections (see also Medford, Middlesex Fells Reservation, Western Section, in this chapter). Although you get less terrain and limited parking, you'll still find some worthwhile trails to explore here. Chief among them are the section's two main hiking routes, the Crystal Spring Trail and the Cross Fells Trail.

The Crystal Spring Trail covers the reservation's northeastern corner and leads to the top of Whip Hill. A 1.5-mile loop, the route gets a little marshy in places. On the hilltop, you're not high enough above the surrounding trees to get much of a view, but your pooch should enjoy the woodsy hike anyway.

The Cross Fells Trail connects to the western section of the park via the Fellsway West Bridge, which crosses over the Northwest Expressway. The entire trail is 4.5 miles long, but it accesses many other paths if you want to make a shorter loop. Along the way, the route passes Quarter Mile Pond, a pleasant spot to take a break. You can get to the trailhead off the Fellsway East; park at the small pullout south of the Crystal Spring parking lot. Be cautious when crossing Woodland Road.

Be sure to pick up a trail map at the park headquarters (see directions below). The map costs $4, but it's invaluable. Dogs need to be kept on a leash. Two spots that are off-limits to everyone are Spot Pond Reservoir and Fells Reservoir, which hold protected public water supplies.

To reach the park headquarters from the Northwest Expressway, take Exit 33 to the Roosevelt Circle rotary. Follow the Fellsway West/Route 28 north. Turn right on Elm Street and then head left on Woodland Road at Molyneaux Circle. The office is on the right, just past Ravine Road, at the intersection with Pond Street.

To get to eastern trailhead from the Northwest Expressway, take Exit 33 to the Roosevelt Circle rotary. Follow the Fellsway West/Route 28 north. Turn right on Elm Street and then head left on Woodland Road at Molyneaux Circle. Turn right on Pond Street and then left on Lynn Fells Parkway. The Crystal Spring parking area is immediately on the left. Open dawn–dusk. 781/322-2851.

PLACES TO EAT

Dairy Dome: For a quick ice-cream stop, try this little drive-up. It also serves sandwiches and breakfast items. The outdoor seating area (three tables) isn't very scenic, but your dog is welcome. 474 Main Street; 781/438-9425.

Swampscott

PARKS, BEACHES, AND RECREATION AREAS

22 Fisherman's Beach

😺😺🐕 (See North of the Hub map on page 52)

This is a good news/bad news deal. Here's the bad news: dogs aren't even allowed to set paw on Fisherman's Beach (also called Blaney Beach) from May 1–October 1. The good news? The rest of the year, dogs can romp leash-free as long as they're under voice control and you're nearby to pick up after them.

Flat and open, Fisherman's Beach overlooks Swampscott Harbor and is protected from the large ocean waves by Nahant Bay and Lincoln House Point. It still gets its share of rough surf, so people might not find the swimming all that great. Your sea dog will love bodysurfing here, but she needs to take care not to venture into tricky waters. Keep a close eye on her from the beachside benches.

From Route 1A, take Eastern Avenue/Route 129 east. After a leftward turn, Eastern Avenue becomes Humphrey Street. Fisherman's Beach and the town pier are across from Greenwood Avenue. Park on Humphrey Street. Open dawn–dusk. 781/596-8871.

23 Phillips Beach

😺😺🐕 (See North of the Hub map on page 52)

Like Fisherman's Beach (see previous entry), your dog is welcome off leash during the winter and spring, but he's not allowed here at all from May 1–October 1. Also, the surf is strong here because half-mile-long Phillips Beach opens on the Atlantic Ocean. Inu loves to jump the waves as they come rolling in here. While your dog romps in the surf, watch him to make sure he doesn't get carried away (literally).

The sea breezes can be brisk, so if it gets too chilly for you and your pooch, forgo the water and hike the short, crisscrossing trails along Palmer Pond. The pond lies right over the sand dunes, beyond the low-lying beach shrubs. The rambling walk is about a mile long.

The no-dogs-in-summer rule is just as well, because in the summer months, only residents are allowed to park on the nearby streets. In the off-season, remember that a strict pooper-scooper law is enforced here, and your dog must be under voice control. Residents have complained about owners not picking up after their dogs on this beach, and you know the trouble that can lead to.

From Route 1A, take Eastern Avenue/Route 129 east. Where Eastern Avenue turns left into Humphrey Street, continue straight on Atlantic Avenue/Route 129. Turn right on Ocean or Longley Avenues. Park on Ocean, Longley, or Shepard Avenues. Open dawn–dusk. 781/596-8871.

PLACES TO EAT

Dale's Red Rock: This fine seafood restaurant along Nahant Bay has a take-out window and a couple of tables on the patio. The ocean views are reserved for the indoor seating, but we enjoy feasting on the clams and watching the beach traffic idle by outside. 141 Humphrey Street; 781/595-9339.

Popo's Hot Dogs: It may not have the recognition of Coney Island and Nathan's, but Swampscott and Popo's is just right for this dog. Choose your favorite frank and assorted toppings, then sit outside on the bench and watch the world go by. Fisherman's Beach is right across the street if you want a little sand with your dog. 168 Humphrey Street; 781/592-9992.

Wakefield

PARKS, BEACHES, AND RECREATION AREAS

24 Lake Quannapowitt

🐾🐾 (See North of the Hub map on page 52)

The three-mile loop around the lake makes a terrific weekend walk. Of course, you'll have to share the path with half the town, but that just means that it's a great community gathering place. Although it's popular with residents, the real local color is provided by the ducks and geese who angle for handouts on the lake. You'll love watching the windsurfers cut across the sparkling water, and your leashed dog will love taking a cool dip on a warm summer's day.

Park at manicured Veterans Field and walk the entire loop. Or if you don't want to do the whole route, start near the Boston Technologies plant on the north side. Here a large grassy area runs right along the lake off Quannapowitt Parkway, off the path that's so well beaten by the walkers, strollers, and in-line skaters on the lake's other side.

DOG-EAR YOUR CALENDAR—SEPTEMBER

Walk 9K with your canine: Amble around Lake Quannapowitt and raise money for the worthy cause of the Muscular Dystrophy Association. You and your dog can join the throngs on a New England fall day. It's held on the last Sunday in September. For more details, contact the K-9 Walk for the Muscular Dystrophy Association, 20 Conant Street, Danvers, MA 01923; 978/720-2800.

The lake is bordered by Main Street/Route 129, Church Street, North Avenue, and Quannapowitt Parkway. From Route 128, take Exit 39 to North Avenue south. The main parking area is at Veterans Field. Additional parking is along Main Street. Open dawn–dusk. 781/246-6345.

PLACES TO EAT

Liberty Bell: Subs, salads, spaghetti, and seafood come with a homemade taste and go in a fast-food style. Sit at the tables out front or scoot into the drive-through. 894 Main Street; 781/246-1155.

Winthrop

PARKS, BEACHES, AND RECREATION AREAS

25 Deer Island

🐾🐾 (See North of the Hub map on page 52)

Massachusetts once sent its prisoners to Deer Island. Then came the mentally ill, next those with infectious diseases, then the, um, trash, in the form of a massive sewage treatment plant that did the cleanup on Boston Harbor. This isn't what we'd call an attractive history.

Fortunately, Deer Island has undergone an "island makeover." In fact, it isn't even an island anymore. As part of the Boston redevelopment project, a causeway was recently built, connecting it to the southern tip of Winthrop. And in this case, if you build, they will definitely come!

Come for the new bike path which is over two miles, or the scenic landscaping and spectacular ocean views. Best of all, come for the plentiful beach areas where your dog can take a dip. Officially Deer Island is part of the City of Boston, but you can't get there from here. The only access is from Winthrop. Dogs need to be leashed.

From the intersection of Washington Avenue/Route 145, Veterans Road, and Shirley Street, take Shirley Street south onto Taft Avenue for a mile into the park. Open sunrise–sunset. 617/482-1722; website: www.bostonharborwalk.com.

26 Winthrop Beach

🐾🐾 (See North of the Hub map on page 52)

It's a bird! It's a plane! It's... both! Winthrop Beach isn't as noisy as Yirrell Beach (see next entry), and its shoreline is larger, but this is the first beach where we've encountered pigeons. And, yes, those other objects flying overhead are jumbo jets departing from Logan Airport. Our dogs don't seem to mind the planes or the pigeons, however. They just go on about their business of rolling in seaweed and looking for stinky stuff. It's a dirty job, but they've got to do it. The gentle waves of Broad Sound should lure your pooch in for a dip.

Dogs aren't allowed here from May 1–September 30; at all other times, your pooch must be on a leash.

From Route 1A, take Route 145 to Winthrop Shore Drive. Park along the seawall. Open dawn–dusk. 617/536-1160.

27 Yirrell Beach

🐾🐾🐕 (See North of the Hub map on page 52)

If you miss your flight out of Logan Airport, you can try to catch up with it here. Just reach up and grab one of the wheels as it flies right over you. Beachgoers can also check out the Deer Island Sewage Treatment Plant on the tip of Winthrop Peninsula. What a deal!

On the positive side, you'll find good waves here and a healthy population of seabirds. It's also the local dog-walking spot, so there are plenty of friendly walkers and pups frolicking in the waves. And, best of all, dogs are allowed off leash if they're under voice control.

From Route 1A, take Route 145 to Shirley Street. Park along the seawall. Open dawn–dusk. 617/536-1160.

PLACES TO STAY

The Inn at Crystal Cove: This charming 37-room hotel is located on Boston Harbor. Many of the rooms have a view of the water, some include kitchenettes, and all welcome you and your pet. Close to downtown Boston and area beaches, this is one place that is reasonably priced, comfortable, and convenient. Rates are $99–169 per night. 600 Shirley Street Winthrop, MA 02152; 617/846-9217 or 877/966-8447; website: www.inncrystalcove.com.

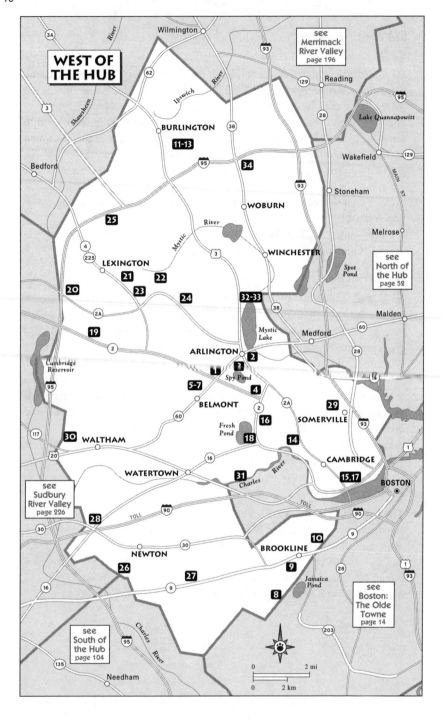

WEST OF
THE HUB

Wilmington

see
Merrimack
River Valley
page 196

3A

62

Ipswich River

River

129

Reading

95

3

Shawsheen

BURLINGTON

38

11-13

95

34

Bedford

25

River

Mystic

River

3

WOBURN

93

Stoneham

129

Wakefield

MAIN ST

Lake Quannapowitt

Melrose

WINCHESTER

Spot
Pond

see
North of
the Hub
page 52

4

225

LEXINGTON

21

22

20

23

24

32-33

38

Malden

60

2A

Mystic
Lake

Medford

28

19

2

ARLINGTON

2

Cambridge
Reservoir

Spy Pond

95

5-7

4

29

BELMONT

2

2A

SOMERVILLE

16

93

Fresh
Pond

18

14

117

30

WALTHAM

CAMBRIDGE

1

20

16

15,17

BOSTON

WATERTOWN

31

Charles   River

see
Sudbury
River Valley
page 226

28

TOLL

90

TOLL

90

30

30

10

9

NEWTON

BROOKLINE

26

27

9

Jamaica
Pond

9

28

1

93

8

203

see
Boston:
The Olde
Towne
page 14

see
South of
the Hub
page 104

95

135

Charles   River

Needham

0   2 mi

0   2 km

CHAPTER 3

West of the Hub

The towns due west of downtown Boston share one thing in common—geography. Otherwise, they're as different in population and terrain as you can get. Cambridge and Brookline, for example, boast lively political and intellectual communities centered around Coolidge Corner and Harvard Square, respectively. Arlington, Lexington, and Winchester are "suburbs in the country" that still retain the charming feel of early America, along with a shared legacy as Revolutionary War sites. Stately homes line the tree-shaded streets of Newton and Belmont, while working-class communities thrive in Waltham and Watertown, where early textile and paper mills first sprang up along the Charles River. All have deep historical and cultural roots, but the parks and pursuits they offer you and your dog vary greatly from town to town.

The Department of Conservation and Recreation's Division of Urban Parks and Recreation (DCR): Managing the Metropolitan Parks System, the DCR administers recreation areas in 34 towns and cities in the Greater Boston area, including many parks in this chapter. In all DCR areas, dogs

PICK OF THE LITTER—WEST OF THE HUB

BEST WALKWAY AND BIKEPATH
Fresh Pond Park, Cambridge (page 90)

BEST LEASH-FREE PARK
Willard's Woods Conservation Area, Lexington (page 95)

BEST COOLIDGE CORNER PLACE TO STAY
Bertram Inn, Brookline (page 85)

BEST PLACE TO STAY
Hotel Marlowe, Cambridge (page 92)

must be leashed. For more information on its history and holdings, see the Resources section.

Minuteman Bike Trail: This 11-mile paved bike path runs from Cambridge and Somerville all the way out to Bedford, passing through the towns of Arlington and Lexington along the way. Bikers who yell "The British are coming! The British are coming!" come as close as one can to re-creating Paul Revere's famous ride.

Built in 1846 as the route of the Boston-Maine Railroad, the original track has been replaced with blacktop as part of the national Rails-to-Trails program. It's now extremely popular for cyclists as well as walkers and in-line skaters. Leashed dogs are welcome, but they and their human companions must be alert, especially on Saturday and Sunday, when the number of bicyclists and skaters on the Minuteman Bike Trail can rival the number of runners in the Boston Marathon.

The best starting point is at the Alewife T Station in Cambridge, which is found at the intersection of the Concord Turnpike/Route 2 and Alewife Brook Road/Routes 2 and 3. Parking is available at the train station for a fee. For free parking, try Spy Pond Field and Park (see Arlington in this chapter) or park on the street near the trailhead. Open 24 hours; 781/646-1000.

The Trustees of Reservations: This preservation organization manages more than 75 parks and reservations located on nearly 18,000 acres throughout the Commonwealth, including lands in this chapter. Dogs must be leashed on Trustees properties. For more information on its history and holdings, see the Resources section.

Arlington

PARKS, BEACHES, AND RECREATION AREAS

1 Menotomy Rocks Park

🐾🐾🐾 (See West of the Hub map on page 76)

This wonderful neighborhood park is pint-sized—one square quarter mile all the way around. Hills Pond, in the center, is circled by a dirt path, three grassy fields, and a ring of woods that separates the park from the surrounding houses. The area takes its name from south Arlington's small rises or hummocks, of which Menotomy Rocks make up the highest point.

On a typical visit, the four of us receive a tail-wagging, dog-frisking welcome from local pooches already on the scene. Inu usually says hello and then quickly joins the water dogs for a swim. Except for the occasional duck, the pond is clear and uncluttered. A neighborhood group, the Friends of Menotomy Rocks Park, sponsors community events here and handles the upkeep of the place. The town leash law applies.

From Route 60, take Gray Street west. Turn left on Jason Street. The entrance is at the intersection of Jason Street and Brantwood and Hillsdale Roads. No parking is allowed near the gate, but you can leave your car nearby on the neighborhood streets. Open dawn 9 P.M. 781/316-3000.

2 Mystic River Reservation, Mystic Valley Parkway Section

🐾 (See West of the Hub map on page 76)

Stretching three-quarters of a mile along the pretty Mystic River, this thin strip of parkland nestles cozily between Lower Mystic Lake at the Somerville border and the Mystic Valley Parkway. Although it's not an extraordinary find, residents and their leashed dogs can get in a decent walk here. Pups will enjoy sniffing out the great smells along the water's edge and looking for remnants of the long-gone Mystic Canal. Alas, no swimming is allowed in the lake. Street traffic can be busy—keep an eye on your dog.

No parking is allowed on Mystic Valley Parkway. Try one of the side streets. From Medford Street/Route 60, take the Mystic Valley Parkway east. Open dawn–dusk. 781/662-5230.

3 Spy Pond Field and Park

🐾🐾 (See West of the Hub map on page 76)

Cyclists and runners on the adjacent Minuteman Bike Trail (see listing at the beginning of this chapter) like to cool their jets here, but this park caters mostly to residents. A narrow but pleasant strip along Spy Pond, the park features a popular children's playground and duck-feeding area. George's rubber-beak imitation didn't fool any of the feeders, but he did have a pretty good waddle. The peaceful lake is clean and big enough for windsurfing and swimming. A decent-sized green provides an alternative to the hubbub of the playground area, complete with picnic tables and benches along the water. Leashed dogs who want to stretch their legs may yearn for a bit more room than Spy Pond Field offers.

The entrance is on Pond Lane off Massachusetts Avenue/Route 3, near Arlington Center. Free parking is available in a lot. Open dawn–9 P.M. 781/316-3880.

4 Thorndike Field

😺 (See West of the Hub map on page 76)

Just off Route 2 in a corner of East Arlington, this tiny stretch of woods and marshes isn't much of a park. The main attractions are a couple of ball fields and a parking area for the Minuteman Bike Trail, which runs beside it. In the woods beyond the ball fields, you'll find a quarter-mile path, but it's trash-ridden and in spring, very wet.

At best, the park offers a doggy pit stop along the Minuteman Bike Trail. Whenever we run the route, Inu and George find a number of local pals with whom to mix and mingle. Dogs must be leashed.

From Route 3, take Lake Street west. Turn left on Margaret Street. The park and a parking lot are at the road's end. Open dawn–9 P.M. 781/316-3880.

PLACES TO EAT

Starbucks: This coffeehouse is one of the few places in Arlington Center with outdoor seating. In close walking distance to Spy Pond Field and the Minuteman Bike Trail, it's popular with the local dog community. Look for it on the corner of Massachusetts Avenue and Medford Street. 327 Massachusetts Avenue; 781/641-2893.

Belmont

PARKS, BEACHES, AND RECREATION AREAS

5 Beaver Brook Reservation

(See West of the Hub map on page 76)

John Winthrop, Boston's founder and the first governor of the Massachusetts Bay Colony, discovered many a beaver here and named the spot after the lot of –'em. The 59 acres were set aside in 1893, the year Charles Eliot and Sylvester Baxter began the Department of Conservation, so Beaver Brook became the first reservation in the DCR park system. Trapelo Street/Route 60 divides the park into two sections, Mill Pond and Waverly Oaks. Dogs must be leashed in both areas. Both sections are open dawn–dusk. 617/484-6357.

Mill Pond Section

The beavers are long gone, but you'll still find plenty of wildlife at this small recreation area. Canada geese, mallards, swans, and even cormorants flock to the aptly named Duck Pond—and with good reason! Bagels, day-old rolls, and scraps of Wonder Bread fly in all directions, flung by enthusiastic duck feeders.

If you can get by this flurry of activity, beyond the pond you'll discover some short but good trails that you can hike in the dry season. Use the path to the pond's left to pass the feeding frenzy and then follow the trail downhill to romp around the rocks, waterfalls, and greenery of Beaver Brook and Waverly Oaks. If you take the uphill trail, you'll reach Mill Pond, a peaceful spot compared to Duck Pond. Both ponds are about a quarter mile around, but we can't recommended them for swimming as they're awfully muddy. Picnic tables are available if you plan to spend the afternoon.

The ponds are on Mill Street .1 mile north of the intersection of Mill Street, Trapelo Road, and Waverly Oaks Road/Route 60. There is a small parking lot off Mill Street.

Waverly Oaks Section

If your dog wants a short walk or a fun ball-tossing session, head here. Waverly Oaks has a spacious field in the center, a bike path that circles it, and picnic areas. It's especially popular with picnickers and usually gets very crowded on Saturday afternoons. For longer walks or forays into the woods, you and your dog will probably want to stick to the Mill Pond Section.

The park borders both Waltham and Belmont. A parking lot is on Waverly

DOG-EAR YOUR CALENDAR—MAY

Town Day: Held in Belmont Center, this annual street fair is a great excuse for Belmont residents to invite themselves and the rest of the world to a big block party. Traffic is closed on Leonard Street for the day as local merchants share their wares, food, and fun. The Belmont Animal Hospital always has a booth for dog lovers, and you and your pooch will enjoy wandering through this quaint little town on a spring day. The festival runs 8 A.M.–4 P.M. on the third Saturday in May. For more information, call 617/489-4930.

Oaks Road/Route 60, just south of the intersection of Mill Street, Trapelo Road, and Waverly Oaks Road.

6 Highland Farm Wildlife Sanctuary

 (See West of the Hub map on page 76)

The Massachusetts Audubon Society manages this small tract of meadow and forests nestled into the surrounding Belmont community. Leashed dogs are allowed here, **but be respectful** of the bird-watchers and wildlife.

Short paths offer brief excursions into the wilderness. The main trail wanders through a corridor of tree-lined fields, and side paths branch off to the right into the secluded oak and pine woods.

The four of us usually make a couple of loops around to get in a decent workout. George and Inu don't mind repeating a few trails, as it gives them a chance to revisit some of the spots they missed the first time around. Wouldn't want to miss all those delicious smells!

The entrance is along Somerset Road, which is off Concord Avenue between Mill Street and Pleasant Street/Route 60. Park along the dirt pullouts. Open from 6 A.M.–8 P.M. 617/489-5050.

7 Rock Meadow Reservation

 (See West of the Hub map on page 76)

Once farmland and fruit orchards owned by McLean Hospital, today Rock Meadow offers hikers a sea of rolling hills covered with grass and woodlands. Three miles of trails wind among the meadows here. For a longer hike, follow one of the trails deeper into the woods across McLean Brook in the western part of the park. George, full of energy, always wants to explore every inch of the place. Inu, social butterfly that he is, usually sets his sights on greeting the other dog walkers we meet along the way. The town of Belmont and the Department of Conservation manage the park. Dogs must be leashed, primarily because of the many nesting birds here.

You can enter the park from the southwestern corner of the Mill Street and Concord Avenue intersection. The main entrance is off Mill Street, just north of Beaver Brook Reservation. The parking lot here can hold 15–20 cars. The other entrance, along Concord Avenue, is really just a turnout. It's a mile west of Highland Farm Wildlife Sanctuary. Open dawn–dusk. 617/489-8255.

Brookline

PARKS, BEACHES, AND RECREATION AREAS

There is continued talk in Brookline about establishing a dog run in one of the existing parks for leash-free roaming, but at press time no firm plans had been established. Yes, we also told you that in our last edition, but the situation is still the same. The subject continues to be discussed by the city council. We suggest that you call the Brookline Parks and Recreation for updates (617/730-2069).

8 Larz Anderson Memorial Park

🐾🐾🐾 (See West of the Hub map on page 76)

Donated to Brookline in the 1960s by philanthropist Larz Anderson, this lovely park used to be one of the best doggy hangouts in the city. We use the past tense because this once-upon-a-timeleash-freepark is no longer a leash-free space. That's right, George. Because of a few thoughtless dog owners who refused to pick up after their dogs (and a little help from a non-dog-loving constituency who seized upon every opportunity to complain to city officials about any dog infraction), dogs must bring their leashes when visiting here.

The park has two main parking areas and entrances. From the Newton Street entrance at the Massachusetts Museum of Transportation, you can drive up to the hilltop and enjoy views over the park and the cities of Brookline and Boston. Walk down the large grassy hill toward Avon Street on weekend mornings, and you'll meet many other dogs and their owners. This is a perfect spot for your pup to chase balls and romp with other canines. Or if you venture over the other side of the hill, you can roam through small clusters of woods.

Enter at Goddard Street and park either in the designated area on the street or in the parking area at the foot of the western slope. From here, you can make your way across the ball field to a rotunda and pond. The pond is small, but your dog can take a quick dip from the shore area or just sniff around the edges. Plenty of picnic tables and benches provide spots to sit and have a bite to eat. Because you're fairly close to the ball field, though, be sure your dog doesn't decide to crash someone else's party uninvited.

Make your way from the pond up through the woods to the ice rink and back to the hilltop again. The rink is off-limits, but since the only dog we've ever seen on skates was Snoopy at the Ice Capades, we doubt your dog will mind too much.

From Route 9, take Lee Street south; follow Lee Street until it turns into

DIVERSION

Book 'em, Fido: Normally we wouldn't include a retail store that allows dogs, but we have to make an exception for **Brookline Booksmith & Soundsmith.** Not only are four-footed patrons welcome inside the shop, but regulars know that all they have to do is sit politely by the front counter, and they'll be rewarded with a dog biscuit. No purchase necessary! Of course, once you're in the store, you'll have a hard time leaving without getting the latest pet book, always prominently displayed for their best customers. Want more proof that the place has gone to the dogs? Every few months the store's newsletter features a new Dog of Distinction, which includes a Miss America–style Q&A with the lucky pooch. In August, the store's windows have a Dog Days display with all the great, soon-to-be-dog-eared books you and your pooch will enjoy. 279 Harvard Street; 617/566-6660.

Clyde Street and then turn left on Newton Street. Take an immediate left on Goddard Street and turn right into the parking area, or follow Newton Street one block and turn left into the Museum of Transportation. Open dawn–dusk. 617/730-2069.

9 Reservoir Park

(See West of the Hub map on page 76)

There's more reservoir than park here, but a quick run or walk along the water's perimeter makes a pleasant outing. Bikes are not allowed here, so if you like to jog with your dog, this is prime real estate. Bench huggers can take a seat along the water and enjoy the view as it runs or walks by.

Dogs must be leashed here, and parking is scarce. Nonresidents must park on Dudley Street, a short one-way street that's somewhat difficult to find. The community was planned to prohibit shortcuts through the area, so you may have to navigate through one-way streets that lead in the opposite direction from where you want to go.

From Route 9, take Warren Street south. Turn left on Walnut Street and then left again on Dudley Street. Open from 5 A.M.–11 P.M. 617/730-2069.

10 The Riverway

(See West of the Hub map on page 76)

Established in 1890 and added as a link in the Emerald Necklace in 1893, this park laces its way along the Muddy River—an appropriate name unfortunately. The entire route is an easy walk of about a half mile. The terrain isn't diverse, and you have to walk close to the fumes of Route 1, but if you want trees and water to gaze at as you take a light stroll, this place will do the trick. Your dog must be leashed.

From Route 1, take Longwood Avenue west or Brookline Avenue south. Park on the street along either Brookline or Longwood Avenues. Open dawn–11:30 P.M. 617/635-4505.

PLACES TO STAY

Beech Tree Inn: This family-style bed-and-breakfast is located in a 100-year-old Victorian home. Modest and clean, it offers 11 rooms, each decorated differently. All of Boston's university medical schools, as well as some major hospitals, are nearby. The inn gets a lot of traffic; plan on booking well in advance. Make sure you inform them when you make your reservation that you'll be bringing Rover along. It's a stone's throw from the Coolidge Corner shops. Rates are $90–200 per night, depending on whether you share a bath or not. Continental breakfast is provided. 83 Longwood Avenue, Brookline, MA 02146; 617/277-1620 or 800/544-9660; website: www.thebeechtreeinn.com.

The Bertram Inn: Built in 1907, this stately manor home in Coolidge Corner is within easy walking distance of shopping and restaurants. Each of the 14 rooms is carefully decorated (two have fireplaces). Continental breakfast is served in the dining room each morning. Rates are $110–250. Dogs stay free, but they must promise to wipe their muddy paws on the welcome mat before entering. That's not a bad idea for humans, either. 92 Sewall Avenue, Brookline, MA 02146; 617/566-2234 or 800/295-3822; website: www.bertraminn.com.

Burlington

Alas, Burlington isn't the best place to take your dog in the Boston area. Dog-park advocates were lobbying for the creation of a canine park here, but like many well-laid plans, this one died when the woman spearheading efforts moved from the area. Probably went to a town that had a few good parks! Anybody want to take up the charge?

PARKS, BEACHES, AND RECREATION AREAS

🔟 Rahanis Park

🦴 (See West of the Hub map on page 76)

This park's electrifying! Your dog will get a real charge out of it! You'll have a powerful experience here! Rahanis Park is small, but it would be even smaller if it didn't contain a parcel of land located directly below power lines.

For people, the area offers a playground, tennis courts, and ball fields. For dogs, however, there's a little field of wildflowers behind the courts and not much else. A meager, half-mile trail works its way along the corridor of power lines; it starts at the end of the soccer field, but it's really not worth the effort. Dogs must be leashed in Burlington. Hopefully, this will keep Tiger out of the muddy brook that runs through the middle of the park.

From Route 128, take Exit 34 to Winn Street north. Turn right on Locust Street and then left on Mill Street. A parking lot is on the left. Open dawn–dusk. 781/270-1695.

12 Simonds Park

 (See West of the Hub map on page 76)

With ball fields, playground, and a picnic area, human recreation takes precedence at this park at the top of town. Stay clear of these areas with your dog. You can explore a shady but tiny pine forest in the corner of the park—it's only good for a sniff or two. All dogs must have their leashes on.

From Route 128, take Exit 33 to Cambridge Street/Route 3A heading north. Turn left on Bedford Street and then take an immediate right into the park's parking lot. The park is open 7 A.M.–11 P.M. 781/270-1695.

13 Town Common

(See West of the Hub map on page 76)

For a town common, this park is beautiful, grassy, and spacious. The well-kept grounds and gardens feature a small paved path and a gazebo. It's in the center of Burlington (where else?), so traffic speeds by on all sides. But we still think it's the best place in town for a walk with your leashed pooch.

From Route 128, take Exit 33 to Cambridge Street/Route 3A north. The common is at the intersection with Bedford Street. Open 24 hours a day. 781/270-1695.

Cambridge

This eclectic college town proudly wears the title of Athens of America. Famous Harvard University and the Massachusetts Institute of Technology (MIT) reside here, and their influences are felt far and wide. Lively Harvard Square and Central Square percolate with canine-friendly folks from the four corners of the world. And countless reminders of the past remain—from George Washington's headquarters during the American Revolution to the lecture halls where Timothy Leary first urged students to "tune in, turn on, and drop out" in the psychedelic '60s. But Cambridge isn't simply a place of the past—it's a cutting-edge town that makes its own history every day.

PARKS, BEACHES, AND RECREATION AREAS

14 Cambridge Common

 (See West of the Hub map on page 76)

Just beyond Harvard Square and Harvard Yard, the Cambridge Common is a swath of greenery in the heart of Cambridge. Surrounded by Massachusetts Avenue and Garden Street, it's a fine place for a quick walk, and a great spot to catch up on your history. A plaque here commemorates George Washington's famous 1775 address to his troops, and you'll find a war memorial and other monuments of historic events. Although not a big park, it has plenty of grass, benches, and scenic sights to keep you busy after an afternoon exploring Harvard Square. A low, wrought-iron fence surrounds the perimeter, so your dog will be safe from busy Massachusetts Avenue. Keep your dog on leash. Metered street parking is available on Massachusetts Avenue or Garden Street.

Harvard Square is in the center of Cambridge. From Harvard Square, continue west on Massachusetts Avenue, and you'll find the Common. Open 24 hours a day. 617/349-4376.

15 Charles River Reservation

(See West of the Hub map on page 76)

The following portion of the reservation runs along Memorial Drive on the Cambridge side of the Charles River. Below, we have divided it into four sections. All are open 24 hours a day. 617/635-4505.

Eliot Bridge to Anderson Bridge Section

This area along Memorial Drive is closed to car traffic on Sunday afternoons. It only provides a small strip of sidewalk, so for your dog's safety, visit on

Sunday, when the road is shut down. You'll enjoy a pleasant afternoon stroll along a lovely stretch of river, close to Harvard Square. It does get busy, so be sure that your dog can handle crowds.

Anderson Bridge to Boston University Bridge Section
🐾🐾

Would you like to journey back in time, to an age when boats were a daily means of transportation? You and your leashed pooch can do it with a walk along this stretch of the Charles River. The highlight of the stroll is the Harvard Boathouse, a well-preserved remnant of a bygone era. Built in the late 1800s and still used by the Harvard crew team, the boathouse's graceful design echoes the gentle curves of the river and blends in perfectly with the area's manicured lawns and stone footbridges.

For a 1.5-mile stroll, walk on the bike path along Memorial Drive from the boathouse at Anderson Bridge and Harvard Square to the ball fields at Magazine Beach. You'll share the path with in-line skaters, joggers, and cyclists. The route cuts through grassy areas where you and your dog can play or just soak up the sun. Separating Anderson Bridge and Western Avenue is the elegant John Weeks, Jr. Bridge, a stone footbridge that provides access to the other side of the river. (Why did the chicken cross the John Weeks, Jr. Bridge? For the great view, of course—and to get to the other side.) Make the trip across for the vista up and down the Charles, if nothing else.

Between Western Avenue and River Street, the area narrows to a single sidewalk, so be careful through this short block. Beyond this block, however, the reservation opens first on a parking lot and then Magazine Beach, a lovely grassy walkway along the river. The beach part of its name is exaggerated—at best you'll find a few rocky clearings close to the water—but the green space is perfect for sunbathing. The ball field here is off-limits when games are in progress, but on weekend mornings, local Cambridge dogs and their owners gather here for some old-fashioned wagging and walking.

Except for the parking area at Magazine Beach, which can hold 40 cars, parking is scarce. To reach the Magazine Beach lot, from the Massachusetts Turnpike/I-90 take the Cambridge/Allston exit onto Cambridge Street. Cross the Charles River into Cambridge and River Street. Turn right immediately on Memorial Drive. The park and a lot are on the right. To get to the Harvard Boathouse and Harvard Square, drive 1.5 miles past the lot. Limited street parking is available along Memorial Drive.

Cambridge Parkway Section

This slender parkway along the river runs about a quarter mile beside Memorial Drive, behind the Sonesta Hotel and condominium high-rises overlooking Boston. There isn't much here, unless you just want a scenic, short walk

DIVERSION

Old Cambridge Walking Tour: Harvard Yard, Harvard Square, Cambridge Common, Tory Row, and the historical district of classic homes from the American Revolution are among the highlights of this self-guided two-mile walk. Free tour maps and brochures are available at the Cambridge Discovery Information Booth in Harvard Square or from the Cambridge Historical Society. For additional information on the walk, call 617/497-1630.

with your leashed dog, but it's quiet and fairly uncluttered by traffic. Parking is scarce; you can park at the few metered spots on Cambridge Parkway.

16 Danehy Park

 (See West of the Hub map on page 76)

Location counts, and this pleasant little park doesn't have the greatest one, but once you get here it's well laid-out and—yippee!—it's got an off-leash dog run. With three main lots, parking is easy, and maps at each entrance make finding your way around a snap.

You'll discover bathroom facilities, drinking fountains, fitness course, and picnic areas. And although she must be leashed elsewhere in the park, your pooch will be thrilled to find a dog run. The enlightened city of Cambridge considers its dogs important citizens and gave them their own space. It has a little pond (well, really a puddle), grass, gravel, and fences on three sides. Okay, it's not very big, only about 600 square feet, but it's popular on weekend mornings, when 15–20 pooches make the most of it. Enter on New Street for quick access to the dog run. The other parking lots are on Sherman Street and Field Street.

From Route 2, follow the Fresh Pond rotary to Concord Street and turn right on New Street. It looks like you are entering the back of Fresh Pond Mall, which you are, but the road also leads to the park. Or take Rindge Street off Route 2 and turn right on Sherman Street. Or from Harvard Square, take Garden Street west and turn right on Field Street. Open 8 A.M.–11 P.M. 617/349-4895.

17 Fort Washington Park

 (See West of the Hub map on page 76)

This park is a great example of what a little persuasion and perseverance can do. Cambridgeport residents were being hounded (and ticketed) for letting their dogs off leash in other Cambridge parks. So they got to doing a bit of howling on their own and lobbied the city to designate a leash-free park for dogs. What they got is leash-free access to Fort Washington Park, a small, out of the way place, where no else visited.

The historic park, once the site of a fort built in 1775, is half a city block in size and almost completely surrounded with an attractive cast-iron fence. There is a fair amount of grass and some trees, too. Our dogs enjoy playing around the remains of the fort, which consists of three cannons and some earthen mounds. Just don't yell "Charge!" or you're likely to start a stampede.

The park is located on Waverly Street between Erie and Putnam Streets. Open dawn–10 P.M., April 1–October 31; dawn–dusk, November 1–March 31. 617/349-4376.

18 Fresh Pond Park

🐾🐾🐾🐾🐕 (See West of the Hub map on page 76)

If you live in Cambridge, this is a fabulous place to go. If you don't live here, it's still pretty terrific, but only if you have wings, because there's no place to park. We suspect Cambridge residents want to keep this little piece of doggy heaven to themselves—the parking lot is for residents only, and you're not supposed to park on nearby streets. (They do ticket occasionally.)

No matter how you get here, Fresh Pond is bound to be popular with your four-legged friend, since dogs can romp here off leash as long as they're under voice control and their owners pick up after them. Fresh Pond got a face-lift in 2000; the city installed a new water treatment plant and master layout which affected leash requirements for awhile, but, thankfully, not permanently. Six mutt mitt dispensers are spread throughout the park, so you've got no excuse not to pick up after your dog. Don't blow it!

When you enter the park, you'll find a pack of happy dogs frolicking at the big grassy area near the parking area. In fact, this spot gets so much use that it must be periodically fenced off in order to let the grass grow back. On muddy fall and spring days, the dogs really tear up the place. But this is a real community gathering place, so if you and your dog want to socialize, come on down.

DIVERSION

Get jazzed with your pup: On Thursday evenings from the end of July through the end of August, listen to jazz in the open-air square next to the Charles Hotel during the **Charles Square Summer Music Series.** Beginning at 8 P.M., the casual concerts feature local and name musicians. You and your dog will enjoy the music and the ambience--unless your pup insists on howling along with the saxophone, that is. 617/536-5352.

DOG-EAR YOUR CALENDAR—
SEPTEMBER, OCTOBER

Cambridge River Festival: On the first weekend of September, Cambridge closes down Memorial Drive and turns it into the site of the annual **River Festival.** Musicians, dancers, artisans of all kinds, and international food booths abound, as the city holds this big block party. You and your dog are invited to the festivities, and it's worth checking out at least once in a lifetime. For details, call 617/349-4332.

Head of the Charles Regatta: It wouldn't be October in New England without a trip to the **Head of the Charles Regatta,** the largest single-day collegiate rowing event in the country. Rowers come from all over the world to participate. The race runs along the Charles River from the Harvard boathouses to the Massachusetts Avenue Bridge; people line up early for a ringside seat. Our dogs love all the commotion, not to mention the tasty morsels dropped on the ground. The regatta is held every year, rain or shine, on the third Sunday in October 8 A.M.–4:30 P.M. 617/864-8415.

Oktoberfest: A traditional German festival, this lively street fair takes over Harvard Square on the second Sunday in October. You'll enjoy the food, entertainment, and craft booths, and your dog will enjoy the food, the food, and the food. Did we mention the food? 617/491-3434.

If you'd rather run or stroll around the reservoir, you can follow a 2.5-mile path along the perimeter that takes you to woods, water (Little Fresh Pond), and fields. Little Fresh Pond is really just a big duck pond outside of the main reservoir, but your dog can dip his paws here. No swimming is allowed in the reservoir itself, so watch out for the breaks in the fence that your dog will be sure to find.

Finding these openings in the fence is George's favorite pastime, much to JoAnna's dismay. The city is pretty good at patching them up, but there always seem to be new ones to sniff out. He's just small enough to wriggle under the tiniest opening. More than once he's dropped his ball at the fence, letting it roll under. Then he looks up longingly, with eyes that say, "That was the best darn ball in the entire world. I know I'll never find another like it!" And off he goes to retrieve it, leaving JoAnna to stand on the other side of the fence, looking like the lookout man during a bank heist.

In addition to the reservoir, another off-limits spot is Kingsley Park, a small peninsula in the park's interior. It's reserved for picnickers, so your dog is not welcome, no matter how enticing the food smells. Given all the other leash-free perks Fresh Pond offers, our dogs agree this is a small price to pay.

From Route 2 and the Fresh Pond rotary, follow the Fresh Pond Parkway east toward Boston. The parking area is located on the right, just before you reach Huron Avenue across from Huron Road. It's not marked, so keep a look-out or you might drive right past it. Open dawn–dusk. 617/349-4793.

PLACES TO EAT

Au Bon Pain: This restaurant in the heart of Harvard Square has ample room for you, chess players, and your dog. (Categories are not mutually exclusive, of course.) Directly across from Harvard Yard and right off the Red Line T Station, the outdoor area gets more than enough activity to delight people- and dog-watchers alike. You and your pup can nosh on a croissant as local chess pros match wits at the table beside you. With fresh lemonade in the summer and hot cider in the winter, it makes a great beverage stop after a walk along the river and shopping in the Harvard Square shops. 1360 Massachusetts Avenue; 617/497-9797.

Carberry's Bakery & Coffee House: With more than 15 varieties of fresh bread baked on the premises, this delightful Central Square establishment produces the best loaves in town. We're partial to the rosemary French bread, but the cheese bread is pretty tasty, too. The coffee drinks and light menu are also terrific. In addition to outdoor tables, it's got a small parking lot—a big plus in parking-starved Cambridge—so you can enjoy this great little spot with Spot, stress free. 74-76 Prospect Street; 617/576-3530.

Kendall Square cafés: The restaurants in this little, lively outdoor enclave between Broadway and Hampshire Streets change regularly, but no matter the name, there are always plenty of dining choices to enjoy with your dog. Eat your take-out food on outdoor benches along the street.

PLACES TO STAY

The Charles Hotel: This pricey but outstanding hotel will put you right where the action is. Located in Harvard Square, the hotel is close to just about everything. There is no size restriction, but management requests you not leave your dog in the room unattended. A refundable $100 deposit is required. Rates are $199–389. 1 Bennett Street, Cambridge, MA 02138; 617/864-1200 or 800/882-1818; website: www.charleshotel.com.

Hotel Marlowe: This new luxury hotel is operated by San Francisco-based Kimpton Hotels, and Rover will get the red carpet treatment here. Upon check-in, your pup will receive a welcome package, complete with doggie treats and fleece blanket. Pet spa and dog-walking services are also available. And they should be at these prices: Rates are $280–450. No extra charge for Fido. 25 Edwin Land Blvd, Cambridge, MA 02141; 617/868-8000; website: www.hotelmarlowe.com.

Residence Inn: This suite-style hotel features full kitchens in all rooms, refrigerators, full amenities, and a complimentary buffet breakfast each morning. It's also located on the Red Line for easy trips into downtown Boston. You probably wouldn't stay here on a short visit, but if you are expecting an extended stay, dogs are allowed for an additional, nonrefundable $100 fee per stay plus $10 per night. Rates are $129–250 per night. 6 Cambridge Center Cambridge, MA 02142; 617/349-0700; website: www.residenceinn.com.

Lexington

What schoolkid hasn't heard of Lexington, the minutemen, and the events that occurred here on April 19, 1775? Well, this is the place to see where the history of our country began. Remarkably well preserved from the days of the Revolutionary War, this area feels like a 200-year-old time capsule. White colonial buildings with black and green shutters dot the streets, and you and your dog will love sniffing out all of the notable spots in this beautiful town.

Lexington has a "flexible" leash law, meaning that in city parks you may forgo the leash if your dog is truly under voice control. (Otherwise, she must remain leashed.) Let's hear it for flexible and farsighted Lexington! Of course, the same flexibility does not apply in Minute Man National Historical Park, where your history-loving pooch must stay on leash.

PARKS, BEACHES, AND RECREATION AREAS

19 Hayden Woods Conservation Area

🐾 🐕 (See West of the Hub map on page 76)

The Lexington Conservation Commission, a group formed in 1963 to protect the town's natural resources, maintains 94-acre Hayden Woods' wetlands and forest. Although the park offers a few trails, most of them bring our leash-free dogs closer to the swamps than we like them to be.

The main trail begins on Valleyfield Street, passing through an open field and the Valleyfield Playground Area. From there, it enters a moist forest of pine, maple, and oak. After a half mile, the trail splits into two. The path to the right eventually works its way to Cutler Farm Road. The trail to the left continues out to a nearby driving range. Both routes are about a quarter mile long one-way, and neither is particularly exciting.

From Route 2, take Exit 54 to Waltham Street north. Turn left on Bridge Street and then take another left on Valleyfield Street. Parking is at the road's end. Open dawn–dusk. 781/862-0500.

20 Minute Man National Historical Park, Battle Road Section

🐾 🐾 🐕 (See West of the Hub map on page 76)

Ever hear of the "shot heard 'round the world"? Well, this entire park is dedicated to that shot and the events of April 19, 1775. On that day, the British took

Battle Road through Lexington and Lincoln to reach the patriots' arms supply in Concord, and the minutemen bravely defeated them here upon their return. You and your leashed dog are welcome to walk the quarter-mile-long restored portion of Battle Road. As you do, try to imagine that you're British redcoats marching on the road, as the local militia wait in ambush behind every stone wall and tree you pass.

Other historic trails are at Fiske Hill and Hartwell Farm. Both offer roughly one-mile-long hikes in a preserved country setting. Dogs are not allowed in the park's visitor center.

From Route 128, take Exit 30B to Marrett Street/Route 2A west. Follow the signs to the national park and a parking area. Open 9 A.M.–5 P.M. 978/369-6993.

21 Parker Meadow Conservation Area

🐾🐾🐕 (See West of the Hub map on page 76)

Here the North Lexington Brook flows through 17.5 acres of wetlands, meadows, and woods. If your dog is under voice control, he can run off leash along North Lexington Brook and through a mowed grassy field on a half-mile trail that begins on Revere Street. Beyond the field, the path circles around a pond before heading into marshy woods. You may want to avoid the pond area unless your dog is an accomplished hopper of lily pads. If you drive here, you could have a muddy dog in the backseat on the way home. Neighborhood dog walkers can risk it without fear.

From Route 128, take Exit 31 to Bedford Street/Route 4 south. Turn left on Hancock Street and then right on Revere Street. A tiny parking lot is on the left, just before the Minuteman Bike Trail, which parallels the park but doesn't connect to it. Open dawn–dusk. 781/862-0500.

22 Shaker Glen Conservation Area

🐾🐾🐕 (See West of the Hub map on page 76)

Another area managed by the Lexington Conservation Commission, 16-acre Shaker Glen resides on former farmland, as does much of Lexington. These days, a forest of oak, ash, and hickory is quickly reclaiming the land. Shaker Glen Brook flows here, keeping the wetlands soggy.

In this cozy little park, hikers and their leash-free dogs can follow narrow trails through soft grassy meadows. The woodland trails range beneath a canopy of young trees that tucks you in tight. As chipmunks, squirrels, woodpeckers, and sparrows cross your path, you may feel that you've wandered into a scene from *Snow White and the Seven Dwarfs,* but don't worry. We haven't encountered any poisoned apples or wicked stepmothers here yet.

From Route 128, take Exit 32 to Middlesex Turnpike south, which becomes Lowell Street. Turn left on Fulton Road and then right on Rolfe Road. The park and a parking area are at the end of the street. Open dawn–dusk. 781/862-0500.

23 Tower Park

🐾 🐾 🐕 (See West of the Hub map on page 76)

Even though this simple woodland park won't wow you, it might provide a bit of grass, shade, and exercise. Stretching along Massachusetts Avenue at the end of town, this clean, well-maintained city park makes a decent stop if you're passing through Lexington or if you're a resident. A path runs along the avenue and through a grassy area where you can throw the ball, go for a short run, or just let Rover out for a quick, leash-free sniff. Keep an eye on him along busy Massachusetts Avenue, however.

From Route 2, take Exit 56 to Watertown Street north/Routes 4 and 225 on Massachusetts Avenue. The park is on the right; park along the street. Open dawn–dusk. 781/862-0500.

24 Whipple Hill Conservation Area

🐾 🐾 (See West of the Hub map on page 76)

At an elevation of 374 feet, Whipple Hill earns its place as Lexington's highest point. Although it falls short of being the tallest peak in the Commonwealth, the views are still breathtaking. This park encompasses the hill, along with more than 150 acres in Lexington's southeastern corner.

The short climb to the top of Whipple Hill is a perfect way to get some exercise on a summer day. The trail to the right of the parking lot quickly ascends the hill. From the rocky top, you get views over Boston and across Lexington, as well as cool and refreshing breezes. An assortment of unmarked trails head down from here, but the main path continues onto Little's Pond.

From the trailhead, the path to the left goes directly to Little's Pond, or what's left of it. It's really nothing but a puddle now. From the pond, you can wander along the streambed for a half mile across the park to Summer Street.

From Route 2, take Exit 56 to Watertown Street north/Routes 4 and 225. Turn right on Maple Street/Route 2A and head straight onto Winchester Drive at the Lowell Street intersection. A parking lot is on the right, just past Russell Drive. Open dawn–dusk. 781/862-0500.

25 Willard's Woods Conservation Area

🐾 🐾 🐾 🐕 🐕 (See West of the Hub map on page 76)

In Willard's Woods' 100 acres, you'll find a picturesque setting of pine forests, open meadows, wetlands, and a few orchards that were once used for farming. It's also a popular place for dog walking. You and your leash-free dog will love hiking through the woods on cushioned paths of pine needles or through the fields along trails lined with old stone walls.

Near the parking lot, the main trail departs from an orchard that has picnic tables and barbecue pits. From here, the trail drops down into a meadow and splits in two. The trail to the left runs along the meadow to a bike path. The trail to the right crosses Willard's Brook and enters the woods. Eventually both trails meet up again in a meadow in the park's center, creating a pleasant loop.

The Lexington Conservation Commission protects and maintains these woods. As you explore the area, you will see signs that the forest is reclaiming pastures that once were cleared for farming. Young trees and thickets now blur the line between wild woods and cultivated fields. The flexible leash law applies here, as in the rest of Lexington, so your dog may go off leash if she obeys your commands.

From Route 128, take Exit 32 to Middlesex Turnpike south, which becomes Lowell Street. Turn right on Adams Street and then right again on North Street. Turn left on Willard's Woods Road and continue a quarter mile to the park. A parking lot is at the end of the dirt road. Open dawn–dusk. 781/862-0500.

PLACES TO EAT

Bertucci's: Can we have more rolls, please? Bertucci's Italian menu is a hit all over New England, but the brick-oven rolls are what bring us back. That and the sidewalk seating area in the heart of Lexington. With George and Inu under the table, those rolls go even faster. 1777 Massachusetts Avenue; 781/860-9000.

Wilson's Farm: Fall doesn't officially start until you make a trip to Wilson's and have your caramel nut candy apple. Savor it while overlooking the farm from one of the available benches. Your dog will be sitting happily right at your feet. (It's amazing how well she'll behave here.) Wilson's isn't a restaurant, but a food shop selling plenty of fruits and vegetables, jams and preserves, pies and breads, and flowers and seasonal decorations. 10 Pleasant Street, between Routes 4 and 225; 781/862-3900.

PLACES TO STAY

Battle Green Motor Inn: Don't let the name fool you. This quaint little spot is really more like a bed-and-breakfast than a motor inn, even though you can park your car in a lot under the facilities. Set in the heart of historic Lexington, this is a perfect place to stay if you're taking in the American Revolution sites. You'll enjoy the easy walking distance to the Lexington Visitor Center, Battle Green, and Minuteman Bike Trail. Small dogs are preferred, but management will consider larger dogs on request. Rates are $89–109 per night; there is a $20 pet fee per stay. 1720 Massachusetts Avenue, Lexington, MA 02173; 781/862-6100; website: www.battlegreeninn.com.

Newton

PARKS, BEACHES, AND RECREATION AREAS

In our last edition, we told you that while no decision had been made regarding adding a dog park in Newton, this is always a hot topic. Well nothing has changed. The neighbors around Crystal Lake and Normumbega Parks are still unhappy about the doggy-action these parks get. We suggest checking with the Parks and Recreation Department (617/552-7120) for the latest update, as this situation could change at any time.

26 Crystal Lake

☙ (See West of the Hub map on page 76)

This serene little slice of suburban solitude is in an elegant neighborhood just off busy Newton Centre. For a quick walk, follow the short, quarter-mile path along the lake off Lake Street. Used mostly by residents and local dog walkers, it's a lovely surprise in the middle of bustling suburbia. Dogs must be leashed, and swimming in the lake is not allowed.

From Route 128, take Exit 21 to Washington Street/Route 16 east. Turn right on Beacon Street and then left on Lake Avenue. Limited street parking is available. Open dawn–dusk. 617/552-7120.

27 Hammond Pond Reservation

☙ ☙ (See West of the Hub map on page 76)

Part of the Department of Conservation system, this reservation borders the Webster Conservation Area and the Mall at Chestnut Hill. Hammond Pond itself is in the park's eastern corner, near the parking lot. Your dog can take a dip here, but she'll rub elbows with the anglers and geese who frequent the shore. From the pond, short and easy-to-follow trails head west and north into some densely wooded, rocky areas.

The drawback to the reservation is Hammond Pond Parkway, which tears right through the middle of the park. A four-lane road, it can be hard to cross, especially on a shopper's Saturday. This is a shame, because the park's western portion has the better trails. To access this area, try taking advantage of some of the mall parking lots on the western side of Hammond Pond Parkway. Dogs must be leashed.

DOG-EAR YOUR CALENDAR—JULY, AUGUST

Sunday Evening Ethnic Festivals: Almost every Sunday afternoon into early evening, from July–August, the town of Newton sponsors an ethnic food festival at the town common between Centre and Beacon Streets. Each week it features a different cuisine, representing the multicultural spirit of the place. In the past there have been Guyanese, Italian, Indian, and many other food fairs. You and your dog can stroll through town and catch the good vibes—not to mention the great eats. For details, call 617/527-8283.

DIVERSION

Tip a canoe and your puppy, too: If your pooch dreams of high-seas adventures, she's bound to enjoy a refreshing day canoeing the Charles River. (Make sure she has her sea legs, or you'll be swabbin' the deck.) Rent a canoe, and your crew can coast along some of the more peaceful parts of the upper Charles River in Newton, Weston, and Waltham. Daily and hourly rates are available. Contact the Charles River Canoe and Kayak Center, 2401 Commonwealth Avenue; 617/965-5110.

From Route 9, take Hammond Pond Parkway heading north. The parking lot is immediately on the right. Open dawn–dusk. 617/698-1802.

Hemlock Gorge

See the listing in the Needham section of the South of the Hub chapter.

28 Normumbega Park

 (See West of the Hub map on page 76)

Leashed dogs are welcome in this small park along the Charles River in the northwestern corner of Newton. You can play in an open field or walk the quarter-mile dirt path around it. Yes, the park has some nature—a small stand of woods separates the field from the river—but it has even more pavement. Someone must have made a good deal on blacktop. The river is fairly clean, but some debris does get trapped in the coves along the shoreline. Part of the park borders the other side of the river in Weston.

From Route 128, take Exit 25 to Commonwealth Avenue and Newton. Turn left on Woodbine Street and proceed to the park gate at the road's end. Street parking is available. Open dawn–dusk. 617/552-7120.

PLACES TO EAT

Newton Centre: Downtown Newton's shopping plaza offers many outdoor dining options. Order your food to go and eat it outside on one of the benches that loop around Centre Street or Union Avenue by the T station. Some restaurants, listed below, have outdoor seating in warm weather.

Sabra: Eat in or take out a delicious meal from this Middle Eastern restaurant to share with your dog. The stuffed grape leaves are terrific. Enjoy the outdoor seating in the hub of Newton Centre. 57 Langley Road; 617/964-9275.

Starbucks: Apparently, no town is complete without one. One of the more spacious locations, this coffeehouse is set in the old Newton train station, now a T stop. Sit at a shaded outdoor table by the tracks or grab your coffee and muffin to go. 70 Union Street; 617/332-7086.

PLACES TO STAY

Sheraton Newton Hotel: With 272 rooms to choose from, there should always be room at this inn! Luckily, they also take dogs. Right off the Massachusetts Turnpike/I-90 at Exit 17, you are near local shopping and within easy distance to many area universities and parks. Dogs under 40 pounds preferred. Room rates are $150–280. 320 Washington Street, Newton, MA 02458; 617/969-3010; website: www.sheraton.com.

Somerville

Good news for Somerville dogs. After years of lamenting all those "No Dogs Allowed" signs at every park entrance, you finally have a place to call your own. Due to the tireless efforts of the Somerville Dog Owners Group, the first dog park opened in 2006. To get involved with this group, visit the website: www.somdog.org.

PARKS, BEACHES, AND RECREATION AREAS

29 Nunziato Field Off-Leash Recreational Area

🐾🐾🐕 (See West of the Hub map on page 76)

We are excited about this dog run because it is a major step in improving the life of Somerville dogs. Unfortunately, if you don't live in Somerville, it's not much to get excited about.

The run is small, abut 90 by 40 feet, and most of the grass is worn out from use. It does have a nice fence, a couple of shade trees, and a few picnic tables. There is also a separate area for small dogs. Dogs are not allowed on Nunziato Field.

The park is located at the intersection of Summer and Putnam Streets in the center of the city, near City Hall. Open 8 A.M.–10 P.M.; website: www.somdog.org.

DIVERSION

Fi-Dough: This specialty pet bakery features homemade delicacies for your pampered pup. Offering dreamy "desserts," gourmet dog biscuits, and specialty pet accessories, this one-stop store should satisfy all doggie tastes. Tell 'em George and Inu sent you. 70-E Beacon Street, Somerville, MA 02143; 617/661-3436; website: www.fidough.com.

DOG-EAR YOUR CALENDAR—MAY

When the Saint Bernards Go Marching In: You and your own saintly dog can be in that number when you join the Somerville Dog Owners Group each year for the annual Somerville Memorial Day Parade. The parade starts at City Hall, runs past Nunziato Field, through Davis Square, and ends at Teele Square. Dogs are welcome to join their owners for a day of fun, civic pride, and to provide a reminder to the city how important open space is for our best friends. A $5 donation is recommended for this 2.5-mile event. Register at the group's website: www.somdog.org.

PLACES TO EAT

Davis Square: Davis Square is one of the busiest and happening places in Somerville. But restaurants come and go as fast as the people, so we only list a few of the cafés with staying power. Suffice it to say that most of the eateries in Davis Square that have outdoor areas allow dogs.

Mike's Restaurant: One of the most recognizable establishments in Davis Square is Mike's. It also happens to be the most accommodating to dogs. Serving a menu that includes breakfast right through dinner, there is plenty of outdoor seating on the square. 9 Davis Square; 617/628-2379; website: www.mikesondavis.com.

O'Naturel's Cafe: Formerly Carberry's, this café is part hangout, part study spot, and most importantly, a full-on eatery. There are plenty of tables outside in warmer weather so you and your hound can share a turkey or veggie sandwich. 187 Elm Street; 617/666-2233.

Waltham

PARKS, BEACHES, AND RECREATION AREAS

Beaver Brook Reservation

See the listing in the Belmont section of the West of the Hub chapter.

30 Prospect Hill Park

🐾 🐾 (See West of the Hub map on page 76)

The park is open year-round, but Prospect Hill Road, which runs through the middle, only allows vehicles from April–October. You and your leashed dog can always walk the 1.5-mile route—just be prepared for a hardy climb at the start. Want to know how steep it is? Well, in winter, Prospect Hill offers

a small downhill ski area. On top, however, the terrain levels out. The access gate to Prospect Hill Road is on the right at the park entrance.

Whether you walk or drive, you'll find Prospect Hill Park to be a pleasant woodland with trails, picnic areas, and fine views over Waltham and the Cambridge Reservoir. Park at the main entrance and walk or jog the entire road to the other end of the park and back. For a little more of a workout, include the side road to the top of Prospect Hill. It branches to the left off Prospect Hill Road about three-quarters of a mile from the start.

If you and your pup just want to nosh in nature, drive into the interior to any of the numerous picnic areas. Each site has a small pullout to park along the road, as well as picnic tables and a barbecue grill.

From Route 128, take Exit 27 to Totten Pond Road. The park entrance is on the right. Open dawn–dusk. 781/893-4040.

PLACES TO STAY

Homestead Studio Suites Hotel: This extended-stay hotel features studio apartments equipped with all the amenities and full kitchens. Dogs are welcome for $25 per stay. Rates are around $109–189 per night, depending on length of visit. 52 Fourth Avenue, Waltham, MA 02254; 781/890-1333; website: www.homesteadhotels.com.

Summerfield Suites Hotel: This extended-stay hotel features one- and two-bedroom suites with full amenities and kitchen facilities. Dogs under 60 pounds are welcome; no more than two dogs allowed per suite. Rates are around $119–299 per night, with an additional pet fee of $150 per stay. 54 Fourth Avenue, Waltham, MA 02451; 781/290-0026; website: www.summerfieldsuites.com.

Westin Hotel: Perched above Route 128 but well away from the traffic noise, this hilltop luxury hotel rolls out the red carpet for its four-footed guests. Rates are $119–329. 70 Third Avenue, Waltham, MA 02154; 781/290-5600; website: www.westin.com.

Watertown

PARKS, BEACHES, AND RECREATION AREAS

🐾 Charles River Reservation, Charles River Road Section

🐾🐾 (See West of the Hub map on page 76)

From the intersection of Main and Mount Auburn Streets, follow the bike path along the river on Charles River Road to the Watertown Yacht Club. The river is very sleepy at this juncture, and there isn't much traffic along the road, so enjoy the peace and quiet. A short, half-mile stroll, it's a fine stretch of the reservation to take in a little fresh air, grass, trees, shade, and the soothing sound of the river rolling by. Two-hour parking is allowed along Charles River Road. The path is less pleasant farther up on Greenough Boulevard. Dogs must be leashed.

Take either Route 16 or Route 20 until you reach the intersection of Main Street, Mount Auburn Street, and Charles River Road, right by the Watertown Bridge. The reservation is open dawn–dusk. 617/727-0988.

Winchester

PARKS, BEACHES, AND RECREATION AREAS

🐾 Brooks-Parkhurst Town Forest

🐾🐾 (See West of the Hub map on page 76)

Nestled among the many homes of southeastern Winchester, these woods make a pretty spot for a quick walk with your four-footed friend. The 25-acre forest features a well-marked, half-mile loop trail. The hilly terrain is clean and safe for your leashed dog.

From Main Street/Route 38, take Grove Street southwest. Turn left on either West Chardon Road or Sussex Road. The town forest and street parking are at the road's end. Open dawn–dusk. 781/729-5151.

Middlesex Fells Reservation, Western Section

See the listing in the Medford section of the North of the Hub chapter.

🐾 Mystic River Reservation, Mystic Lakes Section

🐾🐾🐾 (See West of the Hub map on page 76)

Although parkland covers much of the eastern shoreline of Upper and Lower Mystic Lakes, it's the Sandy Beach Peninsula that your dog will love the most. Safely tucked away from the busy traffic of the Mystic Valley Parkway, it allows plenty of room where she can kick up her canine heels and just be a dog.

Sandy Beach juts out into Upper Mystic Lake, offering fine views and refreshing breezes. Our dogs like to stroll along the paved walkway, sniffing out secret shoreline scents. In the wooded section at the tip of the peninsula, you'll find a picnic area and a large open lawn to stretch your legs.

Serious dog walkers like to use this area as a home base and journey down the trail that runs between Upper Mystic Lake and the Mystic Valley Parkway. You can follow it all the way into Medford and to Lower Mystic Lake. Although the path narrows in a few places, it's still a pleasant one-mile walk.

If only your dog were allowed to ramble off leash here! The Department of Conservation manages the area and requires that dogs remain on leashes. Another doggy downer is that canines are not permitted into the Sandy Beach swimming area. Oh well. Your pooch will have to content herself with the other pleasures this spot provides. A mystical note: Although this is part of the Mystic River Reservation, the river itself doesn't cross this section. Hmm. Kind of spooky.

The park is located off the Mystic Valley Parkway, just south of Bacon Street and Lake View Terrace. There is a large parking lot at the park's northern end and small turnouts at its southern end. Open dawn–dusk. 781/662-5230.

Woburn

PARKS, BEACHES, AND RECREATION AREAS

🐾 34 Forest Park

🐾 (See West of the Hub map on page 76)

When you and your pooch arrive, you won't have trouble finding the forest, but you both may ask, "Where's the park?" There's not much of a park here, but, hey, you do get a few decent acres of woods where a dog can enjoy a little exercise. The forest, though, isn't big enough to hide nearby homes or drown out the hum of Route 128. The thin oak and pine woods begin just past the upper ball field. Dogs must be leashed and aren't welcome on the ball fields.

From Route 128, take Exit 35 to Main Street south. Turn left on Brentwood Road after .2 mile, then left again on Forest Park Road. Leave your car at the Weafer Little League Park. Open dawn–dusk. 781/932-4400.

PLACES TO STAY

Holiday Inn Select: Formerly the Radisson Inn, this hotel is within easy access of major routes into and out of Boston. Best of all, they allow dogs of all sizes. Rates are around $109–159 per night with an additional pet fee of $25 per stay. 15 Middlesex Canal Road, Woburn, MA 01801; 781/935-8760; website: www.ichotels.com.

Red Roof Inn: Although you won't find many parks nearby, this dog-friendly motel provides easy access to Boston and the North Shore. Rates are around $75–95. 19 Commerce Way, Woburn, MA 01801; 781/935-7110; website: www.redroof.com.

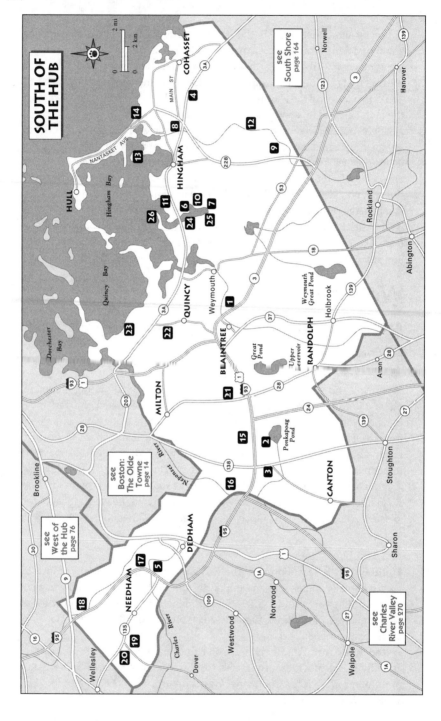

CHAPTER 4

SOUTH OF
THE HUB

see
South Shore
page 164

see
Boston:
The Olde
Towne
page 14

see
West of
the Hub
page 76

see
Charles
River Valley
page 270

South of the Hub

In the 1800s, hard-working immigrant families arriving in New England settled the region along the coastline south of Boston. Unlike the whaling ports north of the city, this area's granite quarries and shipping yards attracted craftsmen and laborers from all corners of Europe. In bygone summers, wealthy Boston families escaped the city to the cool shores and sprawling residences here. Today, Victorian clapboard houses border the estates, and beaches meld into gentle hillsides along the coast. Easily accessible from anywhere in the Greater Boston area and just a hop and a skip from downtown, this region is home to some of our favorite haunts.

The Department of Conservation and Recreation's Division of Urban Parks and Recreation (DCR): Managing the Metropolitan Parks System, the DCR administers recreation areas in 34 towns and cities in the Greater Boston area, including many parks in this chapter. In all DCR areas, dogs must be leashed. For more information on its history and holdings, see the Resources section.

PICK OF THE LITTER—SOUTH OF THE HUB

BEST OFF-LEASH ROMP
Whitney and Thayer Woods, Cohasset (page 109)

BEST OF EVERYTHING
World's End Reservation, Hingham (page 117)

BEST VIEW OF BOSTON SKYLINE
Blue Hills Reservation, Milton (page 120)

BEST EVENT NAME
Folk and Fur Fest, Hingham (page 117)

The Trustees of Reservations: This preservation organization manages more than 75 parks and reservations on nearly 18,000 acres throughout the Commonwealth, including lands in this chapter. Dogs must be leashed on Trustees properties. For more information on the group, see the Resources section.

Braintree

PARKS, BEACHES, AND RECREATION AREAS

Blue Hills Reservation
See the listing in the Quincy section of this chapter.

Pond Meadow Park
🐾 🐾 (See South of the Hub map on page 104)

Part of the Weymouth Braintree Regional Recreation Conservation Area (whew, what a mouthful!), this park covers much of the southeastern corner of Braintree. An assortment of trails crisscross its 320 acres, looping around Pond Meadow. The pond lies at the park's center; on any given day, its serene beauty attracts plenty of wildlife, visitors, and at least two thirsty dogs we know. It's a perfect spot for a summertime doggy dip.

On weekend afternoons, this place can get crowded. The park's entrance trail, which runs a quarter mile from the parking lot to the pond, is always busy with strollers, bicycles, and off-road vehicles (ORVs). Luckily, a divider separates the baby strollers from the trucks. Just before the pond, the path splits into three side trails: hiking trail, biking path, and ORV route.

If you're walking your dog, head for the hiking trail (with red markers), which goes just over a mile along the water's edge. It's less crowded than some of the wider trails and paved paths. The route ventures through exposed rock and woods down to the wetlands that surround the pond and Smelt Brook.

The off-road-vehicle trail doesn't get much use. As long as you steer clear of the four-wheelers, it's a decent walk through the woods. Stay away from the bike trail, however; it can get a bit like an expressway during rush hour. Neither you nor your dog will enjoy eating the dust of all the 10-year-old speedsters racing by. Dogs must be leashed.

From Route 3, take Exit 17 onto Union Street toward Weymouth. Turn right on Middle Street and then left on Liberty Street. The park and a parking lot are on the right. Open sunrise–sunset. 781/843-7147.

PLACES TO STAY

Holiday Inn Express: Formerly the Days Inn, this hotel allows well-behaved dogs as long as you don't leave them unattended. Just notify the front desk at check-in that you're letting sleeping dogs lie. Rates are around $119–149 plus a $10 pet fee per night. 190 Wood Road, Braintree, MA 02184; 781/848-1260; website: www.hiexpress.com/braintree.

Motel 6: All Motel 6 locations allow dogs as long as you don't leave your pet unattended. This well-situated inn is just south of downtown Boston and on the way to South Shore parks and beaches. One dog is welcome per room. Rates are $75–85. 125 Union Street, Braintree, MA 02184; 781/848-7890; website: www.motel6.com.

 DIVERSION

Santa, baby: If your pup is worried that her wish list of diamond-studded collars, gourmet dog biscuits, and a weekend visit to Camp Gone to the Dogs (see the Putney, Vermont, section in the Beyond Beantown chapter) isn't going to reach Santa in time, let her give it to the Jolly One himself at the annual **Santa Photo Day.** Sponsored by the Friends of the Plymouth Pound, this annual event is held at the PetSmart Store in Braintree (in the Kmart Plaza). Call for exact dates and times. 508/356-5980 or 508/224-6651.

Canton

PARKS, BEACHES, AND RECREATION AREAS

2 Blue Hills Reservation, Ponkapoag Pond Section

🐾🐾🐾🐾 (See South of the Hub map on page 104)

Many visitors use Route 128 to reach the Blue Hills Reservation, and who can blame them—it runs right through the middle of the park. But the highway, also known as I-93, can feel a lot like Mr. Toad's Wild Ride, with cars jockeying frantically for position. Most drivers are so busy navigating the traffic that they don't even notice the lovely, peaceful wilderness surrounding them.

If you're one of the lucky drivers taking the Ponkapoag Trail exit (yes, the trailhead has its own exit), get ready for a wonderful transformation. Soon, the drone of the traffic begins to fade, and color returns to your knuckles. You realize that the leaves are changing, the dog pops his head out the window to breathe in the fresh scents, and your heart rate slows to less than a high-speed hum.

The sunshine sparkles off the ripples on Ponkapoag Pond. In the eastern corner of the lake, marsh grasses sway in the cool breeze, and across the water, the many colors dapple the Blue Hills in the fall. The Great Blue Hill itself towers over all this beauty in silent repose. (For details on the hill, see the Blue Hills Reservation in the Milton section, later in this chapter.)

The best hiking route is the Ponkapoag Trail, which loops around Ponkapoag Pond. A flat, dry run about four miles long, it passes through thick woods, along numerous shore points, and over marshes.

Also be sure to visit the innovative Boardwalk Trail. Built in the 1930s by a professor from a local college, it is constructed out of a base of logs placed hydroponically in the marsh. Then other flat-cut logs are placed over that. The trail rises and falls depending on how wet the season is, and it's a bit like walking on a rope extension bridge. Find the trail off the Ponkapoag Trail at the northwestern corner of the pond. Your tippy, tottering hike traverses the Ponkapoag Bog for almost a half mile, leading you into the middle of a wonderful, solitary, wet wilderness. The terrain is unlike any you have seen before, mainly because the area around it is like quicksand. Without a proper walkway, it would be impassable. At the end of the trail is the extra treat of the clear, clean water of Ponkapoag Pond; our dogs love to "walk the plank" (or dive, in Inu's case) as they swim after sticks. On a hot summer day, you'll probably want to go for a dip, too.

The Blue Hills attract many visitors year-round, but most of the crowds who come to climb the Great Blue Hill miss the Ponkapoag Pond section. In fact, Inu and George often have the pond to themselves.

Leashed dogs are welcome in the Department of Conservation park. Free trail maps are available at the park headquarters in Milton, and for $1 you can get a large color map.

From Route 128/I-93, take Exit 3 to Ponkapoag Trail south. The northern parking lot and trailhead are right at the highway exit. To reach other park access points from Route 128, take Exit 2A to Route 138 south/Washington Street. For the eastern parking lot, turn left into the DCR Ponkapoag Golf Course at the Turnpike Street/Route 138 intersection. For the southern parking lot, continue straight on Turnpike Street and then turn left on Randolph Street. Turn left into the Blue Hills Reservation parking lot at the Westdale Road intersection. The park is open dawn–dusk, but the southern parking lot is only open 9 A.M.–4:30 P.M. 781/698-1802.

🖪 Eleanor Cabot Bradley Reservation

🐾🐾🐾 (See South of the Hub map on page 104)

A certain air of elegance pervades the properties in the Trustees of Reservations system, especially the Eleanor Cabot Bradley Reservation. Old cart paths wind through pleasant green pastures, flower gardens, small ponds, and pine forests. All are separated by graceful stone walls.

The park occupies 84 acres surrounding the Bradley Home and gardens. Your leashed dog isn't allowed inside the historic house, but he'll probably have a good time taking a short walk along the 1.5 miles of trails around the promises.

Just over a mile in length, the main trail leaves from the parking lot heading away from the Bradley Home. It slopes down through the pastures and enters the piney woods in the park's back section before looping back around to the house. Two quarter-mile trails branch off the loop and skirt to the edge of the property.

From Route 128, take Exit 2A to Route 138 south/Washington Street. Turn into the very first driveway on your right. A small parking lot is available. Open sunrise–sunset. 781/821-2977.

Cohasset

Hooray for Cohasset! The town has a flexible leash law. That means your well-behaved dog may walk around leash free as long as she is under voice control and accompanied by her owner.

PARKS, BEACHES, AND RECREATION AREAS

🖪 Whitney and Thayer Woods

🐾🐾🐾🐾🐾 (See South of the Hub map on page 104)

South Shore dogs know a good thing when they sniff it. And they'll find an abundance of exceptional sniffing spots on the 800 acres of beautiful woods and marshlands here. They'll also discover 12 miles of cart paths and trails to romp on leash free. That's right, dogs are allowed off leash as long as they obey their owners' voice commands and their human pals pick up after them.

Lush groves of rhododendron and azalea bushes border and at times jut into the trails in the park's southern portion. In spring, the area's foliage can be especially pretty. Follow the Milliken Memorial Path to take in the full bloom. The Great Swamp dominates the park's northern section, and the trails here can get extremely wet. The swamp drains south through the middle of the park. Boots come in handy but aren't mandatory.

Enormous, glacially formed boulders dot the park, making fine rest stops or destinations. Trail maps indicate the locations of Bigelow Boulder and Ode's Den, both of which are worth visiting. Ode takes its name from the hermit who made a home among the rocks in a gorgeous hollow. You'll find it well worth the short hike.

Whitney and Thayer Woods is adjacent to Wompatuck State Park, making it easy to expand your hike by connecting to the numerous trails in the state park.

The two parks are divided by privately owned land. Plenty of routes connect the areas, and thankfully you're free to pass on all of them. In fact, most people don't realize they have left the park until they pass the private residence on Howe's Road. Although landowners don't roll out the red carpet, it is a public byway.

George and JoAnna enjoy cross-country running here. The dirt trails are ideal for George because he doesn't like to run on pavement, and the varied terrain ensures that JoAnna gets a solid workout. Stay on the wider cart paths as these tend to be drier and less rocky. You can keep track of your mileage by checking the distances listed on the park map. Maps are available for $1.25 at the Mobil Mart across Route 3A. They're invaluable because the trail system can be confusing.

From Route 3, take Exit 14 to Pond Street/Route 228 north into Hingham. Turn right on Chief Justice Cushing Highway/Route 3A and head east into Cohasset. The park is on the right at Sohier Street. A parking lot is available. Open sunrise–sunset. 781/821-2977.

Wompatuck State Park

See the listing in the Hingham section of this chapter.

PLACES TO EAT

French Memories Bakery: Pick up a cup of cappuccino and a to-die-for cinnamon roll before you hit the trails on a sleepy Saturday morning. If the smell of the fabulous baked goods doesn't wake you up, the espresso will. 60 South Main Street; 781/383-2216.

JJ's Dairy Hut: When you've been together as long as Chris and Inu have, there are no arguments about sharing a spoon and a dish of vanilla. But in the beginning, Inu wasn't too sure about the vanilla shakes. Fortunately, it was here at JJ's that Inu mastered the art of drinking from a straw. Now Chris has to share that, too. *Slurp!* There is outdoor seating for those lovely summer beach days. Open April–October. 140 Chief Justice Cushing Highway/Route 3A; 781/383-1880.

Dedham

PARKS, BEACHES, AND RECREATION AREAS

Cutler Park

See the listing in the Needham section of this chapter.

Neponset River Reservation, Fowl Meadow Section

See the listing in the Milton section of this chapter.

5 Wilson Mountain Reservation

🐾🐾🐾 (See South of the Hub map on page 104)

This 207-acre park is the largest remaining open space in Dedham. Purchased by the Department of Conservation in 1995, the park offers scenic views of the distant Boston skyline and the Blue Hills.

There are two hiking trails: the longer two-mile loop covers a good portion of the park's perimeter, winding through a hilly terrain of granite outcroppings

DOG-EAR YOUR CALENDAR—OCTOBER

Petoberfest: Every October head on over to the Animal Rescue League in Dedham for their yearly fur-, er, fund-raising fair at Pine Ridge Animal Center. This family event features games, crafts, a petting zoo, animal awareness education, food, and tons of fun for you and your pet. Take part in a pet talent show, training session with local animal experts, and lots of mingling with other dog folk. Call for exact date and details. 55 Annas Place; 781/326-0729 or 617/426-9170.

and hemlock forest. The shorter three-quarter-mile loop doesn't fool around. It takes you right where every hiker wants to go—to the top of Mount Wilson. Note that the trail here is steep and slippery in some places but negotiable for all but the tiniest of dogs.

From I-95/Route 128, take Exit 17 to Needham Avenue/Route 135, then east onto Common Street for a quarter mile. The park and parking lot are on the right. Maps are displayed in the parking lot. Open dawn–dusk. 617/698-1802.

Hingham

PARKS, BEACHES, AND RECREATION AREAS

6 Bare-Cove Park

🐾🐾🐾 (See South of the Hub map on page 104)

We started bringing George and Inu here because we hoped to instill in them a sense of strict military discipline. Since a military base once occupied Bare-Cove, we thought the place might have an inspirational effect on them. Maybe if we visited often enough, we reasoned, our dogs would begin to obey our every command and march beside us in unison.

Well, as you probably guessed, we're not there yet. But the Rescue Dogs of New England train here, so we aren't the only ones who thought this would make a good disciplinary setting.

During most evenings and weekends, this park is a popular place for local

DOG-EAR YOUR CALENDAR—MAY, JUNE

Bless your pooch: This annual event has now become part of **That Doggone Walk** (see the South Boston section in the Boston chapter) at Castle Island. In the 10-minute service, an Episcopal priest will bless your dog and lead a prayer for animals. The free event is nondenominational, and all are welcome. It's held on the first Sunday in May. For more information, call 617/426-9170.

Teach your children: Each June the Pine Ridge Animal Shelter sponsors a one-day obedience training course specifically for children and their pets. Kids are taught how to care for their animals responsibly. The course festivities conclude with a pet show featuring the most talented, best behaved, and cutest pets, and whatever other categories they can dream up. It's a great day for children and even better for their dogs. Call for more details and the exact date; 781/326-0729.

dogs and their owners to meet and mingle. If you like socializing, you probably won't venture much farther than the front entrance. But if you want a lovely walk, there's plenty of pretty terrain to explore.

Set along the picturesque Weymouth Back River, Bare-Cove has three miles of hiking trails and paved roads. The roads are closed to vehicle traffic and plowed in the winter. Along with a few empty buildings, they're remnants of the military days. Some of the buildings are open, including the observation deck on the south side of Beal Cove.

The Weymouth Back River is home to a variety of waterfowl, including ducks, cormorants, herons, and egrets. Although there is a lot of old, bumpy pavement here, you and your leashed dog will love roaming through the surrounding woods and fields. And if you're traveling with a water dog, there are numerous access points that lead into the drink.

From the Southeast Expressway/I-93/Routes 1 and 3 in Quincy, take Exit 12 to Route 3A south. Continue on Route 3A through Weymouth into Hingham. Take the first right after the Hingham town line on Beal Street. Travel a quarter mile. The northern parking lot is on the right. To reach the southern parking lot, continue on Beal Street to West Street. Turn right on Fort Hill Street and then immediately turn right again on the Fire Museum/Wildlife Center access road. Follow the access road to the park gate. Open dawn–dusk. 781/741-1464.

7 Cranberry Pond Conservation Area

🐾🐾 (See South of the Hub map on page 104)

Surrounded by a small woodland, this serene little pond is a perfect spot if you and your dog want some peace and quiet. It won't give you a lot of exercise, however. The short trip around the pond is only a quarter mile; to fully explore the woods, you'll only need about 15 minutes. Don't expect to find any cranberries; years ago the area was a cranberry bog, but it has since become a pond.

From Route 3A, take Beal Street into West Street. Turn right on Fort Hill Street and then left on French Street. The park and a parking area are on the left. Open from a half hour before sunrise to a half hour after sunset. 781/741-1464.

8 Foundry Pond Conservation Area

🐾🐾🐾 🐕 (See South of the Hub map on page 104)

Quaint, lovely Foundry Pond is the centerpiece of this 32-acre leash-free park on the Weir River. Thick woods blanket the pond banks, and scattered lily pads and majestic swans add just the right amount of color. It's a popular place for strolling along the water's edge or even putting in a canoe.

A few trails branch off from the pond. One runs down from Foundry Pond Dam near the parking area and follows the Weir River into the salt marsh for a short distance. It's a swampy route, so you'll need your mud boots if you're planning on hiking it.

On the other side of the pond, you'll find some slightly longer trails that run through the woods and an old quarry. Getting to these trails, however, can be tricky. Crossing over the dam isn't safe for several reasons, not the least of them nesting swans. No complete path surrounds the pond, but you can push through the woods and cross over an abandoned railroad bridge to reach the other side. Inu and George, who are always up for roughing it, find this is a great adventure.

In spring when many birds and other animals are raising their young, a walk in the woods at Foundry Pond can bring another kind of adventure altogether. Most wildlife avoid confrontations by fleeing at the sound of an approaching human or canine. When their young are not yet ready to travel, however, they're prepared to take on all comers, including you and your dog, as we discovered here.

During one visit, as Inu and Chris neared the pond from the woods, they heard a pounding "Whomp! Whomp! Whomp!" The sound came from the other side of the pond, where a large mute swan was beating his giant wings on the water.

The pounding stopped when they turned from the swan to the dam. It began again as they forged their way closer to the dam, where the swan took off and flew just above the crest of the water, its wings beating the surface. Expecting the bird to fly right over them, Chris prepared to get a close look at him, but the swan never rose off the water. Instead, it soared directly toward them with an evil and sinister glare.

Hissing horribly through its outstretched beak, the gigantic swan landed with a tremendous splash at the water's edge before Inu, its three-foot-long wings still thrashing the water. Inu responded with a couple of half-friendly barks as he ran back and forth on the shoreline before the angry bird.

The great swan, still hissing, started pushing into the reeds. Inu gave a departing bark and joined Chris on the trail back into the woods. The mutant, er, mute swan took a few victory laps near the dam to fluff its feathers and then thundered back to the pond's far end.

Peeking out of the woods and believing that the coast was clear, Chris and Inu made another run for the dam, but—"Whomp! Whomp! Whomp!" Once again, the swan took off after them.

Chris retreated again to the woods, expecting to find Inu behind him, but he turned to see Inu leaping over the reeds into the pond. That's Inu, a typical golden retriever. He has to stop and chat with everyone and everything: other dogs, cats, people with food, people without food, axe murderers, and even swans possessed by the devil.

Inu did his best to be friendly and get a good sniff of this wondrous creature. The swan did its best to remove every piece of fur from Inu's coat. Luckily, before incurring a serious attack, Inu got tired of the game and left the bird and the pond. On the way out, Chris noticed a second swan nesting behind a reedy bog. No doubt the reasons for the great swan's bravery could be found there, among the eggs or cygnets steadfastly guarded by its mate.

From the intersection of Chief Justice Cushing Highway/Route 3A and East Street/Route 228, take Chief Justice Cushing Highway east to Kilby Street. Turn right on Foundry Pond Lane, just past Rockfall Road. Open from a half hour before sunrise to a half hour after sunset. 781/741-1464.

🔟 George Washington Forest

🐾🐾🐕 (See South of the Hub map on page 104)

We'd like to wax poetic about this spot, but here's the plain truth: you get woods here, beautiful woods, and that's it. Circled by a residential area, the small pine forest is only about a mile long and a quarter mile wide. You can disappear into the woods with your leash-free pooch on the wide, flat, and easy-to-follow fire road. Access is difficult because parking is only available at pullouts along Charles Street and South Pleasant Street.

From Route 3 in Rockland, take Exit 14 to Route 228/Main Street north to Hingham. Turn right on South Pleasant Street and right again on Charles Street. Open dawn–dusk. 781/741-1464.

🔟 More-Brewer Park

🐾🐾🐕 (See South of the Hub map on page 104)

Hingham has the More-Brewer family to thank for donating the 140 acres that make up this park. Here you and your pup can wander among grassy knolls, pine forests, and tranquil ponds, all connected by old, winding carriage roads.

From the main parking area, the trail leads along the outer perimeter to Brewer Pond. The water gets a little swampy, so it's not great for swimming. On the right is a pretty meadow where you and your off-leash dog can picnic, roll down the hill, toss a ball, or just lie out in the sun. Follow the trail up the hill to reach a beautiful grove of trees where your dog can snoop and sniff to her heart's content.

Across Hobart Street is the Brewer Reservation, the first section of land donated by the Brewers. It offers a lovely 40 acres, but your dogs will quickly sniff out the town dump, which is right next door to the reservation. Our spirits plunged as our walk took us from wildflowers and soft pines to a forest floor covered in trash. Then our hearts crashed as we came upon a huge, open pit of garbage and bulldozers. Our advice: Stick with the trails in More-Brewer Park and recycle.

From Route 3A, take Beal Street into West Street. Turn right on Fort Hill Street and then left on New Bridge Street. Turn right on Hobart Street. A parking lot is located on the right. Open dawn–dusk. 781/741-1464.

11 Stodder's Neck Reservation

😾😾😾 (See South of the Hub map on page 104)

This harbor peninsula near the mouth of the Weymouth Back River was once a gravel pit. But don't let that little bit of historical trivia deter you. The Department of Conservation reclaimed the land and created a wonderful park with rolling hills, green lawns, and well-placed trees and shrubs. Although just a small peninsula and the shore is more stone than sand, it is a popular place for pups because you won't have to worry about Fido running off—there is only one way out.

A simple half-mile path takes you and your leashed dog around the reservation. To take in views of the scenery and the many pleasure boats on the river, head for the tip of the peninsula. And make time for a refreshing dip when you arrive. The water is clean and easily accessible.

Dogs are to be leashed.

From the Southeast Expressway/I-93/Routes 1 and 3 in Dorchester, take Exit 12 to Route 3A south. Follow Route 3A through Quincy and Weymouth into Hingham. Make a U-turn at the first light after the Hingham town line on Route 3A north. The parking lot is on the right. Open dawn–dusk. 617/727-5293.

12 Wompatuck State Park

😾😾😾😾 (See South of the Hub map on page 104)

With 3,500 acres and miles of trails, this state park offers plenty of uncharted territory for you and your leashed dog to explore. Get a map at the park's visitor center—you'll need it to find your way through the seemingly endless woodlands of maple, oak, and pine.

Don't let the pavement and concrete here scare you off. The roads and odd-shaped buildings are remnants of the park's past as a military base. What these structures were once used for is anyone's guess. It seems almost criminal to have ever allowed such ugly buildings to be built in the first place. Fortunately, Mother Nature is reclaiming the area as her own, just as squirrels and chipmunks are claiming the buildings as their stomping grounds.

Visitors use the numerous old roads, bike paths, and trails that traverse the park year-round. In summer, runners and bikers canvas the trails, while winter brings out cross-country skiers and snowshoers. Spring and fall are popular times for horseback riding. And of course dog walking and hiking are encouraged every month of the year.

From the visitor center, take the trail to the left of the parking area toward Wildcat Pond, a short half mile away. You won't want to swim in it—like all the ponds here, it's mucky, murky, and marshy—but the easy-to-follow walk is through a pleasant pine forest. Continue three-quarters of a mile to Heron Pond, a larger but equally muddy pool.

DIVERSION

Folk and Fur Fest: Take a walk on the Wompatuck side. In Wompatuck State Park, that is. Every September, the Standish Humane Society sponsors a three-mile **Benefit Walk for Animals** to raise money for local spay and neuter programs. Featuring a festive day of prizes, exhibits, canine contests, and dog demonstrations and, yes, even folk music, you and every other dog lover will find this walk in the woods one you won't want to miss. Registration is 10 A.M.–2 P.M. For details, call 781/834-4663; website: www.standishhumanesociety.com.

If you take the trail to the right of the parking area, you'll head to Aaron Reservoir. A mile-long trail, it eventually links to the Heron Pond Trail for a decent four-mile loop. None of the trails is marked, but the occasional sign points you in the direction of the ponds.

Wompatuck has all the accoutrements and rules you'd expect at a state park: restrooms, camping, interpretive programs, and, yes, a pesky leash requirement. The campground offers 400 sites for tents and trailers in a wonderful wooded area. You can book a campsite up to six months in advance by calling the Massachusetts State Camping Reservation Center at 877/422-6762. A minimum stay of two nights is required; you must reserve at least three nights on holiday weekends. It's open for camping April 15–October 15. Showers, electrical hookups, and dump stations are available. Dogs must be leashed when outside of your tent or trailer and cannot be left unattended. Campsites are $10 per night.

Wompatuck State Park extends into Norwell, Cohasset, and Scituate, but Hingham provides the main access. The park's eastern portion, in Cohasset, borders Whitney and Thayer Woods (see listing in the Cohasset section of this chapter) and makes a great place for extended hikes.

From Route 3 in Rockland, take Exit 14 to Route 228 north/Main Street and Hingham. Turn right on Free Street. Take a left on Lazell Street. Turn right on Union Street. Parking is available throughout the park. The visitor center is a quarter mile into the park on the right. Open dawn–dusk. 781/749-7160.

13 World's End Reservation

🐾🐾🐾🐾 ◄ (See South of the Hub map on page 104)

Every time we visit here, we find ourselves wishing that the world were actually flat. That way there would be more ends of the world to visit—and they would all be equally impressive. Two islands connected by a sandbar, 250-acre World's End overlooks Hingham Harbor, Weir River, and Boston Harbor Islands. The grass-covered hills are connected by four miles of well-laid-out, shaded carriage roads and three miles of trails. You and your dog can hike through a variety of terrain, including meadows, woods, and seashore.

The one-mile main trail, a cart path, leads straight from the ranger's station and makes its way up grassy Planter's Hill. This is the highest point in the reservation, rising 120 feet above the treetops and offering fine views in all directions. The tree-lined path continues down the hill's other side to the Bar, a thin causeway that connects with the outer island of World's End.

Here again, you'll find leisurely trails, spectacular views, open fields, and more woods. The cart paths loop around the outer hill in and out of the meadows and forest. Although the shore can be rocky in places, it is passable and well worth visiting. With the peaceful harbor waters lapping the small beaches, you and your dog will be in heaven. A cool swim is an option here if the weather's hot enough.

World's End is a major stop for migratory birds, such as plovers, ducks, herons, egrets, and finches. It's also an extremely popular park with people, so arrive early to get one of the few parking spaces. Dogs, alas, must be leashed here. A bit of history and a cautionary word: World's End has always had a leash law, but for a long time the rule was not strictly enforced. This fact and the area's beauty attracted many dog walkers. Most were responsible; others were not, which caused tranquil World's End to become the center of a swirling canine controversy.

In 1994, after receiving numerous complaints about disruptive pooches and scattered doggy waste, the Trustees of Reservations established some simple guidelines for dogs in the park: keep your dog under control and pick up after him. Apparently, this wasn't enough, because problems persisted, and in 1995 the Trustees began enforcing a strict leash law at World's End. And they do ticket here! In fact, some folks want to ban dogs entirely from this beautiful park. But as of this printing, that hasn't occurred. All because a few dog owners decided the rules didn't apply to them.

So what's the bottom line? As dog owners, it's up to us to keep our pets under control and the parks clean. Ninety-nine percent of us are good owners. But it's that 1 percent that ends up on the front page of the *Boston Herald*.

The day-use fee is $6. From the Southeast Expressway/I-93/Routes 1 and 3 in Dorchester, take Exit 12 to Route 3A south. Continue on Route 3A through Quincy and Weymouth into Hingham. At the Hingham Harbor traffic circle, leave Route 3A via Summer Street. Turn left on Martin's Lane. Parking is at the road's end. Open 8 A.M.–8 P.M. in summer, and 8 A.M.–5 P.M. in winter. 781/749-8956.

PLACES TO STAY

Wompatuck State Park Campground: See Wompatuck State Park listing, above.

Hull

PARKS, BEACHES, AND RECREATION AREAS

It's early. The sun, a brilliant fireball in the eastern sky, breaks free of the horizon. The morning mist begins to clear. The waves prepare for another cycle.

A golden retriever with a steely eyed glare sits motionless on the beach. Inside, his heart is racing. With total concentration, he watches. He waits. The tennis ball rests silently in the sand.

The man, immersed in the sports section, begins to move toward the ball. The dog salivates with anticipation. The hand reaches down and picks it up for the zillionth time. The eyes grow gigantic and appear as if they'll work their way out of the dog's head. Without so much as a thought, the man lets go with a mighty heave.

The ball sails out into the rising sun and splashes into the sea. Instantly the retriever explodes with an energy found only in canines. In an all-out sprint, the crazed animal crosses the sand, hits the water, and leaps the first two waves. As the water deepens, the dog begins to swim. A wake big enough to require a small-craft warning forms. He splits the third wave and grabs the helpless object. Then, on a dime, the dog cuts back to shore, riding in on the next two waves. With a proud trot, he emerges from the ocean and drops the ball.

A golden retriever with a steely-eyed glare sits motionless on the beach. Inside, his heart is racing. With total concentration, he watches. He waits. The tennis ball rests silently in the sand ....

🐾 Nantasket Beach

🐾🐾🐾 (See South of the Hub map on page 104)

Inu just loves the beach; Nantasket is high on his list of favorites, and with good reason. During low tide, the grainy beach is wide and easy to run or walk. And it's 3.5 miles long, which means we won't be going back to the car for at least an hour!

If you don't want to get sand between your toes, you and your dog can stay on the walkway that runs along the seawall spanning the length of the beach. There's plenty of parking available off Nantasket Avenue. Leashed dogs are only welcome on the beach October 1–April 30.

From Chief Justice Cushing Highway/Route 3A in Hingham, take East Street/Route 228 east. Turn left on Hull Street/Route 228 into Nantasket Avenue/Route 228 and Hull. The beach and a parking lot are located on the right. Open dawn–dusk. 781/727-8856.

PLACES TO EAT

Weinberg's Bakery: Coffee, bagels, pastries, the morning paper, and glorious sunshine. After a good workout on the beach, we like to head to Weinberg's for a break. Even when the weather is cooler, the small sidewalk tables really soak up the morning sun. 519 Nantasket Avenue; 781/925-9879.

Milton

"I got the doggone blues, oh yeah. I got the bluuues real bad.

Wanna be walkin' down the road, but my owner's nowhere to be had .... "

Sometimes Chris gets busy at work and has to put in extra hours to get the next big project done. So he gets home late, and Inu's walks get shorter. After about a week of this, he can expect to come home and find the dog howlin' the blues in that hurts-real-bad Mississippi Delta voice of his. Whenever that happens, it's time to head for the hills. The Blue Hills, that is.

PARKS, BEACHES, AND RECREATION AREAS

15 Blue Hills Reservation, Great Blue Hill Section

🐾🐾🐾🐾 🐾 (See South of the Hub map on page 104)

A vast wilderness covering almost 6,000 acres across five towns, the Blue Hills Reservation is the single largest conservation area within 35 miles of Boston. The trail system here encompasses 125 miles, and the views from the hilltops are downright spectacular. For details on the park's other sections, see the Blue Hills Reservation listings in the Canton and Quincy sections.

If this is your first visit to the Blue Hills, then it's a must that you and your leashed dog make the climb to the top of Great Blue Hill. At 635 feet, it's one of the highest points on the Atlantic coast; you should be able to see your house from the observation tower. The two principal trails to the summit are the Great Blue Hill Trail and the Skyline Trail.

The Great Blue Hill Trail leaves from the Trailside Museum off Washington Street/Route 138. The fairly steep, one-mile (round-trip) route is popular with summer weekend hikers. Running east to west along the Blue Hill Range for the park's length, the Skyline Trail covers nine miles; don't worry, you don't have to do the whole thing. Hikers can pick up the Skyline Trail at several access points, but the easiest starting place is at the reservation's headquarters. From here, you can make a loop using the north and south branches of the Skyline Trail. Go up one and return on the other for a three-mile round-trip. Along the way, you'll pass a number of excellent vantage points with views over Boston.

If your feet and your pup's paws want a somewhat flatter route, try the easy path around Houghton's Pond. It's only about a half-mile walk, and the clean lake is good for a refreshing swim. Or you can explore one of the many other trails in the park; you'll find enough to keep you busy for countless return visits.

From Route 128/I-93, take Exit 3 to Blue Hills River Road. Turn right on Hillside Street. A parking lot is on the right at Houghton's Pond. You can also park on Hillside Street, a quarter mile beyond the pond, at the reservation's headquarters. Obtain a free trail map here or buy a large, colorful park map for $1.

To reach the Trailside Museum from Route 128/I-93, take Exit 4 to Washington Street/Route 138 north. It's on the right, just past Blue Hills River Road. There are also many other smaller parking areas throughout the park. Most are simple pullouts along the road. Open dawn–dusk. 617/698-1802.

🐾 Neponset River Reservation, Fowl Meadow Section

🐾 (See South of the Hub map on page 104)

Marsh grasses, the Neponset River, and the Blue Hills dominate the scenery here. You and your dog can trot along a straight, two-mile gravel path called Burma Road. Keep your pet close at hand here because the route crosses plenty of swamps and muddy areas.

On your way out, be sure to cross the reed-lined Neponset River on Paul's Bridge, a historic stone span built in the 1700s. The Department of Conservation requires dogs to be leashed.

From Route 128/I-93, take Exit 2 to Washington Street/Route 138 north. Turn left on Neponset Valley Parkway. The park and a small parking lot are at the intersection with Brush Hill Road. Open dawn–dusk. 617/698-1802.

PLACES TO EAT

Newcomb Farms Restaurant: One of our favorite things about hiking is starting off with a hearty meal. So before we hit the trail in the nearby Blue Hills, we stop at Newcomb Farms. There's no place to sit with your dog, but

DIVERSION

Hiking hounds: What a wonderful world it can be. Not only is the Blue Hills Reservation a great place for you and your dog to explore, but twice a year (in spring and fall) rangers sponsor a free, one- to two-hour hike called **Canine Capers**, just for dog walkers. The hike starts with information about how to keep your dog happy and healthy while out on the trail, and then a ranger guides everyone on a special hike. It's a terrific way to explore out-of-the-way spots on the reservation, and for once you won't feel like you're in the minority. You'll just be one of the pack. Dates and hikes are subject to change; for details, call 617/698-1802.

takeout is just fine and the food's great. It has a full breakfast menu, served anytime, and a lunch and dinner menu of charburgers, roll-ups, and hot and cold sandwiches.

While you wait (they draw big crowds on weekends), you can have free coffee outside, or you can fill up your water bottles at the Milton Spring, behind the restaurant at the Pepsi-Cola Center.

After getting our take-out food, we eat it at the picnic area at the Chickatawbut Overlook. Only a mile away via Route 28 south, turn left on Chickatawbut Road. From here, you get breathtaking views of Boston and the surrounding woods. 1139 Randolph Avenue/Route 28; 617/698-9547.

Needham

PARKS, BEACHES, AND RECREATION AREAS

🔢 Cutler Park

😺 (See South of the Hub map on page 104)

Sometimes you just can't escape civilization. Take the Department of Conservation's Cutler Park, for example. This beautiful area is tucked into the eastern corners of Needham and Dedham on the Charles River. But Route 128 forms the western boundary of the park, and there's just no getting away from the highway's rumble. For that extra touch, an industrial office complex marks the northern border.

A dirt road, softly covered with pine needles and leaves, circles Cutler Pond and ventures deep into the park. The 1.25-mile path leads you along many fine viewing points along the Charles River. It's pleasing to the eye, but to the ear—well, there's still that darn highway clamoring off in the distance.

The trail departing from the parking lot ambles through the woods near the water's edge. It becomes a wide path as soon as you leave the office parking lot. Dogs must be leashed.

From Route 128, take Exit 19 to Highland Avenue in Needham. Turn left on Hunting Road and then left again on Kendrick Street. The park is on the right, just past the Polaroid plant. Use the parking lot to the left of the entrance.

You can also access a trailhead in Dedham along Needham Street, which connects with the Cutler Pond loop after 1.5 miles. To reach it from Route 128, take Exit 18 to Needham Street east; parking pullouts are on the left. Open dawn–dusk. 781/455-7500.

18 Hemlock Gorge

🐾 🐾 🐾 (See South of the Hub map on page 104)

"Inuuu... Inuuu." At Hemlock Gorge, calling your dog is easier than in any other park. That's because no other park has Echo Bridge. This National Historic Landmark, built by Boston Water Works in 1877, supports the Boston aqueduct over the Charles River, and doggone, is it impressive! The bridge itself is an elegant granite structure surrounded by—you guessed it—a forest of hemlocks. But to really appreciate its span, you need to listen to it.

The name Echo Bridge comes from the reverberations under its huge arch. Call your dog, and she won't have any excuse to ignore you as her name echoes over and over across the glimmering water and beyond. Dogs are to be leashed here, and you'll want to be sure to follow this advice as the railings are short and the walkway is pitched to both sides.

To access the park, use the stairway at the Newton end of the bridge. The park itself is 23 acres and straddles the Needham and Newton sides of the river. Managed by the Department of Conservation, this park allows you to explore the steep hiking trails along the gorge or access the trails that lead north into Wellesley.

From I-95, take Exit 20 to Route 9 east into Newton. Turn right onto Chestnut Street, right onto Elliott Street, and back into Needham. The park and a parking lot are on the right immediately after crossing the Charles River. Open dawn–dusk. 617/698-1802.

19 Horsford Pond Recreation Area and Town Forest

🐾 (See South of the Hub map on page 104)

This small, scenic picnic area is located at Horsford Pond. Around the pond are benches, tables, and some trails that wander off into the forest. You and your leashed dog can sit and enjoy the reflections in the pond or take a half-mile hike into the oak and pine woods. Don't expect to encounter crowds at this out-of-the-way spot in the woods. Parking is plentiful here.

From Route 128/I-95 in Dedham, take Exit 17 to Needham Street/Route 135 north and Needham. Turn left on South Street and then right on High Rock Street. Turn left on Marked Tree Road and then left on Central Avenue. Take an immediate left into the park. Open dawn–dusk. 781/455-7510.

20 Ridge Hill Reservation

🐾🐾🐾 (See South of the Hub map on page 104)

Although it's only 220 acres, this manicured park offers enough goodies to entertain even the most finicky of dogs. Does your pup long to explore rolling meadows, thick woods, wetlands, and eskers? Does your pup know what an esker is? Well, it's a high ridge formed from deposits left by a river or stream flowing under a glacier. And if both of you want to see two of 'em, head on over to Ridge Hill.

The entrance and short park road open on a grand meadow speckled with pine trees. This field alone is a fine place for you and your dog to romp and play. Most of the trails lead from various points in the grassy clearing.

One popular 1.5-mile hiking route is really a combination of three short paths. Begin with the Esker Trail, which begins in the northwestern corner of the meadow. The path gradually rises as the ridge climbs 30 feet over the forest floor. A half mile in, the Swamp Trail leaves the esker to the left and enters a marshy woodland. The route through the swamp alternates between a dry, spongelike path of mulch in drier sections and a railed boardwalk in the wetter areas. This trail connects with the Chestnut Trail, which veers left, returning you to the meadow.

Park headquarters are at the road's end and meadow. Facilities include a restroom and warming room after winter activities, but they're a bit run-down. Dogs must be leashed.

From Route 128/I-95 in Dedham, take Exit 17 to Needham Street/Route 135 north and Needham. Turn left on South Street and then right on Charles River Street. The park and a small parking lot are on the right. Open dawn–dusk. 781/449-4923.

Quincy

PARKS, BEACHES, AND RECREATION AREAS

21 Blue Hills Reservation, Chickatawbut Section

🐾🐾🐾🐾 (See South of the Hub map on page 104)

Set in the eastern half of the Blue Hills, the Chickatawbut Section of the reservation is home to Chickatawbut Hill, the Great Cedar Swamp, Blue Hill Reservoir (off-limits to dogs), and miles and miles of hilly and rocky woodlands. As in the other parts of the reservation, this portion offers many hiking routes of varying degrees of difficulty. Be sure to pick up a $1 trail map at the

reservation headquarters on Hillside Street in Milton. (Also, see the Blue Hills Reservation listing in the Milton section of this chapter.)

You can access two of the more popular trailheads off Chickatawbut Road. Both are good places to set off for Chickatawbut Hill (517 feet high) and the Blue Hills backcountry. The first begins at the Chickatawbut Overlook, where you'll find parking, picnic tables, and a great view of the Boston skyline. A short distance up the trail is the observation tower for an even higher panorama and the starting point for more trails.

The second trailhead starts at the intersection of Randolph Avenue/Route 28 and Chickatawbut Road. From here you can make a three- to four-mile loop to Chickatawbut Hill by following the Braintree Pass, Bouncing Brook, and Skyline Trails. The route is only sporadically marked, so the map is essential. The Randolph Avenue intersection also marks the starting point of the six-mile Massachuseuck Trail, which traverses much of the park, including Ponkapoag Pond. (For a description of the area, see the Blue Hills Reservation listing in the Canton section of this chapter.) Look for the rectangular orange trail markers. Parking is available. Dogs must be leashed.

From the Southeast Expressway/I-93/Routes 1 and 3, take Exit 8 to Willard Road/Route 37 south. Turn right immediately on Wampatuck Road into the Blue Hills. Turn left on Chickatawbut Road. Open dawn–dusk. 617/698-1802.

22 Faxon Park

🐾🐾 (See South of the Hub map on page 104)

For those dog owners in walking distance of Faxon Park, this is the local doggy hangout. The park underwent a major face-lift in 1997, and unfortunately for

DIVERSION

Quincy Historic Walking Trail: Although most of the notable sights are indoors, and consequently closed to dogs, you can still get a sense of Quincy's rich history on this short, 1.25-mile walk through downtown. Points of interest focus on the homes of Quincy's famous families, the Adams and Hancocks. For a free detailed map to help you on this self-guided tour, stop by the Adams National Historic Site Visitor Center at 135 Adams Street; 617/770-1175.

the pooches, the beautiful 10 acres of woods shrank down to about two. The rest became a new ball field and playground in the middle of the park. No dogs allowed on the playing fields, and your pup must be leashed at all times.

From the intersection of Hancock Street and Washington Street in downtown Quincy, head south on Hancock Street, which becomes Quincy Street. Turn right on Faxon Park Road. Open dawn–dusk. 617/727-9547, ext. 450.

🐾 Wollaston Beach Reservation

(See South of the Hub map on page 104)

This Department of Conservation park on Quincy Bay is divided into three sections: Wollaston Beach, Caddy Memorial Park, and Moswetuset Hummock (say that three times fast!). At any time of day, any day of the week, you can find plenty of people and dogs here enjoying the sea air. Most of them are taking advantage of the 2.5-mile walkway that runs between Wollaston Beach and Quincy Shore Drive. Dogs are allowed on Wollaston Beach only between September 30 and May 1 but can enjoy the walkway year-round.

From the Southeast Expressway/I-93/Routes 1 and 3, take Exit 12 to Route 3A south. Turn left on Quincy Shore Drive. Parking is available along the beach and in the parking lots at Caddy Memorial Park and Moswetuset Hummock. 617/727-5293, or, in the summer, 617/773-7954.

Caddy Memorial Park Section

Set in the southern portion of the reservation, on the other side of Quincy Shore Drive from the beach, the park encompasses 20 acres along Black Creek. From here you can view the salt marshes and their abundant bird life, including ducks, herons, egrets, and gulls. You'll find a .75-mile bike path/walkway that leads to Wollaston Beach, a small observation deck, picnic tables, and some grassy areas for your leashed pooch.

Moswetuset Hummock Section

This tiny wooded peninsula along Quincy Bay occupies the reservation's northern end. It's a National Historic Site, honored as the early capital of the Massachusetts (or Moswetuset) Indians under Sachem Chickatawbut. In the early 1600s, the Massachusetts Bay Colony settled the area, supplanting the Massachusetts tribe, whose members suffered great losses due to diseases introduced by European settlers. The trail around the peninsula is about one-third mile long.

Wollaston Beach Section

Most people and some of their pooches shy away from swimming here because of the brownish water, but not Inu. After a dip, he smells no worse than a wet dog. Our policy is don't smell, don't tell. As long as he doesn't reek, we prefer not to know what gives the water its murky hue. The beach itself is rocky in some areas, sandy in others, and not very wide. But since it's not really a popular spot for sunbathers, a leashed dawg can romp here to his heart's content between September 30 and May 1.

PLACES TO EAT

The Clam Box: This local restaurant features the usual seafood fare of fried clams and french fries. From the outdoor tables, you can watch the action along Quincy Shore Drive and the beach walkway. 789 Quincy Shore Drive; 617/773-6677.

Tony's Clam Shop: Here's another place for all the old salty dogs who have an appetite for fried clams and a view of Wollaston Beach. Enjoy them both from the outdoor picnic tables. 861 Quincy Shore Drive; 617/773-5090.

Randolph

PARKS, BEACHES, AND RECREATION AREAS

Blue Hills Reservation

See the listing in the Canton section of this chapter.

PLACES TO STAY

Holiday Inn: Dogs are allowed in rooms on the first floor. When you make your reservation, let the management know your pooch will be staying with you. Rates are around $79–139. 1374 North Main Street, Randolph, MA 02368; 781/961-1000; website: www.ichotels.com.

Weymouth

PARKS, BEACHES, AND RECREATION AREAS

24 Great Esker Park

🐾🐾🐾🐾 (See South of the Hub map on page 104)

An amazingly varied, seemingly undiscovered world, Great Esker offers a wild adventure for you and your intrepid, leashed dog. Take your pick of terrain: hardwood forest high atop the Great Esker, marshy grassland in the low-lying country, or shoreline along the Weymouth Back River. Visit all three areas and marvel that so many different landscapes exist so close together.

The Great Esker itself extends about two miles and in places towers 90 feet above the surrounding marshland before dipping down like a roller-coaster. A paved service road, closed to vehicles, runs along the top of the thin ridge. George and Inu like to barnstorm down the side of the esker after chipmunks. George gives a good chase; Inu just takes out small shrubs.

Two main trails, the Marsh Trail and the Reversing Falls Trail, head down from the service road to the water. You'll need boots for both trails and possibly a flotation device during high tide. The paths wander through the fields, marshes, and small islands along the Back River. And, yes, the Reversing Falls actually exist, created by the changing tides that send water in and out of one of the inlets. It's a very cool sight, if you catch it at just the right time. Check the tide tables for high or low tide.

The southern terminus of the road is a heavenly point of solitude. Relax on the shores of Pyramid Hill and you'll feel as if you're almost in the middle of the Back River. When you come out of the woods into the marsh grass, the view is especially lovely. Here a small beach with a picnic table makes a great place to stop for lunch. Follow the shoreline around, and you can take advantage of a shortcut in the shape of a footbridge that leads back to the service road.

From the Southeast Expressway/I-93/Routes 1 and 3 in Dorchester, take Exit 12 to Route 3A south. Continue on Route 3A through Quincy into Weymouth. Turn right on Green Street and then left on Julia Road. A parking lot is at the road's end. Open dawn–dusk. 781/337-3342.

25 Stephen Rennie Herring Run Park

🐾 (See South of the Hub map on page 104)

To call this a park would be stretching the definition, but we mention it because it's a fun place to visit when the fish are running. Every year from April–May, the alewife herring make their way upstream to their spawning grounds, assisted by the fish run built here by the town of Weymouth. The park is a tiny spot of grass surrounding the canal, but it offers picnic tables and benches if you want to stop for lunch and a sniff. And if you plan it right, two months out of the year you can catch Mother Nature working her aquatic miracles. It's really a sight to behold. Dogs must be leashed.

From Route 3, take Exit 16 to Main Street/Route 18 north; it merges into Washington Street/Route 53. Turn right on Broad Street. The park and a parking area are on the left, just before Commercial Street. Open dawn–dusk. 781/337-3342.

26 Webb Memorial State Park

🐾🐾🐾🐕 (See South of the Hub map on page 104)

Dogs aren't allowed to set paw on the Boston Harbor Islands, but they're welcome here on this majestic peninsula as long as they're wearing their leashes. The park juts out far enough into Hingham Bay to give your dog an island experience. Follow the crushed-stone paths over the rolling, grassy hills to the outermost points of the peninsula. Along the shore, you'll find a mix of sand and pebble beaches. All have great views of Boston and the surrounding islands, including Grape and Slate Islands. Keep an eye out for harbor seals, which are being sighted more frequently in the harbor.

We like to pack a lunch and two old tennis balls for the boys and head for one of the outer picnic tables along the water. Here you can spend an afternoon tossing tennis balls into the waves, rolling in the grass, and lazing about in the sun. Woof!

From the Southeast Expressway/I-93/Routes 1 and 3 in Dorchester, take Exit 12 to Route 3A south. Continue on Route 3A through Quincy into Weymouth. Turn left on Neck Street and continue on as it becomes River Street. The park is on the left. A large parking lot is available. Open dawn–dusk. 781/740-1605.

PLACES TO EAT

Mary Lou's News: For headline coffee, bagels, sandwiches, beverages, and more, take out the news at Mary Lou's. It's the top story in town for breakfast or lunch. Read all about it with your pup on the bench outside or pack your meal for the trail. 768 Main Street; 781/340-5146.

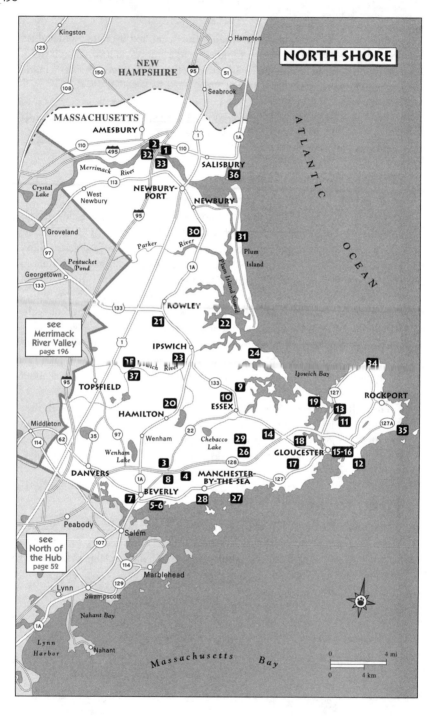

NORTH SHORE

NEW HAMPSHIRE

MASSACHUSETTS

AMESBURY

SALISBURY

NEWBURY-
PORT

NEWBURY

ROWLEY

IPSWICH

TOPSFIELD

HAMILTON

ESSEX

ROCKPORT

GLOUCESTER

MANCHESTER-
BY-THE-SEA

DANVERS

BEVERLY

ATLANTIC OCEAN

Ipswich Bay

Plum Island

Plum Island Sound

Massachusetts Bay

Nahant Bay

Lynn Harbor

see
Merrimack
River Valley
page 196

see
North of
the Hub
page 52

Kingston

Hampton

Seabrook

Crystal Lake

West Newbury

Groveland

Georgetown

Pentucket Pond

Parker River

Ipswich River

Middleton

Wenham

Wenham Lake

Chebacco Lake

Peabody

Salem

Marblehead

Lynn

Swampscott

Nahant

Merrimack River

0   4 mi
0   4 km

CHAPTER 5
North Shore

Running along the coast from Beverly to the New Hampshire border, the North Shore encompasses the classic New England seaports of Gloucester, Manchester-By-The-Sea, Newburyport, and Rockport. Rich in American history, these communities served as centers of the whaling industry during the last century. Today they continue to make a living from the sea, but many have also become popular tourist sites because of their picturesque fishing villages and artists' colonies. All of the towns fall within Essex County's borders.

Geographically the area offers varied hiking terrain to dogs and their owners. Along the water, you'll find vast sandy shorelines such as Crane Beach, Plum Island, and Salisbury Beach, as well as rocky cliffs, like those on Cape Ann. The interior is dominated by hardwood forests, horse farms, and the salt marshes of the Ipswich, Merrimack, and Parker Rivers.

Thanks to its winding rivers and miles of coastline, the North Shore can be a very wet area year-round. If your pup is a water dog, he should be more than happy to visit all the parks listed in this chapter. Almost every

PICK OF THE LITTER—NORTH SHORE

BEST WILD PLACE
Dogtown Commons, Gloucester (page 140)

BEST PLACE TO WATCH BOATS
Wingaersheek Beach, Gloucester (page 145)

BEST BOARDWALK
Wilderness Conservation Area, Manchester-By-the-Sea
(page 154)

BEST SEAFOOD & VIEWS
Lobster Pool, Rockport (page 160)

BEST SEASIDE RESORT
Cape Ann Motor Inn, Gloucester (page 146)

BEST SEAPORT VILLAGE RESORT
Morrill Place Inn, Newburyport (page 157)

park has some kind of water source, so be prepared for a soggy dog when it's time to head home.

During the summer months, dogs aren't allowed on most of the beaches, so visit the rivers to keep cool. Beginning in September, the beaches open up to our pawed pals. Take advantage of the spring season for beach-going, too. Some beaches permit leashed dogs to romp until the end of May.

Bay Circuit Trail: Linking parks and reservations between Plum Island on the North Shore and Kingston Bay on the South Shore, this trail will eventually connect more than 30 towns across 200 miles, including Ipswich, Newbury, Newburyport, and Rowley. For details, see the Extended Hiking Trails section of the Resources.

Essex County Greenbelt Association: For the past 27 years, the Essex County Greenbelt Association's efforts have led to the preservation of more than 4,000 acres in the Essex County region. Dogs are allowed leash free on all of its properties. For more information on how to get involved with this great conservation group, see the Land Conservation Groups section of the Resources.

Merrimack River Trail: Administered by the Merrimack River Watershed Council, this pathway follows the Merrimack River from the New Hampshire border to Newburyport on the Atlantic Ocean. In this chapter, the towns of Amesbury, Newburyport, and Salisbury include trail sections. For details, see the Extended Hiking Trails section of the Resources.

Amesbury

PARKS, BEACHES, AND RECREATION AREAS

1 Deer Island

🐾🐾🐾🐕 (See North Shore map on page 130)

Not to be confused with Deer Island in Boston Harbor (see Chapter One), this Deer Island is on the Merrimack River and provides a cool spot for a swim. In previous editions, we downgraded this lovely park to a two-paw rating because of a trash problem. We're happy to report that things have improved, and this leash-free park has returned to its previous scenic splendor. The effort to clean the Merrimack River also continues, and one result is the gradual return of the eagle population to this beautiful valley. Deer Island sits in the middle of the river, offering wonderful views downstream. The Amesbury Conservation Commission manages the area, and you may bring your dog here off leash as long as she is under voice control.

On our visits to the island, we've rubbed shoulders with bird-watchers and anglers. Although the area is small, less than a half mile around, it provides enough room for everyone—that is, if you come for the right reason. Inu will be the first to tell you that Deer Island is the place for a cool swim and not for a run or a long walk. (There's just not enough land for it.) Chris brings his binoculars for bird-watching. Inu hauls along his tennis ball for Chris to toss for him; he usually ends up dodging in and out of the river a hundred times an hour. The Merrimack has a strong current, so don't throw for distance here.

From the parking lot, follow the quarter-mile trail through the small pine forest out to the island's eastern tip, where the landscape changes to sand and tall grasses.

The Merrimack River is a winter home for bald eagles. November–March is the prime time to watch them soar above the river.

From I-95, take Exit 58 to Elm Street/Route 110 east. Take a quick right on Merrill Street and cross the Essex-Merrimack Bridge to the island. It's easy to miss the small parking lot on your left, but if you do, you get a chance to go over the Chain Bridge, one of the classic uncovered New England bridges. Open dawn–dusk. 978/388-8100.

2 Pow Wow River Conservation Area

😺😺😺😺 🐾 (See North Shore map on page 130)

For a walk on over 200 acres near and around Lake Gardner, hightail it to this fabulous conservation area, which borders Southhampton, New Hampshire, and Amesbury. Countless interconnecting trails weave through the area, attracting dogs and their owners from all over. The trails are well mapped at each trail intersection and on the map board at the parking area off Route 107A.

George likes to pretend he is living in the Wild West when he trots along the Stagecoach Trail Road to Lake Gardner. Taking a swim is mandatory, and the dogs race towards the water's edge as soon as we are within sight of the lake. Inu and all the other retrievers take a break from swimming for a little ball throwing in the open meadows of the Community Gardens. And since this park is leash free, there isn't a spot that won't be enjoyed by Spot.

Dogs are not allowed in the adjoining Camp Kent Environmental Center; just watch for boundary signs.

From Route 150, take Route 107A north for a half mile. Signs for Battice Farm and the park entrance are on your left. Park in the farm lot and proceed to the trailhead. Open dawn–dusk. 978/388-8100.

Beverly

PARKS, BEACHES, AND RECREATION AREAS

3 Alt Woodland

😺😺 🐾 (See North Shore map on page 130)

Looking for an enjoyable 45-minute walk? Then head over to this lovely 61-acre park. Part of the Essex County Greenbelt Association, the well-groomed woodland has a gentle but varied terrain for you and your off-leash dog to traverse. The trails aren't well marked, so you may find yourself roaming a bit off course. Stick to the main trail, which leads off to the left at the trailhead; it eventually loops a half mile back to the starting point.

Woodlands surrounded by several small open meadows occupy the heart of this acreage. Ticks are just waiting to tackle you in the spring and the fall, so make sure you give your dog (and yourself) a thorough checking for a few days after your walk. But we don't want to discourage you. This seldom-used spot is a wonderful place to visit. And best of all, dogs are allowed off leash. For a detailed trail map, call the Essex County Greenbelt Association at the number listed below.

From Route 128, take Exit 18 to Essex Street/Route 22 north. Turn left on Grover Street. The park is on the left; you can leave your car at the small pull-out. Open dawn–dusk. 978/768-7241.

4 Beverly Conservation Area

🐾🐾🐾 (See North Shore map on page 130)

Mountain bikers love this place, and it's no mystery why. The many rolling hills and rocky passageways give the most avid hiker or biker a thorough workout. Nestled in a countrified residential area on more than 150 acres, the park still offers plenty of privacy for you and your off-leash dog. The cart roads are fairly easy to follow, but foot trails here can be confusing. No matter how lost you get, though, you'll find your way back with a little exploring. In the meantime, you'll also discover some delightful country. Some trails lead through leaf-covered glades; others shoot straight up rocky hillsides. In the wet season, some of the low-lying trails can get swampy, so bring a pair of sturdy boots. A jaunt around the entire reservation should take you well over an hour.

A word of warning: In spring and fall, the ticks will find you. Make sure you check your dog from top to bottom for a few days after your visit. The Essex County Greenbelt Association manages the conservation area. Call them for a detailed map. Even with their map in hand, however, we've found the trails can be hard to follow.

From Route 128 in Wenham, take Exit 17 to Grapevine Road. Continue onto Hart Road in Beverly. Turn right on Greenwood Avenue. The park is at the road's end; street parking is available on the corner of Greenwood and Webster Avenues. Open dawn–dusk. 978/768-7241.

5 Lynch Park

🐾🐾🐾 (See North Shore map on page 130)

This may be the most scenic spot in Beverly. Here's the good news: It's got access to three white-sand beaches; a tree-lined, shady park area with picnic facilities; a walled-in grassy lawn on Woodbury Point at its southeastern end; and a great view of the North Shore Islands offshore. Between the road and the spacious parking lot, you'll find another fenced-in hilly and grassy area where you and your leashed dog can play. There are restrooms for you, and lots of bushes and trees for your canine pal.

Okay, now that you're ready to jump in the car, we have to break the bad news: No dogs are allowed from Memorial Day–Labor Day. On our first visit, we reenacted that telephone commercial where the excited dog bounds out of the car and runs right past the big No Dogs Allowed sign. (Or, in our case, George lifted his leg on the sign. Who says that dogs can't read?)

But we're counting the days until Labor Day, because this makes a terrific morning or afternoon outing on a crisp fall (or spring) New England day. Best of all, you'll probably have the place to yourself, as the beachgoers will have gone into hibernation for the winter. Dogs must be leashed at all times.

From Route 128, take Exit 18 to Essex Street/Route 22 south. Turn left on Dane Street at the Beverly Common and then left again on Hale Street/

Routes 62 and 127. Turn right on Obear Street. The park is on the right. Open 7 A.M.–10 P.M. 978/921-6067.

6 Lyons Park/Dane Street Beach

🐾 (See North Shore map on page 130)

These two tiny beach parks run along Lothrop Street, separated only by a group of three houses in the middle. Dane Street Beach is the smaller of the two, running about two blocks long. It has a white sandy beach that runs into a quiet cove of clean water. A seawall separates the beach from the grassy area along the street, so your dog is somewhat contained from car traffic. Five-block-long Lyons Park is practically Dane Street Beach's twin in all respects.

The only catch is that no dogs are allowed from Memorial Day–Labor Day, so this spot is out in summer. If you like the beach on cool fall days, you'll find this a clean, safe, and scenic place to go. And what a great view of the North Shore Islands! Dogs must be leashed.

From Route 128, take Exit 18 to Essex Street/Route 22 south. Turn left on Dane Street at the Beverly Common. Turn right on Lothrop Street/Route 127. Park at one of the many spots along the street. Open from 7 A.M.–10 P.M. For canine restrictions, call 978/921-6040, ext. 311.

7 Obear Park

🐾 (See North Shore map on page 130)

If you're a Beverly resident, this small park makes a decent locale for your dog's daily walk. It also works if you're on your way up north and want to pause for a scenic rest stop. Located at the west end of Beverly Harbor, it offers good water access and a strip of sandy beach for your dog to run on. There are picnic tables, a partially enclosed grassy area, and ample parking at the end of a dead-end street. Every time we've visited we've had the park to ourselves.

We can't recommend this as a must-do trip if you're traveling from other places in the Boston area, but it's clean, has a lovely view of the harbor, and provides your leashed dog with a place to enjoy the three S's: swimming, sniffing, and squatting. Sadly, the park is off-limits to Rover from Memorial Day–Labor Day.

From Route 128, take Exit 22 to Elliot Street/Route 62 east. Turn right on Bridge Street at the Beverly town line and then turn right on Kernwood Avenue. Turn right on Upland Road and left on Livingstone Avenue. The park and a parking lot are at the end of the drive. Open dawn–10 P.M. For canine restrictions, call 978/921-6040, ext. 311.

8 Sally Milligan Park

🐾🐾🦮 (See North Shore map on page 130)

For folks who like the peace and quiet of open woods, we've got a real find for you. Established by a son in memory of his mother in 1933, Sally Milligan

Park occupies 40 acres of prime woodland property off Cross Lane. Unfortunately, this park is off-limits to dogs from Memorial Day–Labor Day. You'll have to visit the area in spring, fall, or winter instead.

The forest terrain doesn't have much variety, but it's cool, shady, and well maintained, with lots of trails. Best of all, your dog can roam without a leash. Come here to enjoy a quiet picnic or an hour hike through gentle woodlands.

From Route 128, take Exit 18 to Essex Street/Route 22 south. Turn left on Cole Street, which becomes Cross Lane. The park is on the right. There's no developed parking area, but you can park at the turnout on Cross Lane or along Jewett Road or Bonad Road (off Lakeshore Avenue) on the northeast boundary. Street parking is limited to two hours. Open 6 A.M.–9 P.M. For canine restrictions, call 978/921-6040, ext. 311.

PLACES TO EAT

Captain Dusty's Ice Cream: Every sailor signs on for another trip when the port o' call is Captain Dusty's. This popular Pride's Crossing ice-cream store serves up heaping scoops of hard-pack and soft-serve ice cream and frozen yogurt. 642 Hale Street; 978/921-5311.

Taste Buds: This nifty little gourmet food shop is a real dog-friendly zone. The canine clientele waits impatiently outside while human friends get the goods inside: specialty sandwiches on homemade bread, muffins, gourmet coffees, and desserts.

We knew we liked this store when we noticed they had homemade dog biscuits for sale, right next to the fresh-baked chocolate-chip and oatmeal cookies. Then we turned to the ice-cream case. Alongside the Dove Bars, we found—are you ready?—Frosty Paws, frozen treats for your dog. Yes, we definitely came to the right place. 151 Hale Street; 978/922-0151.

Danvers

PLACES TO STAY

Motel 6: All Motel 6 locations allow dogs as long as they are not left unattended. Located near the intersection of I-95 and Route 1, you'll find this a convenient stopover. Rates are $56 per night. 65 Newbury Street, Danvers, MA 01923; 978/774-8045; website: www.motel6.com.

Residence Inn: A cross between a hotel and a motel, this inn has spacious rooms with small efficiencies included. The kitchen really comes in handy when you have your pooch along. Right off Route 128, it's a great one-night stopover on your way to North Shore parks and beaches. A $100 refundable deposit is required. Rates are around $169–289, plus $7 for the dog. 51 Newbury Street, Danvers, MA 01876; 978/777-7171; website: www.residenceinn.com.

Essex

PARKS, BEACHES, AND RECREATION AREAS

🖸 James N. and Mary F. Stavros Reservation

🐾🐾 (See North Shore map on page 130)

The Stavros family donated this 73-acre park to the Trustees of Reservations. A prime spot of real estate, the views will be the reason to come back here again and again. As you make your way up the easy, grassy grade to the top of White Hill, you'll pass groves of red cedar and devil's walking stick. The path is just over a quarter mile long, but you climb high enough to enjoy spectacular vistas of Hog Island, Crane Beach, and the salt marshes of the Essex and Castle Neck Rivers. On the top of White Hill, you can relax in a pretty clearing that is naturally fenced in by woods and thick brush.

The short stroll, however, is only enough to whet the appetite of our dogs, so we usually come here on our way to somewhere else. The panorama from the hill makes this site a favorite of ours, but our dogs prefer a little more stimulation. Dogs must be leashed.

The park is off John Wise Avenue/Route 133 on Island Road; park at the small pullout. James and Mary once owned the adjacent Cape Ann Golf Course as well. Open dawn–dusk. 970/921-1911.

🔟 Warren-Weld Woodland

🐾🐾🐕 (See North Shore map on page 130)

The hilly terrain, rich forest, and babbling brooks of 106-acre Warren-Weld Woodland make for a pleasant, if short, walk in the woods. Here you can explore a few hiking trails and some old cart roads that crisscross the woods. And since it's part of the Essex County Greenbelt Association, your dog will have the chance to roam through the forest off leash.

The main trail, Caesar's Lane, follows a brook up backcountry roads, past a private pond (sorry, no swimming). The dogs just seem to love the muddy route—as always, the muddier the trail, the better.

Along the cart roads, you'll pass some fine woods, but more and more development is encroaching on the area. You won't find these outer roads as private as the trail along the interior.

DOG-EAR YOUR CALENDAR—DECEMBER

Christmas on the Corner: Although Inu is generally quite dignified, he just couldn't hold back. He saw Santa, hopped onto his lap, and pulled out a list about a mile long. We didn't get a close look at it, but the word "biscuit" appeared a lot. While Inu and Santa reviewed the list, the rest of us watched the tree-lighting ceremony and even joined in some caroling. The street festival is held on the second Friday in December, along Main Street in Essex; 978/283-1601.

From the town center at the intersection of Martin Street/Route 22, John Wise Avenue, and Main Street/Route 133, take Main Street east. Turn right on Southern Avenue and then take a sharp right on Apple Street. After a mile, look for a small pullout on the left; parking is allowed below the Essex County Greenbelt Association sign. Open dawn–dusk. 978/768-7241.

Wilderness Conservation Area

See the listing in the Manchester By The Sea section of this chapter.

PLACES TO EAT

Woodman's of Essex: Enjoy a feast of fried clams and lobster rolls while sitting at one of the 10 tables under the big tent out back. It's a beautiful setting for lunch or dinner because of the well-maintained lawn and the breathtaking views of the Essex River. There's also plenty of space to take an after-dinner stroll along the river with your dog. 125 Main Street/Route 133; 978/768-6451 or 800/649-1773.

Gloucester

In the 1800s, Gloucester stood as America's largest fishing port, and in the 1700s, it was among the major Eastern hubs of the whaling industry. Even though its historic schooners are long gone, the town still retains the flavor of a rustic, weathered fishing village. Today whale-watching tours circle Stillwagon Bank, where humpback whales are returning after being nearly depleted 150 years ago. And landlubbers will be glad to know there's a lot more to Gloucester than *The Perfect Storm*. The beaches are beautiful and, if your pooch has an aesthetic bent, he may want to browse the many art galleries in the thriving artist's colony of Rocky Neck in eastern Gloucester.

PARKS, BEACHES, AND RECREATION AREAS

11 Dogtown Commons

🐾🐾🐾🐾🦮🔊 (See North Shore map on page 130)

Could there really be such a place? The answer is yes. Well, at least there once was. In the early 1700s, Dogtown was primarily a farming community. However, after the American Revolution, the population declined sharply. Many local men did not return from the war, and those who did moved on to the coastal regions of Cape Ann. Left behind were the widows, the poor, and the abandoned family dogs. Eventually all the people left, and the area literally went to the dogs.

As you wander the more than 3,000 acres here, both you and your leash-free pooch can search for remnants of the past. After a mile, George and Inu like to sniff out ancient scents from the days of adventure and glory when dogs were dogs and cats were scared. They take off crashing through the woods like the wild animals they are. As for us, we prefer to explore Dogtown Square for stone walls and other reminders of the town and its old homesteads.

Real treasures to search for are the carvings that Roger Babson commissioned during the 1930s. You'll find two types. The first feature numbers marking significant sites in Dogtown; the second offer inspirational sayings such as "Never Try, Never Win." Both are forged in many stones and boulders in the area, printed in black lettering. We encountered about 20 sayings and at least 18 numbers. Most are difficult to find and require that you wander off Dogtown Road.

A variety of trails traverse Dogtown. The easiest is the paved path around scenic Goose Cove Reservoir. Slightly fewer than two miles long, the loop attracts joggers, walkers, and cyclists. The leaf-covered route makes its way through the woods, along the shore, and across several dams.

DIVERSION

Gloucester Maritime Trails: Gloucester is the oldest working harbor in America and one of the world's major fishing ports. Its harbor is also a popular setting for local artists. The city has four self-guided, quarter- to half-mile walking tours that highlight the picturesque seaport. The trails focus on Pavilion Beach and Stage Fort Park, Gloucester Harbor, and the waterfront, Main Street and downtown, and the Rocky Neck artist's colony. All of the walks are short, close together, and marked by signs and a painted red line on the sidewalk. Free maps are available at the Gloucester Visitor Welcome Center in Stage Fort Park; 978/283-1601 or 800/321-0133.

Off this path on the eastern side of Goose Cove Reservoir and almost directly across the water from the parking lot is the start of Common Road. This old three-mile cart path winds its way through Dogtown into Rockport. Along the way, you cross the rich forest and rocky terrain that typifies Cape Ann.

You can make a 3.5-mile loop by following the Goose Cove Reservoir path to Common Road, Wharf Road, and Dogtown Road. Dogtown Road returns you to civilization and pavement, but not to your car. To return to the parking lot, continue on the paved portion of Dogtown Road and take a right onto Cherry Street. After a country quarter mile, turn right on Gee Avenue. The lot is at the road's end.

A word of caution: One reader alerted us to the fact that there were target practice sounds on his last visit, and his dog spooked and was lost for four hours. We checked it out, and the city assures us there is neither a rifle range nor an authorized target practice site in the area, but this is a big park and we can't assure you that people aren't out shooting cans. If your dog bolts easily, we advise you to keep him on a leash.

Dogs are not allowed to swim in the Goose Cove and Babson Reservoirs, but they can run free under voice command in the rest of Dogtown.

To reach the Goose Cove Reservoir parking area from Route 128, take Exit 11 to Route 127/Washington Street north. Turn right on Stanwood Street. Merge left onto Gee Avenue. The parking lot is at the road's end.

To get to the Dogtown Road parking area from Route 128, take Exit 11 to Route 127/Washington Street north. Turn right on Reynard Street and then left on Cherry Street. Turn right on Dogtown Road. (The street sign says Historic Dogtown.) Park at the gate at the end of the pavement. Open dawn–dusk. 978/281-9720.

12 Good Harbor Beach

🐾🐾🐾 (See North Shore map on page 130)

Once upon a time, dogs were allowed here off leash in the off-season and after 5 P.M. during the summer. Catch a tolerant ranger and you still might get away with those privileges, but the official rules are: no dogs allowed from May 1–September 15, and then they need to be leashed.

We love Good Harbor Beach for its beauty and peacefulness. The wide-open area offers plenty of room to run, and our dogs just love to romp through the moist sand. If you're at Good Harbor at low tide, you can walk out to Salt Island, a large hunk of rock resting just offshore. George and JoAnna canoed out to the island one bright summer day and had it all to themselves for swimming, sunning, and off-leash bliss. But when the tide is low, you have to share it and must abide by the summer hours and leash laws.

From Route 128, take Exit 9 (the last exit) to the intersection of Bass Avenue and East Main Street. Turn left on Bass Avenue/Route 127A, then left on

Thatcher Road/Route 127A. The beach and a parking lot are on the right. Open dawn–dusk. 978/281-9720.

13 Goose Cove Reservation

🐾🐾🐕 (See North Shore map on page 130)

Whether it's high or low tide, Inu loves coming to Goose Cove. Given his choice, of course, he checks the tables for low tide. That's when he'll find more muddy, fishy places to sniff out, and best of all he can paddle out to the sandbars, where he declares himself supreme alpha dog of the islands. As top dog, he eats all the shellfish he wants and rolls in as much seaweed as he feels is necessary to get just the right scent.

The main trail cuts right through the middle of the reservation's thick woods. The walk from the trailhead to the farthest point is almost a mile long. The pathway brings you out to an open spit of land overlooking scenic Goose Cove. This is a great spot for swimming; the water is shallow, and during low tide, several sandbars lie within easy walking distance. Just watch out for some of the muckier spots.

Another trail ventures off to the left of the parking lot and leads to the marshy coast of the cove. The short spur is overgrown and takes you through muck and mud. If that sounds good to you, then be our guest. But if not, stick to the main trail. You'll get a much better walk and views of the cove.

The Essex County Greenbelt Association manages this conservation area, so dogs are allowed off leash. Make sure your pooch is trail wise; otherwise he'll pick up countless burrs and tangles if he races off the beaten path into the vines and thickets.

When it's time to head home, Inu faces the difficult decision of choosing between his vast empire and a biscuit. Let's just say you would be left high and dry as a subject of his court.

From Route 128, take Exit 11 to Washington Street/Route 127 north. The reservation's entrance is on the right, just past Holly Street. A parking lot is available. Open dawn–dusk. 978/768-7241.

14 Hardy Mountain Park

🐾🐾🐾🐕 (See North Shore map on page 130)

If you've been searching high and higher for a decent place to take your Bernese mountain dog, then you should visit Hardy Mountain Park. The rocky terrain and dense woods of Hardy Mountain provide the perfect place for the lofty adventures that all dogs enjoy. And, as long as your canine companion is under voice control, he's allowed to enjoy it all off leash.

The park is tucked away in the western corner of Cape Ann along Route 128. The park entrance feels like a secret passageway that opens up onto a room full of gold and silver—only here the treasure is a mountain of trails and woods. And to a dog's eyes, that's worth far more than the loot.

Hardy Mountain lies on private land, and it's only due to the goodwill of the owners that hikers and dogs have access to the park. People are allowed to use a narrow brook trail to cross the property.

Once in the park, the two-mile trail quickly climbs through the trees to the mountaintop where you'll find excellent views over the entire cape. You're sure to share the path with the many rock climbers who come to scale the steep cliffs.

If you and your dog aren't into altitude, there are many other great trails here that circumvent the peak and run deep into the woods through small hills and valleys. A two-mile trail extends all the way out to the park's western border and Haskell Reservoir. Dogs are not permitted in the water, but the serene beauty makes it a worthwhile destination.

From Route 128, take Exit 14 to Essex Avenue/Route 133 west. Head to mile marker 38, next to the storage company. Leave your car at the small roadside pullout and walk into the park. Open sunrise–sunset. 978/281-9720.

15 Miles Beach

 (See North Shore map on page 130)

Set on the scenic East Gloucester Peninsula, this pleasant, small beach attracts most people for its views over Gloucester Harbor and the Boston skyline in the distance. In fact, most people seem to prefer taking in the sights from the parking area. That leaves all the more room on the sand for the dogs, but even so, there's not much room; the beach might be better named Quarter-Mile Beach. Still, it's clean and boasts a hard, flat surface for running or playing.

Dogs are prohibited from May 1–September 15. After that, your dog may accompany you on leash.

From Route 128, take Exit 9 (the last exit) to the intersection of Bass Avenue and East Main Street. Continue straight on East Main Street; it becomes Eastern Point Road. The beach and a parking lot are on the right. Open dawn–dusk. 978/281-9720.

DOG-EAR YOUR CALENDAR—JUNE, AUGUST

St. Peter's Fiesta: Celebrating the Italian feasts of the saints, this party is held in St. Peter's Square at the end of June each year. The four-day event includes a carnival, games, live entertainment, fun for the kids, and lots of food. 978/283-1601.

Gloucester Waterfront Festival: An annual arts-and-crafts event, this festival shows off many of Gloucester's fine artisans. Although dogs aren't the focus, it's still a terrific outing in town. The festival is held the third weekend in August. 978/283-1601.

16 Pavilion Beach

☙ (See North Shore map on page 130)

The Fisherman's Memorial, a statue of the salty seafarer leaning against a wheel as he peers into the ocean, watches over this small beach in the heart of town. The weary fellow may look familiar. You've probably seen the image a thousand times on boxes of Gorton's frozen fish sticks. In fact, Gorton's factory is located right in Gloucester, but not along the beach.

Pavilion Beach's central location means it gets a lot of activity, but most of the commotion occurs on the walkway along Western Avenue. The smooth sidewalks and spectacular views of the harbor and cliffs of Stage Fort Park make it a popular spot for walking or jogging. The beach is small and rocky, so it doesn't attract many swimmers of the human variety. Inu, however, is not terribly picky. He just needs a little room to run and some water to dive into. After a refreshing dip, we walk the length of the pavilion to dry off and enjoy a little exercise.

During the summer, dogs are not allowed on the beach. During the off-season, dogs must be leashed.

From Route 128, take Exit 11 to Washington Street south. Turn right on Western Avenue/Route 127 south. Street parking is available. Open dawn–dusk. 978/283-1601.

17 Ravenswood Park

☙☙☙ (See North Shore map on page 130)

Occupying 500 acres, this protected woodland makes a fine outing for hikers, both the two- and four-legged kind. As a Trustees of Reservations holding, it requires that dogs wear a leash. Still it's well worth a peek. It offers seven miles of trails, three miles of carriage roads, and an outstanding vista point on Ledge Hill overlooking the Atlantic Ocean. During the spring and summer, you and your dog will enjoy the well-maintained hiking trails and quiet forest shade; in the winter, the carriage roads are perfect for cross-country skiing and snowshoeing.

At the trailhead, you'll find ample parking and a detailed map of the hiking routes. The terrain is varied enough to provide a pleasant, quiet walk with some flavor. The Ledge Hill Trail leads to the vista. Or you could follow the Magnolia Swamp Trail, where your dog can sniff at the scent of magnolia blossoms growing along the swamp's edge.

From Route 128, take Exit 14 to Essex Avenue/Route 133 east. Turn right on Western Avenue/Route 127 south. The park is on the right. Keep a close eye out for the park sign; it isn't well placed. Open 8 A.M.–sunset. 978/921-1944.

18 Stoney Cove Reservation

☙☙🐕 (See North Shore map on page 130)

These rarely visited 53 acres along the Little River are part of the Essex County Greenbelt Association and offer visitors a chance at a little peace and quiet—

in any season. Choose between walking in the woods or exploring the salt marshes and tidal pool along the river's edge. When the tide is in, your dog can take a cooling dip on a hot summer's day. The park is located off the northbound lane of Route 128 just after Exit 13. Use caution exiting and entering the parking area. Open 4 A.M.–10 P.M. 978/768-7241.

19 Wingaersheek Beach

🐾🐾🐾🐾🐾 (See North Shore map on page 130)

This has to rank as our favorite beach in the Boston area. Absolutely beautiful, and secluded on one end, this heavenly slice of sand overlooks an inlet across from the Annisquam Lighthouse. You get your choice of white sandy beaches nestled alongside grassy dunes, wooded hillsides surrounding the bay, or the open sea and large weathered rock formations splashed by the surf. Dogs even get a choice of waves.

Stay to the right of the rocks, and the waves gently roll in for those dogs who just like to get their feet wet, like George. Stay to the left, where the beach is more exposed to the sea, and the waves come in with a little more spirit. This side is perfect for those high-energy dogs who need a day in the surf to wear them out. Wingaersheek Beach, in the secluded northwestern corner of Gloucester, is about a mile long. After October, you'll have the place to yourselves, but the official rule still calls for a leash. During the summer months, however, dogs are prohibited.

From Route 128, take Exit 13 to Concord Street north. Turn right on Atlantic Street. The beach and a parking lot are at the road's end. Open dawn–dusk. 978/281-9720.

PLACES TO EAT

Boulevard Ocean View Restaurant: What a great place to take a break from dog walking and the usual New England cuisine. The American and Portuguese menu is not as bizarre as it sounds, and the small, umbrella-covered outdoor deck will allow you and your dog to enjoy the chow and the view. 25 Western Avenue; 978/281-2949.

Harbor Point Ice Cream: Even though this treat shop doesn't have outdoor seating, it serves some good ice cream. And since Pavilion Beach is right across the street, you can pick up your favorite flavor and enjoy a pleasant harbor view from one of the beachside benches. 29 Western Avenue; 978/283-1789.

PLACES TO STAY

Cape Ann Campsite: This 200-site camping area is close to all the area beaches and offers secluded camp and RV sites in a lovely natural setting.

Close to town and the area beaches, you and your dog will enjoy getting out in nature here. Beach permits are available if you want to go down the street to Wingaersheek Beach. Sites are $25–30 per night. Dogs are welcome but must be leashed. Atlantic Street, West Gloucester, MA 01930; 978/283-8683; website: www.cape-ann.com/campsite.

Cape Ann Motor Inn: Nestled on the edge of Long Beach on the border of Rockport and Gloucester, this clean, well-maintained inn can't be beat for location. Not only do the proprietors welcome dogs, they're proud to be the first motel on Cape Ann to do so. The 31 rooms are new and spacious, all with balconies overlooking the beach and ocean. There are no size restrictions, but a one night's room deposit is required for your pet. Rates range from $70–130 (the honeymoon suite is more expensive); an additional $15 fee is required for rooms with a kitchen. This is a great find for you and your pet. 33 Rockport Road, Gloucester, MA 01930; 978/281-2900 or 800/464-VIEW (800/464-8139); website: www.capeannmotorinn.com.

Hamilton

PARKS, BEACHES, AND RECREATION AREAS

20 Appleton Farms Grass Rides

🐾🐾🐾◀● (See North Shore map on page 130)

How many times have you driven past a private farm with rolling hills and hay bales and had to tell your excited pooch that he couldn't get out and run? Probably so many times that you're still in therapy to get rid of the guilt. One way to feel better is to visit the Trustees of Reservations' 228-acre Appleton Farms Grass Rides. (Yes, the name's confusing. A "ride" is a path made for horseback riding through the woods. Today, the paths are open to people and dogs, but not to horses because of the delicate nature of the soil.)

First tilled by Thomas Appleton in 1638, Appleton Farms just may be the oldest working farm in the United States. Be sure to stay on the trail as you pass right through the middle of corn and wild grass fields. The four-mile route leads from the farm into glorious woodlands, which are crisscrossed with a maze of old grass-covered carriage paths.

All of the trails eventually lead to the circular clearing in the park's center, known as Roundpoint. Here you'll discover a granite pinnacle that was salvaged from Gore Hall before the former Harvard College Library was torn down. The school bestowed the monument on Francis Appleton, who once served as the library's chairman.

Michael Tougias's book *Nature Walks in Eastern Massachusetts* features an accurate and probably life-saving map of the carriage paths. It's especially handy as the trails are beautiful but confusing, and the park offers no maps. Dogs must be leashed here.

You can find Appleton in northern Hamilton. From Route 1A in Wenham, take Arbor Street north for 3.5 miles. Arbor Street becomes Highland Street in Hamilton. Turn right on Cutler Street. A parking lot is on the immediate right. The trailhead is across Cutler Street on the right. Open dawn–dusk. 978/921-1944.

PLACES TO EAT

The Junction: Have you noticed that we have a nose for ice cream? Well, we've got another hot spot for Spot (and you). This little roadside creamery has plenty of parking and benches lining the surrounding woods, offering a great setting to set awhile and enjoy a cone after a day's outing. The trees provide plenty of shade for weary human travelers and doggy explorers alike. 600 Essex Street; 978/468-2163.

Ipswich

A booming industrial center in the late 19th century, Ipswich earned its reputation with famous shoe, hosiery, and paper factories. Wealthy Bostonians also vacationed here in summer, enjoying the sweet ocean breezes that drift in over the dunes and marshes. Since the Depression, the factories have departed. Currently much of Ipswich is protected as one of the last major wetlands on the Eastern seaboard. You and your canine companion will enjoy the beauty of the marshy grasslands stretching out over gentle hills and white sand beaches, as well as the old-fashioned splendor of this quiet seaside town.

PARKS, BEACHES, AND RECREATION AREAS

🐾🐾 Dow Brook and Bull Brook Conservation Lands

🐾🐾 (See North Shore map on page 130)

It may not look like much at the start, but persevere and you'll discover some great woodland hiking here. The main trail, part of the Bay Circuit Trail, is an old cart road that starts near the farms of Mile Lane. Here the road is covered with grass until it enters the dense woods. Then the trail crosses over Bull Brook Reservoir, Prospect Hill, and Dow Brook and goes all the way out to Prospect Street in Rowley for a three-mile, one-way hike. The brooks are clean, clear, and slow moving.

From the top of Prospect Hill, you can look out over the 486 acres of the park. When the foliage is down, you get an endless panorama. In summer, you'll have to make do with a lovely, lush view of the thick tree cover. But do take the quick trot up to the top, both for the aerobics and the exhilaration of being up there. You can tell people you climbed it because it was there.

Dogs must be leashed. Keep an eye out for horses on the three miles of trails.

From the town center at the intersection of South Main Street and County Road/Routes 1A and 133, take South Main Street northwest; it becomes Central Street. Turn left on Linebrook Road. Turn right on Mile Lane. A small pullout and a weathered park sign are on the left. Parking is permitted at Doyon Elementary School on Linebrook Road when school is not in session. Open dawn–dusk. 978/768-7241.

22 Greenwood Farms

🐾 🐾 🐾 (See North Shore map on page 130)

So you and your canine companion have been getting out there, visiting quite a few parks with all sorts of terrain, everything from beach to woods. Maybe you've even run with the big dogs at some of the city parks. You're feeling pretty confident. Yup, you and your pup can handle just about any trail that comes down the pike.

Well, good for you. But *The Dog Lover's Companion to Boston* has a little challenge for you. Greenwood Farms just might have enough of a twist to give the two of you a little trail test.

The 120-acre park, managed by the Trustees of Reservations, starts out nice and easy. Open fields of cut grass lead you from the parking lot to the historic homes of the Paine family, who established the estate in the 1600s, and the Dodge family, who restored and donated the property. It's a quick walk up the gradual slope. From here, you'll enjoy fine views of the tidal basin of the Ipswich River.

Just beyond the houses, however, you leave the high ground of the estate and enter the salt marshes to the left. And this is where the challenge begins.

How many of the marsh islands can your elite expedition team visit? You'll find five tiny islands on the estate, each a solid plot of land with trees and shrubs. Many marsh birds, such as blue herons and northern harrier hawks, use them for feeding areas. Separating the islands are soft, grassy wetlands and Greenwood Creek. The marshy trail runs from island to island (reaching at least three of them). It gives you bridges to cross the two branches of the creek, but during high tide, you'll have to navigate the flooded banks all by yourselves.

We made it to three of the islands, risking life and limb (not to mention a big laundry bill) in the process. It was worth it, though, just for the chance to experience the scenic beauty of the Ipswich River. We offer two helpful tips: Wear boots, and check your charts for low tide. It's a rough-and-ready trip, but if you're both rough and ready yourselves, we say, "Go for it!"

From Route 1A and Route 133 in central Ipswich, take County Road north. Turn right on East Street and then turn left on Jeffrey Neck Road. Go half a mile to the park on the right. Look for a small gravel parking lot; the Trustees of Reservations sign is hard to see. Dogs must be leashed. Open dawn–dusk. 978/921-1944.

23 Julia Bird Reservation

🐾 🐾 🐕 (See North Shore map on page 130)

An Essex County Greenbelt Association property, the Julia Bird Reservation offers a pleasant, off-leash walk through woods and grassy fields, a refreshing swim in the Ipswich River, and perhaps a game of polo with the big boys.

From the trailhead, follow the path along the brook through the woods. (Be sure not to head onto the dirt road to the left—it's private property.) Although the trail's a little swampy at the start, it's not long before you reach greener pastures. A polo field is part of the park and, if it's not covered with horses, makes a great place to play. Inu and George always head for the field and chase each other over a stick. Guess it's just something about the grass.

Horse farms are plentiful in the area, so you and your canine companion are bound to share the trail with equestrians. Beyond the field to the left and the right, the wide trail continues into the forest. And the beautiful Ipswich River rushes nearby. Let your dog cool off in these waters after a good, tiring romp.

From the town center at the intersection of South Main Street and County Road/Routes 1A and 133, take County Road heading south and then turn right on Wadingfield Road. The park is located on the right; look for the Essex County Greenbelt Association sign. Leave your car at the roadside pullout. Julia Bird Reservation is open dawn–dusk. 978/356-6607.

24 Richard T. Crane Jr. Memorial Reservation

🐾 🐾 🐾 ◖● (See North Shore map on page 130)

In 1916 Richard Crane, a Chicago millionaire, bought this 800-acre parcel of Atlantic coast and built a 17th-century-style, 59-room mansion known as the Great House. Now a historical landmark—*The Witches of Eastwick* was filmed here—the land has been managed by the Trustees of Reservations since Crane's death. Aside from being one of the most beautiful beaches in Massachusetts, the wetland provides a home to thousands of coastal birds and animals. Because of the delicacy of the wetland preserve, you're not allowed to tramp through the protected areas. From October–May, however, leashed dogs are welcome on one of New England's most popular and well-known shore points, Crane Beach, a four-mile-long barrier beach that acts as a kind of seawall to the Essex and Ipswich River estuaries.

Although it gets crowded around the mouth of the parking area, once you set off in either direction along the beach, you'll soon find you have the beach practically to yourselves. Sometimes the Atlantic pounds furiously at the sand; at other times it rolls quietly into shore. Either way, this makes a lovely, deserted place to get away from it all. Watch out for greenfly season, which usually hits in late May. These flies are nasty—very nasty!

From Route 128 in Beverly, take Exit 20N to Route 1A north and the Ipswich town center. Turn right on Argilla Road. The beach gate is at the road's end. There is a $4 parking fee. Open dawn–dusk. 978/356-4351.

25 Willowdale State Forest

☙ ☙ ☙ (See North Shore map on page 130)

As in most of Massachusetts's state forests, limited services are available at Willowdale State Forest. Depending on how you like to experience the outdoors, this can be a plus or a minus. The lack of parking, infrequently maintained trails and restroom facilities, and scarcity of park rangers may be a hindrance to some. Others, however, find the secluded, rugged woods here make for perfect wilderness outings.

You and your leashed dog will find an extensive trail system on Willowdale's 2,400 acres, but many of the routes, although passable, can be wet or swampy. If your dogs are like ours, they'll love it. "The muddier the better" is their motto. We simply bring along a high-pressure fire hose (and a lot of towels) to wash them down before allowing them back in the car. For a guaranteed mucky hike, try the red-and-blue marked trail that loops around Dismal Swamp. (What a name!)

The Bay Circuit Trail runs through the state forest from Pine Swamp Road to East Street. You can also take the Bay Circuit Trail one mile west to the Hood Pond section of Willowdale State Forest, but to do so, you must cross Route 1. Because of car traffic, it's not the best area for dogs.

DIVERSIONS

Pick an apple a day: In summer and fall, try apple picking on one of the most scenic farms on the North Shore. **Goodale Orchards,** just up the road from Crane Beach, is the perfect place to pluck a basket of apples. If you want your dog to help, put a doggy knapsack on her and fill the pouch along with your own. Call for seasonal conditions. 123 Argilla Road; 978/356-5366.

Take a three-hour tour, a three-hour tour: There's no telling when you'll want to return from your canoeing adventure on the Ipswich River. Its beauty and serenity will captivate you and your dog all day long. Renting a canoe is a perfect way to explore this quiet, winding three-mile section of the river that glides ever so gently between the Willowdale State Forest and Bradley-Palmer State Park (in Topsfield). Make sure your pooch is of the calm variety, or you'll play tippy-canoe all day. A canoe costs $25 per day; reservations are recommended for weekends. Visit Foote Brothers Canoe Rentals at Willowdale Dam, 230 Topsfield Road, or call 978/356-9771.

To reach the park's southern portion and the main trailhead from Route 1, take Ipswich Road east. Ipswich Road becomes Topsfield Road at the Asbury Street intersection. The park is on the left. Use the car pullouts on your left at Gravely Park Road, at the sign for the Topsfield and Ipswich town line. On the southern side of Topsfield Road is Bradley-Palmer State Park (see the listing in the Topsfield section of this chapter).

To access the park's northern section from Route 1, take Linebrook Road east. The forest is on the right. Park along the shoulder or at the Doyon Elementary School when classes are not in session. Open sunrise–sunset. 978/887-5931.

PLACES TO EAT

Bruni's: We mention this gourmet grocery store because it has easy, self-serve sandwiches, bakery goods, soups, salad bar, and deli items. The food's delicious, outdoor seating is available, and there's a yogurt shop right next door just in case you aren't full enough after feasting on Bruni's many delicacies. Fast, easy, and dog friendly, this is our kind of place. Pick up something on your way in or out of town. 24 Essex Road; 978/356-4877.

White Cap Restaurant: What else should you eat in Ipswich besides Ipswich clams? In our opinion, there is no "what else!" And this is the place to get them. Eat your clams and other baked, broiled, or fried seafood on the outdoor picnic tables. There's a big backyard for your faithful friend. Water is on the house (and under the deck). 141 High Street/Route 133; 978/356-5276.

White Farms Ice Cream Sandwich Shop: This is the place, or at least George thinks so. Doggy dishes of soft vanilla with a big biscuit are 25 cents or free with another purchase. So of course we had to get something. JoAnna went with the popular Oinker Sandwich—ham, three kinds of cheese, tomatoes, onions, and a special mustard sauce. And then on to the ice cream! Outdoor seating is available. 1326 High Street; 978/356-2633.

PLACES TO STAY

Whittier Motel: Just outside of town, this 20-room motel is still close to walking trails and a small park across the street. It has a coffee shop that serves breakfast, and the rooms are clean, if a bit dated. But they allow you to bring your dog, so it's okay in our book, and the price is right. Rates are $70–100; it's $10 extra per night for your dog. There's no size restriction, but the management requests that you not leave your dog unattended in the room. 120 County Road/Route 1A, Ipswich, MA 01938; 978/356-5205 or 877/418-0622; website: www.whittiermotel.com.

Manchester-by-the-Sea

PARKS, BEACHES, AND RECREATION AREAS

🐾 Agassiz Rock

🐾🐾🐾 (See North Shore map on page 130)

Short and sweet describes the trail up Beaverdam Hill. It's short, because the 1.5-mile loop quickly lets you and your leashed canine pal escape into the wilderness. It's sweet, because the trail is covered with pine needles, which give off a fresh scent as you hike.

This 101-acre Trustees of Reservations area is named for Louis Agassiz, a Harvard professor who studied glacial movement here. Agassiz first noted that the two giant boulders on the hilltop here were deposited there by the glaciers that once moved across New England. The boulders are glacial erratics, a designation that refers to the random way they've settled. Little Agassiz is easily climbable and has great views over the reservation. The second, Big Agassiz, lies on the back loop and rises 30 feet out of the marsh. Because of the surrounding swamp, it's not possible to climb it.

The main trail to the hilltop and Agassiz Rock ascends gradually. A number of excursion paths branch off from the main trail. As long as you stay with the wider path at the intersections, you should have no problem remaining on course. George and Inu are pretty good scouts for us. If we're unsure about going left or right, we let them decide. They tend to follow the better-traveled trail because the scents on it are stronger. Of course, this system breaks down if a chipmunk has recently crossed the path. But we generally try the other route after two or three loops around a fallen tree.

From Route 128, take Exit 15 to School Street north for about a half mile. The parking area is on the right; it's little more than a pullout off the road. Open sunrise–sunset. 978/921-1944.

🐾 Coolidge Reservation

🐾🐾 (See North Shore map on page 130)

Part of the Trustees of Reservations system, this 58-acre parcel of land on Route 127 is a mixed bag. Hiking trails are plentiful and varied—you can walk on hilly or flat terrain, with great vistas over the ocean. The forest is made up mainly of pine trees mixed with oaks and maples, and it opens onto the Great Lawn and Clark Pond. But the best path, the Great Lawn Trail, which leads down to the ocean, is only open on Saturdays, and dogs are not allowed on the lawn itself.

Another word of caution: Clark Pond is a swampy, muddy pond with no shore area. We found out the hard way, as our dogs eagerly followed the scent of water. But in order to reach the pond, you must wade tummy deep into

thick muck. Inu and George came out covered in black gunk, looking less like dogs than great gooey globs. Although they were both happy campers, we had major second thoughts about letting them jump back into the car covered from head to toe. So unless you stick to the forest trails or drive a pickup truck, beware the Black Muck! Dogs must be leashed.

From Route 128, take Exit 15 to School Street south. Turn left on Lincoln Avenue, which becomes Lincoln Street. Turn left again on Summer Street/Route 127. The park is two miles up Summer Street on the right, just before Raymond Street. Open 8 A.M.–sunset. 978/921-1944.

28 Singing Beach

🐾🐾 🐾 (See North Shore map on page 130)

As scenic spots go, they don't get any better than Singing Beach. No, this beach doesn't get its name from anything dramatic like sirens singing on the rock, luring sailors to their destruction. In fact, when we asked how it came to be named Singing Beach, we were told that when the wind blows, the movement of the sands creates a kind of "song."

Set at the end of Beach Street through Manchester Center, this big, open sandy beach overlooks the Northern Harbor Islands. It'll seem like a dream to you, but not necessarily to your dog. As with all the prime beaches on the North Shore, your dog can't visit from May 1–October 31. When you're both allowed, however, it's a terrific spot for a good hard run and a ball-tossing session.

During high season, parking can be expensive. On one of our summertime visits, the guards asked us to pay $15 for a spot. But since your dog isn't welcome anyway, why bother until autumn? After Labor Day, the parking area is open free of charge. Your canine pal must be leashed.

From Route 128, take Exit 15 to School Street south. Turn right on Union Street/Route 127. Turn right again on Sea Street and then left on Beach Street. The beach and a parking lot are at the road's end. Open dawn–dusk. 978/526-2040.

🖭 Wilderness Conservation Area

🐾🐾🐾🐾 (See North Shore map on page 130)

This spectacular reservation is in Essex, Hamilton, and Manchester-By-The Sea. And even though it is composed mainly of swamps and rocky outcroppings, it seems everyone wants a piece of it. That includes developers. Fortunately for all of us, the Manchester Conservation Trust, Essex County Greenbelt Association, Trustees of Reservations, and the three town conservation commissions have been successful in protecting most of the more than 400 acres. The battle to conserve natural resources continues (and sometimes the good guys win).

This is a wonderful place for you and your dog to explore. A wide variety of terrain is available: open ponds, thick swamps, dense forests, rocky summits, and even a few flat, dry areas.

One of the more popular sections is the newly protected Gordon Woods, which is located off Pine Street on the Hamilton-Manchester border. Heron Pond and the Sawmill Swamp, off School Street on Essex-Manchester line, are also worth a visit. The park also encompasses Agassiz Rock. For membership and a good map, write to the Manchester Conservation Trust, P.O. Box 1486, Manchester, MA 01944.

The main parking area is on School Street. From Route 128, take Exit 15 to School Street for a half mile. The parking area is on the left. For the Pine Street parking area, take Exit 16 from Route 128 to Pine Street north. Small pullouts are on the left as the pavement ends. Other parking areas are at Warren-Weld Woodland in Essex and Agassiz Rock in Manchester. Open sunrise–sunset. 978/526-4211.

Newbury

PARKS, BEACHES, AND RECREATION AREAS

🖭 Old Town Hill Reservation

🐾🐾 (See North Shore map on page 130)

We had just pulled off into the small parking area when we saw our tour guide coming down the lane. He sauntered over with a grin, a trot, and a wagging tail that only a jolly Labrador can put together. After George and the Lab had a playful getting-to-know-you romp right there in the road, we followed him on our personal tour of the reservation. JoAnna's only wish was to be able to keep up with the eight legs trotting ahead of her.

The trail, less than half a mile long, gradually climbed up 168 feet to the top of Old Town Hill, which is covered with woods and thick brush. Our energetic guide pointed out Castle Hill and Plum Island in the distance. He also showed us some decent fields to run in and some pleasant places to eat grass. JoAnna stayed with the views.

One word of caution: The low-lying underbrush is a haven for ticks, and George came out covered from head to toe with the little varmints. Tick season runs from August–November, peaking in October, so keep this in mind when you visit. We still think it's worth the trip, but make sure you check your dog thoroughly after a romp in the grass, and absolutely make certain you have him vaccinated for Lyme disease if you travel anywhere in the woods and brush of New England.

The Trustees of Reservations manages the 372-acre park. Dogs must be leashed at all times.

From Route 1 in Newbury, take Boston Road east. Turn right on Hay Street, then right again on Newman Road. The small pullout for parking is on the left. Open dawn–dusk. 978/921-1944.

31 Parker River Wildlife Refuge/Sandy Point State Reservation

😺 😺 (See North Shore map on page 130)

You'll find this vast coastal area encompassing the Parker River and Plum Island wild and beautiful. Since this is a fragile and protected natural environment, you're only allowed to take a quick, careful hike here. Dogs are allowed October 1–March 31, and they must be leashed. Dunes and salt marshes, popular places for nesting birds, are off-limits. And that's all we're going to say. It's a great place, but because our dogs tend to be pretty energetic, we find it's better left to the many resident birds, who probably appreciate the seclusion. Bird-watchers will find the usual shoreline suspects: plovers, herons, cormorants, and the occasional osprey and snowy owl.

From the intersection of Route 1, Route 1A, and Route 113 in Newburyport, follow High Road/Route 1A south. Turn left on Rolfes Lane into Ocean Avenue and Newbury. Turn right on Plum Island Turnpike and right again on Sunset Drive, which leads into the park. There is a $5 day-use fee (or $12 for an annual pass). Open from a half hour before sunrise to a half hour after sundown. 978/465-5753.

Newburyport

PARKS, BEACHES, AND RECREATION AREAS

🐾 Maudslay State Park

🐾🐾🐾 (See North Shore map on page 130)

Flower fans, take note: This 476-acre state park along the Merrimack River is a garden paradise. In May and June, blooming azaleas and rhododendrons entice many hikers. In the winter, the mountain laurels attract nesting eagles. And all year long the charming gardens and ambling carriage trails draw numerous visitors. This park is a popular place for horseback riding in the summer and cross-country skiing and snowshoeing in the winter. Leashed dogs are welcome to enjoy the numerous and varied meadows, ponds, old-growth forests, and cliffs of the former Moseley family estate.

Most of the gardens are in the park's northeastern corner around the estate houses. On our visits, we like to start off with a good hike in the secluded backwoods to give the dogs (and ourselves) some exercise. An enjoyable route is the Pine Hill Road Trail to the North Road or Main Road Trails; from here you can hike out to Castle Hill. Once the dogs have had their fill, we finish up the day with an easy stroll through the gardens.

In the winter, two small sections of the park are closed to the public to avoid disturbing the eagles during breeding season. Maps are available in the parking lot and at the ranger station. Dogs must be leashed.

From I-95, take Exit 57 to Storey Avenue/Route 113 east. Turn left on Ferry Road. Ferry Road becomes Pine Hill Road just after crossing over I-95. Pine Hill Road becomes Curzan's Mill Road upon entering the park. Parking is on the right. Open dawn–dusk. 978/465-7223.

🐾 Moseley Woods Park

🐾🐾 (See North Shore map on page 130)

Talk about a contrast! This park overlooks the peaceful flow of the majestic Merrimack River on one side and the frantic racing of interstate traffic on the other. Just look the right way and you'll be okay. Moseley Woods sits right

🐾 DOG-EAR YOUR CALENDAR—AUGUST

Newburyport Waterfront Festival: Held in mid-August, this annual street fair and craft show is a summer favorite. This isn't an event for hyper or shy dogs, but if your pooch won't mind the crowds, you both will probably enjoy an afternoon exploring festive Newburyport. 978/462-6680.

DIVERSION

Pick a pack of apples: Go apple picking before or after a walk in the woods. **Arrowhead Farms,** right next to Maudslay State Park, lets you pack both activities into one afternoon. Bring an extra backpack for the both of you and fill it with fresh, crisp, ripe apples after a day of hiking. The best times are early spring and late fall. Call for seasonal conditions. 131 Old Ferry Road; 978/462-9482.

between the Chain Bridge and the Whittner Memorial Bridge, which is the crossing for I-95. Keep your eyes on the water and not the road, and you'll do just fine here. The views of the river and nearby Deer Island from the park's cliffs are especially impressive.

Stepping back from the river's edge, the park offers a forest of tall, shady pines with sheltered picnic areas, a small playground, and a few short trails through the woods. The main trail is a segment of the Merrimack River Trail system, which is still being completed through the towns along the river. It's an easy, half-mile loop through a lovely area. The only drawback is that inescapable highway drone in the background. Your dog must be leashed.

From I-95, take Exit 57 to Storey Avenue/Route 113 east. Turn left on Moseley Avenue. The park gate is on the right at the intersection of Merrimac and Spofford Streets. Open dawn–dusk. 978/465-4407.

PLACES TO EAT

Coffee Aroma: You get two benches in front of this quaint breakfast nook. It's perfect for a quick stop for a cup of joe and a nibble before or after a run on the trails. 15 Water Street; there is no phone.

PLACES TO STAY

Morrill Place Inn: This sea captain's mansion dates back to 1806 and features 10 lovely rooms, each with antique furnishings and four-poster beds; some rooms have fireplaces and refrigerators. Breakfast is served each morning. Dogs of all sizes are welcome but must be able to get along with the Hunter's friendly bullmastiff. Rates are $85–125. 209 High Street, Newburyport, MA 01950; 978/462-2808 or 888/594-4667.

Windsor House: This Federal-style brick inn has five beautiful rooms done in English colonial style, some with a private bath. Dogs are welcome on approval in the Merchant Suite, located on the ground floor. Because this lovely home dates back to 1786 and needs tender care, the owners prefer small– to medium dogs. Rates are $120–155, including a full breakfast and afternoon tea. 38 Federal Street, Newburyport, MA 01950; 978/462-3778 or 978/465-3443; website: www.bbhost.com/windsorhouse.

Rockport

Just up the road from Gloucester, on the tip of Cape Ann, is scenic Rockport. Named for its many quarries, the town once provided granite to booming Atlantic coast cities during the Industrial Revolution. Samuel de Champlain first landed here in 1603 and named it Beauport for its stunning beauty. Today, the charming town has small shops, scenic harbors, and quaint B&Bs (sorry, no dogs allowed in most of them). You and your canine pal will love strolling the wharf at Bearskin Neck and dining alfresco over the water in the summer months.

PARKS, BEACHES, AND RECREATION AREAS

Dogtown Commons
See the listing in the Gloucester section of this chapter.

34 Halibut Point State Park/Halibut Point Reservation
🐾🐾 ◄█▶ (See North Shore map on page 130)

If you like rocks, we've got rocks. And more rocks. Encompassing an old quarry and leading down to the edge of the Atlantic Ocean, this park offers a panoramic and almost primeval view of the water from a vast field of glacially formed boulders.

Halibut Point, at the northernmost tip of Rockport, is small, only 68 acres, but big enough to be split between two park systems. The Massachusetts state park system and the Trustees of Reservations share administration duties.

DOG-EAR YOUR CALENDAR—DECEMBER

Rockport Tree Lighting Ceremony: Santa arrives by boat along the wharf at Bearskin Neck on the first weekend in December. What, no reindeer? Your children will be confused, but your dog will have a great time watching the carolers and strolling musicians. 978/546-6575.

Dogs can't really swim here. You won't find a true beach, and the waves beat strongly against the rocks. Still, dogs can enjoy a pleasant walk along the quarry or a rugged walk climbing on and hopping over huge stones. You'll enjoy some of the most breathtaking and unusual views of the sea in New England. George had fun imitating a mountain goat as he skimmed over the rocks, but Inu's size made it a little more difficult to navigate. This is not to everyone's taste and there is a leash law, but if you like rocks, it's a must-visit.

There is a $4 parking fee between Memorial Day and Labor Day.

From Route 128 in Gloucester, take Exit 11 to Washington Street/Route 127 north and Rockport. Washington Street becomes Granite Street. Turn left on Gott Avenue. Parking is on the right. Open sunrise–8 P.M. 978/546-2997 or 978/921-1944.

35 Pebble Beach

 (See North Shore map on page 130)

Just down the road from Long and Cape Hedge Beaches, you'll come upon the smaller Pebble Beach. And, yes, there are plenty of pebbles. Unfortunately, there's also plenty of seaweed. But you can park along the shoulder of the road, and because the beach is less attractive to sunbathers, you'll probably find you have the beach to yourselves. Because the cove is slightly protected, the swimming is great. But be warned: Your leashed pooch will discover lots of stinky sea stuff to roll in (and our dogs are stinky-stuff magnets). So, while this may be a favorite spot for Spot, if you value the smell of your car, you might pick your way carefully through this beach.

From the town center at the intersection of Routes 127 and 127A, follow Route 127A south until it becomes South Street. Turn left on South Street off Route 127A. Turn left on Penzance Road. Parking is on the side of the road. Open sunrise–sunset. 978/546-6894.

PLACES TO EAT

Lobster Pool: Here's where you'll find the best views in Rockport, and guess what? Your dog is invited along. Right at the water's edge in Folly Cove at the tip of Cape Ann, you can catch a great lobster or seafood dinner and take it outside to picnic along the ocean. Prices are moderate for seafood, so if you can accept eating on paper plates in a gorgeous but rustic setting, then we think this restaurant offers the best value in town. 329 Granite Street/Route 127; 978/546-7808.

Sundays: After lunch at the Lobster Pool, stop for ice cream at Sundays. (Hey, it's only a few calories—and you'll be walking it off, right?) There are plenty of ice-cream stops in Rockport, but this cute shop on the wharf at Bearskin Neck has some terrific flavors. Chris had Muddy Sneakers, an appropriate choice considering the state of his own shoes. JoAnna chose Mud Pie. (Is there a theme here?) George and Inu tried both.

Best of all, Sundays features an outdoor garden that overlooks the classic New England fishing harbor. Lots of dogs and their owners roam along the town's wharf, so you'll definitely find this a friendly place to stop after burning a few calories on the hike of your choice. It's along the wharf on Bearskin Neck; there is no phone.

PLACES TO STAY

Hedges by the Sea: Although Rockport has plenty of charm, there are few dog-friendly places to stay. Fortunately you'll find this cozy bed-and-breakfast more than enough. With two guest rooms and a lovely view of the sea, you and your dog will enjoy the peace and quiet here. It's only a short walk to town, and the innkeepers will be happy to recommend other walks you can take with your pup. Rates range from $88–175, depending on the season. There is $20 per stay charge for Rover. 165 Granite Street, Rockport, MA 01966; 978/546-0158; website: www.rockportusa.com/sleep/hedges/home.htm.

Rowley

PARKS, BEACHES, AND RECREATION AREAS

Georgetown-Rowley State Forest

See the listing in the Georgetown section of this chapter.

Salisbury

PARKS, BEACHES, AND RECREATION AREAS

36 Salisbury Beach State Reservation

😺😺😺 (See North Shore map on page 130)

Salisbury Beach measures 520 acres, but its actual size can really vary, depending on the tide. That's because the beach is about a quarter mile wide and five miles long, so when the tide's up, there isn't a lot of sand. But at low tide, it's one of the best beaches we've found for taking a long, healthy run.

The sand is hard and flat, so George always brings the requisite tennis ball with him. The only problem is that he insists on keeping it sand free. When the ball gets gritty pieces of sand rolled onto it, he drops it into the cold Atlantic's waves. And when the waves inevitably pull his ball out into the water, he expects JoAnna to go in to fetch it. Dream on. We usually lose it for good, and like a message in a bottle, it goes bobbing away to intrigue someone in the South Seas. But the chance to take a long, uninterrupted walk on a beautiful beach makes this a worthwhile trip. Just bring extra tennis balls.

For folks who want to camp along the beach, the reservation has 483 campsites with electrical hookups. The campground is really a big parking lot for RVs and trailers. There are no tent sites or restrooms, but it allows dogs. Call the Massachusetts State Camping Reservation Center at 877/422-6762 to make sure you get a site. Dogs cannot be left unattended and must be leashed when outside the RV or trailer. Rates are $10 per night for tent sites; $15 per night for RV hookups.

Dogs are only allowed on the beach during the off-season, from Patriot's Day–Columbus Day; they must be leashed at all times.

From I-95, take Exit 58 to Elm Street east/Route 110. Turn left on Route 1 north. Take an immediate right on Beach Road/Route 1A north. The park and a large parking lot are on the right. Open sunrise–sunset. 978/462-4481, website: www.ReserveAmerica.com.

PLACES TO STAY

Salisbury Beach State Reservation Campground:
See the Salisbury Beach State Reservation listing above.

Topsfield

PARKS, BEACHES, AND RECREATION AREAS

37 Bradley-Palmer State Park

 (See North Shore map on page 130)

This nifty park has something to offer in any season. It features 721 acres of hilly terrain filled with open meadows, woodsy trails, and a serene, pretty section of the Ipswich River. Trails are great for hiking and jogging in summer. In winter, folks can cross-country ski on the paths and snowshoe across the park's wide-open areas. And your leashed canine companion can accompany you everywhere in the area.

The three entrances have formal parking lots, restrooms, and picnic grounds—which, in our view, makes them less attractive to dog lovers. In addition to the main entrance, a second entrance is off Winthrop Street on the park's east side, and a third is on the south side, off Highland Street.

You can also enter the park on the north side along Topsfield Road and the Ipswich River. This allows you to access the park's less cultivated section, the part your dog will like best, away from all that concrete and the uptight folks who glare at a happy trail dog. Park along the shoulder of the road and cross the footbridge to the other side of the river. Here your pooch can stop for a cooling swim before heading up the trail to Moon Hill.

Although Moon Hill is more meadow than hill, you must walk up an incline to reach it; we assume this is why it's called a hill. If you continue up past the meadow, you'll definitely ascend a hill on the steep path to Blueberry Hill. The summit here also has a large meadow, where your canine pal can frolic, chase balls, or retrieve sticks. The highest point of the park, Blueberry Hill is often deserted; most people prefer to linger down at the wading pool at the main entrance. Dogs aren't allowed in the wading pool, so if swimming's a priority, the river will be your best option.

Now, the park does come with some obstacles—to be specific, the 15-hands-high type of obstacle. You're in horse country when you enter Topsfield, and this park is heavily used by the towering, four-hoofed creatures. You must watch out on the trails, and for obvious reasons your dog must remain leashed to prevent either scaring the horses or getting hurt by them. The horse traffic can make your visit a little more stressful than it would otherwise be.

If your pooch is skittish around horses, take the trail that runs several miles along the Ipswich River. A great hike, it's usually not as popular with our tall friends, but you still have to be on the lookout. In the winter months, however, you won't have to be so careful, as the equestrians stay away.

To reach the main entrance from Route 1, take Ipswich Road east. Turn right on Asbury Street. The park entrance is on the left.

To get to the Ipswich River trailheads from Route 1, take Ipswich Road east. Ipswich Road becomes Topsfield Road at the intersection with Asbury Street. The car pullouts are on the right. On the left, the north side of Topsfield Road, is the Willowdale State Forest. Open sunrise–sunset. 978/887-5931.

PLACES TO EAT

Busy B's: We don't know how busy they were "B"-ing, but this roadside eatery offers a wide range of burgers, fried fish, and box lunches in a scenic setting. The prices are moderate, the food is fine, and there's ample outdoor seating to accommodate you, your dog, and the rest of the world. A decent snitting spot behind the restaurant will be a godsend if your dog has been traveling in the car for a while. Grab lunch on the way to or from your hiking destination. 41 Haverhill Road/Route 97; 978/887-8956.

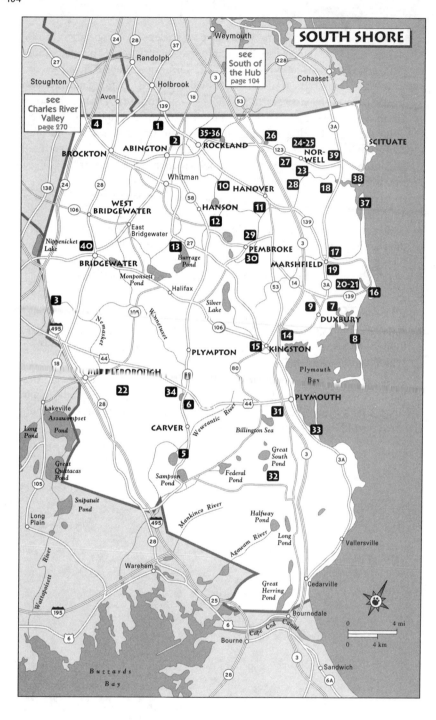

SOUTH SHORE

see
South of
the Hub
page 104

see
Charles River
Valley
page 270

Weymouth

Randolph

Stoughton

Holbrook

Cohasset

Avon

SCITUATE

BROCKTON

ABINGTON

ROCKLAND

NOR-
WELL

Whitman

HANOVER

WEST
BRIDGEWATER

HANSON

East
Bridgewater

Nippenicket
Lake

Burrage
Pond

BRIDGEWATER

PEMBROKE

MARSHFIELD

Monponsett
Pond

Halifax

DUXBURY

Silver
Lake

Nemasket

Wannetuxet

PLYMPTON

KINGSTON

Plymouth
Bay

MIDDLEBOROUGH

Lakeville

CARVER

PLYMOUTH

Assawompset
Pond

Billington Sea

Weweantic River

Long
Pond

Great
South
Pond

Great
Quittacas
Pond

Sampson
Pond

Federal
Pond

Snipatuit
Pond

Mankinco River

Long
Plain

Halfway
Pond

Long
Pond

Vallersville

Agawam River

Wareham

Wankinquoah
River

Great
Herring
Pond

Cedarville

Bournedale

Bourne

Cape Cod Canal

Sandwich

Buzzards
Bay

0   4 mi

0   4 km

CHAPTER 6

South Shore

The South Shore ranges from Brockton in the interior to Scituate and the Cape Cod Canal along the coast, including most of Plymouth County. Its serene coastal towns, like Duxbury and Norwell, are renowned for their cranberry harvests, seafaring communities, and beautiful, white sand beaches. In Plymouth, the Pilgrims first established their twin traditions of hard work and independence, which have become bedrock values for New Englanders. It's here that the sun seems to shine a little brighter and a little longer.

The beaches of the South Shore are some of the best in New England for dogs. They're wide, spacious, and a far cry from their rockier cousins on the North Shore. Duxbury Beach and Plymouth Beach are among the more popular destinations. Heading inland, the flat terrain gives way to forests and cranberry bogs, offering plenty of places for your dog to get wet, dirty, and happy as a canine can be.

PICK OF THE LITTER—SOUTH SHORE

BEST BEACH WALK
Duxbury Beach, Duxbury (page 171)

BEST PLACE TO GET LOST
Myles Standish State Forest, Plymouth (page 188)

BEST PLACE TO STAY
Inn at Scituate Harbor, Scituate (page 194)

BEST PET LOOK-A-LIKE CONTEST
Pet Walk-a-Thon, Plymouth (page 190)

Bay Circuit Trail: Linking parks and reservations between Plum Island on the North Shore and Kingston Bay on the South Shore, this trail will eventually connect more than 50 towns across 200 miles, including piecemeal routes in Duxbury and Kingston. For more information on its history and holdings, see the Resources section.

The Trustees of Reservations: This preservation organization manages more than 75 properties on nearly 18,000 acres throughout the Commonwealth, including lands in this chapter. Dogs must be leashed on all Trustees properties. For more information on the group, see the Resources section.

Wildlands Trust of Southeastern Massachusetts: Formerly named the Plymouth County Wildlands Trust, this nonprofit group has made tremendous strides in its land conservation efforts since its conception in 1973. Today it preserves more than 2,000 acres of wildlands and open spaces in Barnstable, Bristol, and Plymouth Counties. Through its land acquisitions, educational programs, and involvement in community development, the trust is saving the special places of southeastern Massachusetts for the benefit of all. In this chapter, Wildlands Trust properties can be found in Duxbury, Pembroke, and Plymouth. To become a member or to make a donation of funds or property, contact the Wildlands Trust of Southeastern Massachusetts, P.O. Box 2282, Duxbury, MA 02331; 781/934-9018; website: www.wildlandstrust.org.

Abington

PARKS, BEACHES, AND RECREATION AREAS

1 Ames Norwell State Park

🐾🐾 (See South Shore map on page 164)

Cleveland Pond, also known as Ames Pond, lies at the heart of this 607-acre state park. The three miles of trails here roam through a cool forest and around the water's edge, providing your leashed dog with enough room for a refreshing workout. At the trailhead off Linwood Street, you'll find a map that will give you an overview of the area.

Pine trees provide shade along most of the pathways. Sparkling Cleveland Pond is the main draw, attracting both canoeists and anglers. Be careful on the two-mile trail around the shoreline, however; the terrain near the water is rocky and laced with roots. The one-mile path through the woods makes an easier walk.

From the town center at the intersection of Bedford Street/Route 18 and Brockton Avenue/Route 123, take Brockton Avenue west. Turn right on Rockland Street, then right again on Linwood Street. The park and a parking lot are at the road's end. Open 8 A.M.–4 P.M. in winter; 8 A.M.–8 P.M. in summer. 781/857-1336.

2 Island Grove Park

🐾 (See South Shore map on page 164)

Nestled along Island Grove Pond, this quaint little town park can be a pleasant spot if you time your visit right. It's set among tall pines beside a lake—what more could you or your leashed dog ask for? Try a little elbow room. During peak season, especially on warm summer weekends, the place is packed with families on outings and picnics, especially around the swimming hole.

On quieter days, a short walk through the pines and along the shore or across the pedestrian-only Memorial Bridge over Island Grove Pond is just the ticket for a short, scenic quarter-mile stroll. But do yourself and your pooch a favor—come here when the rest of the town isn't trying to picnic on a hot Saturday afternoon.

From the town center at the intersection of Bedford Street/Route 18 and Brockton Avenue/Route 123, take Brockton Avenue east. Turn left on Washington Street/Route 123. Turn right on Centre Avenue/Route 123 and then turn left on Park Avenue. The park is on the left; park on the shoulder on either side of the road. Open dawn–dusk. 781/982-2125.

Bridgewater

PARKS, BEACHES, AND RECREATION AREAS

🖪 Taunton River Conservation Area

😼😼 (See South Shore map on page 164)

Well, it's not the mighty, muddy Mississippi, but the dark, quiet waters of the Taunton River flow by just as if you were down on the bayou.

Along the river, you'll discover this wooded, 50-acre conservation area and about a mile's worth of short, looping trails and dirt paths to stretch your legs on. At times the paths can be a bit trashy, depending on when the last late-night party was held.

But we don't come here on hot summer days for the woods. We come to cool off our Cajun canines. Inu loves to sink his whole body in the river and let the water roll right over him. George, graceful dancer that he is, is the master of some fancy four-stepping along the shoreline. He dips one paw in, then the next, and so on and so on. The technique may be a tad cautious, but it cools him off!

As with any body of water, care should be taken when walking along the edge, because some approaches to the shore are steep and the river can be deceptively quick. For dogs who would like a less adventurous dip, there is also a decent pond close by that's just as refreshing. It's right near the river's edge, and the trails lead to it. Dogs must be leashed.

From Route 24, take Exit 15 to Pleasant Street east. Turn right on Vernon Street and then turn right again on Beech Street. The park is on the left. An unpaved parking area can accommodate a couple of cars. Open sunrise–sunset. 508/697-0907.

Brockton

PARKS, BEACHES, AND RECREATION AREAS

🖪 D. W. Field Park

😼😼 (See South Shore map on page 164)

The towns of Brockton and Avon share this wonderful 50-acre park. Most of the activity is in the park's lower half on the Brockton side. The Avon side encompasses Brockton Reservoir, which is off-limits to the public except for the roadway. For your dog's purposes, the Brockton section is the best half.

Even though D. W. Field Park is only 2.5 miles long and a half mile wide, it offers woods, footpaths, bikeways, and seven sparkling, clear ponds connected by waterfalls and babbling brooks. Of the waters here, Lower Porter Pond, Thirty Acre Pond, and Waldo Lake are the largest and most accessible

DOG-EAR YOUR CALENDAR—SEPTEMBER

Who let the dogs out?: That's what you'll be asking when you join the fun at the MSPCA's annual **Walk for the Animals.** Benefiting the Brockton shelter, this walk takes place in September at D. W. Field Park. After the walk, join the fun at an amateur dog show and contest. Local pet stores share goodies and treats with your pup, and all proceeds go to help find homes for less fortunate dogs than yours. Call for dates and details, 508/586-2053.

for you and your dog. Each has tree-lined shoreline trails and clearings that skirt the water's edge, with plenty of places where your dog can dive in. And be sure to venture out across the land bridge at Waldo Lake.

For longer walks, try the park roadway, which is called D. W. Field Drive in one section and D. W. Field Parkway in the other. It runs the length of the park and loops around most of the ponds. The one-way road has a lane for cars and a lane for pedestrians. Keep a close eye on your dog here. Auto traffic is light, but it's a popular route for pedestrians and cyclists, not to mention ducks and geese.

Summer weekends can be busy, but you can always find a secluded piece of lakefront property around one of the ponds. Try the trails around Thirty Acre Pond for solitude.

From the American Veterans Memorial Highway/Route 24 in Avon, take Exit 19 to Harrison Boulevard east. Turn right on Pond Street into D. W. Field West Parkway and the northern entrance to the park. There are parking lots and pullouts throughout the park. Park roads are open to auto traffic noon–9 P.M. The park itself is open 9 A.M.–9 P.M. 508/580-7860.

Carver

PARKS, BEACHES, AND RECREATION AREAS

Myles Standish State Forest

See the listing in the Plymouth section of this chapter.

5 Savery's Avenue

😊 🐾 (See South Shore map on page 164)

America's first divided highway doesn't get as much traffic as it once did. In 1861, William Savery built the historic road, a quarter-mile dirt path with a row of trees separating its two lanes. Today it's been bypassed by Route 58, but you and your canine pal can walk on the very short trail in the pine forest. You'll see why Savery wanted to keep as many of the trees as possible. The invigorating scent of pine drifts through the woods, and the forest floor is covered in pine needles.

Your leashed dog won't get a lot of exercise here, but it's a handy pit stop in an emergency and a unique piece of the past. Managed by the Savery's Avenue Historic District Commission, the area is part of historic Carver. Aside from this early contribution to the nation's roadways, little remains of the old town, except for some nearby historic homes.

From the town center at the intersection of West Street and Main Street/Route 58, follow Main Street south. Savery's Avenue branches off to the right upon entering the Savery Historic District. Open 9 A.M.–9 P.M., May 1–October 31; open 9 A.M.–6 P.M., November 1–April 30. 508/866-3403.

6 Shurtleff Park

 (See South Shore map on page 164)

At 15 acres, this small park in the town center offers pine trees, band shell, and not much room for a leashed dog to roam. In this rural town where most homes are adjacent to woods or a cranberry bog, most folks just open their back door to let Rover enjoy the outdoors. But Shurtleff Park does offer a space where the community can gather and dogs can frolic with one another.

The park is in town at the intersection of West Street and Main Street/Route 58. Open 9 A.M.–9 P.M., May 1–October 30; 9 A.M.–6 P.M., November 1–April 30. 508/866-3403.

Duxbury

PARKS, BEACHES, AND RECREATION AREAS

Bay Farm Field

See the listing in the Kingston section of this chapter.

7 Cushman Preserve

 (See South Shore map on page 164)

Managed by the Wildlands Trust of Southeastern Massachusetts, this 65-acre reservation is set along the Blue Fish River just before it empties into Duxbury Bay. Once a private farm, the area is now a quiet woodland and marsh preserve for local wildlife. From the entrance, the land opens onto a large meadow, which has a pathway circling it and cutting through the middle. The half-mile-long dividing path takes you beyond the field into a small forest and then—voilà!—the marsh. Here you can actually access the river at the edge of the marsh grasses. The water is deep but clean, and of course our water dog, Inu, plunges right in. He swims a few lazy laps before returning to us on

shore. Then he and George welcome each other like long-lost friends and run exuberant circles around the marshy banks before we return to the car.

This park won't provide you with a long walk, but it's a beautiful spot. You'll probably see quite a few seabirds and herons on your visit. Dogs must be leashed.

From the Southeast Expressway/Route 3, take Exit 11 to Congress Street/Route 14 east. Follow Route 14 onto West Street. Continue straight into St. George Street. Turn right on Anchorage Lane. The park and a parking lot are on the left. Open dawn–dusk. 781/934-9018.

8 Duxbury Beach

🐾🐾🐾🐾 🐾 (See South Shore map on page 164)

If you've ever wanted to know what it feels like to own a deserted island, try a visit to Duxbury Beach. If you're not a billionaire (and there are so few of us these days), it may be as close as you'll come to enjoying your very own private stretch of paradise.

Duxbury Beach is a remarkable geological formation in Cape Cod Bay. A peninsula that's more than four miles long, the beach is only a quarter mile wide at most points. Park in the lots on either side of the Powder Point Bridge—you can park and walk across or not, as traffic and weather dictate—and head to the right along the beach. In high season, you'll need to keep your leashed dog close by you as you both navigate through the beachgoers near the parking area; continue another 500 yards and you'll have an undisturbed walk of approximately 3.5 miles each way.

And what a walk it is. With the Atlantic on one side and Duxbury Bay on the other, this is a beach as Mother Nature intended. The sand is hard packed for a fairly easy stroll, and chances are you won't find other people crowding in on your turf. Bring a good bouncy ball or Frisbee and some treats for you and the dog. You'll enjoy your walk in any weather, although it does get a little breezy on the ocean side in inclement weather. We suggest that you turn around at the cluster of houses at the bend of the finger; there really isn't much to explore beyond this point. Once we made the mistake of continuing another half mile to the very end, which proved uneventful and made for a longer return trip. That extra mile can make your hike feel like a marathon on the way back—especially if you've forgotten to bring the trail mix along.

Of course, at the end of the hike you can close your eyes and imagine you own the place. That way you'd be home already.

From the Southeast Expressway/Route 3, take Exit 11 to Congress Street/Route 14 east. Follow Route 14 onto West Street. Continue straight into St. George Street, which becomes Powder Point Avenue. Park in either lot before or after Powder Point Bridge. Open from 8 A.M.–8 P.M. 781/934-1104.

🐾 North Hill Marsh Wildlife Sanctuary/Round Pond

🐾🐾🐾 (See South Shore map on page 164)

Welcome to a wilderness playground for the big dogs. That's right, this is roll-and-tumble country, with just enough mud to send your leashed canine  home filthy and happy.

The dense woods that surround North Hill Marsh, Round Pond, nearby Island Creek Pond, and Pine Lake are loaded with great trails, adventure, and plenty of swamps and bogs. That's why the area is so popular with mountain bikers, hikers wearing brand-new hiking boots, and dogs who have just had a bath. But we know how to change that in a hurry ....

The main trail partially circles the pond named North Hill Marsh. This big, wide country road bobs and weaves its way through rich woods. At places, it rises over ridges where you can get a better look at the pond. In other spots, the path drops down into small marshy, muddy hollows. This is where our dogs like to practice their tuck-and-roll moves as they barrel down the hillside.

There isn't a complete route around the pond, but from the parking lot, side trails venture to the east and west sides of the pond. On the west side is Waiting Hill, which offers some fine views over the area. On the east side, you'll find more small loop trails and a cranberry bog.

The aptly named Round Pond is across Mayflower Street, about a quarter mile into the woods. Here an easy trail circles the pond and surrounding cranberry bogs. There's plenty of shade in summer and pine cover in winter. This isn't a strenuous or overly long walk, but it's recommended if you want a leisurely 30-minute stroll through a quiet woodland.

From the Southeast Expressway/Route 3, take Exit 11 to Congress Street/Route 14 east. Take an immediate right on Lincoln Street. After Lincoln Street becomes Mayflower Street, stay on Mayflower Street past East Street. Parking for Round Pond is on the right; parking for North Hill Marsh is on the left. Open sunrise–sunset. 781/934-1104.

PLACES TO EAT

French Memories Bakery: After a morning wading through cranberry bogs and playing in the surf on Duxbury Beach, you and your canine companion have enough grime and sand on you to earn the names Grunge Dog and Sandy Pants. It's time for a touch of class. And that's where the French come in. This quiet, outdoor café is the perfect place to relax in an atmosphere of sunny gentility while enjoying gourmet coffee and French pastries. The bakery prepares some delicious sandwiches, too. 459 Washington Street; 781/934-9020.

Hanover

PARKS, BEACHES, AND RECREATION AREAS

10 Fireworks Property Conservation Land

😺 (See South Shore map on page 164)

You won't see us setting off any fireworks to celebrate this park. Although we give the town of Hanover a big paws-up for designating land for public access, this 130-acre conservation area is a letdown. You get two designated trails here, but the first runs along a property fence, and the second dead-ends at the Drinkwater River. The park encompasses both the Drinkwater River and Factory Pond, but thanks to dense brush and woods, you can't actually reach the pond, which is the best of these locations. Ironically, the trail along the fence runs parallel, but inland, to the river, where you'd much rather walk, and Factory Pond is impossible to access unless you cross private property. No one in the Hanover Conservation Commission could tell us why the trails were laid out this way; in fact, its own literature touts this spot as having an "excellent trail system along the banks of the Drinkwater River." Trust us, it doesn't.

From the town center at the intersection of Hanover Street/Route 139 and Main Street, take Hanover Street west. Turn left on Circuit Street. Turn right on King Street. The trailhead is on the left. Look for the forest road and gate. Park along the dirt road. Open dawn–dusk. 781/826-8505.

11 Indian Head River Greenway

(See South Shore map on page 164)

The Hanover Conservation Commission and the Wildlands Trust of Southeastern Massachusetts jointly manage this great park system, which combines the Wampanoag Passage hiking trail with a fine picnic area. The park administration divides the park into three separate areas, which are listed below. Dogs must be leashed here.

From Route 3, take Exit 13 to Washington Street/Route 53 south. Washington Street eventually becomes Columbia Avenue/Route 53. Turn right on Broadway. Turn left on Elm Street. The park entrance and a parking lot are on the right, just before the bridge over the Indian Head River. Open dawn–dusk. Hanover Conservation Commission, 781/826-8505; Wildlands Trust of Southeastern Massachusetts, 781/934-9018.

Luddams Ford Section

This is one of those "something for everyone" places. There are two open meadows for picnicking and playing, shady trees for meditating or napping beneath, a clean stream for swimming, fishing, or fetching, and plenty of parking off Water Street. Anglers also get a fish run here, for the spring shad runs, so you can expect to see people casting away. Luddams Ford is also the entrance to the Wampanoag Passage hiking trail, so after some ball throwing and a picnic lunch, head upstream for a stroll. To reach Water Street and the parking lot here, continue north on Elm Street from the park entrance.

Riverside Drive Section

This 46-acre stretch runs along the North River—a continuation of the Indian Head River—below the dam. You can either park at the Indian Head River dam and cross Water Street, or head down Riverside Drive (called Indian Head Street on some signs) and park at the end of the dirt road. The route here is not nearly as pleasant as the Wampanoag Passage, but if you like swamps and mud, then give it a whirl. You'll find (or you won't find) a poorly marked one-mile trail and access to the river. Be sure to bring sturdy boots for yourself and a towel for your dog. There is talk of sprucing up the trails here, but for now, what you see is what you get.

Wampanoag Passage Section

The Wampanoag tribe once inhabited this land, and one of its riverside trails still remains for you to explore. It's a pretty two- to three-mile hike covering about 20 acres, and you can walk along either side of river. From the trailhead at the Indian Head River dam, you can either take the more leisurely, flat path to the right, or head across the meadow and follow the eastern side of the brook (which is actually in Pembroke). The left fork is a bit more strenuous, leading you along the hillside and up a few slopes. Both routes provide a shady, woodland walk with easy access to the river. Our dogs like to wade in the shallow areas along the trail as we take the more boring land route. Do, however, watch out for the shallow rapids as the water speeds up around the river's boulders. About 1.5 miles up the trail, the path becomes less scenic, so you can either retrace your steps to the dam or forge ahead to the Cross Street Bridge to loop back on the other side.

Hanson

PARKS, BEACHES, AND RECREATION AREAS

🐾🐾 Hanson Town Forest

🐾🐾 (See South Shore map on page 164)

Your first few steps through Hanson Town Forest are about as attractive as a landfill, but make it to the woods, and the landscape brightens up considerably. There are about two miles of trails that lead to and along Wompatuck Pond. Take the trail leading straight ahead to go directly to the pond. Here you'll find easy access to the water and fine swimming on a hot summer day. The woods are made up of white pine, so the forest floor is cushioned by the pine needles. Sit beneath a shady tree on a felled log while your dog splashes around in the water.

If you follow the trail to the left, you'll enjoy a half-mile jaunt around the pond. The walk's pleasant, but it leads you behind several houses built along the water, which diminishes some of the trail's wilderness appeal. Dogs must be leashed.

From the town center at the intersection of Liberty and Winter Streets, take Liberty Street east. Turn right on Indian Head Street. The park is on the right; parking is allowed at the Indian Head School on the left when school is not in session. Open dawn–dusk. 781/293-2772.

🐾 Smith-Nawazelski Conservation Land

🐾 (See South Shore map on page 164)

Even though this conservation area has been named for Smith and Nawazelski, it was donated to the town of Hanson by the Stillman family, whose homestead still stands along Elm Street. A 500-foot trail leads toward Stillman Pond, but you can't walk along the pond because it's located on private property. Unfortunately, a second, half-mile trail runs below some power lines, taking some of the "charge" out of the walk. If you live in the area, you may want to stop here to give your dog some exercise, but otherwise it really isn't worth making the trip. Dogs must be leashed.

From the intersection of Indian Head Street/Route 58 and Main Street/ Route 27, take Main Street west. Turn left on Elm Street. The park is on the right; park on the left at the dirt-road intersection. Open dawn–dusk. 781/293-2772.

PLACES TO EAT

Heidi's Hollow Farm: Look for the pink cone—that's the store's sign. Just off Route 58, this quaint roadside ice-cream parlor has outdoor tables where you and your dog can enjoy a treat at the end of a long, dusty hike. It serves ice cream and frozen yogurt, and it'll even whip up a doggy sundae consisting of vanilla soft serve topped off with a dog biscuit. Just bark and sit pretty, you lucky pooch. 165 Liberty Street/Route 58; 781/294-0131.

Kingston

PARKS, BEACHES, AND RECREATION AREAS

14 Bay Farm Field

🐾🐾🐾 (See South Shore map on page 164)

Perched on quiet Kingston Bay, this beautiful spot is a great place for a picnic. If you park in the small lot on Loring Street and head across the open field on the Orange Loop, you'll reach a grove of oak trees and rocks overlooking the calm water. What could be better on a warm spring or summer day? The trail is only three-quarters of a mile long, so you won't work up a sweat or hunger pangs, but if you bring your appetite with you, along with a picnic basket, it should provide a fun diversion on a lazy afternoon.

If you'd prefer to eat your sandwich on the sand, haul your lunch and your leashed dog over to the Yellow Loop, which leads a half mile through low lying trees and saplings to a small, sandy beach where you both can eat, swim, and sunbathe. A bench at the southern end of the beach provides a fine view of Myles Standish Monument across the bay in Duxbury. At the trail's northern

end, you'll find some open, flat rocks on Rock Ledge for relaxing. There's even a picnic table under the trees for those who want to stay out of the sun.

Trails are well marked and easily accessed; a map at the parking area will give you an overview. Of the routes, only the Blue Loop was somewhat disappointing. It meandered aimlessly through some shrubs and then back to the main trail. Even so, this short amble didn't elicit any complaints from our dogs. After lunch, they just wanted to go back to roam and rove until dinnertime.

From Route 3, take Exit 10 to Route 3A into Duxbury. Turn right on Parks Street. Turn left on Loring Street. The parking area is on the left by the open field. Open sunrise–sunset. 781/585-0537.

15 Sampson Park/Faunce Memorial Forest

🐾🐾 (See South Shore map on page 164)

Yes, there are two park names here, but it's one contiguous forest, and there's no telling where Sampson Park ends and Faunce Memorial Forest begins.

Managed by the Wildlands Trust of Southeastern Massachusetts and the Kingston Conservation Commission, the 160-acre forest makes for a pleasant afternoon of woodland hiking. The well-marked Bay Circuit Trail runs through the park, which abuts the fast-moving Jones River. However, the trail disappointingly leads into the interior of the woods, rather than along the riverbank.

Cushioned by pine needles and shady white pine trees, the mostly flat terrain offers many clearings for picnicking. There are two primitive campsites, available on a first-come, first-served basis. If you're taking a longer trip, this forest should make a very enjoyable, private place to pitch a tent.

Furnace Brook cuts through the interior of the park, but in every season except spring, it's usually a marshy trickle. The Kingston Conservation Commission has maintained the wilderness integrity of the park, so except for the lack of the river view, we can definitely recommend this spot in any season. Every time we've visited, we've had the quiet forest to ourselves. Park at the trailhead off Route 80, where you will also find an easy-to-read trail map.

From Route 3, take Exit 9 to Main Street/Route 3A north. Turn left on Brook Street/Route 80. Turn left on Elm Street. The park and a parking lot are immediately on the right. Open dawn–dusk. 781/585-0537.

PLACES TO EAT

Persy's Place: This place has claimed bragging rights as the best breakfast joint on the South Shore, and you won't get any arguments from us. Dogs are allowed on the outdoor patio on request (and as long as other patrons don't complain), or you can order your food to go and eat it on the bench outside. The menu is extensive, and so are the weekend crowds. Don't be surprised if you have to wait for a table. One note: It's only open for breakfast and lunch, so don't work up an appetite on the trail and then show up at 4 P.M. for an early dinner. If you do, you'll be out of luck. On Route 3A, near Exit 9 by the Independence Mall; 781/585-5464.

PLACES TO STAY

Plymouth Bay Inn and Suites: This attractive inn is right next to Route 3, so it can get a little noisy on the road side of the motel, but it also provides easy access to most of the South Shore towns. Recently renovated to include suite rooms, the rooms are clean and reasonably priced at $99–189. Dogs are welcome, but the management asks that you do not leave your dog unattended in the room. 149 Main Street, Kingston, MA 02364; 781/585-3831 or 800/941-0075; website: www.plymouthbay.com.

Marshfield

PARKS, BEACHES, AND RECREATION AREAS

16 Brant Rock Beach

😾😾 (See South Shore map on page 164)

Dogs are allowed here from Labor Day–Memorial Day, but this two-mile-long beach will only please pups who are part mountain goat. It's a rocky outcrop awash in sea stones, with a little sand thrown in for good measure. The wind whips the shore at a steady clip here in the winter months. George actually likes these conditions, because he's light enough to bound from rock to rock, but Inu has a hard time and prefers a little more sand with his rocks. If you're hardy and enjoy the deserted and chilly conditions of a New England beach in winter, this is the place for you. Dogs must be leashed.

From the town center at the intersection of Ocean Street/Route 139 and Moraine Street/Route 3A, take Ocean Street east all the way to the Brant Rock Peninsula. The beach is on the left. Parking is available on Ocean Avenue. Open dawn–dusk. 781/834-5573.

17 Carolina Hill Conservation Land

😾 (See South Shore map on page 164)

We had high hopes for this place. Hearing it was located on more than 1,000 acres of prime woodland in the heart of Marshfield, we put on our hiking boots, and the dogs had their leashes in their mouths almost immediately. But unfortunately our expectations were not fulfilled. The biggest, widest trail in the park runs beneath power lines. Even worse, the fire roads that make up the majority of the pathways seem to be a favorite of dirt bikers. Some inner paths explore the interior of the pine forest, and at the crest of Carolina Hill, you get a spacious vantage point with a terrific view of Marshfield and its environs. But the forest itself has the unkempt look of a teenagers' partying spot. If you live nearby and need a place to give your dog a lot of room to roam, maybe you'll find this park adequate; otherwise, this is an example of a lot of room without a lot of heart.

From Route 3, take Exit 12 to Route 139/Church Street/Plain Street east. Turn left on Furnace Street, then left again on Eames Way. The park is at the road's end; street parking is available. Another entrance to the park is at the north end of Eames Way, off Pleasant Street. Open dawn–dusk. 781/834-5573.

18 Corn Hill Woodland Conservation Land

 (See South Shore map on page 164)

It's modest and it's swampy, but we like this tranquil little spot. Situated on 132 acres of woodland separated by marshy streams, it offers you and your leashed dog a leisurely hike along well-marked trails through white pine forest.

The main trail, identified with yellow markers, loops for 1.5 miles through the woods. At the far end of the loop, look for a thin path that leads out to the marshy grasses of the North River. You can't reach the river from here without walking over a muddy marshy swamp, but you can get a beautiful view of the river and the rolling hills in the distance. This is a prime bird-watching spot; you'll see many hawks, ospreys, and turkey buzzards lazily circling overhead. The occasional heron and seabird also appears.

Off the main trail, you can follow the enticingly named Swamp Trail, which leads away from the river and up a small slope—Corn Hill—before returning to the Union Street entrance. A local Boy Scout troop has built a welcome boardwalk over most of the truly swampy areas, so you'll find this a fairly muck-free half-mile walk.

From Route 3, take Exit 12 to Route 139/Church Street/Plain Street east. Take an immediate left on Union Street. Turn left on Corn Hill Lane. The park is on the right. Park at the trailhead off Corn Hill Lane. Open dawn–dusk. 781/834-5573.

19 King Phillip's Esker Conservation Land

(See South Shore map on page 164)

You'll be certain you're in the wrong place when you first visit this spot. The trailhead is set in a nice suburban community, identified only by a small sign that announces the name of this nifty little park. The entrance is between two property lines, and the only parking is along the street, but after a short hike from the street, you'll reach the path that takes you to the esker and a lovely woodland.

An esker is a cliff or plateau separated by ravines on each side, and King Phillip's runs along a charming ridge surrounded by trees, flowers, wild blueberries, and open sky. You won't go too far from civilization here—the trail is one-quarter of a mile on only 16.6 acres—but it's a pleasant forest walk that empties on the Green Harbor River estuary and a cranberry bog surrounded by a dry, open walkway. Combine the esker trail with the mile-long cranberry trail, and you'll enjoy an exceptional morning or afternoon walk. Dogs must be leashed.

From the town center at the intersection of Ocean Street/Route 139 and Moraine Street/Route 3A, take Moraine Street south. Turn left on King Phillip's Path. The park is at the far end of the loop. Street parking is available. Open dawn–dusk. 781/834-5573.

20 Webster Wilderness Conservation Land

🐾🐾🐾 (See South Shore map on page 164)

Deep in the jungle of the Webster Wilderness, the trail narrows to just a thin pass through the thick brush. The rich, green canopy of branches and vines blocks out the hot sun. Your imagination begins to run wild... you think you caught a glimpse of a spider monkey swinging through the trees and crocodiles along the shorelines. The sounds of tropical birds fill the air as you track the panting wild creature racing before you... no, wait. That's no exotic animal. That's your dog.

The terrain in the Webster Wilderness is truly junglelike. The Sapsucker and Teal Trails, both one mile long, work their way through the thick, marshy oak, pine, and elm woodland and dense ivy and vine undergrowth along Wharf Creek. Somehow the paths stay dry, even though they skirt dangerously close to the water's edge. When the trails border the water, you get spectacular views of the creek and surrounding ponds. When they turn back toward the trees, the paths lead over land bridges to other corners of the park. It's easy to get disoriented, so be sure to keep track of your route. Remember: It's almost a jungle out there. Dogs must be leashed.

From the town center at the intersection of Ocean Street/Route 139 and Moraine Street/Route 3A, take Ocean Street east. Turn right on Webster Street. The park is on the left, just past Schofield Road. A parking lot is available. Open dawn–dusk. 781/834-5573.

21 Wharf Creek Woodland Conservation Land

🐾🐾 (See South Shore map on page 164)

This quiet, 90-acre park, managed by the Marshfield Conservation Commission, is located off a small easement on Calypso Lane, a sleepy suburban street. We don't know how the neighbors feel about people walking between their houses to get to the trail, but the local dogs are always eager to say hello as we enter the path. From here, there's a short, half-mile trail through a fairly dry forest, ending at a lovely meadow along Wharf Creek. This is good birdwatching territory, so bring binoculars if you want to get a glimpse of the wildfowl along the river, including herons, egrets, ducks, and geese.

Another, shorter trail begins off Route 139 and leads about a quarter mile to the Green Harbor River. But parking is difficult here, as there is no parking on the road, and the only lot is at a nearby store. If the two trails were connected, then you'd really have an ideal place for a walk, but at present there are no plans to combine them. Both entrances are well marked and easy to find.

From the town center at the intersection of Ocean Street/Route 139 and Moraine Street/Route 3A, take Ocean Street east. Turn right on Webster Street, then left on Careswell Street/Route 139. Turn left on Calypso Lane. The park is at the far end of the loop. Street parking is available. Open dawn–dusk. 781/834-5573.

PLACES TO EAT

Johnson's Drive-In: Small-town America lives! This old-fashioned hamburger joint is a throwback to a time when drive-ins meant window service at your car rather than at the establishment's pull-through. April–October you can stop at this great little restaurant and actually be served on a car tray brought to your vehicle. (If you were born after 1970, you may have no idea what we're talking about.) Your dog will eagerly lean over your shoulder from the backseat as you eat, and there are free refills of root beer for the asking. 2105 Ocean Street/Route 139; no phone.

PLACES TO STAY

Ocean Village Motor Inn: This lovely motor inn, located right across from Brant Rock Beach, allows well-behaved pets in select rooms. All the rooms are clean and comfortable and equipped with refrigerators. Rates are $59–115 per night. 875 Ocean Street, Marshfield, MA 02050; 781/837-9901.

Middleborough

PARKS, BEACHES, AND RECREATION AREAS

❷❷ Pratt Farm Conservation Area

🐾🐾🐾 (See South Shore map on page 164)

Whether your dog loves roaming woodsy trails, romping in meadows, or swimming in a sparkling pond, Pratt Farm is a doggone good place. An assortment of trails loop around the ponds and hillsides, so you can pick and choose the distance you and your dog want to go. Or you can head right to one of the ponds for a cooling dip.

From the main trail, take the first side trail to the left to reach Stoney Brook Pond. The trail crosses a small dam that dogs just love to explore. From the pond, you can continue down the path to swing back into the park's main section.

In the center of the 160 acres are Upper Mill Pond and Lower Mill Pond. Despite the power lines that pass over them, you and your dog will still like this section. Around the pond are the remnants of some of the mills that were built on the waterway. The park's main trail, about a mile and a half long, goes directly to the ponds and loops between them. Along the way, it passes through fields, streams, and woodlands. Beyond the ponds are even more side trails if Rover needs a bit more roving to tire him out. The Middleborough Conservation Commission requires dogs to be leashed.

From I-495, take Exit 4 to Route 105/South Main Street north. Follow Route 105 until it becomes East Main Street. The park is on the right. Parking is available. Open sunrise–sunset. 508/946-2406.

PLACES TO STAY

Days Inn: Your dog is welcome here with a $5 charge per night. Rates are in the neighborhood of $60–95. 30 East Clark Street, Middleborough, MA 02346; 508/946-4400; website: www.daysinn-middleboro.com.

Norwell

PARKS, BEACHES, AND RECREATION AREAS

🐾 Albert F. Norris Reservation

🐾🐾🐾 (See South Shore map on page 164)

In the 1700s, this area along the North River hummed with industrial activity. The rich woods, the brooks and ponds, the salt marshes, and the river itself made an ideal locale for mills and shipbuilding. Today the 101 acres of Albert F. Norris Reservation are still filled with activity. The ponds and marshes attract a variety of waterfowl. The forests provide an excellent habitat for numerous species of wildlife, and the easy trails and cool breezes coming off the North River make the area a favorite of hikers and leashed dogs alike.

The park's wide and peaceful trails form a scenic, two-mile loop. The main trail runs straight out through the woods to the North River. On your way, you'll pass an old millpond where your inquisitive dog will want to sniff around the remaining stone foundations of the mills.

Coming out of the woods, the trail turns north to border the North River, which rises and falls with the tide. At low tide, your dog may explore the salt marshes, but it's easy to lose a boot in some of the muddier spots. From the shoreline, two routes head back to the parking lot.

From Route 3, take Exit 13 to Washington Street/Route 53 north. Turn right on Main Street/Route 123 east. Turn right again on West Street and drive to the Dover Street intersection. There's a parking lot at the intersection, off Dover Street. Open sunrise–sunset. 781/821-2977.

24 Cuffey Hill

🐾🐾🐕 (See South Shore map on page 164)

We highly recommend a visit to this park, but you'd better watch your step here. It lies right next to the Black Pond Preserve, where dogs aren't allowed. If you can stick to the trails designated for Cuffey Hill, then go and enjoy yourselves. But steer clear of the preserve land, because you're only allowed there with a permit—and your dog won't qualify.

If your dog is under voice control, take off his leash and start your hike at the trailhead off Mount Blue Road, a hundred yards down from the nature preserve. Although it's officially the Cuffey Hill Trail, at the entrance and at various other intersections it's labeled the Mount Blue Trail. Go figure, and go straight up this path through oak and pine woods and around the Black Pond Swamp, following the orange trail markers. At various points, the path is difficult to see, so keep an eye on the orange tree dots or pointers to remain on the straight and narrow. Otherwise you may veer off the trail along one of the many deer paths that lead into thickets and other dead ends.

At a clearing, you'll have to cross some power lines. Beyond them you'll walk up another slight incline to Cuffey Hill. The elevation is 193 feet, but don't get your hopes up. The "hill" designation is a bit of an exaggeration, and there's no view to be seen.

The path continues in a large arc along a lovely little brook and back to the power lines. Head to the right along the power line trail. Here's where the going gets tricky. About a hundred feet up, you'll reach another unmarked trail to the left. This enters the Black Pond Preserve. There are no signs to tell you that you can't go here, but trust us, you can't. It's a pretty walk that leads to the Black Pond, but the plant life is quite fragile here, and your dog could do a lot of unintentional damage. For everybody's sake, continue to follow the power lines back to the main trail and your starting point.

The 1.5-mile loop should take you about 45 minutes. Conservation Commission maps are recommended and can be obtained at the town hall on Main Street.

From the town center at the intersection of Main Street/Route 123 and Central Street, take Central Street north. Turn right on Old Oaken Bucket Road. Turn left on Mount Blue Street. The park is on the right, past the Black Pond Trailhead. Park on the shoulder. Open dawn–dusk. 781/659-8022.

25 Fogg Forest

🐾🐾🐕 (See South Shore map on page 164)

You get a little bit of everything on this short forest walk. A little, mind you, not a lot, but if you're looking for a quick walk that will give your dog a woodland sniff, a splash in a clear brook, and a romp through a meadow—all off leash—then you're in the right place. You'll find the start of the trail across from 604 Main Street. A big red conservation sign marks the spot. There isn't a parking lot, but you can park on the shoulder by the sign.

Walk across a lovely meadow to the large rock memorial to the Foggs, the family who left the land to the town. In spring, the meadow is fringed with rhododendron bushes. At the rock, head to the right, through the woods and past a series of stone walls. When you pass the second wall, go straight. If you bear right and follow the path along the wall, it will end at private property.

The path leads through a soft pine forest. After about a quarter mile, you'll reach another fork in the road. The right fork leads to the bridge over Black Pond Brook and through the woods to Central Street. The brook is clear and relatively fast flowing here. Our dogs plunge in and do the swallow wallow here. They lie down and let the water wash over them as they lap up the clean liquid, looking happy as hogs in mud.

If you take the left fork, it will lead you to another part of the brook. Here you'll find the ruins of an old, man-made fishing hole, part of the old Fogg homestead; this will be another spot your dog will enjoy plunging into. It's small, but the water's deep and clear. The rest of the trail runs alongside the brook on the way back to the meadow. The whole loop will take you about 20–30 minutes.

The park is located right in the town center on Main Street/Route 123, just west of Central Street. Roadside parking is available. Open dawn–dusk. 781/659-8022.

26 Jacobs Pond

🐾🐾🐾🐕 (See South Shore map on page 164)

This conservation land has all the things your dog will love, including the privilege of sniffing out the good stuff while off leash. The town of Norwell keeps this lovely park well maintained, and there are many trails for you and your dog to get away from it all.

Park at the lot off Jacobs Lane and head for the path that takes you along the pond. The waterside path offers many turnouts where your dog has ample opportunity to swim in the deep, clean pond. If he likes to dive in, like Inu, and swim out a distance, this is the place for him. The trail and the swimming spots tend to be more populated near the parking lot, so we suggest hiking up the trail a bit to find your own little stretch of the pond.

Several side trails cross the main path, giving you the option of looping inland and back to the parking area. If you choose to follow the whole two-mile loop, you'll want to keep veering to the left-hand trail at each intersection. Continue through the piney forest around the marsh, and at the farthest point from the trailhead, you'll reach an overlook with a convenient bench. Here you can rest up a bit and gaze out over Jacobs Pond for as long as you like.

Head back by continuing inland on the trail. It will loop you back through the forest and drop you at the starting point.

Another path veers off to the left and takes you to Prospect Street. You'll have to backtrack to the main path if you want to get back to the parking area, but this path is a good option if you want to prolong your walk a little or give the dog a bit more exercise.

From Route 3 in Hanover, take Exit 13 to Washington Street/Route 53 north towards Norwell. Turn right on Main Street/Route 123 east. Take a quick left on Jacobs Lane. The park and a parking lot are on the left. Open dawn–dusk. 781/659-8022.

27 Miller Woods

🐾🐾🦴 (See South Shore map on page 164)

You won't challenge yourself aerobically on this pleasant hike, but it'll give you an easygoing mile-long walk through pine, oak, and maple woodlands. It's made all the more pleasant by the fact that your pooch is welcome to stroll beside you without wearing a leash.

Park at the small lot and head along the main trail, which leaves to the right. This loop will eventually lead you to a shady, woodsy glen and a bench perfect for a picnic or rest stop.

From here, you can continue straight ahead and return to the parking area. If you follow the trail to your right, however, you can extend your walk another half mile before looping back. You can explore all of the trails here in about an hour. You won't cross any water, unfortunately, except for muddy low points on the trail. But the woods are pleasant, and they're not too buggy in hot weather. Pick up a free trail map at the town hall.

From the town center at the intersection of Main Street/Route 123, Central Street, and River Street, take River Street south. Turn right on Forest Street. A small parking lot is available at the trailhead. Open dawn–dusk. 781/659-8022.

28 Stetson Meadows

🐾🐾🦴 (See South Shore map on page 164)

If you've been longing for a view of the North River, that elusive rolling river that you can never seem to catch sight of, then this is the park for you. Here you'll find a short but pleasant walk through an oak and pine woodland to a lovely overlook by the river. As usual, you can't really get to the river, because it's surrounded by marshland, but the picnic area is shady and comfortable if you want to kick back and enjoy the view while your leash-free dog sniffs his way around the area.

There are two parking areas. The first is at the end of Stetson Shrine Lane. Just park at the cul-de-sac and walk over to the well-marked trailhead. Busy Route 3 isn't far away, but the trail leads you into the woods, where you won't even hear the highway. Follow the orange trail markers, which will lead you to a meadow that's fine for picnicking if you don't want to continue to the overlook.

If you want to circumvent some of the trail and start farther up, there is a small turnout about a quarter mile up the dirt road. Here another trail sets off and eventually connects with the orange-marked trail.

To reach the overlook from the meadow, you can go one of two ways. The first will be the trail to the left, which is marked the Twin Pines Trail. The other path is across the meadow and over the dirt road. Both trails meet to form a loop, so whichever way you choose, you'll end up taking the other trail to return to the meadow.

The entire loop is a little over a mile and will take you about 40 minutes. It's a pleasant and easy walk, and our dogs always seem to find plenty to enjoy here.

From the town center at the intersection of Main Street/Route 123, Central Street, and River Street, take River Street south. Turn left on Stetson Shrine Lane, just before Route 3. The park and a parking area are at the road's end. Open dawn–dusk. 781/659-8022.

Wompatuck State Park
See the listing in the Hingham section of this chapter.

Pembroke

PARKS, BEACHES, AND RECREATION AREAS

29 Herring Run
 (See South Shore map on page 164)

This small, quaint park makes an art form out of function. Created as a herring run for the alewife who swim to their spawning grounds upstream in April and May, this little park features crisscrossing streams amid a grassy, green park. Large trees shade graceful benches, and little footbridges elegantly span the streams. Your big galoot of a dog might think the whole setup is a little too demure for his tastes, but if you want a quiet place to sit or a quick stop to stretch the dog's legs, this is a fine spot to do both.

From the town center at the intersection of Oldham Street and Center Street/Route 14, take Center Street east into Barker Street. The park and a parking area are on the left, just past High Street. Open from 8 A.M.–dusk. 781/293-7211.

30 Hobomock Trails
👣👣👣 (See South Shore map on page 164)

Hidden away behind the elementary school, the wonderful trails here run along Herring Brook and lead to Glover Mill Pond and a lovely woodland. Rather curiously, all routes are marked in white. Every intersection we came to directed us to follow either the white trail or—the white trail. After a while, you just have to give up and go whichever way you choose. As the Caterpillar said to Alice, "If you go somewhere, you'll surely end up there." So trust us, you'll never be far from somewhere worth going when you're on the white trail.

The "somewhere worth going" is Glover Mill Pond. From the trailhead, keep following the trails that lead you downhill and to the left. You'll cross several streams here before you finally find the pond about a half mile away. It's a clean little pool and a great place to swim.

From the pond, head upstream on the path along Herring Brook. Eventually the path turns uphill and veers to the right. There are many crisscrossing trails to wander and explore, but you can't really go too far wrong, even though your only guides will be your instinct and your dog's nose. The trails are wide and well traveled. Even if they aren't well identified, they're easy to follow at least. Dogs must wear their leashes here.

From the town center at the intersection of Oldham Street and Center Street/Route 14, take Center Street west. Follow Center Street into Route 36 south. Turn left on Hobomock Street, then left again on Learning Lane. The park and street parking are at the road's end. Open dawn–dusk. 781/293-7211.

Indian Head River Greenway

See the listing in the Hanover section of this chapter.

Plymouth

If New England has a mecca for visitors, this just might be it. Even the Pilgrims, the first British tourists in New England, grasped this simple truth when they landed here in 1620. History abounds, and you can find fascinating traces of life in the early days of the Massachusetts Bay Colony. Walk along the waterfront to see Plymouth Rock, a replica of the *Mayflower,* and the Statue of Massasoit, the leader of the Native Americans who aided the Pilgrims as they established themselves in the New World. Your dog may not get the significance of these spots, but with all the sights and smells she, too, will be in for a treat.

PARKS, BEACHES, AND RECREATION AREAS

🐾 Morton Park

🐾 🐾 (See South Shore map on page 164)

The town of Plymouth first established this cozy recreation area in 1889. With a sparse pine forest, pond, and sandy beaches, this is the local watering hole for residents who don't want to venture too far for a splash. There's a snack bar, restrooms, and boat rentals. All these facilities add up to thick crowds on summer days, so it might not be the best place for you and your leashed dog to get some exercise.

If you decide to check it out, we can tell you that Little Pond is ringed with three public beaches and some nearby trails, which lead up into the surrounding woods. Dogs must be leashed. There's a $10 parking fee on weekends, $7 on weekdays. It's probably worth a trip in the off-season, but don't bother in summer. You and your dog will be greatly outnumbered by the beachgoers.

From Route 3, take Exit 6 to Samoset Street east. Turn right on Westerly Road and then right again on Summer Street. Turn left on Morton Park Road. Open dawn–9 P.M. 508/830-4095.

🐾 Myles Standish State Forest

🐾 🐾 🐾 🐾 (See South Shore map on page 164)

At 14,635 acres, Myles Standish State Forest is the largest park listed in *The Dog Lover's Companion to Boston*. If your dog can't find the room that he needs here, he'll never find it. Not only do you get acres upon acres of woods, fields, and lakes, but you'll encounter more trails and paths than you could cover in a lifetime. The forest offers trails geared to all sorts of recreational uses: all-terrain vehicles, bicycling, horseback riding, skiing, snowmobiling, and even motorcycling. Dogs and hikers are allowed on all of them, but you should be

DIVERSION

Plymouth Historical Walk: Take a stroll along the lovely waterfront overlooking Plymouth Bay, and you'll end up at historic **Plymouth Rock.** George and Inu eagerly sniffed the area—they could tell something exciting was going on—but they couldn't figure out why the rest of the folks were crowding around the small rock. It looked like—well, a rock. So what if it signifies the European entrance into the New World? They wanted to move on and get to Plymouth Beach. But for you, the significance will not be lost. The coastal walk will take you only about 10 minutes, but you can breathe in the fresh sea air and absorb a little history while you're at it. For more information, stop at the Plymouth Visitor Center at 130 Water Street; 508/747-7525.

alert, especially when on the nonhiking paths. In Myles Standish State Forest, folks take their sports seriously.

Two great trails are designated hiking-only in this state forest, named for the Pilgrim military leader.

The first is the East Head Nature Trail around East Head Reservoir. The three-mile loop is a wonderful walk around the scenic lake. Most of the trail is right on the water's edge, but it does drift into the pines in places. A boardwalk takes you and your dog over the muddier sections. There is a quarter-mile stretch where the trail follows the roadway. The path begins and ends at the parking lot at the forest headquarters. Look for the blue markers.

The second, unnamed trail is a more rugged, five-mile loop into a wilderness of pitch pines and fields. It's a much drier and hillier route, so be sure to carry lots of water on this hike—you'll only cross limited water spots for dogs. It's also a little trickier to follow because many other trails intersect with it. Just stay with the blue markers and watch for horses. Some of the cross trails lead to College Pond and New Long Pond. The trailhead is at the parking lot on Upper College Pond Road.

If your dog is a tenderfoot and would rather walk on smooth pavement, try the bike routes. Fifteen miles of them cover most of the park. What makes these paths especially great to use is that they don't run alongside car-filled roads like some other bike routes do. Instead, they forge into the forests, where you're more likely to dodge a squirrel than a sedan. Bike paths begin at both the forest headquarters and Upper College Pond Road parking lots.

If you want to stay overnight, the forest's campground offers 475 campsites, all available on a first-come, first-served basis. You can secure a spot at the main headquarters on Cranberry Road. There are no hookups, but people with tents and trailers can stay for $10 per night or $12 per night with a shower.

DIVERSION

A day on the bay: You and your seaworthy dog can catch the approximately two-hour boat ride from Plymouth Harbor to Provincetown at the tip of Cape Cod. Leashed dogs are welcome aboard the small cruise boat, but you must get permission from the captain. The trip leaves every day at 10 A.M. from mid-June–Labor Day. After four hours of roaming around scenic Provincetown, return to the boat for the trip back to Plymouth Bay. The ride costs $35 per adult, with no extra charge for your four-pawed matey. For reservations, call Captain John Boats, 508/746-2670 or 800/242-2469.

Leashed dogs are allowed. All trails are closed on Saturday and holidays from mid-October–January 2 and for one week in the late fall during hunting season. Hunting is not permitted on Sunday. Free park maps and information are available at forest headquarters. Spread across the towns of Plymouth and Carver, two-thirds of the park's acreage is on the Plymouth side.

From Route 3, take Exit 5 to Long Pond Road south. The park entrance, Alden Road, is on the right. Follow the signs to the forest headquarters.

From I-495, take Exit 2 in Wareham to Tremont Street/Route 58 and Carver. Turn right on Cranberry Road and continue into the park. The forest headquarters is on the left. Open dawn–dusk. 508/866-2526.

33 Plymouth Beach

🐾🐾🐾 (See South Shore map on page 164)

More than 3.5 miles long, this thin peninsula stretches into Plymouth Harbor and overlooks the town center. From downtown, you can easily reach the sandy beach by car or foot. It's long and wide, and if you get past the main area near

DOG-EAR YOUR CALENDAR—SEPTEMBER

Be a friend! Help a friend in need when you attend the annual **Pet Walk-a-Thon** sponsored by Friends of the Plymouth Pound. Held on the second Saturday in September, this walk to raise funds for needy animals is a worthy event that feels like a whole lot of fun. Held at Morton Pond Park, 9 A.M.–2 P.M., you and your pooch can participate in contests, races, training tips, and a cook out (our dogs think the wienie roast is the best). For more information and exact date, call 508/224-6651; website: www.gis.net/~fpp.

the snack bar and parking lot, chances are you'll have a long uninterrupted walk. The local canine elite flock here in the morning and on weekends for doggy socializing. You'll be more interested in the beautiful view than all the gossip and lore that the dogs are barking about. Dogs must be leashed here.

There's ample parking, but you must pay $8 to park here Memorial Day–Labor Day.

From Route 3, take Exit 4 to Plimoth Plantation Highway. Turn left on Warren Avenue/Route 3A. The beach and a parking lot are on the right. Open 8 A.M.–8 P.M. 508/830-4050.

PLACES TO EAT

Lobster Hut: Serving fresh and fried fish at reasonable prices, this outdoor restaurant on the tip of the waterfront wharf has outside tables where you can perch with your dog. Town Wharf Road; 508/746-2270.

Wood's Seafood Market & Restaurant: Our favorite fish place on the waterfront, it's got plenty of picnic-style seating outside, where you can eat with Rover. Town Wharf Road; 508/746-0261;

PLACES TO STAY

Auberge Gladstone: Built in 1848, this stately inn welcomes well-behaved dogs in all rooms. Each room is cozy and unique, some have fireplaces, private entrances, and most have private bathrooms. The inn is close to the town center and a hop, skip, and a jump from the beach. Rates are $100–125 plus a $10 pet fee per night. 8 Vernon Street, Plymouth, MA 02360; 508/830-1890; website: www.aubergegladstone.com.

Myles Standish State Forest Campground: See Wompatuck State Park listing, above.

Plympton

PARKS, BEACHES, AND RECREATION AREAS

🔢 Winnetuxet River Park

🐾🐾 (See South Shore map on page 164)

"Look out, guys! Here I come! Cannonball!"

Water dogs, take note: This little riverside park is the local hot spot to dunk yourselves in cool water. George and Inu have not yet perfected their diving technique, but no one can beat Inu's belly flop.

The park's a grassy knoll with some picnic tables, a couple of trees, and a simple pond that's fed by the Winnetuxet River. There are no trails here, but even if there were, we wouldn't be able to get the dogs out of the water to go explore them. All dogs must be leashed.

From the town center at the intersection of Main Street and Palmer Road/ Route 58, take Main Street south. Turn right on Winnetuxet Road. The park is on the right. A grassy parking area is available. Open dawn–dusk. 508/585-3868.

Rockland

PARKS, BEACHES, AND RECREATION AREAS

35 Hartstuff Park/Fox Run Conservation Area

 (See South Shore map on page 164)

Does the dog need a quick trot—hold the ambience? That's what she'll get on the short trails at Hartstuff Park, home of Rockland's ball fields and play-grounds, and the Fox Run Conservation Area, the woods next door.

You'll find the trails on the other side of the playground from the parking lot. If you can look beyond the trash and oil slicks at Hartstuff Park, your dog can enjoy a little exercise in Fox Run. The main trail, a little less than a mile long, loops through the forest over the hilly terrain and passes by a creek that flows through the park. The woods are certainly cleaner than the playground.

From the town center at the intersection of Market Street/Route 123 and Plain Street/Route 139, take Market Street east. Turn left on Liberty Street, then right on Webster Street. Turn left on Hingham Street. The park entrance is on the left. A parking lot is available. Open dawn–9 P.M. 781/871-1730.

36 Studley's Pond Park

 (See South Shore map on page 164)

The two-acre stretch of land on Studley's Pond has seen better days, but to a dog's eyes, it won't look too bad. That's because the pond offers a chance for a summer dip, and there's room enough to shake off the water on some grass when it's time to get back in the car.

The park is in the town center off Market Street/Route 123, just north of the intersection of Central, Market, and Spring Streets. Drive in on the gravel path and park along the road. Open dawn–8 P.M. 781/871-0579.

PLACES TO STAY

Holiday Inn Express: Call in advance and let the folks here know your dog will be in tow. New and roomy, the place offers reasonable rates: $89–115 per night, including breakfast. There is a pet fee of $6 per night. It's right off Route 3 at Exit 14. 909 Hingham Street, Rockland, MA 02370; 781/871-5660; website: www.holiday-inn.com.

Scituate

PARKS, BEACHES, AND RECREATION AREAS

37 Humarock Beach

😊😊 (See South Shore map on page 164)

We'd like to imagine that at one time this spot was called Bringarock Beach. Back then it was a white, sandy stretch of coast, but the name inspired people to actually haul stones and rocks here, and that's why the beach is now completely covered with them. The town of Scituate renamed the place so that folks would come down and hum a rock out into the sea, thus restoring the sandy shore. So far, it hasn't happened.

This peninsula juts out into the Atlantic Ocean and seems to be the first beach on the homeward journey of many a sea rock. The beach is full of 'em. It runs about three miles, so you can get in a great workout here. There's only a small stretch of sand when the tide is low; otherwise, it's a rocky road. Unless your dog has figured out how to skip stones, the going can be tough on the paws. There are leash and pooper-scooper laws here, but dogs are welcome year-round, even in summer. Park at the lot on Marshfield Avenue, a block from the beach. Open 6 A.M.–10 P.M. 781/545-8743.

38 Scituate Driftway Recreation Fish & Wildlife Development

😊😊😊 (See South Shore map on page 164)

For such a simple, rustic place, this park has an awfully long name. But no matter the name, your dog won't be the first to blaze the trails here. There's an easy trail that loops about a mile along First Herring Brook. The river part of the trail can be a bit muddy, so if you want to avoid wet feet, stick to the inland path that ventures through the sand dunes. Benches along the way make fine resting spots.

Your dog will be sure to meet other canines on the visit, as this is a popular gathering place for four-footed friends. In our last edition, however, we told you that there was a poop problem and that the off-leash deal seemed to have led to a "look the other way" attitude on pooper-scooper rules. Well, the good news is that there is no longer a poop problem here. The bad news? You guessed it. Leash-free privileges have been revoked. This is still a great park to visit, but it "coulda been a contender." What can we say?

From the intersection of Routes 3A and 123, take Country Way to New Driftway into Driftway. The park and a parking lot are on the right. Open dawn–dusk. 781/545-8721.

39 Teak Sherman Park

☙ (See South Shore map on page 164)

This is a small, peaceful park with a well-groomed, quarter-mile path leading through a rich pine forest to a shady pine wood and an open field. Since there's not much else, visitors are few, and it's a relaxing place for a picnic or to simply sit and reflect on the joys of a dog's life. And wearing a leash, as your pooch must do here, is not among them.

The park is in the southwestern corner of the intersection of Chief Justice Cushing Highway/Route 3A and First Parish Road, just north of Route 123. The entrance is located off Chief Justice Cushing Highway. Parking is available. Open sunrise–sunset. 781/545-8743.

PLACES TO EAT

Dribbles Ice Cream: In the heart of Scituate Harbor, this little creamery makes a good stop on a hot summer's day. Sit at an outdoor table or take your treat across the street to the benches overlooking the harbor. 4 Brook Street; 781/544-3600.

Morning Glories Bakery: Dogs aren't allowed inside, but they're more than welcome to pop their noses out the car window as you pull up to the drive-in. This country bakery is a great morning stop for muffins and coffee to go on the way to Scituate Driftway Recreation Fish & Wildlife Development 52 Country Way; 781/545-3400.

PLACES TO STAY

Inn at Scituate Harbor: Formerly the Clipper Ship Lodge, this convenient and comfortable hotel is right in the heart of town overlooking lovely Scituate Harbor. The hotel has been recently renovated, and dogs are welcome in selected rooms, so make your reservation early. Room rates are $79–189. There is an additional $20 charge for your dog per stay. 7 Beaver Dam Road, Scituate, MA 02066; 781/545-5550 or 800/368-3818; website: www.innatscituateharbor.com.

West Bridgewater

PARKS, BEACHES, AND RECREATION AREAS

40 Town River Conservation Public Land

☙☙ (See South Shore map on page 164)

When you're a dog, there's never enough places to go for a swim, especially in the summer. Most beaches are off-limits by May, ponds dry up by late July, and fountains are turned off to conserve water. What's a dog to do? If you were George or Inu, you'd head to the Town River and the small wood that runs alongside it.

A single path leads through the forest from the road pullout to the river's edge. The trail can be a little swampy and vague in places, but it's not hard to find the river. Your leashed dog is sure to lead you right there, especially on hot days. There isn't much of a beach at the clearing, but the inviting Town River is cool and clean. Just remember, with any river or body of water, be sure your dog is up to the test of swimming in it. The water does move fast here at certain points.

From Route 24, take Exit 16 to West Center Street/Route 106 east. Turn right on Howard Street, then right on River Street. Turn left on Forest Street. The park is on the left, as is a small pullout for parking. Open dawn–dusk. 781/588-4820.

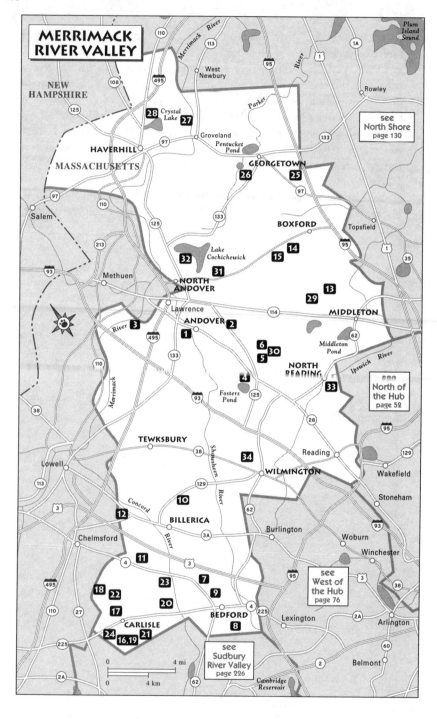

MERRIMACK RIVER VALLEY

NEW HAMPSHIRE

MASSACHUSETTS

Plum Island Sound

Merrimack River

West Newbury

Rowley

Crystal Lake **28** **27**

Groveland

Pentucket Pond

HAVERHILL

Salem

Methuen

GEORGETOWN **26** **25**

see North Shore page 130

BOXFORD

Topsfield

Lake Cochichewick **32** **14** **15** **31**

NORTH ANDOVER

Lawrence

ANDOVER **1** **2** **3**

29 **13** MIDDLETON

Middleton Pond

6 **30** **5**

NORTH READING **4** **33**

Fosters Pond

North of the Hub page 52

TEWKSBURY **34** Reading

Lowell

WILMINGTON

Wakefield

Stoneham

10 **12** BILLERICA

Burlington

Chelmsford

Woburn

Winchester

11 **23** **7** **9**

see West of the Hub page 76

18 **22** **20** **17** BEDFORD **8**

CARLISLE **24** **16,19** **21**

Lexington

Arlington

Belmont

see Sudbury River Valley page 226

Cambridge Reservoir

0   4 mi

0   4 km

CHAPTER 7

Merrimack
River Valley

Some of the Commonwealth's most traditional New England communities can be found in the area north of Boston and south of the Merrimack River. Spread across Middlesex and Essex Counties, these towns first sprang up as settlers began pushing west and north in search of fertile farmland. With the farms came what is now regarded as the quintessential New England landscape: the town center, composed of a square or common; the community meeting hall; and the classic, austere church with its white steeple rising above the trees.

Today many of these farms have disappeared. Some have given way to new homes, but many have been reclaimed by the woodlands that were once cleared to make way for fields and homesteads. These forests are now great places to hike with your dog.

You'll discover some of Massachusetts's best state parks here, including Harold Parker State Forest in North Andover and Great Brook Farm State Park in Carlisle. But what really makes this area stand out are the strong conservation

PICK OF THE LITTER—
MERRIMACK RIVER VALLEY

BEST LAKE SWIMMING
Harold Parker State Forest, Andover (page 202)

BEST HILLS FOR HIKING
Bald Hill Reservation, Boxford (page 208)

BEST VIEW OF THE VALLEY
Weir Hill Reservation, North Andover (page 222)

BEST NORTH SHORE DOG RUN
North Reading Dog Park, North Reading (page 224)

BEST PARK WITH ICE CREAM
Great Brook Farm State Park, Carlisle (page 214)

BEST ICE CREAM WITH A PARK
Great Brook Farm Ice Cream, Carlisle (page 216)

efforts its communities have exerted to preserve public open spaces. Towns like Andover, Bedford, and Carlisle not only protect their valuable land, but they've also established exceptional trail systems to provide people and dogs with access to these natural resources.

Bay Circuit Trail: Linking parks and reservations between Plum Island on the North Shore and Kingston Bay on the South Shore, this trail will eventually connect more than 30 towns across 200 miles, including completed routes in Andover, Bedford, Billerica, Boxford, Carlisle, Georgetown, North Andover, and Tewksbury. For details, see the Extended Hiking Trails section of the Resources.

Essex County Greenbelt Association: For nearly 30 years, the Essex County Greenbelt Association's efforts have led to the preservation of more than 4,000 acres in the Essex County region. Dogs are allowed leash free on all of its properties. For more information on how to get involved with this great conservation group, see the Extended Hiking Trails section of the Resources.

Merrimack River Trail: Administered by the Merrimack River Watershed Council, this pathway follows the Merrimack River from the New Hampshire border to Newburyport on the Atlantic Ocean. In this chapter, the towns of

Andover, Haverhill, North Andover, and Tewksbury include trail sections. For more information on the trail and the watershed council, see the Extended Hiking Trails section of the Resources.

The Trustees of Reservations: This preservation organization manages more than 75 properties on nearly 18,000 acres throughout the Commonwealth, including lands in this chapter. Dogs must be leashed on all Trustees properties. For more information on its history and holdings, see the Resources section.

Andover

During the American Revolution, some of the most valiant militia groups to fight for the colonists lived in this historic town. On Holt Hill, one of the highest points in Essex County, the citizens of Andover gathered to watch the British burn Charlestown on June 17, 1775. Andover is also home to the famed Phillips Academy, prep school to George Bush Sr. and other American presidents. You and your dog can stroll the quiet streets among well-preserved houses and picturesque churches in this beautiful old city.

PARKS, BEACHES, AND RECREATION AREAS

All of the parks listed in Andover are managed by the Andover Village Improvement Society (AVIS), a nonprofit, private organization. We've featured the parks that offer the best recreational options for you and your dog. Some of the smaller reservations not included here may not be big enough or may be too fragile for your dog to enjoy. You can obtain maps of all of the group's trails and reservations for $10.95 from the conservation office at Andover Town Hall or by writing to the group at P.O. Box 5097, Andover, MA 01810; maps are also available on the website: www.avisandover.org. AVIS relies on memberships, volunteers, and private donations. Dogs must be leashed in all AVIS parks.

🐾 Baker's Meadow/Indian Ridge/ West Parish Meadow Reservations

🐾🐾🐾 (See Merrimack River Valley map on page 196)

Running across three great reservations, Reservation Road is aptly named. In reality, all of the reserves share the same 120-acre parcel of land, divided down the middle by Reservation Road. For a terrific three-mile hike with your leashed dog, follow the main trail through all three areas.

Park at the back of Andover High School and walk south on the sidewalk along Red Spring Road. The trailhead into the woods and Indian Ridge Reservation is 100 yards down the road. Stay to the right to access the main route. About a quarter of a mile down the path, you'll climb the end of an esker to reach a four-trail crossroads. The main trail meets two trails along the esker. Another trail runs downhill to the right and leads back to the school.

The entire loop is clearly marked by splotches of white paint; stick with the paint and you won't get lost. Both esker trails lead you in a three-mile arc back to this spot, so it's up to your dog to choose which way to go. Our pooches always prefer to go to the left, probably because it's closer to the pond and their sensitive nostrils smell the water.

The trail to the left first brings you to Baker's Meadow Reservation. Cross Reservation Road and continue along the trail to Baker's Meadow Pond. The trail circles the pond, a fantastic stroll, offering plenty of water access for your dogs and a wide, easy trail for you. Well-placed boardwalks allow you to cross low-lying muddy areas without covering your shoes in muck. You might even see some wildlife if you're quiet. There's an active beaver lodge in this section and plenty of wildfowl nesting along the water's edge. Although some folks want to make Baker's Meadow a protected nature area, at present you and your leashed dog are welcome here.

On the pond's far side, you'll cross the road again into West Parish Meadow. Here another boardwalk takes you over the last vestiges of the marsh and leads into the open meadow beyond. In the meadow, you'll encounter another small pond where the dogs can rinse off if they've gotten muddy in the swamp.

Past West Parish Meadow, the trail returns you to the Indian Ridge Reservation and up the esker trail back to your starting point. Canine tongues will be hanging, but if you've done it right, tails should be wagging, too.

The Andover Village Improvement Society manages the reservations. Dogs must be leashed.

From the town center at the intersection of Central Street, Elm Street, and Main Street, take Central Street south. Turn right on Red Spring Road. The park is on the left; parking is available at the Andover High School auxiliary parking lot. Open sunrise–sunset. 978/623-8311.

🐾 Charles Ward Reservation

🐾🐾🐾 (See Merrimack River Valley map on page 196)

So what will it be, the high road or the low road? Your experience at this lovely 640-acre park will depend entirely on which path you choose. No matter which route you follow, however, you and your leashed dog should enjoy a hike here. Begin at the parking area at the base of Holt Hill, and you'll have several choices.

The low road is a mile-long woodsy stroll. Cross over the meadow to the far left of the field and enter an oak woodland. Take this trail along the base of the hill, and you'll reach a boardwalk on your right. The route winds through a fascinating black spruce bog and out to Pine Hole Pond. Your dog can swim here, but because of limited access, she'll have to dive in.

The high-road alternative is to cross Prospect Road, heading up the hill from the parking area to the Holt Hill Trailhead. From here, we recommend that you follow the dirt trail rather than the fire road. Although the sporadically paved fire road leads to the top of Holt Hill and the fire tower, it's not particularly scenic. Instead, take the half-mile dirt route up through the meadow and the hillside forest to the top.

At 420 feet, Holt Hill is the highest point in Essex County. On a clear day you can't see forever, but you can catch a glimpse of Great Blue Hill in the Blue Hills Reservation and the Boston skyline. The story goes that on June 17, 1775, the town of Andover gathered here to watch the burning of Charlestown by the British. You'll also find the remains of the "solstice stones" put here by the widow of Charles Ward in 1940. Fascinated by Stonehenge after a visit to Britain, Mrs. Ward built her own miniature version of it in this meadow.

For an even better view of Boston, take the low-lying one-mile path through the pine forest to Boston Hill. Here you'll find a 180-degree view of the area, without the distraction of the unsightly fire tower atop Holt Hill. From this trail, you can also walk up Old Chestnut Street, an overgrown 18th-century carriage trail. In all, this hike will give you and your canine pal an enjoyable three-mile walk. Consult the map at the trailhead in order to get your bearings before setting out.

From I-93 in Wilmington, take Exit 41 to Ballardvale Street/Route 125 north into Andover and the Andover Bypass. Turn right on Prospect Road. The park is on the right, as is the parking lot. Open sunrise–sunset. 978/356-4351.

🔢 Deer Jump Reservation

🐾🐾🐾🐾 (See Merrimack River Valley map on page 196)

Another beautiful spot managed by the Andover Village Improvement Society, this park is a wonderful surprise. Six miles of trails crisscross 147 acres, all running along the Merrimack River. Deer Jump Reservation is really a long strip of forest bordering the river's edge; the best public access is off Launching Road, at the reservation's midpoint.

The trail begins through a lovely pine forest that leads down to the river. You can follow the Merrimack in either direction; we suggest heading to the right. After a half-mile hike along the river, you'll cross Fish Brook, a fast-moving, clear, clean stream. Past the brook, the trail continues along the Merrimack for another mile. For a shorter route (about 40 minutes round-trip), follow Fish Brook through the woods as it loops back to the original trailhead.

If you take the route to the left, you can walk alongside the river for four more miles. No matter which direction you choose, you should enjoy your hike in relative solitude. The reservation is hard enough to find that you won't be joined by a lot of weekend river rats. It's a well-kept secret—and let's keep it that way, okay? The trail links with the Merrimack River Trail. Dogs are required to be leashed.

From I-93, take Exit 45 to River Road west. Turn right on Launching Road. The park and street parking are on the right, near the road's end. Open sunrise–sunset. 978/623-8311.

4 The Goldsmith Woodlands

🐾 🐾 🐾 (See Merrimack River Valley map on page 196)

Here's a personal favorite of ours and another example of the excellent stewardship of the Andover Village Improvement Society. This lovely, 170-acre woodland offers well-marked, easy-to-follow trails and a perfect swimming spot. It's along the peninsula at the end of the main trail and is named, appropriately enough, Journey's End.

On your way in, stick to the main trail, which is marked Zack's Way. You won't go wrong if you "follow the yellow brick road." Or, in this case, the yellow paint-splotched trees. Many smaller paths peel off the main trail into the woods, leading to picnic areas and vista points overlooking Foster's Pond. The best of these include Scout's Hollow and Bessy's Point (named for Bess Goldsmith, who, along with her husband, Clarence, originally donated this land for public use). Both spots offer excellent views of the water and shady places to rest. Dogs can swim here, but the water is a little marshy; our advice is to continue to Journey's End and let your water dog take a dip there.

Continue on the yellow trail as it borders the pond. Passing Scout's Hollow, you'll reach a loose chain across the path. Don't worry—this isn't the end of the line. The chain's only there to stop car traffic from crossing the park, not foot and paw traffic. Continue another mile to a fork and head to the right; the path to the left ends up along Route 125, beyond the park's border. The right fork takes you to the peninsula called Journey's End, a great swimming spot. It extends quite far into the water, and the water is clean and fresh and the view spectacular. You can sit peacefully overlooking the water while your dog chases after sticks and refreshes himself in the cool, clear water.

On the way back, follow Zack's Way until you reach the intersection with the Pine Trail, just past Bessy's Point. (The Pine Trail is marked by red paint splotches.) If you don't want to backtrack on the main trail, you can take the Pine Trail all the way back to the park entrance or follow the High Trail (identified by blue paint splotches), an esker trail that connects a short way up the Pine Trail. Both the Pine and High Trails run near the water and Old Mill Reservoir, which is on private property. Dogs must be leashed.

From the town center at the intersection of Elm Street and Main Street/Route 28, take Main Street south. The park is on the right, just past Gould Road. Parking is in a small lot across the street from the entrance. Open sunrise–sunset. 978/623-8311.

5 Harold Parker State Forest

🐾 🐾 🐾 🐾 (See Merrimack River Valley map on page 196)

With more than 3,500 acres and 25 miles of hiking trails, this terrific state forest offers enough sniffs and smells to satisfy the pickiest of pooches. Numerous ponds for swimming invite a dip, and thick and varied woods beg to be explored. Straddling Andover and North Andover (see also the Harold Parker

State Forest listing in the North Andover section of this chapter), the forest here is a blend of old and young groves, with ancient pines growing alongside relatively young, hundred-year-old trees.

In Andover, you'll enter off Route 125 and drive up Harold Parker Road. Almost immediately you'll enter a lovely old forest that surrounds several clear ponds. Park at any of the small turnouts; we recommend the first turnout on the left, near Field Pond. From here, a one-mile trail circles Collins and Brackett Ponds. Follow either the long route around both ponds or take a shortcut over the old dam that separates them. You'll find many spots for swimming and picnicking along the water. The old-growth pine forest here stands in contrast to the younger trees in the North Andover section of the park. Clear-cut in the 18th and 19th centuries, that forest is slowly returning to its former grandeur.

Across the street and a little farther up the road is the Field Pond Trailhead, where you can access a short trail to the edge of the pond. You can't walk all the way around this pond, but canoeing is allowed.

Harold Parker State Forest has countless other forest trails for you and your dog to explore. We strongly recommend that you pick up a free trail map at the forest headquarters on Salem Street before setting out. The area is popular in summer so you might want to plan your visits to avoid the weekend. At other times you may find you have this special park all to yourselves.

You'll find a great campground here. Open May–October, it has more than 130 campsites where you can pitch a pup tent with your pup, or just park your trailer for the night. Dogs cannot be left unattended and must be leashed when outside your tent or trailer. There are no RV hookups. Rates are $10 per night, and reservations are recommended; reservations are available by writing to 1951 Turnpike Road, North Andover, MA 01845; calling 877/422-6762; or visiting the website: www.massparks.org.

From I-93 in Wilmington, take Exit 41 to Ballardvale Street/Route 125 north into Andover and the Andover Bypass. Turn right on Harold Parker Road and continue into the park. Parking is available at most of the trailheads. Open from a half hour before sunrise to a half hour after sunset. 978/686-3391.

Skug River Reservation

😺 😺 (See Merrimack River Valley map on page 196)

Remember when your mother used to say, "The fork goes on the left"? The same rule applies here. From the parking area, take the trail to the left to reach the heart of the reservation and, eventually, the Skug River. The path to the right also leads into the interior, but not this park's interior: instead, it heads into neighboring Harold Parker State Forest. Looks like mother knew best.

Your 1.5-mile hike starts with a forest of thick hardwoods and some quiet streams where your dog can refresh himself. The scenic Skug River runs by you on the right, but the thick brush makes it difficult to reach. A few small paths along the way access the shoreline.

The path crosses the river as it begins looping back. On your return, the terrain becomes hilly as you walk along diverse glacial formations. The jagged ground and giant rocks are remnants of the last ice age. The biggest of the boulders (called a glacial erratic) stands 20 feet high at the turning point in the trail. Make sure you follow the trail to the left around this impressive rock; it will take you back to the starting point, while the other trail leads to private property. Dogs must be leashed.

From I-93 in Wilmington, take Exit 41 to Ballardvale Street/Route 125 north into Andover and the Andover Bypass. Turn right on Salem Street. The park and a parking lot are on the right. Open sunrise–sunset. 978/623-8311.

PLACES TO EAT

Larry D's Village Deli: This busy little place serves only breakfast and lunch. You can get sandwiches, muffins, and bacon and eggs, among other selections. There are plenty of picnic tables out back. And across the road is Duck Pond, where there are more tables to enjoy your meal while watching Daffy, Donald, and their ilk. The deli's just a stone's throw from Reservation Road, which runs through a wonderful trio of parks—the Baker's Meadow, Indian Ridge, and West Parish Meadow Reservations. Pick up a picnic lunch and enjoy your day. 22 Andover Street; 978/470-1492.

Phil's Roast Beef: After a long hike, stop for some of the best roast beef sandwiches around at this roadside establishment. Only five minutes away from Baker's Meadow and the other conservation areas along Reservation Road, it's an easy stop on your way home. Also, there's a grassy area with views over the Shawsheen River. The menu includes burgers, shakes, and ice cream. 32 Andover Street; 978/475-2626.

PLACES TO STAY

We're sad to report that one of our favorite inns, Andover Inn, no longer allows pets. Here are a few other choices to take its place.

Staybridge Suites: Dogs under 30 pounds are welcome at this suite-style hotel. With studios and one- and two-bedroom suites to choose from, this is a perfect place for an extended stay. All suites include a kitchen, full amenities, and a buffet breakfast each morning. There is a nonrefundable $50 pet fee per stay. Rates are $99–180 per night. 4 Technology Drive, Andover, MA 01810; 978/686-2000; website: www.ichotels.com.

Wyndham Hotel: Dogs are welcome at this conveniently located hotel, but please let the management know before you arrive that you will be bringing your pet. Rooms are around $129–159. No extra charge for Rover. 123 Old River Road, Andover, MA 01810; 978/475-5903; website: www.wyndham.com.

Harold Parker State Forest Campground: See Harold Parker State Forest listing, above.

Bedford

PARKS, BEACHES, AND RECREATION AREAS

◼ Fawn Lake Conservation Area

🐾🐾🐾 🐕 (See Merrimack River Valley map on page 196)

For years, the magical waters of Fawn Lake have lured visitors to its shores. The Pawtucket Indians, early American farmers, spring water bottlers, and resort mavens all believed the lake and nearby springs had a medicinal power that could restore and maintain one's health. In the 1800s, a health spa named Bedford Springs drew people here with promises of the water's curative properties. While we don't recommend that you drink the water, we do think that a short walk around the pond could do wonders for both you and your dog.

Park at the spacious lot off Sweetwater Avenue. From here, you can follow the quarter-mile trail around the lake or picnic on the large grassy area overlooking the water. Picnic tables are available on a first-come, first-served basis, and the lawn is a great spot for your dog to roll himself dry after a dip in the clean, cool lake.

For a longer walk, head off into the woods on the far side of the lake. Here a trail leads south through the pines along the railroad bed; eventually it hooks up with a yellow-marked trail that leads into the Wilderness Park Conservation Area about half a mile away. Dogs are allowed leash-free at Fawn Lake if under voice control. The park is managed by the Bedford Conservation Commission.

From the town center at the intersection of Concord Road/Route 62, Great Road, and Carlisle Road/Routes 4 and 225, take Carlisle Road west. Turn right on North Road/Route 4, then right again on Sweetwater Avenue. The park and a parking lot are at the road's end. Open from a half hour before sunrise to a half hour after sunset. 781/275-6211.

◼ Hartwell Town Forest/Jordan Conservation Area

🐾🐾🐾 🐕 (See Merrimack River Valley map on page 196)

These two forests together combine for a leash-free 150 acres, thanks to the Hartwell family who deeded this land to the Bedford Conservation Commission. Explore a still dense forest of tall hard wood trees, Hartwell Brook, abandoned cranberry bogs, and even the town gardens on a number of intertwining trails. Camping is also permitted with permission from the Conservation Commission.

From the town center at the intersection of Concord Road/Route 62, Great Road, and Carlisle Road/Route 4, take Great Road east for a quarter mile. Turn right onto South Road for a third of a mile. Turn right onto Hartwell Road for another quarter mile. The park and a small parking area are on the left. Open from a half hour before sunrise to a half hour after sunset. 781/275-6211.

🄩 Wilderness Park Conservation Area

🐾🐾🐾🐕 (See Merrimack River Valley map on page 196)

This 74-acre park isn't exactly a wilderness, but you and your leash-free dog will certainly enjoy visiting the lovely little forest. The 1.5-mile trail starts across from Middlesex Community College, where you'll find a huge parking area. Walk across the street and head down the dirt trail. Marked with blue paint, it serves as the main trail. There's also a paved bike trail leading off to the right, but that only leads alongside the road, so we don't recommend it.

Early on you'll find the main pathway intersected by green and yellow trails. These side trails crisscross the blue trail throughout the park. If you've been here before and want to explore the woods, follow one of the side trails. If this is your first visit, stick to the blue trail, the longest and clearest path. Leading through pine trees and over the three streams that trickle through the park, the blue trail covers all of the area's main attractions. The trail ends behind the Veteran's Administration Hospital. For a shorter trip back to the parking lot, you might consider following the yellow or green path.

From the town center at the intersection of Concord Road/Route 62, Great Road, and Carlisle Road/Routes 4 and 225, take Great Road east. Turn left on Spring Road and continue past the Veteran's Administration hospital. The park is on the right; park in the Middlesex Community College auxiliary parking lot on the left. Open from a half hour before sunrise to a half hour after sunset. 781/275-6211.

PLACES TO EAT

Bedford Farms Kitchen: A local spot in the town center, this place is good for a quick sandwich or some refreshing ice cream after a run in the park. If you want a meal, go for the Smokey Joe sandwich with smoked turkey, bacon, barbecue sauce, and Swiss cheese. During the summer, you can order from the outdoor windows and if it's not too crowded, sit on the bench out front. 18 North Road; 781/275-3040.

Carriage House Café: This small café has outdoor tables when the weather's warm. Soups, salads, gourmet muffins, coffee, and sandwiches are among its specialties. Take your meal to go or enjoy it outside. It's only minutes from the Wilderness Park Conservation Area. 200 Great Road; 781/275-0095.

Billerica

PARKS, BEACHES, AND RECREATION AREAS

🄩🄪 Fox Hill Conservation Land

🐾 (See Merrimack River Valley map on page 196)

In winter, this vista point makes for great sledding or skiing, but as a place to hike with your dog, its charms are limited. At the crest of the hill, a firebreak

offers breathtaking views of downtown Boston and the surrounding valley. But this area, which the town of Billerica recently acquired, doesn't have many formal or well-maintained trails yet. A residential area surrounds the woods, and you and your pooch will only find a few paths to explore. Give it a few years and it will probably improve. Dogs must be leashed.

From the intersection of Boston Road/Route 3A and Floyd Street/Route 129, take Floyd Street east; it becomes Salem Street. Turn right on Woodbury Road and then left on Gail Ann Drive. The park is at the road's end. Park at the dirt pullout beside the entrance. Open sunrise–sunset. 978/671-0966.

🄌🄌 Veteran's Park

 (See Merrimack River Valley map on page 196)

This beautiful park, with wide open grassy areas, has a fabulous swimming pond—Winning's Pond—and trails leading through a lovely forest. But it's right off Route 3, and the woods, unfortunately, have become a popular spot for anonymous trysts. The pond is one of the best swimming holes we've found, so if you stick to the grassy areas around the water and parking area, you and your dog should find plenty to enjoy. Dogs must be leashed here.

From Route 3, take Exit 28 to Treble Cove Road south. Turn left on Golden Rod Lane. The park and a parking area are on the left. Open sunrise–sunset. 978/671-0966.

🄌🄌 Warren H. Manning State Forest

 (See Merrimack River Valley map on page 196)

Route 129 bisects this little state park. The main entrance is on the north side of Chelmsford Road. This is the more manicured section of the park, with restrooms, picnic tables, and a children's wading pool. If your leashed dog has any say in the matter, you'll skirt all this commotion and head for the area behind the picnic area. Here a trail offers you a quiet loop through a pine forest. Although it's a short walk—it will take you only about 30 minutes—it brings you across a clear brook and near shady spots with benches for a rest stop. The trail is scenic and enjoyable. The only downside is that you can't get away from the noise of nearby Route 3 and Chelmsford Road.

Across the road is another, less developed section. The trails here are in decent shape, but they crisscross each other. Eventually, they all lead to the small pond in the center. This is good bird-watching territory—you'll see ducks and geese—but it can get a bit swampy. If your dog tends to dive into any and all puddles of water, you might want to avoid this side of the park.

From Route 3 in Chelmsford, take Exit 29 to Route 129 east. The park is on the left and right sides of the road; the parking lot is on the left. Open from 9 A.M.–sunset. 978/671-0966.

PLACES TO STAY

Homewood Suites: This suite-style hotel offers studio and one-bedroom suites, each equipped with full kitchens and amenities. Dogs are welcome here with a $50 fee per stay. Rates range from $89–189 per night. 35 Middlesex Turnpike, Billerica, MA 01821; 978/670-7111; website: www.homewoodsuites.com.

Boxford

PARKS, BEACHES, AND RECREATION AREAS

13 Bald Hill Reservation, Eastern Section

🐾🐾🐾🐾 🐾 (See Merrimack River Valley map on page 196)

If you and your dog didn't get enough of the Waltons, then you're sure to enjoy a hike up Bald Hill. Only here it's the Russells: James, Rebecca, Perkins, and Peabody. The Russell family occupied Bald Hill from the mid-1700s to the mid-1800s, and many signs of the old farm remain: the foundations for the barns and homes, open fields and orchards, and even the family graveyard.

The main trail up the mountain is a country lane named Bald Hill Road. It winds past beautiful, tall forests, scenic ponds, and marshes. Along the way, the intersections are coded to make it easier to find your way. To reach the hilltop, you'll just need to stay with the road until Intersection 12, where you turn right to complete the ascent. Up top the views are limited, but there is a wonderful, open field, probably cleared by the Russells.

Follow the trail out of the field to the south; it leads into the heart of the farm. This tranquil setting is a great place for either a picnic or just to wander through the meadows.

To make the two-mile loop around Bald Hill, follow the path west from

Intersection 10 on the Bald Hill Trail. Take a right on the side trail at Intersection 8A. This path passes a lush grove of tall pines and stone walls designating the old boundaries of Peabody Pasture. Continue to Intersection 26 and take a right to cross marshes and complete the loop back to Bald Hill Road.

Other side trails intersect with Bald Hill Road and the Bald Hill Trail. Check the maps at the trailhead for guidance. Dogs must be leashed.

This section of Bald Hill Reservation contains properties managed by the Essex County Greenbelt Association, John Phillips Wildlife Sanctuary, and Boxford State Forest. Free park maps are available at the trailhead, at Harold Parker State Forest Headquarters, and from the Essex County Greenbelt Association. See the Bald Hill Reservation, Western Section listing in the North Andover section of this chapter.

From I-95, take Exit 51 to Endicott Road west. Turn right on Middleton Road and continue to the park and parking lot on the right. Open sunrise–sunset. 978/369-3350.

14 Boxford State Forest, North Section

🐾 (See Merrimack River Valley map on page 196)

Parking is difficult, the trails are short, but wow, what a pond! Baldpate Pond is sparkling and spectacular. Alas, swimming isn't allowed in the tempting water. Party poopers.

Another small downer: the park's bisected by an impassable swamp. Believe us, George and Inu have tried every way imaginable to cross it. On each side of the swampy muck you'll find a small, wooded area that slopes down to the water's edge and some short trails. Access the western section from Baldpate Road and the eastern section from Nelson Street in Georgetown. Your dog must be leashed.

To reach the park's western section from I-95, take Exit 53 to Killam Hill Road west. Turn left on Kelsey Road. Take a right onto Ipswich Road and another right onto Baldpate Road. The park and a roadside pullout are on the right, just after Baldpate Pond.

To reach the eastern section, continue on Nelson Street; the entrance is on the right. Look for a forest road blocked by boulders. Open dawn–dusk. 978/887-8181.

15 Wildcat Conservation Area

🐾🐾🐾 (See Merrimack River Valley map on page 196)

Wetlands and woodlands and wildcats—oh my! These comprise the highlights of Wildcat Conservation Area. Well, maybe just the wetlands and woodlands, but you never know what's out there. We'd like to think that there are still a few wildcats in the woods. When one shows up, we'll be ready.

Years ago, the Boxford/Georgetown area (and much of New England) boasted abundant wildlife populations, including bears, foxes, and wolves.

Today most of these animals are gone, or have learned to avoid humans at every turn. Among the techniques that early colonists and farmers used to trap the creatures was a large, baited hole in the ground, called a wolf pit. Apparently, you can still find some of these pits in and around the woods of Wildcat Conservation Area.

Whether or not you encounter any wild beasts, your canine pal will love sharing the main trail here with you. It roams for 2.5 miles through rich forest, passing many ponds and streams. Follow the access trail from the parking lot. At the first intersection, the main loop begins. Take the trail that leads straight ahead. Along the way, be on the lookout for the Ledge Trail, which veers off to the left and climbs for a higher route. The main trail (to the right) is the low road; it has more ponds and streams. The return part of the loop is known as the Wolf-Pit Trail, where, we are told, you may pass an old wolf pit. The entire route makes a wonderful pass through marshes, stone walls, and ridges.

At present, we have yet to find any wolf pits, but we're always on the lookout for wild, woodland creatures. The Boxford Conservation Commission manages the park and requires dogs to be on leash.

From I-95, take Exit 53 to Killam Hill Road west. Turn left on Kelsey Road. Turn right on Ipswich Road. Take a left onto Herrick Road. The park and a parking lot are on the right. Open dawn–dusk. 978/352-2538.

PLACES TO EAT

Benson's Homemade Ice Cream: Of course there's no such thing as bad ice cream, but Benson's has some of the best around. Outdoor seating available for all. 181 Washington Street/Route 3; 978/352-2911.

Carlisle

Here's good news for Carlisle dogs and their out-of-town visitors: If you love to roam leash free and are responsive to the sound of your owner's voice, the town of Carlisle doesn't require you to wear a leash! You know the deal with this privilege. Abuse it and we may lose it. Now let's be careful out there.

PARKS, BEACHES, AND RECREATION AREAS

16 Banta-Davis Land

🐾🐾🐕 (See Merrimack River Valley map on page 196)

This 40-acre park provides an easy, off-leash walk in the woods. There's a large parking area between the athletic field and Green Cemetery; the trail starts past the field on the edge of the woods. It leads through an oak and maple forest, giving you a quiet, 20-minute walk up and back.

Another short trail leads behind the cemetery to a boardwalk through a swamp. It dead-ends at another athletic field. Fox Hill Conservation Area is right next door to the ball field but, unfortunately, no trail connects the two.

The park is just east of the town center, on the south side of Bedford Road/ Route 225 near the Church Street intersection. A parking lot is available. Open dawn–dusk. 978/369-0336.

17 Conant Land

🐾🐾🦮 (See Merrimack River Valley map on page 196)

Managed by the Carlisle Conservation Commission, this 57-acre property makes for a leash-free, private, easy woodland hike. There are two trailheads:

the first is at the fire station off Westport Street; the second is on Rockland Road at the gated turnout. Park at either location. The loop through the forest will begin and end at either location and takes about a half hour.

Our advice is to start at the Rockland Road Trail. You begin in a pine forest, following the pleasant, slightly hilly path as it winds its way over pine needles and past large boulders. At the bend in the trail, you reach Fishtail Pond. The brook that leads into the pond is clear and clean, but the pond itself is a bit swampy, so it doesn't allow for the best swimming.

Either turn around here and backtrack to the starting point, or continue along the road, which runs along the backyards of some houses to the Fire Station Trail. You'll enjoy a hike here best in the spring and fall; it can get buggy in the hot summer months.

From the town center at the intersection of Lowell Street and Westford Street/Route 225, take Westford Street west. Turn right on Rockland Road. The park is on the right. Roadside parking is available at the trailhead. Open dawn–dusk. 978/369-0336.

18 The Cranberry Bog

🐾🐾🐾 🐕 (See Merrimack River Valley map on page 196)

It's a cranberry bog, all right. It looks like a cranberry bog, smells like a cranberry bog, and it's even called "The Cranberry Bog." But unlike most bogs, this one you'll want to visit. In 1986, the towns of Carlisle and Chelmsford bought this private wetland, and now you and your leash-free dog are free to use it. The cities still lease out the bog to private farmers who harvest the berries, but if you stick to the park's path through the area, you'll have your run of this terrific spot.

Set on the border of Carlisle and Chelmsford, it offers a decent-sized parking area off Curve Street. From here, you'll look out over the working bog, but the trails around the harvesting area are wide and clearly marked. For the best hiking, head to your left and out through the center of the bog toward the woods. Here, you'll have to make sure your leashless dog doesn't go tramping through the boggy marsh, despite all the enticing smells. Keep him on the trail with you, and when you get into the woods, he can sniff the place to his heart's delight.

Once you enter the woods, bear left again on the trail. This route leads through a quiet forest and past several small ponds. Depending on the season, these wetlands can get a bit swampy, but in spring, they are usually fine for your dog to get his feet wet without ending up too muddy. If you follow the trail to its end, it will lead you to another small turnout on Elm Street—across the Chelmsford town line. Here's where you'll turn around and retrace your steps to the starting point.

The entire round-trip walk takes about 45 minutes, and the unusual terrain makes it worthwhile. We've seen deer on every visit, and if you're lucky, you might catch a glimpse of the beavers and muskrats who are rumored to reside in the ponds. As for the cranberries, in the fall months you can buy them at Great Brook Farm Ice Cream (see the listing in the Restaurants section), which you'll find just up the road.

From the town center at the intersection of Lowell Street and Westford Street/Route 225, take Lowell Street north. Turn left on Curve Street. The park and a parking area are on the right. Open dawn–dusk. 978/369-0336.

19 Davis Corridor

🐾 🐕 (See Merrimack River Valley map on page 196)

Although this 126-acre stretch of woodland looks great as you approach it, sometimes looks can be deceiving. The trail winds through a greenbelt right behind houses, so you're never too far from the sounds of civilization. And the woods tend to be very swampy, which means lots of muck for your dog and lots of flies for you. Even though your dog is allowed off leash here, she might well prefer to visit another park on leash.

The only smooth part of the trail leads along Two Rod Road, which was named for its width. There are two "rods," or 33 feet, between the two stone walls that run along the trail here. The road itself leads to Estabrook Woods and Punkatasset Hill, both in Concord (see the Estabrook Woods/Punkatasset Conservation Land listing in the Concord section of the Sudbury River Valley chapter). But the land surrounding the trail isn't great, so if you want to visit those areas, just head over to bordering Concord.

Davis Corridor does offer one bit of great local trivia. If you park at the end of Ledge Hill Road, you'll easily find the Blood's Farm Trail, a muddy, buggy path with an intriguing past. Legend has it that Colonel John Blood stole a handful of Britain's royal crown jewels and was apprehended when his horse stumbled and fell. The jewels, however, were never recovered. Locals swear that somewhere on Blood's Farm is buried an "enormous iron pot filled with gold coins and stones that shine like the sun." Sounds like a fine place to get your dog to bury a bone, wouldn't you say?

From the town center at the intersection of Lowell Street and Bedford Road/ Route 225, take Bedford Road east. The park and a parking lot are on the right, just past Red Pine Drive. Open dawn–dusk. 978/369-0336.

20 Foss Farm

🐾 🐕 (See Merrimack River Valley map on page 196)

A farming collective made up of approximately 70 garden plots and horse corrals, Foss Farm sees a lot of activity during the summer—probably too much for a good dog walk. But during the cooler months, things settle down, and the land is pretty much left to leashless dogs and cross-country skiers.

During winter, the parking lot is plowed, which is handy when other parks get snowed in. The land is flat and open with some woods; the trails are simple and short. A hike here will take you about 30 minutes, which may be enough if you only have time for a quick walk.

From the town center at the intersection of Lowell Street and Bedford Road/ Route 225, take Bedford Road east. The park and a parking lot are on the left, past Maple Street. Open dawn–dusk. 978/369-0336.

21 Fox Hill Conservation Area

🐾 🐕 (See Merrimack River Valley map on page 196)

This is really just a large field surrounded by a patch of woods and a small stream. There aren't any trails, but it's a popular gathering place for local residents and their dogs. If she's so inclined, your dog could stop by to meet the town's leashless canine elite. You can park at Banta-Davis next door or at Kimball Farm across the street.

The park is just east of the town center, on the south side of Bedford Road/ Route 225 near the Church Street intersection. Parking is available across the street. Open dawn–dusk. 978/369-0336.

22 Great Brook Farm State Park

🐾🐾🐾🐾 🐕 🐟 (See Merrimack River Valley map on page 196)

With more than 900 acres and nine miles of trails, this is one of those great parks that you'll want to visit again and again. Our readers have told us this is one of their favorite parks in the entire book. In fact, most of the locals can't imagine making the effort to go anywhere else when they have Great Brook Farm in their own backyard. It has a large meadow, pine and woodland forest, esker trail, swamp, and a lovely pond—not to mention a working farm and ice-cream stand. You'll probably discover your favorite trail and stick with it, but there are many combinations that you can put together to keep you and your dog entertained on every visit.

If it's your first visit, we recommend the Pine Point Loop. To reach the trail, follow North Road a quarter mile past Great Brook Farm to the Canoe Launch parking area. Follow the blue arrow to the Pine Point Loop; the trail starts at the fork. You can set out straight ahead or veer to the right. Either way, the trail will loop around and bring you back to the same spot.

The route to the right leads across a little wooden bridge over Meadow Stream, which is at the tail end of Meadow Pond. If your dogs haven't seen water for a while, they might plunge right in. There's easy access and it's clean, but there's plenty more water to come, so don't worry that this will be their last chance to take a dip.

The route, which also serves as a bridle trail, continues into a pine forest. Be forewarned that on busy weekends it can get a little congested with the very large, four-hoofed animals. As you wander alongside Meadow Pond, we suggest that you stick to the outer trail at points where it converges with another pathway. This will take you closer to the water and help you steer clear of the horses. Swimming is allowed in the pond, and the surrounding shady pine forest offers great spots to picnic or just take a rest amid the beautiful trees.

After looping around the pond, the trail enters a large meadow with manicured grass. The pathway is open and flat here. Keep to the left to continue your walk. Veer to the right to reach Great Brook Farm itself, and the summer ice-cream stand. This is the only part of the park where your dog must be leashed.

If you stay on the main trail (and virtuously postpone your ice-cream break until after your walk), the path continues through the forest and loops around the far side of Meadow Pond before returning you to the trailhead. The swimming is best on the first leg of your journey, so if you'd like to cool off after working up a sweat, reverse the trail sequence. This entire loop should take you about an hour to walk. Along the way, you're sure to meet up with many other dog walkers, as this park really packs in the four-legged crowd.

To extend your walk, we recommend taking the Heartbreak Ridge Loop, which veers up a slight incline about a half mile from the meadow. This narrow trail takes you down through the Tophet Swamp on a two-hour walk. A bit more strenuous than the other trails, it's also free of horses because of the mud. This may make it less desirable for you, as well, but we like it because it's off the beaten track. The path leads through the swamp (there are wooden walkways in those hard-to-pass places) and loops back again to the Pine Point Loop.

If you want a quick historical tour, take the Woodchuck Trail, which is off North Road just past the farm. This short trail takes you by "The City," the remains of an early colonists' community dating back to the 1600s. Here you'll only see some decaying stone foundations that are so easy to miss you may not even notice them.

The park offers many other worthwhile trails. Pick up a free map at the regional headquarters on Lowell Road or check out alternative routes on the posted map at the main parking area by the farm. Your dog may be off leash everywhere but Great Brook Farm itself.

From the town center at the intersection of Lowell Street and Westford Street/Route 225, take Lowell Street north. Turn right on Curve Street, which leads into the park. The parking area is on the left. Open sunrise–sunset. 978/369-6312.

23 Greenough Land

🐾🐾🐾 🐕 (See Merrimack River Valley map on page 196)

The trail at this wonderful 242-acre park twists and turns through a pine forest before delivering you and your leash-free dog to Greenough Pond at its center. It offers a decent hike, and the park has plenty of additional trails for those who want to explore the area further.

The main trail leads straight through the woods before connecting with a second trail branching to the left, which will take you to the pond. Even though the junction trail seems to lead away from the pond at points, if you persevere, you'll arrive at the water. In places it can get a little swampy along the pond's edge. The trail traverses three-quarters of the pond, with the best section on the eastern side, where you'll find two additional trails. Take the path to the left, and you can continue a half mile through a swamp to the Concord River; take the path to the right, and you'll follow the boundary of the private homestead until you reach a pine forest and lower Maple Street.

From the town center at the intersection of Lowell Street and Bedford Road/ Route 225, take Bedford Road east. Turn left on East Street, then left again on Maple Street. The park and a parking area are on the right. Open dawn–dusk. 978/369-0336.

24 Towle Field

🐾🐾🐾 🐕 (See Merrimack River Valley map on page 196)

Although it covers only 112 acres, this terrific park feels a lot bigger because it encompasses so many different terrain types. The trails weave their way through forest and field, over hills and rocks, crossing water at many spots where your off-leash dog can stop for a drink or a refreshing splash. There seems to be a wonderful surprise around every bend.

To get the most out of your hike, take the path that leads to the left from the trailhead. From here, you will walk through a quiet pine forest. The well-maintained trail crosses footbridges and walkways cut in rocks. Rather rocky and even hilly in spots, it will give you a good workout. Follow the trail around the outer edges; lots of cutaway paths lead deeper into the woods, but you never know exactly where you're going to end up, so explore these when you're more familiar with the park. The main trail leads to the small brook on the far southwestern side of the park.

Eventually you'll wind your way into the clearing of Towle Field. This expansive meadow is cut through with several paths, and there's a large hillock in the center for picnicking. This is a great spot for bird-watching or rabbit-chasing; your dog's nostrils will quiver at the many smells left by deer and other wildlife. Stay to the southern path and it will return you to the parking area.

From the town center at the intersection of Lowell Street and Westford Street/Route 225, take Westford Street west. The park and a parking lot are on the left, just past Salvation Lane. Open dawn–dusk. 978/369-0336.

PLACES TO EAT

Great Brook Farm Ice Cream: Set within Great Brook Farm State Park, this ice-cream store could be your well-deserved reward after a long day of hiking on the trails. Park your automobile at the main parking area and go up the hill to the farm. There are plenty of signs to guide you; on a hot summer's day, just follow the crowds! Dogs must be leashed here because you're on a working farm, and you won't be welcome if Fido decides to run around and upset the barnyard animals. 247 North Road; 978/371-7083.

Kimball Farm: I scream, you scream, and your dogs will even scream for this great little outdoor ice-cream and sandwich stand right across from Fox Hill and Banta-Davis Land. The menu's gigantic, and there are plenty of benches and picnic tables around the shop where you and your dog can enjoy lunch or a treat. It's open seasonally, April–October. 343 Bedford Road/Route 225, just past Church Street; 978/369-1910.

Georgetown

PARKS, BEACHES, AND RECREATION AREAS

25 Georgetown-Rowley State Forest

(See Merrimack River Valley map on page 196)

This is a great parcel of public land. The only trouble is that it's surrounded by private land. So getting over to the state forest's 1,112 acres can be tricky. The key to solving this dilemma is Pingree Farm Road, an old dirt path that runs through the middle of the park. Most of it is closed to vehicles, but it can get you where you want to go.

Built on an esker that runs the park's length from east to west, Pingree Farm Road is now part of the Bay Circuit Trail. You and your leashed dog can simply walk along the dirt road or take one of the many foot trails that wind through the woods from the road. The state forest is split in half by I-95, and the only way to get to the other side is from Pingree Farm Road via what we imagine is the world's largest footbridge.

Georgetown and its environs are horse country, and this is an especially popular place to ride. Many stables neighbor the state forest, so you'll share the trail with horses, mountain bikers, and at certain times during the year, hunters, so be alert.

From I-95, take Exit 54 to East Main Street/Route 133 west. Turn left on Central Street/Route 97 south and then left again on Pingree Farm Road. The park and a small parking area are at the end of the paved road. Open sunrise–sunset. 978/887-5931.

26 Lufkins Brook Conservation Area

😸 😸 (See Merrimack River Valley map on page 196)

The 223 acres of Lufkins Brook are composed of rich woodlands with a set of forest cart paths and connecting hiking trails. Although the routes through the forest are simple—most of them run from one end of the woods to the other—the scenic surroundings make for an enjoyable walk. Tall hardwood trees create a high canopy cover for the rolling hills and ridges below.

A drawback to the park is the limited water in the conservation area, making a visit on a summer's day that much hotter. Of course, there's Lufkins Brook in the southeastern corner, but it doesn't really provide enough water to wallow in. The Parker River flows through the northern portion of the park, but it's unreachable.

The main route, about a mile in length, is a loop that begins from the parking area. Follow the cart road and stay to the left (red markers) at the first intersection. From this road, you can continue straight by the brook or look for the foot trail (blue markers) on the right. This trail circles back to the first intersection. Dogs must be leashed.

From I-95, take Exit 54 to East Main Street/Route 133 west. Turn left on Central Street. Turn right on Andover Street, then right again on West Street. The park and parking are on the left. Open dawn–dusk. 978/352-5711.

Haverhill

More than a hundred years ago, the shoe industry kicked this sleepy frontier town to worldwide prominence as a major footwear producer. Nestled along the Merrimack River, Haverhill still has many remnants of its booming industrial and frontier past. You and your dog can walk the Hannah Dustin Trail, named for an early settler who was abducted by Native Americans and managed to escape. You can also high-foot it along Washington Street, the heart (or should we say "sole"?) of the 19th-century shoemaking trade.

PARKS, BEACHES, AND RECREATION AREAS

🐾 Meadow Brook Conservation Area

🐾 🐾 🐾 (See Merrimack River Valley map on page 196)

We love this place in any season. It has enough trails to keep you and your leashed dog busy visit after visit. The forest's 248 acres surround Millvale Reservoir; although you can't swim in this glorious pond, you can take a dip in East Meadow Brook, which runs into the reservoir.

There are two main parking areas. Each offers access to one side of the reservoir. The lot on Millvale Road, on the southwestern side of the dam, provides the most varied trails into the forest's interior. Here you can wander the main trail along the reservoir or explore the many esker trails and peninsulas that lead out over the water. The forest is dense and quiet, creating a beautifully hushed atmosphere for your walk. The water will be oh-so-tempting, but off-limits. If you stick to the trails above the reservoir, your dog will probably content herself with the many great sniffs and smells instead of a cool but illegal dip.

If swimming is a priority, we suggest you park on the other side of the water, at the end of Thompson Road. The trail here leads by East Meadow Brook, where your dog can dip his paws. The brook slows down at a small dam here before running into the northeastern end of the reservoir. The dam collects all the leaves and needles that have fallen into the water, coating the top of the brook with a porous layer of natural debris. Apparently, to our dogs it looks like shoreline, because every time they get fooled and try to go in.

George loves the water but, unlike Inu, he doesn't like to dive in or get his head wet. Instead, he goes in the old-fashioned way: one step at a time. Here he thinks he can jump off the small dam onto the dirt below. The problem is that it isn't dirt, but pine needles covering the water. And every time, he gets an enormous shock by plunging headfirst into the deep water. Don't worry; he can swim, and it's a short dog paddle to the shore, but we can hardly stop laughing at poor George's surprise.

The last time we were here and George did his little trick, JoAnna was holding the trail map and giggled so hard that she let go of it. It went gently floating over the water before resting tantalizingly out of reach on the pine needles. Now what were we going to do? George had already been fooled once; he wasn't going to make the same mistake twice. Chris threw a stick in order to push the map back to the shore. But it was Inu, Super Dog, to the rescue. He dove in after the stick and in the process of retrieving it, hooked

DIVERSIONS

The Buttonwoods Trail, Hannah Dustin Trail, and Washington Street Historic District Trail are part of the **Merrimack River Trail.** For more information on the trail and on the Merrimack River Watershed Council, which manages it, see the Extended Hiking Trails section of the Resources section.

Buttonwoods Trail: This 2.5-mile trail in the eastern part of town follows the north shore of the Merrimack River. It runs from the Washington Street Historic District Trail in downtown Haverhill to Riverside Park near the Groveland border.

Parking is available at Riverside Park and in downtown Haverhill. For more information, call the Haverhill Trails Office, 978/374-2334, or the Merrimack River Watershed Council, 978/681-5777.

Hannah Dustin Trail: This 2.25-mile trail follows the northern shoreline of the Merrimack River from the Methuen town line to the Haverhill historic district. Along the way, you get spectacular views over the broad, majestic river, and a number of benches to rest your weary bones.

The trail was named for Hannah Dustin, who was abducted by Native Americans in 1698. She was held upriver in what is now Concord, New Hampshire, before escaping and finding her way back to Haverhill by canoe.

The route is easy to follow, readily accessible from several areas, and connects with the Washington Street Historic District Trail. The Merrimack is a powerful river, so be careful about letting your dog plunge into the water.

The main parking areas are off Merrimack Street/Route 110, Western Avenue, and Bank Road. For more information, call the Haverhill Trails Office, 978/374-2334, or the Merrimack River Watershed Council, 978/681-5777.

Washington Street Historic District Trail: A two-mile trek, it ventures along city streets and sidewalks through the heart of historic Haverhill on Merrimack Street from Julian Street to the Basiliere Bridge.

The trail connects Haverhill's two river paths, the Buttonwoods Trail in the east and the Hannah Dustin Trail in the west. There is plenty of parking available downtown. For more information, call the Haverhill Trails Office, 978/374-2334, or the Merrimack River Watershed Council, 978/681-5777.

the map with the end of the branch, thus bringing it to shore and saving the day. Who said that dogs can't problem-solve? Not us!

If you continue over the dam and into the forest, the trail eventually leads to the main reservoir, covering the area on the northeastern side of the lake along the way. You'll find other flatter, but no less beautiful, trails to explore here. You can pick up an ever-valuable map at the town hall. Just hold onto it.

From I-495, take Exit 52 to Amesbury Road/Route 110 west. Turn left on Kenoza Street. Turn left on Centre Street and then left again on Middle Road. The park begins at the intersection of Middle and Millvale Roads. Parking is available on both roads. Additional parking is available on the shoulder of East Broadway and off Thompson Road. Thompson Road is off Middle Road, north of Millvale Road. Open from a half hour before sunrise to a half hour after sunset. 978/374-2334.

🐾🐾🐾 Winnekenni Park

🐾🐾🐾 👣 (See Merrimack River Valley map on page 196)

Lake of the Pickerel! Let no more

The echoes answer back "Great Pond,"

But sweet Kenoza, from thy shore

And watching hill beyond.

In 1859, John Greenleaf Whittier wrote those words on the occasion of the renaming of Great Pond. Apparently there were so many Great Ponds in Massachusetts that the towns were going to have to assign them numbers. This one was dubbed *Kenoza,* which means "Lake of the Pickerel" in one Native American language. One of the most beautiful areas around, this park circles the lake in a picturesque setting. A simple trail system leads around Kenoza, but you can't swim in the public water supply, so you might want to hike the higher trail to Lake Saltonstall.

To reach Lake Saltonstall, drive past the main entrance (and the lakeside trail system) to the top of Castle Road. Park at the picnic area and follow the path that leads behind the castle and away from Kenoza Lake. The short hike to the clear lake takes about 20 minutes, and you'll be rewarded by a pleasant swim at various points along the shore. Dogs and nonresidents aren't permitted at the public beach on the lake's west end.

Both trails lead through shady pine forests, and your leashed dog will enjoy the woodsy smells of the trees, shrubs, and logs along the way. The view from the grassy clearing by the castle is breathtaking and well worth the trip. Built in 1875, the large stone castle served as the former summer residence of Dr. James Nichols, a local physician and fertilizer experimenter at a nearby local farm called Winnekenni. There's plenty of room to play ball or Frisbee with your dog at the large picnic area.

From I-495, take Exit 52 to Amesbury Road/Route 110 west into Kenoza Street and then into Kenoza Avenue. The park and parking are on the right. Open from 8 A.M.–8 P.M. 978/521-1686.

Middleton

PLACES TO EAT

Richardson's Ice Cream: New England is famous for its many ice-cream makers (and you've probably noticed, we have visited every one of them!), but we have to say that Richardson's is one of the best and probably the oldest. The Middleton farm has been here since 1695; today the ice cream is shipped all over Massachusetts, but you can get it here first. Order your scoop at the walk-up window, and you and your dog can sit happily at any of the picnic tables outside. Take a walk through nearby Harold Parker State Forest in North Andover, and you have a trip everyone will enjoy. 156 South Main Street (Route 114); 978/774-5450.

North Andover

PARKS, BEACHES, AND RECREATION AREAS

🐾 Bald Hill Reservation, Western Section

🐾🐾 (See Merrimack River Valley map on page 196)

Although this section of Bald Hill Reservation is not as grand as the Eastern Section in Boxford (see the listing in the Boxford section of this chapter), its assortment of trails still provides some fine hiking opportunities.

Near the entrance to the park, you and your leashed dog will have to push through some barren terrain, but once you do, the surroundings improve as you enter thicker and taller woods and pass more ponds and streams. This is especially true if you are energetic enough to hike over to the eastern side of Bald Hill.

This section of Bald Hill Reservation contains properties managed by the Essex County Greenbelt Association and Boxford State Forest. Park maps are available at the trailheads, at the Harold Parker State Forest Headquarters (see directions in the listing below), and from the Essex County Greenbelt Association.

From the intersection of the Andover Bypass/Route 125 and Turnpike Street/Route 114, take Turnpike Street heading south. Turn left on Sharpner's Pond Road. The park and a parking lot are located at the road's end. Open from sunrise to a half hour after sunset. 978/369-3350.

30 Harold Parker State Forest

🐾🐾🐾🐾 (See Merrimack River Valley map on page 196)

Straddling the town of Andover, the bulk of this wonderful 3,500-acre state forest lies in North Andover. We recommend that you pick up a trail map at park headquarters to find all the great places for you to explore here. One of our favorite spots, Stearns Pond, is only a short hike through the woods from the headquarters parking area. A beautiful alpine pond, it makes a great swimming spot for both of you and offers lovely views across the water. You can make a loop around the water on unpaved Pond Road. There is beach access here, which can get pretty crowded on a summer day, but you should have it to yourself the rest of the year and in the morning or evening in summer.

You can also branch off of Pond Road by following the blue markers to Sudden Pond. This is a much smaller watering hole, but the trails are for hikers only, so you shouldn't have to dodge the summer crowds.

The trail leading to Berry Pond is new. A snack bar and restrooms are under construction; when they open, the crowds may flock to this portion of the park. There are picnic facilities at the pavilion, so you'll have to head into the woods to find a secluded spot. Dogs must be leashed.

From the intersection of the Andover Bypass/Route 125 and Turnpike Street/Route 114, take Turnpike Street south. Turn right on Harold Parker Road and proceed into the park. To reach park headquarters, continue on Harold Parker Road and turn left on Middleton Street. Headquarters is on the left. Open from a half hour before sunrise to a half hour after sunset. 978/686-3391.

31 Town Forest

🐾 (See Merrimack River Valley map on page 196)

A pleasant little 35-acre woodland behind a set of ball fields, Town Forest only offers limited hiking. In fact, only one dirt road runs through the park. The half-mile trail begins at the far left corner of the fields. The North Andover Trails Committee manages the area.

From the town center at the intersection of Massachusetts Avenue and Great Pond Road, take Great Pond Road east. Turn right on Marbleridge Road. Turn left on Dale Street. The park is on the right, behind the ball field. You can park on the shoulder of the road. Open dawn–dusk. 978/688-9530.

32 Weir Hill Reservation

🐾🐾🐾🐾 🐾 (See Merrimack River Valley map on page 196)

Do you recall the beginning of *The Sound of Music,* when Julie Andrews runs over the hills and bursts into song? Well, that's how your dog will feel on Weir Hill with the entire Merrimack Valley spread out before him. Of course, with a leash on, he won't be able to run quite as exuberantly as Maria von Trapp at this scenic spot, but it's still one of the best parks you'll find. Our dogs always love to kick up their heels like happy jackrabbits here.

Start at the main entrance off Stephens Street. Here you'll find a map that details the trails in the reservation. We suggest you head through the meadow and uphill to the trail that starts behind the meadow to the right. At first, the trail goes straight up, so get ready for a workout. Although rather steep initially, it soon levels off, and it's a short hike to the lower summit of Weir Hill, where the path opens onto a lovely open meadow surrounded by woods. The view of the Merrimack Valley from up here is quite spectacular. This is where our dogs' tails really start to wag, because they know that once they trot down the hill from the meadow, they'll be at Stephens Pond.

At the bottom of the meadow, the trail levels off a bit. After another quarter mile, you'll reach a signed intersection; head to the bridge between Stephens Pond and Lake Cochichewick. You can swim in the first, but not the second. Both are clean, pretty ponds, but Lake Cochichewick holds the town of Andover's public water supply. So pick the pond to your right and plunge on in.

After a swim, take the Hatch Trail to the top of Weir Hill. The up-and-down trail passes low-lying shrubbery mixed with pine forests that shade the walk. At the top of Weir Hill is another even more beautiful view of the hilltops and church spires throughout the valley. Choose a spot for a picnic or just breathe in the invigorating air.

The entire loop takes about an hour, not including time to rest, swim, or picnic. There are plenty of places to stop along the trail, but the hike can be vigorous in spots, so if either you or your dog is out of shape, you might want to take it slowly. If you're looking for a good hike that will give you a solid workout, however, we guarantee that you'll return to this park again and again.

From the intersection of Andover Street/Route 125 and Turnpike Street/ Route 114, take Andover Street heading north. Stay with Andover Street when it turns to the right off Route 125. Turn left on Stephens Street. The park is located on the right. There is plenty of parking available on the shoulder of the road. Another entrance and additional parking are located off Pleasant Street. Open dawn–dusk. 978/356-4351.

PLACES TO EAT

Bay State Chowda Company: Grab a great cup o' chowda or just about anything else you can imagine at this terrific café. Right in the heart of town, it has outdoor seating where your well-behaved dog will feel welcome. The food is delicious; eat it here or take it on a picnic. 109 Main Street; 978/685-9610.

North Reading

PARKS, BEACHES, AND RECREATION AREAS

🐾🐾🐾 North Reading Dog Park

🐾🐾🐾🐕 (See Merrimack River Valley map on page 196)

There is nothing extravagant about this new dog run, but just the fact that it exists is something to celebrate. The park is smallish but is well fenced and large enough for dogs to chase a ball or two. The run is surrounded with trees and shrubs, providing much-needed shade on a hot summer day.

From the Town Common at the intersection of Park Street/Route 62 and Haverhill Street, take Haverhill Street south for a half mile. Turn left onto Chestnut Street and proceed for a mile. Turn left onto Park Street, and the park and parking area is on your left. Open 10 A.M.–dusk; 978/664-6016.

Tewksbury

PLACES TO EAT

Mac's Dairy Barn: Pull on over and try the best ice cream this side of I-495! You'll have to fight through the Little League teams, soccer teams, and Girl Scout troops, but there is plenty of seating and lots of ice cream. This makes a great stop on the way home from hiking the dusty trails. 1863 Main Street; 978/851-9565.

PLACES TO STAY

Holiday Inn: This 237-room hotel welcomes dogs in its first-floor rooms. The rooms are clean and comfortable and there is no pet fee, although a refundable deposit is required on check in. Rooms are $89–129. 4 Highwood Drive, Tewksbury, MA 01876; 978/640-9000; website: www.holiday-inn.com.

Motel 6: All Motel 6 locations allow dogs as long as you don't leave your pet unattended. This motel is located right off I-495 at Exit 38. One dog welcome per room. Rates are $65. 95 Main Street, Tewksbury, MA 01876; 978/851-8677; website: www.motel6.com.

Residence Inn: Each room in this inn is like a mini apartment, complete with kitchen, bedroom, and living area. Canine guests are welcome for $10 extra per night plus a one-time $75 cleaning fee. Rates are around $109–189. 1775 Andover Street, Tewksbury, MA 01876; 978/640-1003; website: www.residenceinn.com.

Wilmington

PARKS, BEACHES, AND RECREATION AREAS

🐾 Glen Road Berry Bog and Recreation Area

🐾 (See Merrimack River Valley map on page 196)

Right behind the town hall, this is a small but well-maintained park. The marsh beside it is an old cranberry bog that has been allowed to grow back to its natural state. You'll get trails through the adjoining forest and a short boardwalk that extends out over the marsh. You won't get a lot of exercise here, but there's a picnic area with ample parking. From Route 38, take Glen Road east for four blocks. Turn left into the park access road. Open 8 A.M.– 6 P.M. 978/658-3511.

226

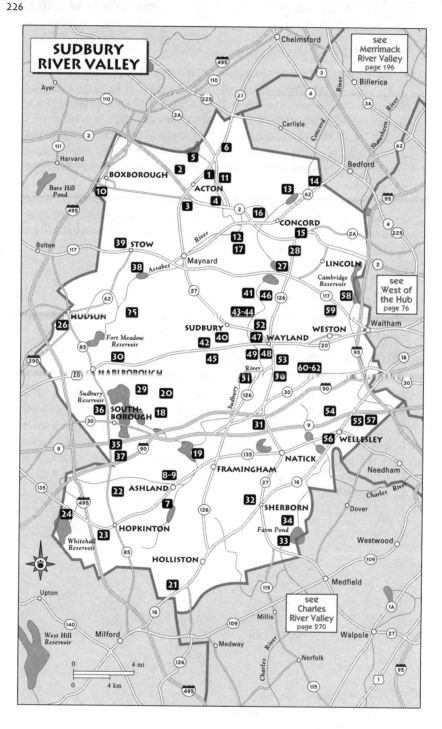

SUDBURY
RIVER VALLEY

Chelmsford

see
Merrimack
River Valley
page 196

Ayer

Billerica

Harvard

Carlisle

Bedford

5
2
6

BOXBOROUGH

1 **11**
ACTON
4
3

13 **14**

16
CONCORD

15

Bare Hill
Pond

10

39 STOW

Bolton

12
17

28
27

LINCOLN

see
West of
the Hub
page 76

38 Assabet

Maynard

River

Cambridge
Reservoir

41 **46**

58

26 HUDSON

75

43-44

59

52
SUDBURY **40**
42

47 WAYLAND

WESTON
Waltham

Fort Meadow
Reservoir

30

45

49 **48** **53**
51 **50** **60-62**

MARLBOROUGH

29 **20**

Sudbury River

54

Sudbury
Reservoir

36 SOUTH-
BOROUGH **18**

55 **57**
31

56 WELLESLEY

35
37

19

NATICK

Needham

FRAMINGHAM

8-9

Charles River

22 ASHLAND

7

32
SHERBORN

Dover

24

HOPKINTON

34
Farm Pond
33

Westwood

23

Whitehall
Reservoir

HOLLISTON

21

Medfield

Upton

West Hill
Reservoir

Milford

Millis

see
Charles
River Valley
page 270

Walpole

Medway

Norfolk

0   4 mi
0   4 km

CHAPTER 8

Sudbury River Valley

Some very lucky dogs live in the region that stretches west of Boston to I-495. The towns here offer some of the best parks featured in this book. Simply put, they are doggone fantastic. Not only are the forests and rivers graced with incomparable natural beauty, but there are more leash-free romping grounds than you can shake a stick at.

The Sudbury River Valley was the cradle of the American Revolution, and much of the landscape including woods, farmland, and town centers—remains as it was in the early days of Massachusetts. There are fascinating historic districts in Concord, Lincoln, Sudbury, and other towns. Acton, Wayland, and Weston have thriving conservation programs. Ashland, Framingham, and Marlborough offer beautiful state-run parks where dogs are welcome visitors. As George and Inu will attest, the pages in this chapter will be dog-eared in no time.

Bay Circuit Trail: Linking parks and reservations between Plum Island on the North Shore and Kingston Bay on the South Shore, this trail will eventually connect more than 30 towns across 200 miles, including Acton,

PICK OF THE LITTER—SUDBURY

BEST SWIMMING HOLE
Estabrook Woods, Concord (page 237)

BEST MEADOW
Callahan State Park, Framingham (page 241)

BEST CONSERVATION LAND
Greenways Conservation Area, Wayland (page 261)

BEST ON-CAMPUS PARK
Lake Waban at Wellesley College, Wellesley (page 266)

BEST PLACE FOR FINE DINING
John Stone's Inn, Ashland (page 234)

BEST FRAPPES
Dairy Joy, Weston (page 269)

BEST HISTORICAL TOUR
Historic Concord Walking Tour, Concord (page 236)

Ashland, Concord, Framingham, Lincoln, Marlborough, Sherborn, South-borough, Sudbury, and Wayland. For details, see the Extended Hiking Trails section of the Resources.

Sudbury Valley Trustees: For more than 40 years, this land preservation association has acquired and protected land in the Concord River Basin. Currently it manages more than 80 properties covering more than 6,000 acres in the communities along the Assabet, Concord, and Sudbury Rivers. With the additional goals of education and recreation, the organization helps to promote the value and enjoyment of open spaces for everyone. To become a member, make a contribution, or obtain additional information, contact: Sudbury Valley Trustees, P.O. Box 7, Wayland, MA 01778; 978/443-6300; website: www.sudburyvalleytrustees.org.

The Trustees of Reservations: This preservation organization manages more than 75 parks and reservations on nearly 18,000 acres throughout the Commonwealth, including lands in this chapter. Dogs must be leashed on Trustees properties. For more information on the group, see the Resources section.

Acton

We tip our hats to the people of Acton for securing so many beautiful areas for the enjoyment of the public, canine as well as human. The leash laws are flexible: to run freely, your dog must obey voice commands, and as a courtesy, you should carry a leash to use in case other walkers are uncomfortable around untethered dogs.

PARKS, BEACHES, AND RECREATION AREAS

1 Arboretum Conservation Land

🐾🐾🐕🦴 (See Sudbury River Valley map on page 226)

The winding trails and pathways of the 53-acre arboretum allow you and your dog to stroll from garden to garden along stone walls, through a variety of woods, and over boardwalks and bridges that traverse streams and bogs. Best of all, if your dog is well behaved enough to obey your commands, she can go leash free and sniff out trees and flowers without dragging you everywhere. The rich, diverse environment attracts hikers and wildlife, so you will likely encounter butterflies, songbirds, squirrels, and a few creatures in Reebok sneakers as you walk.

Marvelous garden aromas that will set doggy noses to twitching fill the many looping trails, which provide an assortment of routes and distances to choose from. Each visit can be different, and you can tailor your walks to suit both your mood and your pooch's.

During the winter, the grounds are popular with cross-country skiers. Picnicking and bird-watching are the favorite summertime activities.

From Route 2, take Main Street/Route 27 north. Turn right on Taylor Road and continue to the arboretum. Parking is available. Open sunrise–sunset. 978/264-9631.

2 Grassy Pond Conservation Area

🐾🐾🐕 (See Sudbury River Valley map on page 226)

The Nagog Hill Conservation Area lies across from this 89-acre parcel of land, and the two are technically connected, although separated by Nagog Hill Road. You could visit both parks in one afternoon—if you don't mind crossing the road and ruining that good country feeling. The good news is that your furry companion can shed the leash at both parks as long as he is under voice control.

Three main trails lead to or around the park's centerpiece, Grassy Pond. The Willis Holden Trail (.6 mile each way) heads southwest through the woods. The Grassy Pond Trail, the most direct route, covers .7 mile. The Newtown Road Trail loops one mile around the perimeter of the water and can be accessed on the opposite side off Newtown Road. The good-sized pond is suitable for swimming, and ice-skating is allowed in the winter. (Do they make skates for dogs?) None of these walks will tire you out, but if you just want to go for a leisurely and quiet stroll with your pooch, give it a try.

From Route 2, take Main Street/Route 27 north. Turn left on Nagog Hill Road. The parking lot is on the left at the hilltop. Open sunrise–sunset. 978/264-9631.

🖪 Great Hill Recreation Area

😗😗🐾 (See Sudbury River Valley map on page 226)

Locals have made this a popular dog-walking spot, especially in the winter when the ball fields behind the fire department are not in use. But even when games are under way, there is room enough to bypass the action and get to the pond and the hiking trails of Great Hill.

Two main trails access the half-mile-square hill, which is covered with woods. A trail to the left runs west from the pond to Main Street. The trail to the right climbs the hill, offering possibilities of canine adventures in the deep woods. In all, the area covers 185 acres. Dogs that are under voice control may wander off leash throughout the park.

To get to the west parking lot from Route 2, take Main Street/Route 27 south. The parking lot is on the left at the Prospect Street intersection. To get to the south parking lot, continue south on Main Street. Turn left on School Street. Parking is available on the left behind the Acton Firehouse. Open sunrise–sunset. 978/264-9631.

🖪 Ice House Pond Conservation Area

😗😗🐾 (See Sudbury River Valley map on page 226)

Several trails in this woodland conservation area wind around Ice House Pond and along the outer walls of the Woodlawn Cemetery. Although the cemetery is off-limits to dogs, your dog is permitted to roam off leash along the edges of the good-sized pond, which has a perimeter of about two miles. The western trails are wider, cut through denser woods, and provide the best water access. The eastern side of the pond sits a little too close to Route 2A. Although you're protected from the road, a walk on this side won't be as relaxing because you can hear the passing cars. We suggest you park at the small lot off Concord Road and head to the western trails, where there are plenty of sticks, sand, water, and trees to keep most dogs happy.

Dogs under voice control don't have to wear leashes on these 60 acres, but their human companions should keep leashes handy as a courtesy to other walkers.

From Route 2, take Wetherbee Street north. Turn left onto Great Road/ Routes 2A and 119, and then make a quick left onto Concord Road. The pond and a small parking lot are just ahead on the right. Open sunrise–sunset. 978/264-9631.

🐾 Nagog Hill Conservation Area

🐾🐾🐾🐕 (See Sudbury River Valley map on page 226)

This is bird-watching territory, so be sure to bring binoculars if you want to observe herons, hawks, phoebes, cardinals, and numerous other species. Whether or not your furry friend is a bird dog, she can feel as free as a bird here, because as long as she obeys your commands, a leash is not required. Walk through a small woody area, and you'll come to a large grassy, swampy field. Then go through the gate across the field to enter the next section of hilly woodland. Conveniently raised walkways lead over the swampy areas, and the trail is well marked. As you approach the woods, one trail leads to the right and another leads to the left. The right option provides a short jaunt through the woods and back to the main road. Choose the left for a pleasant, peaceful woodland walk, with some slight inclines, to Nagog Pond a mile away. At the pond—really a reservoir, so no swimming is allowed—there is shore access for hiking and puddle jumping around the water's edge. In the winter, trails are excellent for cross-country skiing; in the spring, birds are plentiful. In all, the 158-acre park is a good place to spend an hour or an afternoon with your dog.

Parking for approximately 10 cars is available at the trailhead. Across Nagog Hill Road is Grassy Pond Conservation Area, another spot you may want to visit in the same afternoon.

From Route 2, take Main Street/Route 27 north. Turn left on Nagog Hill Road and proceed to the parking lot on the right. Open sunrise–sunset. 978/264-9631.

🐾 Nashoba Brook Conservation Area/
Spring Hill Conservation Area

🐾🐾🐾🐕 (See Sudbury River Valley map on page 226)

Nothing but a stone wall divides these twin conservation areas, which together offer lucky dogs more than 300 acres of leash-free romping territory. The wall is more of a demarcation point than a barrier, so easy movement between the two areas is possible.

Inu and George recommend that you start at the Nashoba Brook trailhead and hike for about 1.5 miles toward Spring Hill. Park at the Wheeler Road entrance; picnic tables are available there, and you can chart your course using the well-placed map at the trailhead. The Nashoba Brook Trail leads over Nashoba Brook and up the hill into the woods. The trails are clearly marked and will help you track your mileage (turn back before your pooch tuckers out). The western trail leads to the right along the brook to a large grassy area that's good for sledding in the winter and chasing Frisbees in the summer. To the left, the eastern trail leads to the Spring Hill area and eventually Red Swamp. The terrain is varied, providing inclines for a good workout, as well as flat, soft areas through pine forest. The trails are clear, perfect for cross-country skiing and snowshoeing in the winter months.

If you enter on the Spring Hill side, you will find another map to help you chart your course through the area. The Spring Hill Trail covers almost three miles as it traces a large circle through a young forest of cedar, birch, and pine trees and around Red Swamp. Well-placed walkways have been built around and over the mucky ground in the swamp, but it might be wise to avoid this area unless your dog will not wander from the trails and bridges. There is simply too much mud and mush that's begging to be wallowed in. Not that this isn't a wonderful spot—it is, after all, great for bird-watching—but if your dogs are like ours, they will appreciate the mud more than the birds. So for the sake of your clothing and car upholstery, you might want to stick to the shorter Spring Hill Trail. Follow this section for almost a mile to the Nashoba Brook connection trail, leading you to the brook and the picnic tables.

To reach the main trailheads of Nashoba Brook from Route 2, take Main Street/Route 27 north and cross Great Road/Route 2A. Turn right onto Wheeler Lane and continue to the entrance and a parking area at the road's end. To get to the main trailheads of Spring Hill from Route 2, take Wetherbee Street north. Turn left on Great Road/Routes 2A and 119, and then make a quick right on Pope Road. Head left on Spring Hill Road and park at the end of the cul-de-sac. Open sunrise–sunset. 978/264-9631.

PLACES TO EAT

Continental Cafe: This café/bakery has had many name changes over the years but still offers a hospitable stop before or after your hike. Grab a cup of coffee, fresh pastry, or a sandwich and beverage and take it outside to one of the benches in front to enjoy your refreshments in the afternoon sunshine. The café is located in the heart of town near the intersection of Massachusetts Avenue and Central Street. 5 Spruce Street; 978/263-2233.

Ashland

PARKS, BEACHES, AND RECREATION AREAS

7 Ashland State Park

🐾🐾 (See Sudbury River Valley map on page 226)

Dogs who desire little more than fresh air and scenic beauty will enjoy a trip to 47-acre Ashland State Park. Here the sparkling waters of Ashland Reservoir reflect the surrounding thick green pine trees. A single trail, carpeted in pine needles, follows the shoreline and crosses over the dam that created the reservoir. Alas, water dogs will get a tempting glimpse of the swimming area,

where they are not permitted. Dogs are required to be leashed at all times. Entrance costs $2 per carload.

From I-495 in Hopkinton, take Exit 21 and head east on West Main Street to East Main Street/Route 135. Continue into Ashland and to West Union Street. Turn right on State Park Road and proceed into the park. Parking is available. Open 9 A.M.–6 P.M. or as otherwise posted. 508/435-4303.

8 Ashland Town Forest/Cowassock Woods

🐾🐾 (See Sudbury River Valley map on page 226)

In the language of the Magunkook, *Cowassock* means "the place of pines," and tree-loving pooches will be thrilled to find that this spot lives up to its name: the combined forest—Ashland Town Forest and Cowassock Woods—is dotted with pines, as well as an assortment of other hardwoods. Six-plus miles of trails traverse the 575-acre parcel of land, and a walk through the hilly terrain will be an enjoyable venture for any leashed dog who wants to exercise his sniffer as well as his legs.

The Ashland Open Space Committee manages the Ashland Town Forest, and Cowassock Woods is the property of the Sudbury Valley Trustees. Each has its own main entrance with parking, but they share a number of the wide dirt trails. The southern trailhead in the town forest begins near the higher hills of the park. The trails break out into three directions: those to the right (with blue markers) ascend to the high point where the town's water tank is located. The red trail runs north to hook up with the paths of the Cowassock Woods. If you stay on the white trail (the main park route and part of the Bay Circuit Trail), you will pass through marshes, overgrown orchards, and old quarries. The trails from the northern trailhead in Cowassock Woods are lush and grassy before meeting up with the paths and woods of the forest.

On a hot day, you'll need to carry plenty of water for you and your pooch, because there's only a small brook to offer respite from the summer heat. Inu follows the same cooling-off routine no matter what the season. He strolls gracefully into a nearby pond or stream, stops and turns to face us, stretches out his front legs so that his belly just touches the crest of the water, and then plops down with a splash and a big, golden grin. George wades in up to his doggy elbows and looks plaintively at us, hoping we'll join him. (Well, maybe he just wants someone to throw the ball.)

To get to the southern entrance from the town center at Main Street and Union Street/Route 135, take Main Street north. Turn left on Pleasant Street and then right on Winter Street. You'll find Ashland Town Forest and parking on the left. To get to the northern entrance, take Main Street north and continue on Myrtle Street into Framingham and onto Badger Road. Turn left on Salem End Road. Cowassock Woods and its parking area are on the left. Open dawn–dusk. Ashland Town Forest, 508/881-0101; Cowassock Woods, 508/443-6300.

Hopkinton State Park

See the listing in the Hopkinton section of this chapter.

◘ Mill Pond Park

 (See Sudbury River Valley map on page 226)

The namesake pond is actually the section of the Sudbury River that swells up behind the Myrtle Street Dam, which was built in 1710. The trail that runs through this park and along this section of the river is known as the Riverwalk. Although the park is quite small and the trail is short, you and your leashed dog can enjoy a quick stroll and take in some sights on the river. The Riverwalk, which provides access to the river, is part of the Bay Circuit Trail, which runs for eight miles through Ashland from Sherborn to Southborough.

From the town center at Main Street and Union Street/Route 135, take Main Street north. Continue onto Myrtle Street and turn left onto Pine Hill Road. The park and parking are immediately ahead on the left. Open dawn–dusk. 508/881-0101.

PLACES TO EAT

John Stone's Inn: Known for its fine food, this 1832 inn is one of the fancier restaurants featured in this book. With old-style gas lamps and a romantic atmosphere, it's a bit too refined for Inu and George (especially after a day on the trail), although smaller pups might love it. Dogs are welcome on the enclosed patio, but if you want to dine with your pooch, she'll have to make an undignified entrance: while you can walk through the inn, dogs must crawl under the fence to reach the patio. The hassle is soon forgotten with the first bite of any of the delicious full-course meals, including traditional preparations of fish, meat, and poultry. 179 Main Street; 508/881-1778.

Boxborough

PARKS, BEACHES, AND RECREATION AREAS

🔟 Wolf Swamp Conservation Land

😼 (See Sudbury River Valley map on page 226)

Although determined dogs may very well want to challenge the idea, most of this 207-acre wetland is inaccessible. There is, however, a half-mile loop trail that allows you to venture into the heart of a wonderfully different environment that's abundant with wildlife and blueberries. The ground can get muddy, so keep an eye open for puddles while you are picking berries or watching a heron in flight. Dogs must be leashed.

From I-495, take Exit 28 to Massachusetts Avenue/Route 111 east. Take the first right onto Burroughs Road and proceed to the small parking lot on the right. Open sunrise–sunset. 978/543-1251.

Concord

The first skirmish between the British and the colonists took place in this famous New England town, which dates back to the late 1600s. The Old North Bridge, still standing, is the site of the "shot heard 'round the world" on April 19, 1775. You can visit many other historical points of interest, from Nathaniel Hawthorne's house to the home where Louisa May Alcott penned *Little Women*. You and your dog will enjoy strolling through this town, which has preserved its colonial charm. You'll even discover old stone markers on the trails of some of the many leash-free parks here.

PARKS, BEACHES, AND RECREATION AREAS

1️⃣1️⃣ Annursnac Conservation Land

😼😼🐕 (See Sudbury River Valley map on page 226)

At 118 acres, this is one of the larger conservation lands in Concord. Dogs who explore these woodlands will discover an unusual variety of flowering trees, meadows, pine forests, and wetlands. If your dog is obedient, she can run off leash. Unfortunately, the trails are popular with the horsey set, so the paths are a bit torn up. On busy summer weekends, you may have to vie for space on the trails with horses and their riders. But otherwise, you and your furry friend should find plenty of solitude.

For a pleasant 30- to 45-minute walk, begin at the Strawberry Hill entrance and follow the wide trail through the pine trees. After about a quarter mile, you'll reach a triangular area with trails that connect before splitting to the right and the left.

The left path leads along a very narrow, leafy woodland where flowering

DIVERSION

Historic Concord Walking Tour: Pick up a map at the North Bridge Visitor Center and treat yourself and your dog to a stroll through town and a lesson in American history. Sites along the way include the Old Manse (Nathaniel Hawthorne's home), the Ralph Waldo Emerson House, the Main Street Burial Ground, the Orchard House (Louisa May Alcott's home), and countless sites from the Revolutionary War. Dogs aren't allowed to participate in any of the museum tours, but you're free to leave your pooch outside while you enter any of the houses. (The houses are small, so she won't be waiting long.) For information, call 978/369-3120.

pears and dogwoods are interspersed with pine trees. The trail follows the outer edge of the wetland and does get a bit muddy in places. Eventually you'll enter a shady pine forest with a few easy-flowing streams before ending at a meadow on Annursnac Hill, more of a gentle incline than a true hill.

To walk through the middle of the wetland, take the trail to the right. It's a wet one, but logs have been placed over the more swampy spots. Here, you are in a traditional pine forest, which ends in a large open meadow that crosses the border into Acton. The meadow is part of the Stoneymeade Conservation Area; you'll find entry to that park easier from here than through the residential area off Stoneymeade Way.

From the traffic circle at the intersection of Barretts Hill Road, the Union Turnpike/Route 2, and Elm Street/Routes 2A and 119, take Barretts Hill Road north. Turn left on College Road and then left on Strawberry Hill Road. The park is on the left; parking is available. Open from a half hour before sunrise to a half hour after sunset. 978/371-6265.

12 Cousins Park

 (See Sudbury River Valley map on page 226)

The Assabet River runs along this little park, which George and Inu recommended we include, not because it's an ideal spot for a dog walk, but because it provides access to the great running river. You can hike beside the water should your dog need a quick dip on a hot summer's day. Head down the hill to find a short trail that leads about a quarter mile along the river. In all, it's a quiet and refreshing walk and will probably leave your pooch wishing there were more trails to explore. A bonus is that leashes are not required—if your dog obeys voice commands.

From the intersection of the Concord Turnpike/Route 2 and Main Street/Route 62, take Main Street east. Turn left on Prairie Street. The park is on the right; parking is available. Open sunrise–sunset. 508/371-6265.

13 Estabrook Woods/Punkatasset Conservation Land

🐾🐾🐾🐾 🦴 🎾 (See Sudbury River Valley map on page 226)

Has your furry ruffian been ruffhousing it too much lately? Is it time to hit some trails guaranteed to wear her out? If so, the ponds, pastures, paths, and other offerings of this popular 800-acre spot may be just the thing for your pup. Dogs are permitted to explore these woods leash free, and you will have one happy, exhausted hiking companion on your hands at the day's end. Enter from Monument Street, and you're in the Punkatasset Conservation Land section, managed by the Natural Resource Commission in Concord. Once you leave the pond area, you're in the vast Estabrook Woods, which is overseen by Harvard University.

The Native Americans who once lived in this area were the source of the name *Punkatasset,* which means broad-topped hill, and yes, there is one. The hill is among the highest vantage points in Concord and affords an excellent view of the surrounding countryside. Follow the trail to your left toward the pond. Off this main path are other wide-ranging trails that take you through some fine timbers and open areas in the unpopulated eastern section of Concord. These trails merge into the trails of Estabrook Woods.

It shouldn't take your dog long to find Hutchins Pond, especially on a summer day. This great spot—one of the best pooch-friendly swimming holes featured in this book—will cool off both of you in hot weather. If you veer right at the trailhead, you'll soon come upon a wide beach area that's ideal for doggies who yearn to dive into the water. The last time we were there, Inu and George were so enthralled by their refreshing dip that we couldn't get them back on dry land. Continue past the pond to the old apple orchard, and you will eventually hook up with Two Rod Road, which leads through the northern part of the adjoining Estabrook Woods into Carlisle. This road is defined by a pair of stone walls that are two rods, or 33 feet, apart.

We like to take the other northern route, which follows the western side of Hutchins Pond up to Mink Pond—an even bigger swimming hole although quite muddy and covered with lily pads. Explorer dogs can access a maze of countless trails from here. Veer to the right, and you'll end up on an old carriage road that originally ran from the Old North Bridge in Concord to Chelmsford Center. (The stone markers that once showed travelers the progress of their mileage are still visible.) If you choose to devote your entire hike to this route, you can enter at the end of Estabrook Road on the dirt road that passes through two private properties. Follow this road north about 2.5 miles to Bateman Pond.

Veer to your left, and you'll pass through a beautiful old forest detailed by streams, marshes, and glacial boulders. It is difficult for us to tell you exactly which trail to take here because none are marked. However, all are marvelous. This is one of the best-loved and most-trodden recreational hiking areas in the Boston area, and you will meet up with many dogs, hikers, mountain bikers,

DIVERSION

All paws on deck: Canoeing the beautiful Sudbury River is more enjoyable when your favorite first mate comes along to keep you company. (No chewing the paddles!) Take a leisurely paddle along the slow-moving river and get a different view of Concord and the shoreline. When you move into the quiet coves, you may see a heron or even a muskrat sunning itself in the shallows. Canoes can be rented by the hour or the day from South Bridge Boathouse, 496 Main Street; 978/369-9438.

and other folk. It is also one of the hardest places to find unless you know where you're going. There are no signs, markers, or trail maps to guide you. Luckily, once you're here, even though there will always be others enjoying the spectacular park with you, you'll find there's enough space to get away from the crowds.

Nonbloodhounds take note: it's easy to lose your way around here. Be aware of where you are and how to return to your starting point. There is so much open forest that you can easily spend four or five hours here without retracing your steps.

From the Concord town square, take Monument Street north until you pass the Old North Bridge. The park is on the left, about three-quarters of a mile past the Concord River. Park in one of the small turnouts along Monument Street. Open sunrise–sunset. 978/371-6265.

14 Great Meadows National Wildlife Refuge/Dike Trail

🐾🐾 (See Sudbury River Valley map on page 226)

Teeming with wildlife and scenic beauty, this area of marshes and meadows along the Concord River is a natural wonder that most nature lovers (including pooches) will appreciate. The National Wildlife Refuge protects more than 3,000 acres of wetlands, much of it accessible via some delightful hiking trails. The most astonishing route is the Dike Trail. It starts from the main entrance by the observation tower, then crosses the quarter-mile-long dike that splits the Great Meadow in two. From your vantage point in the middle of the meadow, the trail offers wonderful, wide-open views in all directions. Ducks, geese, herons, trumpeter swans, hawks, and other animals and plants abound, and lucky dogs will get a chance to experience nature close-up.

On the other side of the Great Meadow, the Dike Trail connects with the Edge Trail, an east-west route on the thin stretch of land between the Great Meadow and the Concord River. If you take it to your left, the path continues for over a mile to the Minute Man National Historical Park and the Old North Bridge. To the right, the trail borders the river for half a mile and then loops around the eastern half of the Great Meadow, eventually connecting with an abandoned railroad-bed trail that takes you back to the main entrance.

Dogs must be leashed, and everyone must remain on designated trails. Great Meadows is a fragile environment; it's home to hundreds of migrating and nesting birds and other wildlife, including muskrats and beavers. The simple bark of a dog can disturb a nest or an entire flock.

From Route 2, take the Concord Turnpike cutoff/Route 2A east. Turn left on Lexington Road, right on Old Bedford Road, left on Bedford Road/Route 62, and then right on Monsen Road. The park entrance is on the left. The parking lot is open April–Thanksgiving; during the winter, park on Monsen Road. Open 8 A.M.–4 P.M. on weekdays, 10 A.M.–5 P.M. on weekends. 617/443-4661.

15 Hapgood Wright Town Forest

🐾🐾🐾🦮 (See Sudbury River Valley map on page 226)

In a startling new discovery, *The Dog Lover's Companion to Boston* announces that Henry David Thoreau's cabin was not on the shores of Walden Pond. The writer actually spent two years in solitude at nearby Fairyland Pond, located in what is known today as Hapgood Wright Town Forest. Thoreau feared that his paradise would be overrun with visitors and subject to too many leash laws once his book *Fairyland* was published. His agent worried that the book's title might not have enough punch, so at the last minute he replaced all references to Fairyland Pond with Walden Pond.

The plan worked. Today, Walden Pond gets the crowds, and dogs have been banned from the pond and the surrounding Walden Woods. Yet half a mile away, in peace and solitude, fortunate dogs and nature lovers can enjoy the beauty and serenity of Fairyland Pond and the town forest that inspired Thoreau to write *Fairyland,* ah, *Walden.*

Leg pulling aside, a forest of majestic pines shelters Fairyland Pond, which is just large enough for a hot dog to take a refreshing dip on a summer day. In any season the hilly terrain is ideal for a short hike. Trails encircle the pond and crisscross the woods in various directions, and a few well-placed benches are situated along the way for pooches to sit a spell with their owners and contemplate the joys of few crowds and a leash-free walk.

From Route 2 at the intersection with Route 126, take Walden Street north. The park is on the right, across from the Concord-Carlisle High School. A paved parking lot is provided. Open from a half hour before sunrise to a half hour after sunset. 978/371-6265.

16 Minute Man National Historical Park, North Bridge Section

🐾🐾🦮 (See Sudbury River Valley map on page 226)

You and your dog can reenact the "shot heard 'round the world" (the first time colonists fired upon British forces) and the historic confrontation on the North Bridge. Take a self-guided tour in which you'll learn all about the battle or just stroll the grounds of the park along this scenic stretch of the Concord River. Dogs must be leashed, which might curb their firing power but not their fun. For information on the Battle Road Section, see the listing in the Lexington section of the West of the Hub chapter.

From Route 2, take Walden Street north to the town center. Turn right on Main Street. Loop around the town square and take Monument Street north. The park is on the left, and a parking area is on the right. Open 8 A.M.– sundown. 978/369-6993.

🞄🞄 Old Rifle Range Conservation Land

😺 😺 🐕 (See Sudbury River Valley map on page 226)

During World War I, the army trained troops on a rifle range that sat on the same land that currently encompasses this out-of-the-way park. Gun-shy doggies will be pleased to know that any traces of this activity are long gone. Instead, this 122-acre park is now a peaceful and quiet spot for a morning walk.

The single trail starts at Williams Street and leads about a mile through a pine forest. It is somewhat steep in spots, so you and your leash-free dog will get a bit of a workout. Your walk will also take you past Ministerial Swamp. Keep your dog out of the muck there; it is quite rich in nutrients and the black mire will stick to him like an extra coat.

On our last trip to Old Rifle Range, we made the mistake of not giving the dogs a drink of water before hitting the trail. We like to make sure their thirst is quenched beforehand so they're not tempted to lap up unsightly or undrinkable water (their favorite, by the way). This time caution was thrown to the wind, however, and we were immediately sorry. Both dogs kept edging toward the swamp and would return reluctantly each time we called. We were hoping to keep them out of the mud until we got to the fresh pond at the end of the trail. No matter how many times we told them they would drink soon, they didn't believe us. Finally, Inu could wait no longer. He plunged into the black gunk like a pig in mud and came out covered in the filth. We stopped to let him pass, but just as he was about to go by, he decided to share his experience with us, halting midstep and shaking himself on JoAnna.

Needless to say, she looked like something out of the B version of the *Creature from the Black Lagoon*. Mud was dripping from her face, hair, clothes, you name it. Life with a dog is never dull—or for the fastidious. So here's to mud in yer eye! And hair and clothes and ....

If your dog does venture into the muck, the good news is that you can wash him off at the end of the trail. You'll cross a dirt road, Old Mill Road, and pick up the trail across the way. Almost immediately you'll head down a short hill and come upon a lovely little lake. The trail leads partway around the lake on both the left and the right. Go to the left and you'll dead-end at private property. Go to the right for better water access and to scrub down a muck-covered dog. The water is murky at the edges but is cleaner deeper down, so if your hound is the wash-and-wear type (as ours are), go ahead and take the plunge.

From the intersection of the Concord Turnpike/Route 2 and Main Street/ Route 62, take the Concord Turnpike east. Turn right on Old Road to Nine Acre Corner and make a right on Old Marlboro Road. The park is on the right, and you can park on the shoulder. Open a half hour before sunrise to a half hour after sunset. 978/371-6265.

PLACES TO EAT

Back Alley Café: This cute shop makes a good stop for sandwiches on six-grain bread, salads topped with sprouts, finger pastries, and gourmet coffee. If your dog doesn't mind waiting outside, you can sit at one of the tiny tables with the cool coffee-crowd scenesters. But if your furry friend is all the company you need, there's a wobbly bench outside, just right for relaxing on a sunny day. 12 Walden Street; 978/369-6636.

Sally Ann Food Shop: All sorts of hidden delights await at this gourmet food shop. If you crave it, they've probably got it: fresh breads, muffins, sweets .... There are no outdoor tables, but it's a great place to pick up something tasty to eat on the trail—or, most likely, on the way to the trail. Before you head out to Estabrook Woods or Fairyland Pond, we suggest stopping here for a loaf of fresh bread, some juice or gourmet coffee, and the famous fruit salad. 73 Main Street; 978/369-4558.

PLACES TO STAY

Best Western Concord: Well-behaved canines are allowed to stay with their well-behaved owners. The inn is conveniently located near the historic sites in Concord, not to mention the many great parks. There is a pet fee of $10 per night. Rooms are around $109–124. 740 Elm Street, Concord, MA 01742; 978/369-6100; website: www.bestwestern.com.

Framingham

PARKS, BEACHES, AND RECREATION AREAS

18 Callahan State Park, South Section

🐾🐾🐾🐾 ◀ (See Sudbury River Valley map on page 226)

If your dog has never set paw in this beautiful state park, she's in for a major treat. George and Inu think these 423 acres are among the loveliest of the pooch-friendly parks in the Boston area. When you drive up to the parking area off Millwood Street, you'll be greeted by an expansive, scenic meadow. Spreading out across several acres, it is divided only by long trails that lead into the woods beyond.

Set off across the meadow, and you'll soon reach two clean brooks that cut through the property. Just past the second brook, you'll encounter another meadow and, nestled there like a jewel, Eagle Pond, which looks more like an alpine pond than the typical New England swimming hole. Several small beaches provide easy access, and a large rock that your dog will enjoy wading to and playing on sits in the middle  of the water. The pond usually gets a lot of visitors on the weekends, but even though the water is perfectly clean, not many humans swim in it.

Continue into the woods for a long hike, about a mile or two depending on your doggy's energy and fitness level. Head up to the western end of the pond, and you'll eventually reach the Packard Trail, which leads into the neighboring Welch Reservation and to Packard Pond. This pathway can get a bit muddy and sludgy in spots, so bring a pair of sturdy boots. If you head back through the center of the meadow, you'll be on either the Juniper Trail or the Deer Run Trail. Both take you through the pine forest, where the other major trails intersect. All the passages are very clearly marked at most intersections.

The Red Tail Trail and Rocky Road (they're one and the same, but when you're headed north, the signs say Red Tail, and when you're headed south, the signs say Rocky Road) lead along a beautiful private meadow. Continue on the Red Tail Trail and you'll cross Edmands Road into the park's northern section (see the listing in the Marlborough section of this chapter). We think the southern portion is the most scenic and spectacular, but you'll enjoy visiting both to vary the dog-walking routine. The Bay Circuit Trail runs through Callahan State Park and Welch Reservation, and you can access it off the Pioneer Trail near Edmands Road.

Equestrians use the trails, so some sections are muddy and torn up. Makeshift trails lead around the offending terrain in most of these spots, but undainty dogs may not be inclined to use them. You'll meet up with a lot of potential canine pals as you hike, but the park is so big you'll feel that you have enough room to yourselves. As in all state parks, dogs are required to wear their leashes.

From Worcester Road/Route 9, take Pleasant Street/Route 30 west. Turn right on Belknap Road and then left on Millwood Street. The park and a parking area are on the left. Open a half hour before sunrise to a half hour after sunset. 508/653-9641.

🔟 Farm Pond Park

🐾🐾 (See Sudbury River Valley map on page 226)

You always knew your dog was worthy of sainthood, and here she can walk on water—with the assistance of a land dam that splits Farm Pond, that is.

This 43-acre park runs along the western edge of the pond, which is managed by the Metropolitan District Commission. There is a small wooded area next to Dudley Road, but when you and your leashed dog emerge from the trees, you can walk on a dry, flat, grassy area along the pond. She will probably love swimming here, and you'll love not having to haul her out of muddy water for a change. You can walk across the pond to the far southern side on the land bridge. It's wide and flat, so there's no danger of falling in, and you'll get a great view of the pond and the shoreline.

From one end to the other, the walk covers about 1.5 miles. The grassy area by the road gets busy with picnickers on weekends. But there's not much of a beach area at the pond, so for once you'll actually have a great place to go to beat the heat *and* the crowds in the summer. Maybe you'll be walking on water, after all.

From Waverley Street/Route 135, take Fountain Street west. Head right on Dudley Road. The park and a parking area are on the right. Open 8 A.M.–8 P.M. 508/620-4834.

20 Welch Reservation

🐾🐾🐾🐕 (See Sudbury River Valley map on page 226)

The main pathway through this 300-acre conservation area, owned by the Sudbury Valley Trustees, will take you along a private meadow and through a bucolic woodland of pine and oak. Follow it for 1.5 miles—a quiet and isolated walk—and you'll arrive at Packard Pond. The path around the pond can get a bit swampy, but the water is clean and clear, ideal for dogs who like to splash around.

The trail leading north from the pond hooks up with Callahan State Park's Pipeline Trail. So called because it follows a hidden water pipeline, it isn't the most scenic route, but it clearly delineates the boundary between the two parks. Other trails that intersect with the main trail will also take you into Callahan State Park (see the north and south sections of Callahan State Park in the Framingham and Marlborough sections of this chapter), if your unleashed dog has the energy to continue exploring. The full loop to the pond and back covers approximately 2.5 miles and provides a thoroughly enjoyable walk.

You can enter from either Callahan State Park or the main entrance off Edmands Road. From Worcester Road/Route 9, take Pleasant Street/Route 30 west. Turn right on Belknap Road. Turn left on Grove Street, then left again on Edmands Road. Watch for the tiny driveway across from Barnbridge Farm; there is space for about three cars down the driveway. The park is on the left, just past Nixon Road. Open dawn–dusk. 508/443-6300.

PLACES TO STAY

Motel 6: All Motel 6s permit one small pooch per room. Rates for a double room are $65. 1668 Worcester Road, Framingham, MA 01701; 508/620-0500; website: www.motel6.com.

Red Roof Inn: Dogs who weigh under 50 pounds are allowed to stay in this clean, fairly new motel with good-sized rooms. The Massachusetts Turnpike is far enough away that the traffic noise shouldn't disturb you. Rates are about $72–109. 650 Cochituate Road, Framingham, MA 01701; 508/872-4499 or 800/ THE-ROOF (800/843 7663); website: www.redroof.com.

Holliston

PARKS, BEACHES, AND RECREATION AREAS

🐾 Brentwood Conservation Land

🐾 (See Sudbury River Valley map on page 226)

Dogs and hikers alike would love these 400 acres if only it had more of the right stuff or, we should say, less of the wrong stuff. There's plenty of trails, woods, and water, but right next door is the town's recycling depot and landfill.

From the parking area, you quickly pass through some abandoned gravel pits before continuing to the right into the woods and then out into an open field. The trail runs right between a pair of frog ponds in the field. George and Inu always enjoy stopping here, but instead of frolicking they stand with raised ears and tilted heads, trying to get a better idea of just what's jumping around in the grass and making those croaking sounds. Even when we follow the trail back into the woods, they keep a watchful eye on the ribbiting reeds.

This is where the main trail system starts, and the footing can be very soggy. The trail follows the southeast edge of a swamp until it splits into two routes. The path to the right proceeds for a short distance into some hardwood forests. Turn to the left, and you'll continue around the eastern side of the swamp to a small pine forest. As you emerge from the pine trees, a huge, stunning grassy meadow slopes upward before you. Then, just as you think the struggle through the swamp was worth the effort, you see the recycling bins and landfill. You might begin to wonder just what is leaching down into the swamp. By now, your boots are glowing and your dog has grown a fifth leg.

Dogs must be leashed on this property.

From the intersection of Washington Street/Route 16 and Summer Street/ Route 126, take Washington Street west to Courtland Street and make a right. Turn right on Marshall Street, then right on Gorwin Drive. The park and parking are on the left. Open dawn–dusk. 508/491-0601.

Hopkinton

PARKS, BEACHES, AND RECREATION AREAS

🐾🐾🐾 Hopkinton State Park

🐾🐾🐾 (See Sudbury River Valley map on page 226)

The average dog could get a good workout on the trails in this 1,450-acre park. But for some dogs—at least those who have an inexhaustible supply of energy—these trails are not enough. If that's the case with your canine, you'll want to head here on Patriot's Day for the annual Boston Marathon, which covers 26.2 miles from Hopkinton to Boston. (Actually, in order to qualify you must run on two legs and wear elasticized shorts, so maybe this isn't such a good idea.)

For normal dogs, the paths within the confines of the park and around Hopkinton Reservoir are just fine. Pick up a trail map at the main entrance or at park headquarters.

The northern or main portion of the state park is in Ashland. It's a busy place on any given summer weekend, but there is always room on the intertwining trail system for you and your leashed dog. The trails are short, but they are accessible from all the parking areas.

Longer trails are found in the southern, less-used portion of the park, located in Hopkinton. From park headquarters, you can take the Duck Pond Trail out to Duck Pond. This route can be a bit trashy behind the headquarters, but it soon becomes a pleasant cart path that runs for a mile through the woods and streams out to the pond.

Off Duck Pond Trail at the big trail intersection is the Indian Brook Trail, which connects to the northern part of the park. You can use this route to go all the way to the main area of the park or, better yet, loop back on the Glebe Trail around the southern tail of Hopkinton Reservoir and back to the park headquarters. And if that still isn't enough, there is always the Boston Marathon.

From I-495, take Exit 21 to West Main Street heading east. Turn left on Cedar Street/Route 85 north. The southern part of the park, park headquarters, and parking are on the left. Continue north on Cedar Street to get to the northern portion of the park and the main entrance, which is on the right. Open 8 A.M.–9 P.M. unless otherwise posted. 508/435-4303.

🐾 Ice House Pond Recreation Area

🐾 (See Sudbury River Valley map on page 226)

A peaceful retreat, Ice House Pond is located just off busy Main Street. The crushed-gravel path around the half-mile perimeter is fine for a quick stroll with your leashed pooch. Swimming is not permitted, but a dog with itchy feet will find other things to keep him interested: the resident marsh birds, including great blue herons, and a small wooded area to sniff out at the north end.

From I-495, take Exit 21 to West Main Street east. The pond and parking are on the left. Open dawn–dusk. 508/497-9755.

24 Whitehall State Park

😊😊 (See Sudbury River Valley map on page 226)

At 909 acres, Whitehall State Park is big. But don't start straining at the leash, because 800 of those acres are off-limits to dogs. You see, the bulk of the park is covered by Whitehall Reservoir, and swimming is not permitted. The remaining 100-plus acres form a thin strip of scenic, wooded land around the reservoir. A trail follows much of the shoreline, and your pooch is allowed to explore it (leashed, of course, as in all state parks). If you can put up with a pouting pup staring longingly at the water, then this place is worth a visit.

From I-495, take Exit 21 to West Main Street east. Turn left (west) on Wood Street/Route 135. The park and a parking lot are located on the left. Open from a half hour before sunrise to 8 P.M. 508/435-4303.

PLACES TO EAT

Golden Spoon: Lumberjacks, truckers, railroad workers, and dog walkers have one thing in common: they all need a big, hearty breakfast before they can get out and do the job. Sit at the picnic table outside with your pal Joe and enjoy a cup of joe, flapjacks, and taters. There's no need to ask for extra butter. Don't forget your flannel shirt. 85 West Main Street; 508/435-6922.

Hudson

PARKS, BEACHES, AND RECREATION AREAS

25 Sudbury State Forest

😊😊 (See Sudbury River Valley map on page 226)

The most energetic of dogs will find enough trails here to satisfy their exercise needs. The paths don't really lead anywhere, but if you think the process of get-

ting somewhere is more important than the destination itself (as many dogs do), then you'll like this forest. There's no formal entrance or trailhead; just park at any turnout along White Pond Road, and you can access well-groomed trails into an old pine forest. Much of the woodland hasn't been logged in a century, and the foliage is dense and shady. Most routes within the park loop around to their starting point, so you won't have trouble finding your way back. Leash your dog.

From the town center at the intersection of Main Street/Route 62 and Washington Street/Route 85, take Main Street east. Turn right on White Pond Road. The park and roadside pullouts are on the right. Open from a half hour before sunrise to a half hour after sunset. 978/435-4303.

26 Wood Park

 (See Sudbury River Valley map on page 226)

If your Fido is a resident of Hudson, she probably frequents this quaint local park on a regular basis. The park has large grassy areas to romp in on both sides of the Concord River and wooded areas with trails. An arched bridge joins the park with the grass on the other side, where several additional trails await whiskered wanderers. We're not talking about long walks and worn-out dogs, but you will be able to stretch your legs in a beautiful setting. Dogs must be leashed.

From the town center at the intersection of Main Street/Route 62 and Washington Street/Route 85, take Washington Street south. Turn right on Brigham Park Road. The park and a parking area are on the right. Open dawn–dusk. 978/568-9642.

PLACES TO EAT

Dairy Joy: Formerly P. C. Creams, this roadside eatery (and a sister to the Dairy Joy in Weston) has a menu that's so extensive you'll probably give up perusing it and choose a meal before you can finish reading. The same goes for the selection of ice-cream flavors. But no matter what you decide on, you won't be disappointed. There are picnic tables outside where you and your dog can have your scoop and eat it, too. 418 Main Street; 978/568-1775.

Lincoln

Lincoln's civic leaders are lax on leashes. If your dog is obedient enough to follow your voice commands at all times, he can shed the dreaded leash. Otherwise you must tether up when you go for walks in this town.

PARKS, BEACHES, AND RECREATION AREAS

27 Mount Misery Conservation Land

(See Sudbury River Valley map on page 226)

Misery loves company, and you'll get both of those when you visit this park. Mount Misery is the most popular dog-walking spot in Lincoln. Fortunately,

DOG-EAR YOUR CALENDAR—JUNE

Art in the Park Festival: Set on 35 acres that were once part of the DeCordova family estate, the unusual DeCordova Museum celebrates contemporary Massachusetts artists. During its annual outdoor art show, which is held the first Sunday in June, you can stroll around the sculpture garden on the beautiful grassy lawn and check out the many booths selling crafts and international foods. Your well-behaved dog is welcome to join you at the festival, on what is typically a lovely day. There are musicians, magicians, and interactive art stations. The festivities run from 11 A.M.–5 P.M. Entrance to the museum is usually free, but there is a small admission fee for the festival. 51 Sandy Pond Road; 781/259-8355.

you'll only feel miserable trying to figure out why they gave this place such an inappropriate name. It's as scenic as nearby Walden Woods, but unlike at that bucolic haven, dogs are allowed here. Because of this, the trails tend to get crowded on sunny weekend afternoons, a growing concern to the Lincoln Conservation Commission and many hikers.

Luckily the landscape is punctuated with hills and valleys that make it possible to simply disappear over the next ridge. Numerous trails crisscross the wooded terrain, and it's easy to switch from one path to the next. This is especially important if your leash-free dog gets excitable around mountain bikers, horses, or cross-country skiers.

On the other hand, if your Labrador is a social butterfly who loves going on group hikes and exchanging tail wags with passing canines, opportunities abound to meet other trail hounds. George and Inu like to mix it up. First they explore on their own around Beaver Dam Brook, and then they travel down the trail to report their findings to any dog who will listen.

The Mount Misery area covers 227 acres of conservation land, consisting mostly of pine forest. Atop Mount Misery itself and from some of the higher ridges, you can look down on the Sudbury River, Fairhaven Bay, and the Great Meadows National Wildlife Refuge (see below and in the Concord section of this chapter). From here there are a number of minor connecting trails to other conservation areas in Lincoln, including Sandy Pond. Dogs must be under voice control at all times.

From Route 2 in Concord, head south on Walden Street/Route 126, which becomes Lincoln-Concord Road. Turn right on South Great Road/Route 117. The park is on the right. There are three parking lots. The first is the main lot, where most of the trails start. The other two, located on the western border of the park along the Sudbury River, also have trailheads and access to the canoe launch. Open sunrise–sunset. 781/259-2612.

28 Sandy Pond Conservation Land

🐾🐾🐈 (See Sudbury River Valley map on page 226)

Sometimes referred to as Flint's Pond, Sandy Pond is off-limits to all in order to protect the public water supply. Still, the surrounding forest offers opportunities to hike and get some fresh air. Trails lead about three-quarters of the way around the pond. You can't make a loop, but the trails and woods are scenic enough that your dog will certainly delight in retracing her pawprints. And delight she will when she learns leashes are not required for dogs who obey voice commands. (Don't let your canine companion stray too far; the fine for swimming in the pond is $100.)

We recommend you take this route: From the trailhead, trot around the north side of Sandy Pond, where the woods open up and there are a number of small looping paths.

From the town center at the intersection of Bedford, Lincoln, Sandy Pond, Trapelo, and Weston Roads, take Sandy Pond Road west for 1.5 miles. A small pullout on the right is available for parking. The trailhead is the fire road into the woods. To explore more of Lincoln's woods, try the Pine Hill section to the west of Sandy Pond Road. The trailhead is 30 yards north of the Sandy Pond pullout. Open sunrise–sunset. 781/259-2612.

Marlborough

PARKS, BEACHES, AND RECREATION AREAS

29 Callahan State Park, North Section

🐾🐾🐾 (See Sudbury River Valley map on page 226)

Although not as scenic as its southern counterpart in Framingham, this 369-acre portion of the park is still worth checking out. The best parts are the trails around pretty Beebe Pond, which is accessible via two roads.

There's a high road that heads north from the main parking area and follows the Backpacker Trail. On this meandering 1.5-mile trek to the pond, you'll walk north through a pine forest. You can loop around the pond and head back on the shorter Pine Tree Trail or follow the Backpacker Trail into Callahan's southern section. Here you can hike up Gibb Mountain, the highest point in the park at 480 feet.

Take the low road and park on the shoulder off Parmenter Road just west of Pine Hill Road. Two trails lead from either turnout to the pond, about a quarter-mile walk. On those hot summer days when you just can't bear the thought of subjecting your leashed pooch to the long, dusty trail, take the short route and hit the water pronto. Once there, you can take the pleasant loop around the pond before heading back to your car. In all, this hike takes 30–40 minutes.

From Boston Post Road/Route 20, take Farm Road south. Turn left on Broadmeadow Street. The park and a parking lot are on the left. Parking is also available on pullouts off Parmenter Road. Open from a half hour before sunrise to a half hour after sunset. 508/653-9641.

⅏ Ghiloni Park, Concord Recreation Area/ Marlborough State Forest

🐾🐾🐾 (See Sudbury River Valley map on page 226)

To show your nature-loving companion a prime example of a planned recreation area that preserves the natural resources of the surrounding area, head to this beautiful park. The recreation area offers plenty of parking, restrooms, a ball field, and the spacious, open Ghiloni Park, around which are breathtaking woods and well-manicured, paved trails. You and your leashed friend can wander through the woods, play Frisbee on the grass, and explore everywhere except the ball field. To escape the activity, head across the access road into Marlborough State Forest. Although more rustic, these trails are equally pleasing to the eye, taking happy pooches through quiet woods with small gurgling streams. All in all, the park is a doggy delight and earns the town of Marlborough a tail-wagging salute for designing a big city park with all the amenities, yet preserving the innate beauty of the forest for those who desire a more natural retreat.

From I-495, take Exit 24 to Route 20 east. Go left on Concord Road. The park and parking are on the left. Open 7 A.M.–10 P.M. 508/624-6925.

Natick

PARKS, BEACHES, AND RECREATION AREAS

⅏ Cochituate State Park

🐾🐾 (See Sudbury River Valley map on page 226)

George and Inu love few things more than a trip to the swimming hole here— that is, when we can get our act together and time it just right. The best feature of the park is the big, clean lake. What's not so great is that your pooch won't be permitted on the beach on crowded summer weekends—and there aren't many trails to keep you otherwise occupied. So if you can visit on warm spring and fall days during the week, you should have one satisfied dog.

Landlubber dogs will find a few trails leading through a pine forest on the hill behind the picnic area. They don't wind up anywhere in particular; in fact, they dead-end at the railroad tracks about a quarter mile from the lake. There are some short, narrow pathways around the eastern parking lot that offer water access. Watch out for trout anglers, who frown upon dogs who gallop through their fishing lines. That shouldn't be a problem, because dogs are supposed to be leashed.

From the Massachusetts Turnpike/I-90, take Exit 13 to Commonwealth Road/Route 30 east. The park and a parking lot are on the right. Open 9 A.M.–8 P.M. 508/653-9641.

Sherborn

Fortunately for dogs, Sherborn has a flexible leash law: You may walk your dog unleashed in all parks and recreation areas if she is under voice control. Otherwise she must wear a leash. We think this is mighty civilized and generous, and our dogs have solemnly promised to behave here.

PARKS, BEACHES, AND RECREATION AREAS

32 Barber Reservation

🐾🐾🐾🐕 (See Sudbury River Valley map on page 226)

Your Yorkshire terrier may think of the English countryside when he lays eyes on this gentle 189-acre reservation. Beautiful meadows are surrounded by fruit trees and old stone walls. Once used for farming, the land is now a well-maintained open space that the public can enjoy. Your pup will love shedding his leash and kicking up his paws in the meadow grasses, while you might be drawn to the cooling shade of the nearby woods.

Start at the trail to the right of the parking area. Immediately you enter a shady glen of trees. Walk between the stone walls to find three spacious meadows, accessible through various openings in the walls. It is an intriguing venture: Each meadow is divided by the walls as well as foliage. You actually have to walk down a path to enter the open area; if you're not looking, you'll walk right past them.

The first meadow you'll encounter is also the best, located about a quarter mile down the trail. It's all a dog lover could ask for: open, scenic, and fairly dry. The others, although appealing, can be a little wet, especially in the spring.

The trail passes through the last meadow after about a half mile, then passes under some power lines. This isn't the most attractive leg of the journey, but keep going and you'll soon be rewarded; you'll enter more woods and wind up at a small pond where your dog can get soaked on a hot day.

For a shorter walk, head across the first field and explore the smaller woods on the far southern (left) side of the property. You'll avoid the power lines, and your dog will get to scamper through light woods and leafy trees.

You'll occasionally have to share the trails with people on horseback. Jumps have been set up for the horses, but there is plenty of space for everyone to coexist.

From the town center at the intersection of Routes 16 and 27, take Washington Street/Route 16 west. Turn right on Western Avenue. The park and parking are on the left. Open dawn–dusk. 508/921-1944.

33 Rocky Narrows Reservation
🐾🐾🐾 (See Sudbury River Valley map on page 226)
Boston may be only half an hour away by car, but this unique plot of land feels much more isolated than it is. Although the 157-acre reservation is accessible only by canoe, trails reach up and over the Charles River, providing a steep path down to the river and a great vantage point for watching the waters slide by. From the Forest Street entrance, take the pathway across the meadow on your left and follow it through the hemlock and pine forest for almost a mile until you reach the vista point overlooking the Charles River. There is actually a pretty steep drop here, suitable only for agile dogs. You can scramble down to the banks on a very narrow path if you choose, or enjoy the views from above. The trails wind about above the river, and the terrain is quite pretty: gently rolling open fields surrounded by pine, oak, and hemlock.

If you take the trail to the right, through the grove of fruit trees, you will end up in Sherborn Town Forest. Eventually, this trail leads to the river; if your little companion is game, you might try to do the entire loop of approximately three miles, a very enjoyable walk.

The river area is quite steep in places—probably not wise for children or small dogs—so be careful going down. Canoeists can launch at the Bridge Street bridge and paddle to the reservation. Once there, be careful to note your location, as the trails can get somewhat confusing and are not very well marked. Dogs must be leashed throughout.

From the town center at the intersection of Routes 16 and 27, take Main Street/Route 27 south. Turn left on Goulding Street. The park entrance is at the Forest Street intersection, across the road. Open 9 A.M.–sunset. 508/921-1944.

34 Sherborn Town Forest
🐾🐾🐾🐕 (See Sudbury River Valley map on page 226)
Really three separate woodlands, this town forest is broken up by the roads that run through them. The section between Lake and Goulding Streets runs into the neighboring Rocky Narrows Reservation, the segment between Eliot Street and Farm Road features a nature trail and untrammeled woods, and the portion between Main Street and Hunting Lane offers a quick escape from the nearby bustling retail district. We recommend you stop first at City Hall to pick up maps, which you'll find invaluable when charting your course on all the trails.

For the easiest access, go behind Pine Hill School, where there is ample parking and a shady, well-maintained picnic area. Don't be afraid to park on school grounds; you can pull in at the back so you won't disturb the school-children. The David Doering self-guided nature trail—a quarter-mile walk ending at an amphitheater where nature talks are given—starts here.

Across from a playing field, there's another series of footpaths. Take the trail marked with red blazes for the longest loop, about two miles from start to finish. If you desire something shorter, take the various cutoffs along the main trail. The entire route leads through a quiet, lush forest. However, horses are allowed here, and you'll need to be wary on busy weekends. The only thing you won't get here is water, so be sure to bring plenty for you and your dog. Hikers can get parched on the long, dusty trail.

The least appealing section is between Main Street and Hunting Lane. This area is divided by the Shell Oil pipeline, a minor detraction from the getting-away-from-it-all experience. Still, there are many woodland trails, and you'll get in a good hour's walk if you venture on all the pathways. This trailhead is also behind the Pine Hill School.

To reach the last portion, park off Forest Road. This section abuts Rocky Narrows Reservation, and we suggest you take in both in one walk. Strike out across the open meadow and small orchard into the woodland trails on your right. There are myriad trails leading to and from each other. Don't worry, you can't get lost; they all lead back to your starting point eventually. At the far edge of the property is the oil pipeline, so you might want to skirt around this side. Head down toward the Charles River, and you'll reach the Rocky Narrows Reservation and the scenic cliffs above the river. This walk should take just over an hour, although we like to extend it by picnicking above the river under some shade trees.

The Pine Hill School is located in the town center at the intersection of Routes 27 and 16 by Pine Hill Lane. Open dawn–dusk. 508/921-1944.

PLACES TO EAT

C & L Frosty: Your dog is more than welcome to join you at one of the picnic tables outside this nifty burger joint, which makes a great stop after a hot day on the trails. The extensive menu lists full dinners, sandwiches, and ice-cream sundaes. 27B North Main Street; 508/655-7570.

Southborough

PARKS, BEACHES, AND RECREATION AREAS

35 Breakneck Hill Conservation Land

🐾🐾 (See Sudbury River Valley map on page 226)

When those chocolate-brown eyes see the orchards, cows, and alfalfa fields, your dog will know she's in farm country. What's really worth making hay over is that hiking trails lead through all of it. Well, you might want her to steer clear of the cows, but the trails do make for a relaxing down-home country afternoon.

The entire farm is set on the slopes of Breakneck Hill, and the trail system loops around the hilltop for about a mile, offering you and your leashed dog fine views and welcome breezes. A foot-high electrical fence borders most of the route. It's not wired, but it does take some charge out of the walk.

From the intersection of Cordaville Road/Route 85 and the Boston-Worcester Turnpike/Route 9, take the Boston-Worcester Turnpike east. Turn right on Breakneck Hill Road. The park and a grassy parking lot are on the left. Open sunrise–sunset. 508/485-0710.

🐾 Saint Mark's School West Field

🐾 (See Sudbury River Valley map on page 226)

A short trail takes you through a lovely open meadow and a glade of trees on the back side of the Saint Mark's property. From the parking area, head through the field on the paved pathway; at the edge of the woods, the path turns downhill and merges into a regular dirt trail. The entire route traces the fringe between woods and meadow before looping back to the parking area. It can get a little wet in spots, so wear waterproof shoes and bring a towel to wipe off your muddy (read: happy) dog when you get back to the car. Dogs should be leashed.

From the town center at the intersection of Cordaville Road/Route 85 and Main Street/Route 30, take Main Street west. Turn right on Sears Road. The parking area is on the right across from Sadie Hutt Lane. Open sunrise–sunset. 508/485-0710.

🐾 Town Forest/Turenne Wildlife Habitat

🐾🐾 (See Sudbury River Valley map on page 226)

These two individually run areas comprise one park. The town forest is managed by the Southborough Conservation Commission, while the wildlife habitat is managed by the Sudbury Valley Trustees. A long loop trail—clearly marked by blue blazes on trees—goes through both. If you and your leashed dog don't want to complete the entire mile-long loop, you can take the red-marked cutoff and shorten your walk a bit. There's another parking area at the end of Walnut Street, and a connecting trail—a straight, narrow pathway that leads to the main loop and back again.

Pines, maples, and oaks are the most common trees in the forest. A small stream runs through here, so parts of the path do get damp. The walk can be pleasant, but the Massachusetts Turnpike is routed right by the forest, and you are never far from the sound of rushing cars. You'll probably enjoy your nature walk more if you stick to the trail at the top of Walnut Street in the Turenne Wildlife Habitat.

From the intersection of Cordaville Road/Route 85 and the Boston-Worcester Turnpike/Route 9, take the Boston-Worcester Turnpike east. Turn right on Oak Hill Road and then right on Walnut Drive. The park entrance is at 11 Walnut Drive, and there's a parking area on the right. Open dawn–dusk. 508/485-0710 or 508/443-6300.

PLACES TO STAY

Red Roof Inn: This comfy motel offers clean rooms at reasonable prices. Best of all, this is one inn that has room for your pet. Rates are $60–89 per night. 367 Turnpike Road, Southborough, MA 01772; 508/481-3904 or 800/THE-ROOF (800/843-7663); website: www.redroof.com.

Stow

PARKS, BEACHES, AND RECREATION AREAS

38 Gardner Hill Natural Area and Town Forest

🐾🐾🐾 (See Sudbury River Valley map on page 226)

The wonderful woods nestled between the Assabet River and the Assabet Brook offer some great wilderness walks for your leashed dog pack. Wide trails take you through tall pine trees and clearings that give walkers pleasing river views. In the early morning and early evening, keep an eye open for owls perched in the high branches of the pines. These secretive creatures like the thick woods.

Many main trails or fire roads circle Gardner Hill. It's easy to make a loop that's the right distance for both of you. These routes cover about four miles; there are also some short footpaths, some of which ascend the hill's 354-foot summit. Trail maps are available at the town hall.

The woods of Gardner Hill are usually pretty quiet, but if your timing is off, you could encounter a troop of hikers. The southwest corner of the park is used by the Boy Scouts.

From the town center at the intersection of Great Road/Route 117 and Gleasondale Road/Route 62, take Great Road east. Turn right on Bradley Lane. Parking is available at the road's end. Open from a half hour before sunrise to a half hour after sunset. 978/897-5098.

39 Marble Hill Natural Area

🐾🐾 (See Sudbury River Valley map on page 226)

At an elevation of 457 feet, Marble Hill is the geographical matriarch of the woodlands in central Stow. Although the surrounding countryside is visible only during the winter when the trees are bare, you can have an invigorating climb through the young forest at any time.

The grade is not too steep, and the walk covers three-quarters of a mile. Exercise stations have been set up on the main trail, so you can do pull-ups along the way while your puzzled pooch looks on with tilted head and raised ears. (The crazy things these humans will do!) For a secluded trip through less-trammeled terrain, try some of the extended routes that loop around to the northwest of the peak. Leash your dog on this property.

From I-495 in Bolton, take Exit 27 to Route 117 and head east into Stow. Turn left into the Pompositticut Elementary School just past Harvard Road. Parking is available on weekends. Trailheads are in the fields behind the school. Open from a half hour before sunrise to a half hour after sunset. 978/897-5098.

Sudbury

In the 1700s, Sudbury was a thriving town situated on the main thoroughfare between Boston and the western part of Massachusetts. Old Boston Post Road was a major stagecoach route, and the town—with its many taverns, merchants, and mills on the Sudbury River—was a primary stop for travelers. Today, the countrified suburb of Boston boasts one of the best conservation programs anywhere. Not only has the town preserved its past (including the Wayside Inn), but it's preserving its future by purchasing land for people and their dogs to enjoy for years to come.

PARKS, BEACHES, AND RECREATION AREAS

40 Gray Reservation/Haynes Meadow Conservation Land

🐾🐾🐾 🐕 (See Sudbury River Valley map on page 226)

This is one of Inu and George's favorite parks in Sudbury. The 35 acres of the Sudbury Valley Trustees' Gray Reservation and the 37-acre parcel of Haynes Meadow offer a series of varied trails you and your leash-free dog will love. They'll take you through an old pine forest, along several brooks running through an open meadow, on an esker trail (a narrow ridge created by a glacier), and to a freshwater pond where you can take a dip.

Hop Brook runs through Haynes Meadow, feeding the small pond on Gray Reservation. Both have clean and cool water and are deep enough for a dog-paddle. A lovely picnic spot is located by the brook; it overlooks the meadow at the beginning of the main trail. Though easy to find, the various branches of the trail are not well marked, so we suggest you walk over the bridge by the meadow and head to your left through the woods. This will take you on myriad trails that meander through a gracious old pine forest; most routes lead to or near the pond in the center. If you continue past the pond, you'll eventually reach Old Lancaster Road at the end (or the beginning) of Gray Reservation.

Head to your right and you'll walk up an esker trail that offers a view of Hop Brook. Eventually the trail leads to private property and another small pond. The trail leads around the pond, so we suggest you avoid the house nearby and loop back on the forest trail to return to the bridge and your starting point. If you explore the entire 72 acres, it will take you about an hour and a half in all.

From Boston Post Road/Route 20, take Horse Pond Road north. Turn right on Peakham Road and then left on Blueberry Hill Lane. The park and a parking lot are at the road's end. Open dawn–dusk. 978/443-8891 or 978/443-6300.

41 Great Meadows National Wildlife Refuge/Weir Hill Trail

🐾 🐾 (See Sudbury River Valley map on page 226)

Dogs are allowed to pad down this peaceful little trail that runs along the marshes of the Sudbury River if they're on a very short leash—under seven feet, to be exact. Still, you shouldn't come here looking for quality dog-walking territory. We're not sure why they allow canines in the park at all, because this is primarily a haunt of bird-watchers, and you and your pooch will get icy stares from nature lovers on the trail. Frankly, as much as we are eager to take our dogs wherever we go, this is one spot even we don't think you should go with Spot. But the rules say you can, so use your judgment. Visitors are likely to see all kinds of marsh birds, including great blue herons, ducks, and cormorants.

From Boston Post Road/Route 20, take Union Avenue north onto Concord Road. Turn right on Lincoln Road and then left on Weir Hill Road. The park, a visitor center, and parking are on the right. Open weekdays 7:30 A.M.–4 P.M.; weekends 11 A.M.–5 P.M. 617/443-4661.

42 Hop Brook Marsh Conservation Land

🐾 🐾 🐾 🦮 (See Sudbury River Valley map on page 226)

The big challenge of this 80-acre reservation is not the trail itself, but the fitness stations along the way. Your dog won't give two sniffs for the pull-up bars, the step course, the obstacle course, or the jungle gym—mainly because he'll be too preoccupied scampering about leash free. But you might wish to get in a little exercise of your own. It's a great alternative to sweating inside

DIVERSION

Longfellow's Wayside Inn: You and your dog can take a self-guided walking tour of the grounds of this wonderful old tavern, a must-see for Revolutionary War buffs. Immortalized by Henry Wadsworth Longfellow's famous poem "Wayside Inn," this tavern is the oldest operating inn in America. On this walk, you'll see the Redstone School (a former student there was the inspiration for the nursery rhyme "Mary Had a Little Lamb"), the Martha and Mary Chapel, the Wayside Grist Mill, and of course the tavern itself, where revolutionaries met and planned the events of April 19, 1775. You and your dog will feel right at home exploring the well-marked trails through the rustic country grounds. Wayside Inn Road; 978/443-1776 or 800/339-1776.

a gym, but don't feel threatened by the equipment if you just want to go for a gentle stroll through this pine forest.

Hike on the main trail for a quarter mile to Duck Pond. You can circle the entire perimeter of this fairly large pond on a wide, flat trail. There's plenty of shore access for dogs who want a refreshing swim on a sweltering day.

Walk away from the pond on the inland trail, and you'll follow the fitness course or Hop Brook, whichever tempts you most. The route weaves in and out of the wetlands and through a forest of white pines with seemingly endless trails. Exploring the entire area will take an hour and a half, give or take a few hours for a leisurely picnic or a swim—or a few sit-ups.

From Boston Post Road/Route 20, proceed north on Peakham Road. Turn left on Old Garrison Road and then right on Dutton Road. The park and a parking lot are on the left. Open dawn–dusk. 978/443-8891.

43 King Philip Woods Conservation Land

😊 😊 🐕 (See Sudbury River Valley map on page 226)

There's a fascinating history behind this 81-acre leash-free conservation area. It's located on and around the abandoned Old Berlin Road, which was a primary stagecoach route between Boston and Lancaster. You can see the remains of a stone tavern that in the 18th century was a stopping point for coach, human, and beast, as well as a notorious haunt of highway robbers. Legend has it that passengers would disappear from the tavern on a regular basis. Skeletons were found in the basement long after the place had been abandoned, adding to its macabre image.

The main trail loops up and around the tavern site by a marshy pond and an adjoining bog and then back through the forest to your starting point. The entire walk should take about 40 minutes.

In the last edition, we told you that the old inn wasn't the only thing that had fallen into disrepair. The reservation itself had really gone to the dogs (and not in a good way). Fortunately the Sudbury Valley Trustees really have their act together, and the area is now a wonderful place to visit. The trash from the road has been cleared away and the trails are groomed and easy to follow. What an improvement! Thank you to all involved.

From Boston Post Road/Route 20, take Union Avenue north and veer onto Concord Road. Turn right on Old Sudbury Road/Route 27. The park and a parking lot are on the left, just past Rice Road. Open dawn–dusk. 978/443-8891.

44 Lincoln Meadows Conservation Land/Round Hill

😊 😊 🐕 (See Sudbury River Valley map on page 226)

The Great Meadows National Wildlife Refuge surrounds this 78-acre conservation area in the Sudbury River Valley. Although you'll get a great view from atop Round Hill and a good steady hike on the many trails that loop around the bog, the hill, and through the forest, this park isn't maintained as well as some of Sudbury's other parks. Trails in low-lying areas can get muddy because of the nearby bog; on the hilltop, the trails are dusty and dry. On a hot summer day, your dog will be looking for some relief of the watery variety, but alas, the "pond" just past Round Hill is merely a marshy swamp, and Rover would be a mess if he took the plunge.

To get to Round Hill, take the trail just past the root cellar at the parking area. It leads through the meadow at the hilltop and back into the woods to the pond. At the pond, you'll head left and back out to the open meadow and a community garden. You can loop back to the parking area here or walk across the meadow into Lincoln Woods beyond. That trail takes you on another mile-long loop before depositing you at the starting point.

From Boston Post Road/Route 20, take Union Avenue north into Concord Road. Turn right on Lincoln Road. You'll find the park and parking on the left, just past Water Row. Open dawn–dusk. 978/443-8891.

45 Nobscot Conservation Land

😃 😃 😃 🐾 (See Sudbury River Valley map on page 226)

A visit here will take you back to a time when life moved a tad slower and your best friend was your animal. Okay, so maybe people depended on their horses more than anything then, but now the dog is number one, and at this tranquil spot, you can both make believe you're a part of old New England. A short distance from the historic Wayside Inn, the entire 118-acre area looks much as it did in the 18th century. Trails will take you through an old apple orchard, over a dam built to supply running water to the Wayside Inn, and to the top of Nobscot Hill, the highest point in Sudbury. Your dog may not care about the view, but getting to the hilltop will be great fun for all.

The park is split into two sections. From the parking lot, the original trail goes toward Nobscot Hill. Take the rocky road upward; you'll soon reach a lovely pine forest sprinkled with flat glacial rocks perfect for sunning or reading. Several trails converge at the hilltop. You can continue straight through the forest and circle around to the left. The loop will eventually take you through a large meadow with a picnic area and back to the parking area. Veer to the right, and you'll head into the Nobscot Boy Scout Camp next door. Both trails provide a great hike and lots of trees, grass, and shrubs for a leash-free dog to sniff.

The second section was added to the original conservation area in 1985. The trail there begins across Brimstone Lane and heads downhill to the famous Ford's Folly, a dam built in the 1930s by Henry Ford to service the Wayside Inn. Unfortunately, it was never able to hold large quantities of water and was quickly abandoned. Be careful when walking on the top; if your balance isn't good, take one of the additional trails that go around it. You are forewarned: the rest of the area is mostly wetland that gets a bit muddy and marshy—just the stuff to inspire dogs to do their best pig imitations.

From Boston Post Road/Route 20, take Brimstone Lane south. The park and a parking lot are on the left. Open dawn–dusk. 978/443-8891.

Wayland

Throughout Wayland, dogs can go off leash if they obey voice commands and remain in view of the person they're with at all times. Dog owners who let their pets run free must always have a leash in their possession. All the trails in the Wayland conservation areas are well marked with yellow, red, and blue markers to guide you on the path of your choice.

PARKS, BEACHES, AND RECREATION AREAS

46 Castle Hill Conservation Area/
Trout Brook Conservation Area

🐾🐾🐾 🐕 (See Sudbury River Valley map on page 226)

A single road separates these two parks, which we like to think of as one big park waiting for doggy explorers. Start at Castle Hill. You'll find the trailhead just to the left of the ball field. This trail leads up along an esker high above School House Pond. You can wander along the pond at some points, but it can be a bit marshy, so you may not want your dog to swim there. The beautiful esker winds through some lovely, still woods. There is a narrow loop that backtracks on itself. If you follow this trail past the A intersection, it will lead you out to the end of Alpine Road. A quick skip across Sherman's Bridge Road brings you to the trailhead of Trout Brook Conservation Area.

Set in an old pine forest, this park was one of the first conservation lands to be established in Wayland. The well-planned trails loop and meander through 60 stunning acres of woodland. Off the red trail, you'll see a deep kettle hole formed by an ancient glacier. You can't go too far because the trails simply loop around each other, but you can't get lost either. We like to take the trails up and down the hills and through the valleys until George and Inu are dog-tired. Even though you're near homes here, there is something very peaceful about this forest. Take the yellow trail to return to the entrance. Dogs are allowed off leash.

From Boston Post Road/Route 20, take Concord Road/Route 126 north. Turn left on Sherman's Bridge Road and left again on Alpine Road. Parking is available on both sides of the road by the ball fields. Castle Hill is to the left of the ball fields. Trout Brook is at the intersection of Alpine and Sherman's Bridge Roads. Open from a half hour before sunrise to a half hour after sunset. Sudbury Valley Trustees, 978/443-6300; Wayland Conservation Commission, 508/358-3669.

Cochituate State Park

See the listing in the Natick section of this chapter.

47 Cow Common Conservation Area

🐾🐾 🐕 (See Sudbury River Valley map on page 226)

If you like meadows minus the cows, you'll enjoy a trek through here. Once the grazing fields for local farmers, this meadow now serves as a park, picnic area, and a top off-leash dog-walking spot. Trails lead throughout this beautiful open area that's surrounded entirely by woods. In the winter, it's an excellent spot for cross-country skiing; in the summer, you might wish to have a picnic. Downsides are that the ground gets a bit wet in the springtime, and nasty ticks like to hitch rides on dogs in the spring and fall. We recommend that you wear sturdy boots and your pooch wears a tick collar.

From Boston Post Road/Route 20, take Concord Road/Routes 27 and 126 north. Turn left on Old Sudbury Road/Route 27. The park and a parking lot are on the left just past Bow Road. Open from a half hour before sunrise to a half hour after sunset. Sudbury Valley Trustees, 978/443-6300; Wayland Conservation Commission, 508/358-3669.

48 Greenways Conservation Area

🐾🐾🐾 🐕 (See Sudbury River Valley map on page 226)

The latest and greatest of Wayland's parks, 98-acre Greenways was acquired in November 1995. Plans for more trails are in the works, but it is still one of the best parks around.

The trailhead starts to the left of the old family homestead, directly beside and beyond the map board. You and your pooch will enter a narrow woodland before emerging at several lovely meadows. Cross through the middle of two meadows down to the Sudbury River. Picnic tables located along the trail are available on a first-come, first-served basis; the best site is at intersection G overlooking the river on one side and the expansive meadow on the other. Your leashless dog will love romping through the tall grass or going for a swim. You will love the peaceful, pastoral scene.

If you want a more woodsy hike, head right and enter the woods at either intersection N or M. Follow N and you'll come out at the river again. M will take you through the woods a ways to the outskirts of the Sandy Burr Country Club. Follow the trail back through the woods at intersection C, and you'll return to the house.

This loop should take about an hour to complete. You can mix and match trails for shorter or longer walks.

The Wayland Conservation Commission and the Sudbury Valley Trustees are still in the process of studying the wildlife and habitats on this property. Limitations could be imposed in the future, but for now dogs may romp to their hearts' content.

From Boston Post Road/Route 20, take Cochituate Road/Routes 27 and 126 south. The park is on the right, just past Windy Hill Lane. The new "temporary" parking area is across the street at Saint Ann's Church. Please park by the trailhead sign and away from the church facilities. Open from a half hour before sunrise to a half hour after sunset. Sudbury Valley Trustees, 978/443-6300; Wayland Conservation Commission, 508/358-3669.

49 Heard Farm Conservation Area

🐾 🐾 🐕 (See Sudbury River Valley map on page 226)

Until recently this was an active farm. Given to the town of Wayland in 1995, the park is located on a beautiful chunk of land bordering the Sudbury River. Walk with your off-leash pooch through two large fields separated by woods or wander down by the peaceful river to bird-watch or splash around.

The Great Meadows National Wildlife Refuge (see the listing in the Sudbury section of this chapter) surrounds the farm on three sides. A flying duck logo has been posted on trees to alert you to the areas that are off-limits to dogs. There are plenty of trails to explore within the conservation area, however, so your dog shouldn't feel unwelcome.

From Boston Post Road/Route 20, take Pelham Island Road south. Turn left on Heard Road. The park and a parking area are at the road's end. Open from a half hour before sunrise to a half hour after sunset. Sudbury Valley Trustees, 978/443-6300; Wayland Conservation Commission, 508/358-3669.

50 Mainstone Conservation Area

🐾 🐾 🐾 🐕 (See Sudbury River Valley map on page 226)

Together the Hamlen Woods, Turkey Hill, and Wayland Hills Conservation Areas form one continuous pathway around the Mainstone residential district. The town of Wayland and the Sudbury Valley Trustees have done a great job of including so much open space and maintaining the trails. This is one of the prime places in Wayland to visit, and George and Inu think your dog will agree.

Walk through all three areas or devote your time to just one. In our opinion, Hamlen Woods is the best starting point. Contained on more than 50 acres, this section offers a thoroughly enjoyable hour-long walk. The trail starts at the parking area off Rice Road. We suggest you take the red trail, which leads past a tiny pond and Snake Brook. A small peninsula here is perfect for bird-watching over the water, and a small bridge leads over the brook. Continue past the pond into the woods.

Here you can continue on the red trail, which eventually dead-ends on private property about a mile away. Or you can veer to the right on the yellow trail, which leads to a hayfield, where you can continue hiking or loop back to join the red trail and return to the parking area.

For a longer hike, cross the road and head into Wayland Hills Conservation Area. This trail can be picked up across Rice Road and 100 yards to your left. You'll enter a smaller woodland surrounded by marshy wetlands. The trail, however, is fairly dry. Follow the yellow trail for a short walk, or take the red trail to enter Turkey Hill Conservation Area and higher ground.

The trails weave in and out of a well-planned residential area, but the beauty of the design is that you won't intrude on private property and it won't intrude on you. If you explore all three areas, you'll have one pooped pup, and your own dogs will be barking, too. But a tired dog is a good dog (or so we've heard), and we think this is a great woodland hike. Dogs are not required to wear leashes.

From Boston Post Road/Route 20, take Pine Brook Road south to Rice Road. The park and a parking lot are on the right, just past Mainstone Road. Open from a half hour before sunrise to a half hour after sunset. Sudbury Valley Trustees, 978/443-6300; Wayland Conservation Commission, 508/358-3669.

51 Pod Meadow Conservation Area

🐾 🐾 🐕 (See Sudbury River Valley map on page 226)

You can get a lot out of a short walk at this small park. A scenic loop trail takes you past a woodland, a beaver pond, and the Hultman Aqueduct. On our last visit, we observed four great blue herons in their nests at the pond. The beaver dam is active, but you'll have to be an early bird to see the animals busy at their morning's work.

As you enter the park, you'll pass Pod Meadow. There are no trails through this small meadow, so it may not be the best place to trek—though your leash-free dog will probably eye it eagerly.

From Boston Post Road/Route 20, proceed south on Cochituate Road/Routes 27 and 126. Turn right on Old Connecticut Path west/Route 126. The park and a parking lot are on the right, just past Hawthorne Road. Open from a half hour before sunrise to a half hour after sunset. Sudbury Valley Trustees, 978/443-6300; Wayland Conservation Commission, 508/358-3669.

52 Sedge Meadow Conservation Area

🐾 🐾 🐕 (See Sudbury River Valley map on page 226)

Pent-up pooches will want to bound into the large open meadow to play ball or Frisbee, while nature lovers will want to sniff and explore the woods. A trail encompasses the entire meadow, and we recommend you stick to it because the grass gets a bit mushy. On the far left side of the open field, another trail enters the woods. This short path takes you to another grassy hillside perfect for sunning or playing fetch with your pooch. This isn't the place for hard-core hikers, but if you're looking for a short, quiet walk, it just might do.

From Boston Post Road/Route 20, take Concord Road/Route 126 north. Turn left on Glezen Lane and then right on Moore Road. The park and a parking lot are on the left, just past Loblolly Lane. Open from a half hour before sunrise to a half hour after sunset. Sudbury Valley Trustees, 978/443-6300; Wayland Conservation Commission, 508/358-3669.

53 Upper Mill Brook and Lower Mill Brook Conservation Areas

🐾🐾🐾🐕 (See Sudbury River Valley map on page 226)

Many paths and roads at this 200-acre conservation area await dogs with a yen to explore. You won't get to them all in one day, but the place is worth a return trip in any season. Managed in tandem by the Sudbury Valley Trustees and the Wayland Conservation Commission, the park provides something to suit most any doggy's tastes.

The first leg of the trail takes you through an open field and wetland where a dog can muddy her paws. Soon you'll reach the forest and a trail that switchbacks across and over Upper Mill Brook and eventually leads to a pond at intersection F. The pond is swampy, and you may not want your dog to jump in. But she'll still have the brook to satisfy her water needs. It's clean and clear and will wash off any trail dust.

Go a little farther to intersection D and head into the woods. This quiet, pine needle–covered path loops around and back to the pond.

The trails are designated red, blue, and yellow, but they are randomly marked, so we suggest you rely on the intersection markers instead of the trail colors. It's also a good idea to get a map from the conservation office. Obedient dogs can go leash free.

From Boston Post Road/Route 20, take Concord Road/Route 126 north. The park is on the right, just past Claypit Hill Road behind the Peace Lutheran Church. Parking is permitted at the church, except on Sunday morning. Open from a half hour before sunrise to a half hour after sunset. Sudbury Valley Trustees, 978/443-6300; Wayland Conservation Commission, 508/358-3669.

PLACES TO EAT

Caraway's: For all the makings of a great picnic, try this small deli, where you'll find everything from sandwiches, soups, and salads to baked goods, snacks, and frozen yogurt. Or just have a relaxing lunch on the outdoor patio. Either way, your hungry dog gets to sit by your side. 325 Boston Post Road/Route 20; 508/358-5025.

Wellesley

This graceful and wealthy suburb of Boston is home to Wellesley College and a very civilized leash law. Your dog is allowed to go leash free as long as she is under voice control. We love taking our dogs to this homey little town. Your dog will love kicking up her heels while the leash is around your neck, not hers.

PARKS, BEACHES, AND RECREATION AREAS

54 Boulder Brook Reservation/Kelly Memorial Park

🐾🐾🐕 (See Sudbury River Valley map on page 226)

In this small reservation set on approximately 22 acres, you and your dog can take a quick jaunt through the woods and into the open area of Kelly Memorial Park. Surrounded by a pleasant little suburb, this park is popular with locals. There are two well-maintained trails and plenty of trees, bushes, and woodsy smells to keep canine noses twitching and legs lifting.

Park at the small parking area off Elmwood Road and proceed through the woods to the ball field for a game of fetch before your walk. Dogs are allowed to romp without a leash if they obey voice commands, but they must be leashed in the recreation area.

From Route 128, take Exit 20 to Route 9 west. Turn right on Weston Road and then right again on Elmwood Road. You'll find the park on the left. Parking is available. Open 5 A.M.–9 P.M. 781/431-1019, ext. 294.

55 Centennial Park

🐾🐾🐕 (See Sudbury River Valley map on page 226)

Untamed and untrammeled—though we won't go so far as to call it wilderness—this lovely, uncluttered park in the middle of a residential area provides 35 acres of wide-open spaces where you and your dog can wander unfettered by leashes. There are no amenities, but we think that makes the outdoors experience that much better. At any given time of the day, you will probably meet up with other happy canine wanderers and their human companions.

From the parking area, you can head off into the woods across the meadow to your right or climb the small hill directly ahead. There are no maps or special trails, so go in either direction as the whim or the whiff compels you. It will take you and your dog (who must be under voice control to go off leash) about an hour to explore the entire 40-acre park. Longfellow Pond (see the listing below) is just up the road, and you may want to take in both places on the same day.

From Route 128, take Exit 20 to Route 9 west. Exit Route 9, heading south on Cedar Street, and then veer into Hunnewell Street. Turn right on Oakland Street and proceed to the park, which is on the left. Parking is available. Open from 5 A.M.–9 P.M. 781/431-1019, ext. 294.

Elm Bank Reservation

See the listing in the Dover section of the Charles River Valley chapter.

56 Lake Waban at Wellesley College

🐾🐾🐾🐕🐕 (See Sudbury River Valley map on page 226)

A top weekend destination of dog lovers from throughout the Boston area, the attractive grounds of Wellesley College offer one of the best lakes around: Lake Waban. Follow the signs to the visitor parking area and head straight to the heart of campus to find this gem. You may hike along the shoreline here, but the north side of the lake is on private property, so please don't venture all the way around. College officials do not mind people with leash-free pooches using this beautiful space, but they ask that you limit your visits to weekends, holidays, and summer breaks—not when classes are in session. You will meet other dog owners here, and we think it will become one of your favorite spots, if it isn't already.

From Route 128, take Exit 21 to Washington Street/Route 16 west. Cross Route 135, and the campus is on your right. Follow signs to the parking area. Open 9 A.M.–6 P.M. 781/283-2376.

57 Town Forest/Longfellow Pond

🐾🐾🐕 (See Sudbury River Valley map on page 226)

Looking for a good neighborhood meeting place where your dog can run to her heart's content? This forest offers some great trails and a pond—and dogs who obey voice commands can romp here leash free. Very tame ducks who are always on the lookout for free handouts live in the pond, so don't spoil some poor child's idyllic moment by letting your water baby leap from the car and plunge right in, scattering ducks before her. But if the coast is clear, let her go.

This place can get busy with weekend visitors, so you might want to walk up the street to Centennial Park if you're looking for peace and quiet. But if you and your dog like commotion, this is a great spot for a Saturday morning stroll.

From Route 128, take Exit 20 to Route 9 west. Exit Route 9 onto Cedar Street south and continue onto Hunnewell Street. Turn right on Oakland Street and proceed to the park on your right. Ample parking is available off Oakland Street directly in front of Longfellow Pond. Open 5 A.M.–9 P.M. 781/431-1019, ext. 294.

Weston

PARKS, BEACHES, AND RECREATION AREAS

58 Cat Rock Park

🐾🐾🐾 (See Sudbury River Valley map on page 226)

Your dog may have some reservations about visiting Cat Rock Park, but rest assured. Once here, he'll forget all about the name. In fact, this 65-acre park in the northeast corner of town is very popular with the canine set. Even George and Inu have been converted.

The two highlights are Cat Rock Hill and Hobbs Pond. The hill towers over the park, providing grand views of Weston and Waltham to the east. The short climb to the top is strenuous, and you might want to attack it at the beginning of your walk when everyone has energy. You'll also find the town's water tank atop the hill. Dogs may not care about the view or the tank, but they will like sniffing the breezes. In winter, watch for tiny-tot skiers and daredevil sled riders.

A dog who climbs the hill in the summer's heat deserves a refreshing, cooling reward. Head back down the hill and take any of the trails into the woods; they all lead to Hobbs Pond after about half a mile. The invigorating water is clean and cool, and the swimming hole is surrounded by woods. On the western shore there's a grassy field, a good place to dry off after a dip or to play and enjoy the sunshine.

On Saturday in the summer, the place can get crowded with other walkers, so come early. And leash your dog.

From I-95, take Exit 28 to Boston Post Road/Route 20 west. Turn right on School Street, right on Church Street, left on North Avenue/Route 117, and right on Drabbington Way. Parking is available at the road's end, and the trails begin behind the ball field. Open dawn–dusk. 781/893-7320.

59 Cherry Brook Conservation Area

😺 😺 (See Sudbury River Valley map on page 226)

The woodlands and wetlands of Cherry Brook are just the thing for leashed dogs who want to sniff and explore. A vast network of paths in the 65-acre area can provide you and your canine pal with a great afternoon on the trail. These seemingly endless routes—a combination of dirt roads and footpaths—cover much of western Weston, crossing a variety of brooks and streams. The trails are flat and easy to follow, but it's a good idea to stop by the town hall first for a trail map. The map costs $10, but it's well worth it when you're in the backcountry and need to find your way back to the car.

From the Town Common in the town center, take Boston Post Road west to Concord Road and turn right. Look for the pullout on your right just past Merriam Street. Open dawn–dusk. 781/893-7320.

60 Doublet Hill/Elliston Woods Conservation Area

😺 😺 😺 (See Sudbury River Valley map on page 226)

You and your leashed dog are sure to have a wonderfully diverse hiking experience at these two parks, which cover a total of 52 acres. Begin walking near the top of Doublet Hill, just to the left of the town's water tower. Doublet Hill is a rocky outcropping, but it's covered with plenty of shady trees and, in the spring and summer, wildflowers for eager noses to sniff. Follow the main path to the right, and you'll quickly head down the side of the hill until the trail crosses the aqueduct, a giant pipeline that carries water from the Weston Reservoir to the taps of Boston.

The trail picks up again on the south side of the aqueduct and to your right. Here, the woods have grown thick, thanks to the level terrain and ample water supply from Hemlock Pond. The trail skirts the small pond, where the thin shoreline makes a good rest stop. The rich overgrowth around the pond adds to the dark stillness of the water.

The trail continues straight until it just about reaches some nearby homes, then makes a sharp left and begins the gradual climb back to the aqueduct. From here, the path ascends the steep southeastern side of Doublet Hill. The climb to the hilltop is well worth the effort: you wind up back at your car *and* you can sit and enjoy spectacular views of Boston and the Blue Hills after your mile-long walk. There are plenty of great spots on the hill for your dog to explore and for you to set out a picnic lunch.

From the Town Common in the town center, take School Street south into Ash Street. Turn left on Newton Street, then left on Doublet Hill Road. The park and a parking area are at the road's end. Open dawn–dusk. 781/893-7320.

61 Sunset Corner Conservation Area

🐾🐾🐾 (See Sudbury River Valley map on page 226)

Whoever said the West Coast is the only place to see a sunset never made it to Sunset Corner. From high on the hillside, there is an amazing view to the west of Mount Wachussett and, on a clear day, Mount Monadnock in New Hampshire. As evening begins, the sun fades out behind the peaks in a glorious array of colors.

Highland Street divides the 112-acre park into two sections. The upper portion, where you will find the viewpoint, has a number of wide forest roads that are popular with horseback riders and dog walkers alike. To get to the trails, follow the small stone stairway up the ridge. Just as it begins to plateau, take a moment to gaze out over the valley before continuing to the top of the rise.

There are about four miles of looping trails up top, and even if you and your dog cannot be there at sunset, you'll still see a brilliant display of colors. The rich upper woods of pine, maple, and white birch trees are beautiful any time of year.

Your walk through the lower portion of the park begins with a path through a sloping meadow, then turns left to continue downhill into the deep, dark pine woods. Be sure to explore the old chimney off the trail to your right. The route eventually leads to swamps near Westerly Road, but you can follow short loops back up the hill. Leash your dog.

From I-95, take Exit 28 to Boston Post Road/Route 20 west. Turn left on Highland Street. Look for the pullout on your right just after Love Lane. Open dawn–dusk. 781/893-7320.

62 Weston Reservoir Conservation Area

🐾🐾🐾 (See Sudbury River Valley map on page 226)

Dogs agree: this is *the* place for walking in Weston and the most popular hangout in town. The reservoir itself is off-limits, separated by a fence from the rest of the park. But the wonderful country path that leads around the reservoir and through a thick pine forest has local dogs returning weekend after weekend (with their leashes, as required).

The dirt path can be a hound highway on weekend afternoons. Even though dogs cannot go for a dip in the public's water supply, four brooks flow by the path, offering well-placed rest stops along the way. Another good place to take a break is on the far north side at a large clearing overlooking the reservoir. You can't miss it: just look for the pack of happy dogs congregated there.

If you don't have time for the two-mile loop around the reservoir, try the shorter path on the other side of Ash Street. It's only a half mile long, perfect for the short-legged dog in your life.

On the other hand, high-energy pups may find that the longer loop is not enough. If you don't want to make a fifth pass around the lake, there are secondary trails branching off to the south side of the reservoir and a trail that follows the aqueduct to the east. You can take this trail across Newton Street all the way to Elliston Woods.

From I-95, take Exit 28 to Boston Post Road/Route 20 west. Turn left on Wellesley Street, then left on Ash Street. The park and a parking area are on the left and right sides of the road. Open dawn–dusk. 781/893-7320.

PLACES TO EAT

Dairy Joy: The sight of the weekend crowds should tell you just how good the food is here, at one of our favorite places to eat. The full menu offers fish dinners, burgers, ice cream, frappés, the works. There are plenty of picnic tables where a dog can plop down to share the bounty, or you can stroll the grassy areas to escape the masses.

The last time we visited, after a long day at Estabrook Woods (see the Concord section), we stopped for some soft-serve ice cream, along with Bart, a neighbor's springer spaniel. Unlike Bart, George and Inu know the routine by heart and are well versed in ice-cream etiquette. We pass the cone around, and one dog takes a polite lick and then waits for the other to have a chance. On this particular day, a little girl at a nearby table wanted to administer the lickings. She held the cone for George, who took a big slurp, followed by Inu. Bart watched the whole scenario in wonderment. Then the child held the cone for Bart and, gulp, it was gone in one bite and he was off looking for the next one. What can we say? He's an animal. 331 North Avenue; 781/894-7144.

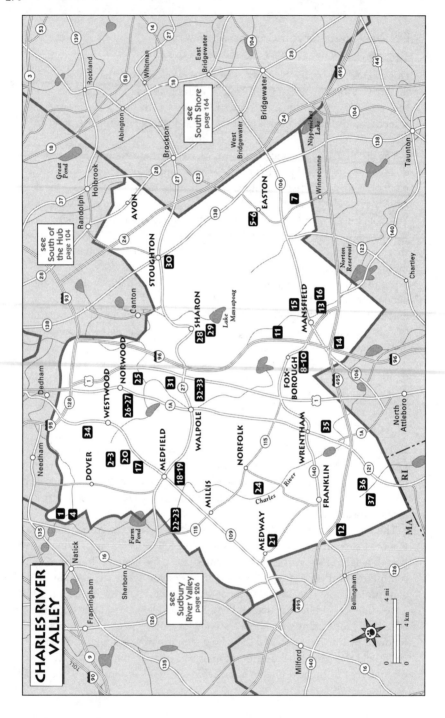

CHARLES RIVER VALLEY

CHAPTER 9

Charles River Valley

Hidden treasures await you and your dog in the region south of the Charles River headwaters and all the way out to I-495. Dover, Medfield, and other secluded country towns along the river offer countless opportunities for outdoor adventures. Communities that are more accessible from the interstates and Route 1, including Foxborough and Stoughton, may not devote as many acres to public parkland as other towns, but they make up for it with high-quality trails. The Trustees of Reservations oversees many of the outstanding parks featured in this chapter, including such gems as Noanet Woodlands and Rocky Woods Reservation. Once you and your trailblazing pooch set off, you'll want to roam the wild and wonderful woods for hours.

Bay Circuit Trail: Linking parks and reservations between Plum Island on the North Shore and Kingston Bay on the South Shore, this trail will eventually connect more than 30 towns across 200 miles, including Walpole. For details, see the Extended Hiking Trails section of the Resources.

The Trustees of Reservations: This preservation organization manages more than 75 parks and reservations on nearly 18,000 acres throughout

PICK OF THE LITTER—CHARLES RIVER VALLEY

BEST RIVERSIDE PARK
Elm Bank Reservation, Dover (page 273)

BEST DOG DAY AFTERNOON PLACE
Noanet Woodlands, Dover (page 274)

BEST OFF-LEASH PARK
Rocky Woods Reservation, Medfield (page 286)

BEST DOG RUN
Henry Garnsey Canine Recreation Park, Medway (page 287)

BEST PLACE TO MEET OTHER DOGS
Sharon Dog Park, Sharon (page 291)

BEST PLACE TO EAT
The Bubbling Brook, Westwood (page 295)

BEST DOG EVENT
Walk for the Animals, Easton (page 277)

the Commonwealth, including lands in this chapter. Dogs must be leashed on all Trustees properties. For more information on the group, see the Resources section.

Warner Trail: If you have a high-energy dog who seems to never tire out, perhaps it's time to hit the Warner Trail. The 30-mile route extends from the Canton Junction T Station in Canton through Sharon, Foxborough, Wrentham, and Plainville before terminating at Diamond Hill State Park in Rhode Island. It passes through several places featured in this chapter: the F. Gilbert Hills and Wrentham State Forests and the Neponset Reservoir.

Be prepared for all kinds of terrain because the trail accesses a variety of parks and neighborhoods. Most of it takes you through woodlands and fields, but there are brooks and marshes to cross, as well as the occasional busy street.

Dogs cannot complete the entire trail, as a portion of it cuts through the Moose Hill Audubon Sanctuary in Sharon, where dogs are not permitted. But don't lose heart—plenty of other spectacular sections are pooch-permissible.

For a trail guide or more information, send a self-addressed envelope and $1.30 postage to: Friends of the Warner Trail, 94 Farnum Pike, Smithfield, RI 02917-3316; 401/231-9431.

Avon

PARKS, BEACHES, AND RECREATION AREAS

D. W. Field Park

See the listing in the Brockton section of the South Shore chapter.

Dover

The rolling hills, grassy town square, and classic New England white church spires rising through the treetops make Dover a beautiful place to live or visit. Taking your dog for a walk here usually means opening the door and letting him explore the backyard woods. Fortunately for those of us who don't live here, there are plenty of leash-free woods you can visit with your dog.

PARKS, BEACHES, AND RECREATION AREAS

1 Elm Bank Reservation

🐾 🐾 🐾 🐾 🚗 🛶 (See Charles River Valley map on page 270)

Here's a well-kept secret to tell your canine friends: the wonderful Elm Bank Reservation is a leash-free romping ground with plenty of trails and wildlife. Once a privately owned estate, it was passed from owner to owner until the state assumed ownership in the 1970s. And for years, the land was slated for the auction block. Fortunately, the Metropolitan District Commission took over management of the 182-acre parcel in 1991. There are activities to suit every taste, and George and Inu think your pooch will enjoy it as much as they did.

The reservation is set on an oblong peninsula surrounded by the Charles River on three sides, and numerous trails have been established. Dogs who obey voice commands are allowed off leash everywhere except the playing fields near the parking areas. From the Old Mansion (the original manor house, which is still standing, although it looks somewhat less stellar than in its heyday), take the loop path leading along the Charles for a great 45-minute walk. You are likely to see muskrats and turtles in the water, and shorebirds such as herons along the riverbank. Little pathways lead down to the river if you want to get a closer look.

At the tip of the peninsula, you'll be treated to a great river view in both directions. This is a good picnic spot. A canoe launch is located down the trail from here, ideal for the dog who wants to be on the water instead of just in it.

The entrance is across the Charles River in Wellesley. From the intersection of Routes 16 and 135 in Wellesley, follow Washington Street/Route 16 west. The park is just past Pond Street on the left. Open 5 A.M.–9 P.M. 617/727-4138.

🟤 Glidden Land Preserve

😸😸🐕 (See Charles River Valley map on page 270)

You can see for miles around from atop Snow Hill and the Ralph MacAllester Fire Tower in this 55-acre preserve set in the high country of Dover. The main route through here is the country road that climbs up and over the hill (elevation 451 feet) from Pine Street to Centre Street. Along the way, you'll encounter a rich pine forest, numerous dips and rises, and a few trails that branch off to the south. Except for the climb, the hike is fairly easy. The pine forest is thick, and through the trees you can see the surrounding countryside, where white church steeples rise out of the green canopy. Even better, it's all leash-free land.

From the town center at the intersection of Centre and Walpole Streets, take Centre Street south to Pine Street and turn left. The park is on the right. Open dawn–dusk. 508/785-8110.

Hale Reservation

See the listing in the Westwood section of this chapter.

🟤 Noanet Woodlands

😸😸😸😸🐕 🦴 (See Charles River Valley map on page 270)

With 10 miles of hiking trails, four ponds, and a view of the Boston skyline from Noanet Peak, this place has it all. There is no better choice in the area for a special outing. The trails are so diverse and immense that your only problem will be deciding which one to take and whether you can get back to the trailhead without completely wearing out your dog.

Local dog owners know that these are 695 pooch-friendly acres. On weekends, a park ranger is often on hand to give directions, and we suggest you pick up a map when the information kiosk is open. It will help you untangle your way through the lush woods to all the best spots in this wonderful reservation. A reminder, however: the reservation is open to dogs for the time being but we implore you not to trample the foliage or forget to pick up after your dog. After all, dogs are allowed to roam here leash free, and it would be sad indeed if that freedom was curtailed due to dog owners who don't appreciate how truly great this place is.

The three main trails (marked blue, red, and yellow) are a bit difficult to figure out at first. We recommend that you follow the blazed trees on the yellow trail and then, when you reach the fork, take the blue trail. After about 15 minutes, you'll arrive at a beautiful waterfall tumbling gently into a pristine millpond on its way to Noanet Brook. Several dogs are usually hanging out

DOG-EAR YOUR CALENDAR—JUNE

Summer Solstice Celebration Reception: Hounds can herald the beginning of summer at this annual event held each June on the Sunday closest to the summer solstice. Festivities include guided hiking and bird-watching excursions through Elm Bank Reservation, and there's a farmer's market and booths where you can get gardening tips and watch demonstrations. Leashed pooches are welcome to participate in all of the activities (bird-watching excluded), and they will have a wonderful time in the great outdoors. The celebration takes place at the reservation 10 A.M.–4 P.M. There's a nominal entry fee on this day only. 617/536-9280.

or swimming here, and it's a favorite spot of canines and their human hiking companions. You'd never know that in the early 1800s, the Dover Union Iron Company operated here.

Take the blue trail up and through the old mill site or turn around here and follow the yellow trail to Noanet Peak. It's a trek of approximately 5.5 miles, so you'll need to bring water for you and your dog. If you keep to the blue trail, however, you'll enter a quiet pine forest and find lots of smaller trails leading to more ponds and hiking slopes.

The red trail traces the western boundary of the reservation. From here, you will find the connector trail to Hale Reservation (see the Westwood section in this chapter). Take the Strawberry Hill Trail to Powissett Pond on the Hale property.

After a few visits here, you'll discover your favorite stomping grounds, but none of the trails is as confusing as the new sign posted at the entrance to the parking lot which says No Dogs! This means no dogs are allowed in Caryl Park, which encompasses the parking lot at the entrance to Noanet Woodlands. Apparently, in a bizarre act of city planning, this means that although your dog can enter Noanet Woodlands, he cannot set foot in the parking lot that leads to the woods. This shouldn't be a problem on weekdays, but on weekends, when the parking lot gets full, you may choose to explore alternative entrances on Walpole and Powissett Streets. Both areas can accommodate up to four cars.

From Route 128 in Dedham, take Exit 17 to Route 135 west and proceed into Needham. Turn left on South Street just past the Charles River. Turn left on Chestnut Street and head into Dover, then make a right on Dedham Street just past the Charles River. The park is on the left, adjacent to Caryl Park. Open sunrise–sunset. 781/821-2977.

4 Pegan Hill Reservation

😾😾 (See Charles River Valley map on page 270)

Right in the heart of farm country, this 32-acre, out-of-the-way drumlin (a small hill left by the retreat of a glacier) offers visitors a break from Dover's larger, more popular parks. You and your four-legged best friend will probably have the oak forest and the lone trail to yourselves. The short and simple path leads to the top of Pegan Hill, where the view through a clearing is of the distant Great Blue Hill. The property is managed by the Trustees of Reservations, who allow dogs to go leash free.

From the intersection of Routes 16 and 135 in Wellesley, follow Washington Street/Route 16 west into Natick. Turn left on Pleasant Street, then right on Pegan Lane on the Dover border. Open sunrise–sunset. 781/821-2977.

Easton

PARKS, BEACHES, AND RECREATION AREAS

5 Borderland State Park

😾😾😾 (See Charles River Valley map on page 270)

With 1,772 acres of open fields, deep woods, and more ponds than you can shake a stick at, this spacious park will have your pooch feeling doggone happy.

The land was once part of the Ames family estate, and many remnants of that past life are visible today. You and your leashed dog can wander by the family mansion, the farmhouses, and the white horse fences that surround the fields and dirt roads. There are six ponds and plenty of trails around. (Swimming is not permitted; this goes for man and beast.)

The main trail is a wide dirt road that circles Leach Pond and Upper Leach Pond, with numerous stopping points and vistas along the way. This is the most popular route in the park, and you'll meet many other dogs in search of adventure. Be sure to take the land-bridge trail between the two ponds. You'll love the views of water on both sides, while your dog will thrill to the cool breezes carrying scents of things we can only imagine.

If you want a more secluded walk, the northern portion of the park offers additional hiking trails. This area is rockier, with denser woods and numerous stream crossings—in other words, perfect for adventure-bound hounds. These trails are like fitness courses to dogs, so don't overdo it. Try the Granite Hills loop trails or the longer Quarry Trail loop.

All of the park's trails are easy to follow, and there are plenty of directional signs. Maps are available at the Ames Mansion.

The park is located on the Easton/Sharon border near the Mansfield town line, hence the name. From Route 24 in West Bridgewater, take Exit 17 to Belmont Street/Route 123 and proceed into Easton. Turn right on Washington

DOG-EAR YOUR CALENDAR—MAY

Calling all canines: Join the puparazzi at Borderland State Park to participate in the **Walk for the Animals,** one of the most fulfilling pet events of the year. Not only do you and your dog get to walk through one of the primo parks in the area and enjoy a day of canine entertainment, you'll also be doing good deeds for dogs not as lucky as yours--all donations go to local animal shelters. There are agility events and obedience contests, and doggy bags for you and your pooch. Sponsored by the Neponset Valley Humane Society, this special event is held in May at Borderland State Park. 508/261-9924; website: www.nvhumanesociety.org.

Street/Route 138, then left on Main Street, which becomes Lincoln Street. At the intersection of Bay Road, the main (west) entrance lies across the road. For the east entrance, take a left on Bay Road and then a right on Rockland Street. Turn right on Massapoag Avenue and the entrance is on the right. Open dawn to the posted closing time, between 4 P.M.–6 P.M. 508/238-6566.

⑥ Town Forest Conservation Area

 (See Charles River Valley map on page 270)

Is the state park across the street too developed for your dog? Do you need a place that offers nothing but plain old woods and trails? Well, you're in luck. This backcountry forest covers 74 acres, all of it protected by the Easton Conservation Commission and all of it leash free.

From the access road off Bay Road, you and your trusty dog will soon pass through a small pine forest. Then it's time to roam the trails and fire roads through the woods and brush. There is no real organization or pattern to the paths, and some get pretty narrow in the thick brush. But after all, isn't that what a dog wants on an excursion?

From the town center at the intersection of Main Street and Washington Street/Route 138, take Main Street west and then veer onto Lincoln Street. Turn left on Bay Road. The dirt entrance road, where you can park, is on the left at the intersection of Randall Street. Open sunrise–sunset. 508/230-3349.

⑦ Wheaton Farm Conservation Area

(See Charles River Valley map on page 270)

Somebody sure was thinking straight when they set aside this land in southern Easton. Ward Pond, Fuller Hammond Pond, the surrounding woodlands, and the cranberry bogs are all protected by the Easton Conservation Commission. It's easy to see why. We still reminisce about our first visit on

DOG-EAR YOUR CALENDAR—OCTOBER

All paws for a golden cause: Join the fun at Borderland State Park for the **Yankee Golden Retriever Rescue Annual Dog Walk.** Held the second Saturday in October, this event not only benefits golden retrievers but is a great day out for *all* dogs. The three-mile walk is open to all breeds and starts at 9 A.M. Later in the day, your dog can bob for dogs (hot dogs, that is), get a "paw" reading, take a canine IQ test (our dogs are smart enough to stay away from that!), and even take a swipe at paw painting. At noon there is the Parade of Rescued Dogs (George likes this event, especially all the four-hanky stories about the pups who go from rags to riches). Spend the rest of the day participating in agility contests, relay races, and more fun than you can shake a stick at. The event runs 11 A.M.–3 P.M. Come for all or part of the festivities. For more information, call the Yankee Golden Retriever Rescue at 978/568-9700 or visit its website: www.ygrr.org.

a sunny afternoon early one winter. A thin layer of ice was clinging to the pond's edge, leaving plenty of room on the water for a handful of ducks. The trails and many pine trees had a light dusting of white from the season's first snowfall. The sun had melted the snowflakes from the boulders and rocks in the woods. As the day wore on, the melting continued, and the water droplets in the sunshine made the entire forest sparkle like a crystal fairyland.

From the parking lot, follow the fire road between Ward Pond and Fuller Hammond Pond. Ward Pond, to the north, is the smaller of the two. After passing the ponds, the dirt road cuts directly south, and a separate hiking trail continues straight into a forest of tall pines.

The road skirts Fuller Hammond Pond and loops through the cranberry bogs. Around the bogs is an open working area, which you might share with tractors or all-terrain vehicles; still, it's a good place for a run or enjoying the sunshine. You can always head into the adjacent woods if it looks like your dog is going to wade into the cranberry bogs. Dogs must be leashed in this open area only.

You'll have a grand time if you take the trails into the forest, a serene setting of pines and hardwoods. The main trail loops for about 1.5 miles through the woods and to the bogs at the south end of Wheaton Farms. Then you can take the dirt road back to the parking lot or explore some of the shorter trails.

From Route 24 in West Bridgewater, take Exit 16 to West Center Street/Route 106 and proceed to Foundry Street and Easton. Turn left on Bay Road. The entrance gate is on the right, but the sign will be on the left. Park at the end of the access road. Open sunrise–sunset. 508/230-3349.

Foxborough

PARKS, BEACHES, AND RECREATION AREAS

8 Cocasset River Park

☷ ☞ (See Charles River Valley map on page 270)

Accessible only to residents of Foxborough, this 112-acre park feels much smaller than it is. Open spaces are limited, and it's really just a ball field backed up by a forest trail. The pathway leads over a small brook (be careful here; the appropriately named Crooked Bridge is a bit slippery and tricky to navigate), and the woods are well kept. But just down the road lies the much larger and more diverse F. Gilbert Hills State Forest. So, unless you're looking for a quick woodland walk with your dog (who doesn't have to wear a leash in Cocasset River Park), you'll probably want to head over there.

From I-95, take Exit 7 to Commercial Street/Route 140 north. Turn left on South Street, then right on Mill Street. The park is on your left, past the F. Gilbert Hills State Forest. Parking is available. Open 9 A.M.–sunset. 508/543-3653.

9 F. Gilbert Hills State Forest

☷ ☷ ☷ ☷ (See Charles River Valley map on page 270)

This excellent 975-acre forest offers more than 10 miles of trails for your leashed dog to explore. You should discover your own favorite route, but for first-time visitors we recommend beginning at the beginning. And that happens to be the main entrance off Mill Street, where park headquarters is located. You can pick up a map, which will definitely come in handy, or study the detailed map at the trailhead to decide where to go.

Our pick is the Acorn Trail, a loop of about 2.5 miles. Just look for the blue sign with an acorn painted on it. Stick to this path, and you'll avoid the mountain bike and bridle trails, although they do intersect at points. The Acorn Trail leads through Wolf Swamp and Wolf Pond Meadow. Various water holes will tempt your dog, and depending on the season, there may be brooks and streams running through the pathway. In the spring, the trail along the swamp can get quite flooded, so you should stick to the loops through the woods and around the main trails whenever possible. At the peak of this route, there's a radio tower that provides a view of the entire area; you might enjoy climbing it to take in the sights, but your dog won't, so you'll probably have to skip it.

Another hikers-only path—a shorter, unnamed loop that veers off to the right of the main trailhead—is also a good choice. It takes about 40 minutes to complete. This shady forest path is great for walks on hot days and is more peaceful than its larger counterparts.

When we go to this park, Inu carries a ball and George plays with it. This teamwork is necessary because George always wants the ball at the park but

gets much too distracted to carry it. Inu, on the other hand, thinks chasing after anything except a potential meal is definitely beneath him. The team-work breaks down, however, when Inu decides to tease George a bit and refuses to give up the ball as soon as we enter the park. Instead, he trots over to a grassy area and rolls all over it. George is left to scramble frantically, hoping to grab his treasured toy. Eventually, Inu tires of tormenting his friend, George grabs the ball, and the games begin.

From I-95, take Exit 7 to Commercial Street/Route 140 north. Turn left on South Street, then right on Mill Street. The state forest and a parking area are on both sides of the road. Two smaller park access points are in Wrentham. The first is on Route 1, just south of the state police headquarters. The other is on Thurston Street off Route 1. The park is open dawn–dusk; park headquarters and the parking area are open weekdays from 8 A.M.–6 P.M.; weekends 10 A.M.–6 P.M. 508/543-5850.

10 Harold B. Clark Town Forest

🐾🐾🐾 (See Charles River Valley map on page 270)

Town forests are usually not high on our list of doggy destinations, but this 300-acre forest is a wonderful exception. There is only one major trail, and it encircles Upper Dam Pond, built over a century ago to serve a mill that once operated here. The walk is easy yet scenic, and your leashed dog will love sniffing the woods along the pond before plunging into the cool, clean water.

The trail starts at the end of Forest Road. Walk a few feet into the woods, keeping to your right. (The trail to the left dead-ends on private property.) In fact, if you veer to the right at every crossroads, you will stay near the pond and won't get lost. The trail loops for 1.5 miles around the pond, and along the way there are flat rocks for sunning and plenty of water-access points so your dog can swim. Among the many wildlife species that live here, geese and herons are the most visible. If you're lucky, you might catch a glimpse of a white-tailed deer in the early or late hours of the day.

At the far side of the lake, the trail intersects with the Warner Trail (see the beginning of this chapter), which leads around the lake a ways before branching off into F. Gilbert Hills State Forest. If you want to extend your hike, this trail is a good option.

From Route 1, take Main Street/Route 140 heading south. Turn right on Lakeview Road and then right again on Forest Road. The forest and a parking area are located at the end of the cul-de-sac. A second access point is off Lakeview Road. Open dawn–dusk. 508/543-1251.

🐾 Wilderness Area/Greeley's Pond

🐾🐾 (See Charles River Valley map on page 270)

These 300 acres are a mixed bag: Although there are lots of woods, it's hardly a wilderness experience. The woods are wet and often buggy, and there's a fair amount of trash. We recommend you head to the Greeley's Pond section off East Street. A small wooden map at the trailhead will help you choose a path; good choices include the longer white trail, the shorter red trail around the pond, and the really short green trail, which volleys between the other two.

The half-mile red trail around the pond is worth a try if you happen to be in the neighborhood and want to take a quick stroll with your leashed dog. The white trail heads into the woods and is a pretty good jaunt, except it gets a bit close to power lines at several junctures. Also, bugs thrive here in hot weather, so you may want to save this one for the cooler months. After walking in the woods for over a mile, you'll loop back to the pond.

The main trailhead is actually located off Willow Street, and ample parking is available. But it's a pitiful little path through swamps and under power lines. Unless you have the patience to endure this leg of the walk before joining up with the white trail, do yourself a favor and bypass this entrance.

From I-95, take Exit 8 to Mechanic Street south, heading toward Foxborough. Turn left on Oak Street, left on Cocasset Street, and left again on East Street. The park is located on the right side of the road. Look for Greeley's Pond and a dirt access road. Open dawn–dusk. 508/543-1251.

Franklin

PARKS, BEACHES, AND RECREATION AREAS

🐾 Franklin State Forest

🐾 (See Charles River Valley map on page 270)

With acres upon acres of woodlands and wetlands, there is plenty of room for your dog to get out and stretch his legs, but that's about all there is to do. A few simple country paths cut through the thick woods, and a couple of trails intersect each other. Depending on the season, the trails can be muddy, but the plus is that you will have them to yourselves—except for the occasional mountain biker. As in all state-owned properties, dogs are required to be on leash.

From I-495, take Exit 17 to West Central Street/Route 140, head west to Grove Street, and turn left. Make a right on Forge Hill Road and follow it to the end. Street parking is available. Open dawn–dusk. 508/543-5850.

Mansfield

PARKS, BEACHES, AND RECREATION AREAS

13 Fulton Pond/Robinson Park

😺 🐾 (See Charles River Valley map on page 270)

This little park in the town center is quite ducky, and your dog will probably be outnumbered by her fair-feathered friends. Fulton Pond makes a good pit stop if you happen to be in the area, but it's really a bird-feeding spot. If your dog thinks chasing ducks and geese is great fun, she won't be very welcome. There are picnic facilities and plenty of benches, but only a small grassy area for walking leashed dogs.

From the intersection of Commercial Street/Route 140 and Chauncey Street/Route 106, take Chauncey Street east. Turn right on North Main Street, right on Fulton Street, and right on Rumford Avenue. The parking lot is on the left. Open dawn–dusk. 508/261-7378.

14 Great Woods Conservation Area

😺 🐾 (See Charles River Valley map on page 270)

Inu and George discovered this place one evening when they were trying to sneak into the Great Woods Performing Arts Center to see their favorite band, Three Dog Night, in a reunion concert. Or was it Los Lobos? Snoop Doggy Dogg? Anyway, they thought they could cut through these woods and dig under the fence. Well, they never got near the place, but they did find a few trails to explore.

The entrance route follows a line of electrical poles, but you can soon cut over to an old dirt cart road that veers to the left. If you continue on the pole line, you'll come to a trail turning off to the right. All three routes are one-way trails, so you will have to double back.

Throughout the park, the terrain is wooded and a little swampy. When you return to your car, your dog will definitely look like he's been out on the trail, not like someone who's going to a show.

From the intersection of Commercial Street/Route 140 and Chauncey Street/Route 106, take Commercial Street south. Turn right on School Street and then veer into Elm Street. Turn left on Oak Street. Parking is available on the shoulder where Elm Street turns to the right. Open dawn–dusk. 508/261-7378.

15 Maple Park Conservation Area

🐾 (See Charles River Valley map on page 270)

The largest of Mansfield's conservation areas at 272 acres, this spot filled us with high hopes the first time we visited. Park at the fire road just past the water station and start walking. You'll soon turn to your left onto the blue trail, which leads through a shady, quiet pine woodland to the yellow trail. This in turn heads over some hills to the muddy, murky, and swampy pond.

Avoid staying on the fire road, even though it's the most open and easiest of the trails, because it leads you nearer than you probably want to go to a very unsightly factory along the park's borders. Chris insisted it's the place where bad puppies are turned into donkeys, but George and Inu weren't buying it. In our dream world, the factory changes dirt bikers into donkeys; if that were the case, we wouldn't mind its ugly presence as much. Unfortunately there are too many of the critters (dirt bikers, we mean) zooming demonically along the trails and not enough trees to hide the industrial buildings. Besides, dogs need to be leashed.

From the intersection of Commercial Street/Route 140 and Chauncey Street/Route 106, take Chauncey Street east. Turn left on Oakland Street, then right on Maple Street. Parking is available on the right shoulder near the fire lane. Open dawn–dusk. 508/261-7378.

16 Marie Strese Conservation Area

🐾🐾 (See Charles River Valley map on page 270)

Also known as the York Conservation Area, this 49-acre parcel of land is located in a quiet little wood. Follow the main path at the Ware Street trailhead, and just past the creek (a branch of the Canoe River), you will come to a fork in the road. You can let your leashed dog decide which way to go, but we suggest taking the right fork because it's easier to loop around and find the left fork trail that brings you back to this intersection. The entire loop is very short (about a 20-minute walk), but your dog will enjoy the woodsy smells of the young pine forest. The Canoe River is enticingly close to this trail, but you can't get there from here so don't bother blazing your own trail.

On our first visit here we got hopelessly lost, although George would say we were just exploring. We had set out on the "short" trail that loops to the left of the main trailhead, then found it was the trail to nowhere. Yes, we had a map, but who needs a map when you've got a great nose? So we forged ahead, certain we could find the Canoe River. After about 30 minutes of roaming hopelessly through shrubs, marsh, and waist-high pine trees, we had to concede defeat. The map was right, and there really wasn't a trail to the river. Maybe one day the town of Mansfield will extend the trail down to the water, but for now, you'll have to be content with the woods.

From the intersection of Commercial Street/Route 140 and Chauncey Street/Route 106, take Chauncey Street east. Turn right on East Street, then left on

Ware Street. The park and a parking area are on the left. Open dawn–dusk. 508/261-7378.

PLACES TO EAT

Sweet 'N' Crafty: We can't vouch for the crafty part, but the candy and baked goods sure are sweet. The ice cream is made on the premises, and your pooch can dine with you on the patio. Sandwiches and breakfasts are also served. Robinson Park is around the corner, just in case you want to walk off those calories. 34 Main Street; 508/339-5202.

Medfield

PARKS, BEACHES, AND RECREATION AREAS

17 Fork Factory Brook Reservation

🐾🐾🐕 (See Charles River Valley map on page 270)

Named after a pitchfork factory that once operated along Mill Brook, this thickly wooded 144 acre park is dotted with swamps that feed off the brook. It's the unknown brother of Rocky Woods Reservation, the prince of parks just across the street, and both are part of the Trustees of Reservations system. There's a 1.5-mile loop trail where your dog can kick up his heels off leash as long as he is under voice control. It begins at Hartford Street across from the Rocky Woods Access Road. Most likely the two of you will be walking in solitude. In the wet season, some of the lower areas can be soggy, but they're always passable. Other portions of the trail pass through pumpkin fields and climb along ridges from which you can view the brook.

Parking and information are available at Rocky Woods Reservation. From the town center at the intersection of Routes 27 and 109, take Main Street/Route 109 east. Turn left on Hartford Street. The Rocky Woods Reservation entrance is on your left. On weekdays, park at the smaller pullouts along the access road. Dogs are not allowed here on the weekends. Open 9 A.M.–6 P.M. 508/359-6333.

18 Henry L. Shattuck Reservation

🐾🐾🐕 (See Charles River Valley map on page 270)

If your dog thinks there are too many people on the trail at Noon Hill Reservation (see below), this place makes a good alternative destination. There are downsides: the trails are limited, and your dog might wander into one of the swampier sections of the Charles River. But there's a good chance you'll have the park to yourselves, and best of all, dogs who obey voice commands are not required to wear leashes.

Three short trails (each about a half mile long) run from Causeway Street down to the Charles River. They'll take you through the woods to wonderful viewing points on the Charles. The area is rich in wildlife: herons, egrets,

DOG-EAR YOUR CALENDAR—JUNE

Paws in the Park: Help promote dog adoptions and have plenty of fun while you're at it when you attend Save A Dog's annual dog walk and festival,**Paws in the Park.** The fundraiser is held at the Norfolk Hunt Club on North Street every June. Events include the mile walk, agility contests, an auction, vendor exhibits, and silly dog games. For more information, contact Save A Dog at 508/877-1407; website: www.saveadog.org.

ducks, and geese are common on the river. Deer and raccoons also call this place home, and your dog might catch their scents in the wind.

From the town center at the intersection of Routes 27 and 109, take Main Street/Route 109 west. Turn left on Causeway Street. After you cross the wetlands of the Stop River, the reservation and a small parking lot are on your left. Another parking area is available at Noon Hill Reservation. To reach it, continue on Causeway Street, then turn left on Noon Hill Road. Open 9 A.M.–6 P.M. 508/921-1944.

19 Noon Hill Reservation

 (See Charles River Valley map on page 270)

Inu and George renamed this large, wooded reservation High Noon Hill and declared it "not big enough for the both of us." Whenever we come here, they battle it out among the trees and rocky outcroppings to see who is king of the hill and who has to get out of Dodge.

From the top of Noon Hill, at an elevation of 369 feet, there are fine views through the trees of the nearby Charles River and Stop River Valleys. The main trail, an old forest road, leads from the parking lot through the woods and nears the top of the rise before continuing into the surrounding woodland.

Because the main objective of every visit is to conquer the hill, you'll want to follow the dirt road upward. The road circles around the back of Noon Hill before splitting. Take the left branch, or the high road, to the top. You and your leashed dog can make a loop by taking one of the foot trails down the north side of the hill. They all lead eventually to the forest road. The entire journey is close to two miles.

There's also a short path around Holt Pond, where a dog can cool off after being crowned king of the hill. The pond and path are near the main trailhead.

The only downside is the nearby rifle range; the echoing gunshots evoke images of a real shoot-out at high noon.

From the town center at the intersection of Routes 27 and 109, take Main Street/Route 109 heading west. Turn left on Causeway Street, then left again on Noon Hill Road. The reservation and a parking area are on the right. Noon Hill Reservation is open 9 A.M.–6 P.M. 508/921-1944.

20 Rocky Woods Reservation

🐾🐾🐾🐾 🐕 🕊️ (See Charles River Valley map on page 270)

Normally, George and Inu are two cool, calm, and collected canines. But they lose it whenever they hear the words "Rock .... " Whew, close call. They lose it whenever they hear "R-O-C-K-Y-W-O-O-D-S." You see, this park, managed by the Trustees of Reservations, is one of their favorite places, and they do a wild dance of anticipation at the thought of bounding down the hilly trails and exploring the rocky formations and refreshing ponds in gleeful, leash-free abandon.

In 2002, our favorite park got a facelift. Usually park renovations are not good news for dogs, but in this case, the nearly 500 acres of woods, rocky bluffs, and numerous ponds were not altered in spirit—just a few cosmetic tweaks, a new parking area, and a lot of behind-the-scenes work to improve drainage, wildlife preservation, and traffic flow. Our dogs still love the twisting, winding trails and cart paths that lead up and over ridges, around giant boulders, and along pools, brooks, and waterfalls. There are plenty of hiking options to choose from and many places to explore. Ask the park ranger for a trail map or just follow other hikers.

One new addition, however, was a pilot program for dogs. Dogs are now required to obtain a Green Dogs Permit to use the property. Annual permits are available for Trustees members at $60 a year for up to two dogs per family. New zones have also been added which include on-leash, off-leash, and off-limit areas. Maps are posted to help you navigate your way. Permits can be purchased at the ranger station each weekend. The Trustees of Reservations is trying to manage this property responsibly for everyone—let's make sure "everyone" includes our dogs! For information on this policy, check out the website: www.thetrustees.org.

Chickering Pond is now off-limits to dogs around the picnic area, located at the main parking area of the reservation. You can trot down the trail beyond the populated areas, however, and take a dip. The water here is too acidic for human swimming but is fine for your pup—just ask the 10 (or 20) or so who are romping in the water at any given time of the day.

If we can pry our dogs away from the great swimming, there are also plenty of great hiking opportunities here. One of our favorite spots here is the Echo Lake Trail to Echo Lake, where a low-lying footbridge crosses over the water. There's something special about bridges and water that makes venturing out on the wooden structure fun for dogs and humans. The Echo Lake Trail can be accessed off the loop trail that runs from the southeast side of Chickering Pond and the parking lot.

Another popular spot is Whale Rock, a huge whale-shaped stone formation that will test your dog's climbing skills and provide views of the surrounding area. Cedar Hill will also elevate canine spirits. To investigate the high, rugged terrain there, take the Noanet or Tower Trails. Most of the trails branch off the Chickering Pond Trail, which begins to the right of the pond in the northeast corner of the parking lot.

Throughout the park, there are many other great places to sniff out and paths to trot down, all but guaranteeing that your dog will have a blast at Rocky Woods.

Dogs must be leashed in the parking area, around Chickering Pond, and near all park buildings. Off-leash areas are posted on the map board at the parking area. Dogs are welcome dawn–dusk every day, except Sunday afternoons from noon–dusk.

Entrance fees are $5 per person on weekends for non-Trustees members. From the town center at the intersection of Routes 27 and 109, take Main Street/Route 109 east. Turn left on Hartford Street. The park is on the left. On weekdays, park in the smaller pullouts along the access road. On weekends and holidays, follow the access road to the large parking area at the road's end. Rocky Woods Reservation is open 9 A.M.–6 P.M. (the gate closes at 5 P.M.). 508/359-6333 or 781/821-2977.

PLACES TO EAT

Casabella Pizza: Inu insisted we list at least one pizza parlor. After all, pizza is his favorite food. Actually he's also happy munching on a sub or calzone as long as it has plenty of cheese. Order whatever cheesy dish your dog prefers and head next door to the gazebo and town green to enjoy it. 454 Main Street; 508/359-4040.

Medway

PARKS, BEACHES, AND RECREATION AREAS

21 Henry Garnsey Canine Recreation Park
🐾🐾🐾🐾🦮 (See Charles River Valley map on page 270)

This large dog park has been a hit since it opened in 2002, and it's easy to see why. It is securely fenced, has plenty of trees, and the mulch-covered grounds keep it looking nice in every season. There are benches and picnic tables for the all-important socializing between human visitors.

Credit then 15-year-old Tim Dumas for making this park a reality. Tim saw the need for a dog park in Medway and worked to create this off-leash area as part of his Eagle Scout project. The park was named for Medway's first settler, Henry Garnsey, whose original home foundation is part of this park. The park is managed by Friends of Medway Dog Park and relies on your donation to maintain the grounds.

From the intersection of Summer Street/Route 126 and Milford Street/Route 9, take Milford Street east for a third of a mile. Turn right onto Franklin Street for one block. Turn left onto Village Street and proceed a half mile. The park is on the left. Limited parking is available around the block on Cottage Street. Open 6:30 A.M.–8 P.M. weekdays and 8 A.M.–8 P.M. weekends. 508/533-3204; website: medwaydogpark.com.

Millis

PARKS, BEACHES, AND RECREATION AREAS

22 Oak Grove Farm

🐾🐾 (See Charles River Valley map on page 270)

Much of these 50 acres were once farmed by the Millis family, for whom the town was named. Today the land is in the process of reverting to a natural state. The plowed fields are once again grassy meadows, and shrubs and young trees have gradually appeared in pockets throughout the meadows. If the growth is allowed to continue, a full forest of tall pines, maples, and oaks will eventually thrive here.

The town of Millis maintains Oak Grove Farm and has been doing a great job of allowing the woods to grow, yet cutting back other areas to keep some of the rolling terrain open for horseback riders, hikers, and of course dogs and dog lovers.

Two miles of trails have been blazed through the meadows, brooks, and the young forest. A grass-lined path circles the outer perimeter of the old farm and takes you from one field to the other. It seems as if rabbits are around every bend in the trail, so it's a good thing dogs need to be leashed.

From the town center at the intersection of Main Street/Route 109 and Plain Street/Route 115, take Plain Street north. Turn right on Exchange Street/Route 115, then left on unpaved Island Road. The park and a parking lot are on the right. Open 5 A.M.–9 P.M. (during daylight saving time) and 6 A.M.–6 P.M. (Eastern Standard Time). 508/376-8011.

23 Richardson's Pond

🐾 (See Charles River Valley map on page 270)

The only things you'll find at this pond are a small beach and a faded-out trail that follows the shoreline. But on a steamy summer day when you and your hot dog have had it with the No Dogs Allowed signs at the Cape and

North Shore beaches, then this is the place. Dogs do have to be leashed, however.

From the town center at the intersection of Main Street/Route 109 and Plain Street/Route 115, take Plain Street north. Turn left on Curve Street. The pond and a parking area are on the right. Open dawn–9 P.M. 508/376-8011.

Norfolk

PARKS, BEACHES, AND RECREATION AREAS

24 Comeys Pond Area

🐾 🐾 (See Charles River Valley map on page 270)

When the dog days of summer set in, you'll be looking for a place where you and Fido can cool off. Comeys Pond is great for beating the heat. The water's the main attraction because there are no trails or even a grassy spot for sunbathing. It's just a pond with a small roadside pullout. But does a pup need anything else on a summer day?

The pond, which is a couple of acres in area, has limited beach access and is popular with anglers, so we advise you to arrive early to grab a spot. Please watch out for old fishing lines and hooks—they can hurt your dog. Dogs are supposed to be leashed to prevent them from disturbing people who are fishing or sunbathing.

From the town center at the intersection of Main Street and Rockwood Road/Route 115, take Main Street west. Continue past Hanover Street to the pond. Open dawn–dusk. 508/541-8455.

Norwood

PARKS, BEACHES, AND RECREATION AREAS

25 Endean Recreation Area/Hawes Brook Walkway

🐾 🐾 (See Charles River Valley map on page 270)

The town of Norwood has put the Endean Recreation Area to many uses. The junior high school is here. There are Little League fields, duck ponds, a public pool, and picnic areas. Most important—from a dog's point of view, anyway—are the woods, fields, and trails.

The Hawes Brook Walkway is a great way to begin your hike. Not only will you bypass all the other activities in the area, but you'll stroll along the stream on a path of crushed gravel. Starting on the north end of the park off Washington Street, it follows Hawes Brook for half a mile until the brook disappears under the esker that supports the railroad tracks. The trail then turns left and follows a dirt path for half a mile along the park's western border.

This brings you to a pair of small meadows with open views of the Great Blue Hill before continuing to the back side of the Endean Woods. The woods are a little trashy in spots, but it's a pleasant walk. As you emerge from the woods, stay to the left of the ball fields, and you'll loop back to the Hawes Brook Walkway. The walk is under two miles, and you and your leashed dog will find good resting stops by the streams.

From Route 1, take Dean Street west. Turn left on Washington Street and proceed to the recreation area on the right. Parking is available near the junior high school, at Hawes Pool Park, and on the street. Open dawn–9 P.M. 781/255-0317.

26 McAleer Park

 (See Charles River Valley map on page 270)

We don't avoid this place because of the swampy section of the woods next to the town ball fields and the junior high school. The trash on the trails is what has us dragging our tails. The forest is thick and encircles a scenic pond, but there's just too much junk, including broken glass, to make it safe for your leashed pup.

From Route 1, take Dean Street west. Turn right on Washington Street and continue until it merges into Upland Road/Route 1A. Turn left on Winter Street, then right on Hawthorne Street. The park and a parking lot are at the road's end. Open dawn–9 P.M. 781/255-0317.

27 Shattuck Park

🐾 (See Charles River Valley map on page 270)

Dogs who are passing through town will find that this wooded park makes an okay pit stop. However, it gets a low paw rating because there are busy roads on all sides and it's very small, just one block. You're sure to get that "is-that-all-there-is?" look from your disappointed friend. Dogs should be leashed.

From Route 1, take Dean Street west. Turn right on Washington Street and continue until it merges into Upland Road/Route 1A. Turn left on Winter Street. The park is on your right at the intersection of Shattuck Park Road. Street parking is available. Open dawn–9 P.M. 781/255-0317.

PLACES TO EAT

Second Cup: Come here for your first, second, or tenth cup of coffee of the day. The takeout menu offers breakfast and lunch items that you and your dog will enjoy, such as eggs, muffins, burgers, and sandwiches. Take your food across the street to one of the picnic tables in the Endean Recreation Area to work off that caffeine-induced energy. 1260 Washington Street; 781/762-8790.

Sharon

PARKS, BEACHES, AND RECREATION AREAS

Borderland State Park

See the listing in the Easton section of this chapter.

28 Massapoag Trail

🐾 🐾 (See Charles River Valley map on page 270)

Citified dogs need not worry: they'll never be far from civilization on this enjoyable walk through four miles of residential forest. It even cuts between some homes. We recommend starting at Lake Massapoag and wandering along Massapoag Brook. After about half a mile, just past Mann's Pond, you'll cross Billings Street and walk a short block on the sidewalk before picking up the trail again. The best portion of the trail ends at Devil's Rock, another half mile farther. The path then becomes indistinct in some spots, trashy in others. But it offers leashed dogs a chance to explore some of the hidden paths of Sharon while getting some fresh air and exercise.

The trailhead is on the northeast shoreline of Lake Massapoag at the intersection of Beach Street, East Street, Massapoag Avenue, and Pond Street. Parking is available off Pond Street, across from Sharon High School. The trail terminates at the intersection of Stonybrook and Winslow Roads, just off North Main Street/Route 27. Parking is available there. Open dawn–dusk. 781/784-1511.

29 Sharon Dog Park

🐾 🐾 🐾 🐕 (See Charles River Valley map on page 270)

Don't judge a book by its cover is the best way to describe this latest and greatest dog park. That's because you have to proceed past an abandoned building, the swamp, and enough "this way to dog park" signs to paper a litter box several times over. But perseverance is rewarded because once you arrive, you'll find one of the best dog parks around. Opened in 2004 and located on the wooded side of Deborah Sampson park, this one-acre off-leash area is surrounded by a lush forest to provide shade and plenty of open area for ball throwing. There are water bowls and folding chairs (no benches yet!) and so far, the park has been a local success. There is even a separate area for small dogs. Eventually, there are plans to link this park to the Massapoag Trail, providing you and your pup with a terrific place to kick up your heels. The dog park is located towards the back of the park, near the skateboard park.

Take Route 128 to Route 95 South. Take Exit 10/Coney Street onto Route 27 to Sharon Center. Take a right onto South Main Street, and the first left onto East Foxboro Street. Proceed a quarter mile to the park. Parking is on the left opposite the ball fields. Open dawn–dusk. 781/784-1530; www.sharondogpark.org

PLACES TO EAT

Crescent Ridge Dairy Bar: Don't you hate it when you have a craving for grapefruit ice cream and just can't find it anywhere? If you're in the mood, head for the working farm at Dairy Ridge and get some to enjoy at the picnic tables. For those who've never had grapefruit ice cream, it tastes like—well, like you would imagine. Next time we'll stick to plain ol' chocolate. 355 Bay Road; 781/784-5892.

Stoughton

PARKS, BEACHES, AND RECREATION AREAS

30 Bird Street Conservation Area

🐾🐾🐾🐾 🐾 (See Charles River Valley map on page 270)

This terrific park is definitely not just for the birds. When you drive to the end of Bird Street, your pup will soon learn that she's in for a "tweet." And you'll find lots to crow about, too. The 450-acre parcel of land can be explored via three main trails: the green and blue trails, which start at the Bird Street entrance, and the orange trail, just off the trailhead at the water tower. All are marked by colors blazed on tree trunks, but they can on occasion be difficult to follow.

If you want to take a short stroll to a great picnic location, hit the blue trail. You'll find it to the right of the trailhead, just past the veteran's memorial plaque. The path leads to Connor's Pond, a clean, clear pool with easy water access and big, flat rocks for sunning or sitting. Your happy dog can dive or wade into the water. Loop back around the pond toward the green trail. The markers are a bit misleading here because they have blue *and* green paint spots; we finally figured out this means that you're on the blue trail and heading for the green trail. In any event, go this way. You will cross the Friberg footbridges, built by Eagle Scouts in 1933 and named for a local family. The entire loop gives hikers a bird's-eye view of the park and takes about half an hour to walk.

Making a larger loop through the park, the green trail also goes by Connor's Pond via Gilbert's Quarry. We always seem to get befuddled on this route; although we've never actually gotten lost (just keep following those markers), there are so many trees with green paint splotches, often leading in opposite directions. Each time we visit we vow that we're going to figure out the logic behind the green trail, but alas, it escapes us. The good news is that we enjoy getting lost on the trail because we always discover new avenues through the park. Those of you who have no trouble will probably think we're hopeless. For the rest, don't say we didn't warn you. This trail—if you do it right—takes about an hour.

The orange trail is the longest, completely encircling the park. You should enjoy the approximately 90 minutes it takes to walk it. Again, don't let those green signposts lead you astray. Just stay the course and ignore them, and you'll make your way through a mossy pine forest, up several hills, and on rocky trails. About half an hour into your walk, you'll reach the exceptionally clean and quiet Welch Pond, a good destination in itself. If you walk the entire trail, you'll eventually wind up at Gilbert's Quarry and, surprise, the green trail. After that, it takes about 15 minutes to return to the veteran's memorial.

Dogs must be leashed on all of the trails. Another drawback is that we occasionally run into those annoying dirt bikers, but they are restricted to the outer edge of the orange trail in the north end of the park by West Street.

From the town center at the intersection of Washington Street/Route 138, Pearl Street, and Canton Street/Route 27, take Washington Street south. Turn right on Plain Street, then left on Morton Street. Make a right on Bird Street and proceed to the end, where you'll find the park. Park on the street. Additional street parking is available at the end of Malcolm Road. To get there, take Marron Avenue south from Bird Street and turn right on Malcolm Road. Open dawn–dusk. 781/341-1300, ext. 262.

Walpole

PARKS, BEACHES, AND RECREATION AREAS

🐾 Francis William Park

🐾🐾 (See Charles River Valley map on page 270)

With manicured fields of grass, winding gravel paths, a small wooded area, and a duck pond, Francis William Park is ideal for a Sunday afternoon stroll. In this quiet setting, locals socialize with one another, children and ducks break bread together, and leashed dogs meet to wag tails and do their circle-and-sniff routines.

Despite its small size and the fact that dogs are prohibited from the duck pond, this park is a popular destination for local canines. Here's the drill: dogs and their human friends hang out on the lawns, then take the quarter-mile trail through the woods to seek out intriguing smells for canine noses.

Some good play spots are also found near the woods and fields on the Washington Street side of the park.

From Route 1, take High Plain Street/Route 27 west and make a right on Old Post Road. Turn left on Wolcott Avenue, follow it around the park, and then head left on Rhoades Avenue. The parking lot on your left is available when there are no church functions. Otherwise, park on the street. Open dawn–dusk. 508/668-6136.

🐾 Spring Brook

🐾 (See Charles River Valley map on page 270)

Begin the short walk by climbing up the grassy ridge that controls the flow of Spring Brook and creates Spring Brook Pond. You and your leashed dog can't walk around the pond, but you can follow the ridge to your right, where you'll find a small, scenic wood and a meadow that's perfect for a picnic and a little doggy playtime.

From Route 1 take High Plain Street/Route 27 west. Turn left on Washington Street. Park on the dirt pullout on the left, just past Stone Street. Open dawn–9 P.M. 508/668-6136.

Town Forest

 (See Charles River Valley map on page 270)

An antsy dog can stretch his legs on the few short trails through this forest, including a section of the Bay Circuit Trail. You'll walk through a dense grove of pine trees not far from the Neponset River. This slow, meandering waterway is difficult to reach because the banks are muddy and lined with thick reeds and grasses. Leash your dogs.

Parking is available at Walpole High School on Common Street when school is not in session. Otherwise, park on the side of the access gate on South Street just east of Washington Street. Open dawn–dusk. 508/668-6136.

PLACES TO EAT

Bristol Square Café: With an outdoor patio overlooking a nearby pond, this cozy café makes having breakfast, lunch, or dinner with your dog much more pleasing. Top selections from the menu are eggs Benedict, a variety of burgers, and Parmesan dinners. 1428 Main Street, in the Bristol Square Mall; 508/668-4342.

Westwood

PARKS, BEACHES, AND RECREATION AREAS

Hale Reservation

(See Charles River Valley map on page 270)

A romp at this 1,200-acre reservation will be a highlight of any dog's trip to Westwood. With myriad trails, ponds, and meadows to sniff out, your pooch will want to return time after time. The good news is that there are over 10 miles of trails to explore. The not-so-good news is that dogs are not allowed around the ponds in the summer, when families buy memberships so they can use the ponds, and children come for the day to swim. No matter, the weather is cooler in the winter, spring, and fall, and chances are good you'll have the place to yourselves then.

Most of the trails lead through a gentle woodland sprinkled with meadows and ponds. The busiest section is around the Cat Rock parking area near the main entrance. This trail leads to Noanet Pond, which is very large (really a lake) and has great beaches along much of the shoreline. If you and your dog want an uninterrupted hike and a little solitude, however, we suggest you head up the road to the trading post parking area. Then follow the Ohio

Trail to Storrow Pond. On the way, you'll pass through a lovely forest and find picnic spots at the pond and Ohio Meadow.

Another favorite spot is up the road at the Strawberry Hill parking area. Take the Strawberry Hill Trail to Powissett Pond, a perfect swimming spot with clean and cool water. Your dog will be in heaven. Surrounding the pond are picnic facilities and open spaces; there's even a forest where you can find some shade. The pond and trail are also accessible from Noanet Woodlands (see the Dover section in this chapter), which abuts the property.

Free maps, which will help guide you on the marked and unmarked trails, are available at the front entrance. Dogs must be leashed.

From I-95, take Exit 16 to High Street/Route 109 west. Turn right on Dover Road. Turn right on Carby Street and proceed into the park. A number of parking lots are available off Carby Street. Open 9 A.M.–dusk. 781/326-1770.

PLACES TO EAT

The Bubbling Brook: After one visit, it's impossible to cross another stream without wanting to return here for a piece of strawberry shortcake or just about any of the items listed on the extensive takeout menu. But don't take our word for it. Just follow the crowds that come from miles around. There are plenty of lunch and dinner specials to choose from and even an ice-cream parlor for dairy-loving dogs. Head out to the picnic tables on the grassy lawn to enjoy your meal. 1652 High Street/Route 109; 781/762-9860.

Wrentham

PARKS, BEACHES, AND RECREATION AREAS

35 Birchwold Farm Conservation Area

🐾🐾🐾 (See Charles River Valley map on page 270)

This is a prime destination for local dogs, and you'll soon learn why. The 80 acres of meadows, forest, and gentle hills are crisscrossed with many trails. Walk to your left or your right from the trailhead. Both paths lead over a small crest and tumble into an expansive meadow. Head across the field toward the fruit trees and explore the orchardlike terrain beyond. Or if your leashed pooch is tired of sniffing trees, go to the left to find more open fields.

For the four-legged wonder who really wants to cover some miles, push on past the power lines, where you can climb rocky ledges or explore back-country trails.

The paths are well trodden, so you won't have any trouble following them. Still, we suggest you look at the map in the open meadow just over the hill from the parking area for more details on the various hikes. The terrain is more or less the same throughout the conservation area, and it won't take long to find the trails that will satisfy your doggy exercise needs.

Be careful of ticks in the spring and fall. These crafty critters really know how to hitch a ride here in the tall grass.

From the town center at the intersection of South Street/Route 1A and East Street/Route 140, take South Street south. Proceed straight onto West Street/ Route 121 and continue for three miles. The park and a large parking area are on the left. Open dawn–dusk. 508/384-5415.

F. Gilbert Hills State Forest

See the listing in the Foxborough section of this chapter.

36 Joe's Rock Conservation Area

🐾🐾🐾 (See Charles River Valley map on page 270)

Named for the towering rock at its center, this conservation area offers a lovely pond, uphill hiking trails, and one of the most beautiful views around from atop Joe's Rock. We recommend coming here just before sunset to sit with the special pooch in your life and watch the glorious display as the sun goes down over the pond. Birchwold Farm is across the street, and you might want to take in both places.

From the parking lot, take the trail to the pond, where you'll have three options. You can veer to the far left for a short walk along the pond. There's a bench to sit on and contemplate in silence, but your dog may feel restless. Choose the trail that lies straight ahead to go along the other side of the pond. A picnic table is available off this trail, but there are few easily accessible entry points to the water here. The path continues to the base of Joe's Rock and back into the woods, ending at a fruit orchard about three-quarters of a mile farther.

The trail to your right is by far the most enjoyable of the three. This path climbs steadily and steeply through the woods and onto the rock, where you can see for miles around. The huge overhanging rock has enough room for you to walk or sit, and you don't need to worry about your dog slipping and falling off. We're certain she'll enjoy sniffing the many nooks and crannies, as George and Inu do. Keep on this trail and it, too, will lead back about half a mile before dead-ending at the privately owned fruit orchard. You can backtrack or take a slightly different path back down to the parking area. Leash your dog.

From the town center at the intersection of South Street/Route 1A and East Street/Route 140, take South Street south. Proceed straight onto West Street/ Route 121 and continue for three miles. The park and a parking area are on the right. Open dawn–dusk. 508/384-5415.

37 Wrentham State Forest

🐾🐾 (See Charles River Valley map on page 270)

The good news is that the trails at this 1,000-acre forest—one of the best state forests we've ever visited—are well marked. The bad news is that you'll have to share some of them with dirt bikers. (Grrrrrr!) The best walk is the Acorn Trail. Follow the blue arrows with the acorn logo and you won't go wrong. It intersects at certain points with the yellow dirt-bike trails, but the deeper you go into the interior (away from busy I-495 and Taunton Street), the farther you'll get from the annoying whine of the motorbikes. This walk is perfect for leashed trailhounds who really want to get out and make a day of it. You'll start at a fairly high elevation and continue uphill at various points. The Warner Trail, which runs from Canton Junction in Massachusetts to Diamond Hill in Rhode Island, links up with the Acorn Trail here. The entire loop takes about 90 minutes.

From I-495 in Plainville, take Exit 14 to Route 1 heading south. Turn right on Old Taunton Street, which leads into Wrentham. You'll see the park just after you cross over I-495. A parking lot is on your left. Open dawn–dusk. 508/543-5850.

PLACES TO EAT

Wampum Corner Drive-Thru: Plenty of outdoor tables are available for doggy diners at this local haunt that serves breakfast, lunch, and ice cream. Located just down the road from two conservation areas, Wampum is a good place to gear up for a hike or relax after one. You can order eggs and coffee in the morning, burgers and fries in the afternoon. 121 South Street; 508/384-7913.

CHAPTER 10

Beyond Beantown

After checking out many of the parks, cafés, and hotels featured in the pre-ceding chapters (not to mention the walks, festivals, and diversions), you and your pup are probably more than pooped. But if you have the energy and desire to explore, you might want to hop back in the car with your trusty canine companion and head out of the state. While researching their book, *The Dog Lover's Companion to New England,* George and Inu discovered hun-dreds of great destinations in all six New England states and feel it's only right to share them with you. Here are a few of their favorites:

Bar Harbor, Maine

Wonderview Motor Lodge: This fabulous motel facility is located on the former estate of mystery writer, Mary Rinehart. And when they say "wonder" view, they mean it. The panorama from atop the hill is simply breathtak-ing. Located less than a mile from town, the shuttle (which is dog friendly) comes right to your door. The rooms are quite large, the service exceptional,

PICK OF THE LITTER—BEYOND BEANTOWN

BEST BEACH
Cape Cod National Seashore, Cape Cod, MA (page 300)

BEST SUMMER CAMP
Camp Gone to the Dogs, Putney, VT (page 302)

BEST PLACE TO STAY
Inn By The Sea, Cape Elizabeth, ME (page 300)

BEST DOG ART
Dog Mountain, Saint Johnsbury, VT (page 303)

and, well, there's that view of Bar Harbor and the islands beyond from your picture window. The rates are quite reasonable given the comfortable accommodations, around $100–220 per night. There is a pet fee of $10 per night or $15 per stay. P.O. Box 25, Bar Harbor, ME 04609; 207/288-3358; website: www .wonderviewinn.com.

While you're here, take a trip into Acadia National Park, one of the most popular parks in the United States. With 200 miles of hiking and carriage trails on over 34,000 acres, you won't have trouble finding a place to kick up your heels. You'll discover plenty of rocky beaches, flat, open hiking areas, dense forests, and even mountains to climb.

At 1,531 feet, Mount Cadillac is a popular destination at sunset, affording 360-degree views from its summit. The peak was named after Antoine de la Mothe Cadillac, a Frenchman who was given Mount Desert Island by Louis XIV in 1688 when France controlled New England, or, as they called it, Acadia. You can drive your own Cadillac up Mount Cadillac or, better yet, climb the peak on a seven-mile trail off Route 3 opposite the entrance to Black Woods Campground.

To help you find the other countless trails and destinations in this popular park, we recommend stopping at the ranger station on your way into Acadia to pick up a park map. The only places off-limits to pups are Sand Beach and any designated lake swimming area; swimming is allowed at any nondesignated area, Aunt Betty's Pond, and along the ocean at the numerous rocky beaches. Leashed dogs are allowed. Day-use admission to the park is $10. Open 24 hours. 207/288-3338.

Cape Cod, Massachusetts

Cape Cod National Seashore: Spanning 40 miles, the Cape Cod National Seashore encompasses most of the endless beaches, sand dunes, salt marshes, and seaside forests between Chatham and Provincetown. The thin peninsula—the elbow-to-hand portion of the Cape Cod arm—is one of the most breathtaking shorelines in the country. This is where the Pilgrims first landed, and the rich history of the seashore also includes the whaling industry, picturesque lighthouses, and tales from the sea.

This end of the Cape is truly beautiful, but it commonly gets high winds and rough seas, especially on the Atlantic Ocean side. The Cape Cod Bay side, the smaller section of the park, is calmer and more protected from the elements. The shoreline is open to all, and designated access points and parking areas make it easier to enjoy the best sections.

Dogs are welcome year-round, but they must be leashed at all times and are not permitted on swimming beaches or on biking and hiking trails. So where can a pooch go? With 40 miles of open beach, there's plenty of room for your dog. He can walk on all beaches that are not part of a lifeguard zone or a posted nesting area and on all fire access roads.

For information or a park map, stop by the Province Lands Visitor Center in Provincetown or the Salt Pond Visitor Center in Eastham, or contact the Cape Cod National Seashore Headquarters at 99 Marconi Site Road, Wellfleet, MA 02667; 508/349-3785; website: www.nps.gov/caco.

If you're planning on staying overnight while visiting The Cape, there are many dog-friendly inns to choose from. To find the one closest to the area you will be staying, check out www.allcapecod.com and look for the pet-friendly icon.

Cape Elizabeth, Maine

Inn By The Sea: This lovely inn is just a few quiet miles south of Portland, Maine, right on the water in Cape Elizabeth. Our friends Beth and Rocky recommended this place to us and we agree—it is a real find. Whether you're on your way up the wild Maine coast or need a weekend getaway only two hours from Boston, this 43-room condo-style hotel will certainly deliver the goods. Each suite includes a kitchenette, living room, and one or two bedrooms. Most have ocean views. Rocky loves the delivered-to-the-room dog biscuits, special pet menu, and all the extra pats he gets from the dog-loving staff. Beth prefers the homemade chocolate chip cookies that are part of the nightly turndown service. For a great morning or afternoon walk, there is access to the beach via a walkway over the wetlands. Suites are $139–449, and there is a two-night minimum stay required on weekends. 40 Bowry Beach Road, Cape Elizabeth, ME 04107; 207/799-3134 or 800/888-4287; website: www.innbythesea.com.

Lincoln, New Hampshire

Lincoln Woods: One of the best destinations for dogs in New England is the White Mountains National Forest—770,000 splendid acres located in mid– and northern New Hampshire. It isn't easy to come up with a single favorite trail in such a vast area, but for sheer variety and scenic beauty, Inu and George confess their favorite doggy haunt is at Lincoln Woods. Once you enter this wonderful wilderness area, you won't need to go anywhere else.

Start at the Lincoln Woods parking area off the Kancamagus Highway/ Route 112, and you'll be on the Lincoln Woods Trail, an old logging road that conveniently runs along the Pemigewasset River. About a mile and a half north you can branch off onto the Osseo and Franconia Ridge Trails, which lead you high into the White Mountains and up onto the spectacular Franconia Ridge. The ridge trail is steep and for experienced hikers, but if you're game, it's definitely worth it.

For a more moderate hike, stay on the Lincoln Woods Trail for another mile and continue east on the Wilderness Trail, which leads you on a lovely walk through forests, streams, and marshes; head north for a picnic at Franconia Falls.

Dogs are allowed off leash on most of the trails as long as they are under voice control at all times. Leashes are required in any public day-use area in the White Mountains, and all vehicles must display a parking pass. The passes cost $5 for a week or $20 for the year and are available from any ranger station or local area business (such as gas stations or convenience stores). At Lincoln Woods, maps, parking permits, and trail information can be obtained at the Lincoln Woods Visitor Center at the main parking area.

From I-93, take Exit 32 at the Kancamagus Highway and head east for 5.5 miles. The trailhead, visitor center, and parking area are on the left. Open 24 hours. 603/528-8721.

Newport, Rhode Island

Sanford-Covell Villa Marina: This elegant 1869 historical landmark offers a rare glimpse of wealthy Newport in the last century. Originally built as a "summer –cottage," this bed-and-breakfast still features a grand staircase rising 35 feet from floor to ceiling, sumptuous wood banisters and balconies, and a sunset view of Naragansett Bay. Some cottage! You are only a short drive from the heart of town and all the many historical and fascinating sights Newport has to offer. Amadeus, the owner's regal standard poodle, will greet you on arrival. There are seven guest rooms and two guest suites. Breakfast is included. Rooms are $85–295. Please inform the management that you will be bringing your dog prior to your arrival. Not all rooms are available to pets. 72 Washington Street, Newport, RI 02840; 401/847-0206; website: www.sanford-covell.com.

Putney, Vermont

A real family vacation: Has the whole world gone to the dogs? Those brown eyes might look at you in disbelief when you tell your pooch that a place like this actually exists: a camp created just for dogs. That's right, dogs and their human companions are happy campers at **Camp Gone to the Dogs,** which is fast becoming a top destination of dog lovers from throughout the country. And it's right here in New England. From the Greater Boston area, you can be blissing out in doggy heaven in about four hours.

Established in 1990, Camp Gone to the Dogs is located on more than 500 acres where you and your dog can hike, swim, and have an all-around fun time together. All activities are optional, so you can go from morning to night until you're dog tired, or relax and let your pooch participate in just a few favorite events. For example, your old dog can learn some new tricks in the tricks class; leap tall obstacles in agility training; enter the tail-wagging, face-kissing, and wienie-retrieving contests; or put on the dog at the weekend costume parade. You can even sign your pup up for square dancing classes. The setting is breathtakingly beautiful, and there are ongoing lectures about canine health, nutrition, special needs, and training problems.

Two week-long full-focus camps are held each year in June and July. A week-long Fall Foliage session takes place in October. At various times of the year, there are weekend sessions focusing on such topics as training, show obedience, and agility. The weekend camps have grown so successful that owner Honey Loring has added weekend sessions in August and July. You must make your reservations far in advance; there is space for 120 humans and 250 dogs, and spots fill up fast.

The cost of a one-week session is $950–1,200 per person and includes all activities and meals. If you stay off-site, $100 is deducted. No more than two dogs per person are allowed. For more information, send a self-addressed stamped envelope to: RR1, Box 958, Putney, VT 05346; 802/387-5673; website: www.camp-gone-tothe-dogs.com.

Saint Johnsbury, Vermont

A nose for art: Yes, George, there really *is* a mountain just for dogs. And all canines are welcome to climb it just because it's there at Stephen Huneck's Gallery at **Dog Mountain.** Located on private land just north of town, you'll feel like the King of the Hill at this 150-acre property surrounding artist Huneck's art gallery and workshop. His commitment to canine visitors means you and your leash-free pooch are invited to explore Dog Mountain's scenic fields, woods, ponds, outdoor sculpture garden, and picnic areas.

Doggy art lovers will also want to visit the gallery with its dog-themed art and furniture inspired by Huneck's Labrador and golden retrievers. Inu's favorite exhibit is the artist's rendering of what really goes on inside your dog's brain. And be sure to check out the Dog Chapel. A beautiful village church designed by Huneck after a near-fatal illness, the chapel is open to all dogs and their owners. Inside there are retriever-styled benches, dog carvings, and even a Labrador with wings on top of the church steeple. The gallery and chapel are open June–October and by appointment in the off-season. The surrounding land is open all year.

From I-93, take Exit 1 to Route 2 west for almost a mile. Turn right onto Spaulding Road for a half mile. The park is on the left. Open Monday–Saturday, 10 A.M.–5 P.M., Sunday 11 A.M.–4 P.M.; 802/748-2700; website: www.huneck.com.

Troy, New Hampshire

The Inn at East Hill Farm: Yes, this is a real farm where you can relax in the shadow of Mount Monadnock or roll up your sleeves and milk the cow while your dog rounds up the sheep. (Okay, just kidding about that last part!) This fabulous complex of cottages and inn rooms is a place the whole family will love—and that includes all four-footed members. All meals and activities are included in the daily or weekly rates. Hiking trails, boat rentals, children's activities, night hikes, and shady picnic spots where you can relax or swim are just some of the fun events waiting for you on a visit here. Dogs are allowed in the upper-floor inn rooms and many of the cottages.

Rates range from $94 daily per person to $625 weekly per person. Dogs are an additional $10 per day and must be leashed while on the property. Monadnock Street, Troy, NH 03465; 603/242-6495 or 800/242-6495; website: www.east-hill-farm.com.

Williamstown, Massachusetts

Jericho Valley Inn: With your own cozy cottage, your dog by your side, and 350 private acres to explore, this lovely inn nestled in the heart of the Berk shire Mountains is about as good as it gets. You'll find plenty of hiking trails on the property, but if that isn't enough, visit nearby Mount Greylock State Reservation (see below) or pop into Williamstown for some window shopping or entertainment.

The main inn includes 12 guest rooms, but dogs are allowed only in the 12 secluded private cottages scattered along the estate. Each cottage features a full kitchen, fireplace, and one–three bedrooms. Prices are $118–258 a night. No extra fee for Fido. 2541 Hancock Road, P.O. Box 239, Williamstown, MA 02167; 413/458-9511 or 800/537-4246; website: www.jerichovalleyinn.com.

Mount Greylock State Reservation: This spectacular park in the Berkshires features the highest point in the Commonwealth—Mount Greylock at 3,491 feet. In 1898, the reservation became Massachusetts' first state park, and local hiking enthusiasts still think this park is one of the best places in all of Massachusetts to stretch your legs. Transcendentalists Ralph Waldo Emerson and Henry David Thoreau were among the many who found inspiration in the 12,500 acres of woods and mountains located here. We think that should be enough for your dog to pack the biscuits and hit the trails, but if you still need a little nudge ....

You can easily spend a day or two hiking, camping, and exploring the terrain. The Appalachian Trail passes through the reservation and is part of an elaborate 45-mile trail system that leads to and around the summit. The Hopper, one of the more popular hiking trails, takes you through a ravine of old-growth spruce trees—some of which are many hundreds of years old. You can reach The Hopper from the summit parking lot by accessing the Overlook Trail directly behind the radio tower.

One of our favorite hikes is the one-mile walk to spectacular March Cataract Falls. Take a picnic and enjoy the rustic beauty of these 30-foot falls (although on summer weekends expect plenty of company!). Both you and your dog may wish to take a plunge in the cool, clean water after your hike. To reach the falls from the Visitor Center, take Rockwell Road up the mountain for 5.5 miles. Go left onto Sperry Road to the parking area and trailhead.

Maps of the entire park are available at the Visitor Center on Rockwell Road, and we recommend you pick one up between 9 A.M.–5 P.M. so as not to miss anything. Dogs must be leashed in all Massachusetts State Parks.

From Route 7 in Lanesborough, take North Main Street north for a half mile. Turn right onto Greylock Road for one mile, then go left onto Rockwell Road into the park. Open sunrise to one half hour past sunset. 413/499-4262.

RESOURCES

24-hour Veterinary Clinics

We were quite surprised to discover that there are only eight 24-hour clinics in the Greater Boston area. Our advice is to know exactly where to go *before* there's an emergency situation. When your pet is sick in the middle of the night, it's scary and bewildering, and chances are you won't have your wits about you, so preparation is always the best solution. What follows is a list of 24-hour animal clinics and where to find them. For those areas that don't have a clinic, we have recommended the nearest one. To be safe, consult your veterinarian about where to get the best care for your dog and know the hours of operation of your regular animal hospital.

BOSTON

Angell Memorial Animal Hospital: The most up-to-date and state-of-the-art facility around, this clinic is open 24 hours a day all year. The emergency room is fully staffed at all times. 350 South Huntington Avenue, Boston, MA 02130; 617/522-7282.

NORTH OF THE HUB

Animal Extra Care: This clinic is open 24 hours a day all year long. 19 Main Street, Wakefield, MA 01880; 617/245-0045 (weekdays 9 A.M.–6 P.M.) or 781/245-0209 (after hours).

WEST OF THE HUB

There are no emergency animal hospitals in the towns listed in this chapter. We recommend going to Boston's Angell Memorial Animal Hospital in the event of an emergency.

SOUTH OF THE HUB

None of the towns featured in this chapter offer emergency animal hospitals. In an emergency, try Angell Memorial Animal Hospital in Boston.

NORTH SHORE

There are no emergency animal hospitals in the towns featured in this chapter. For emergency care, go to Animal Extra Care in Wakefield, in the area North of the Hub.

SOUTH SHORE

Roberts Animal Hospital: Year-round this emergency animal hospital provides 24-hour services. 516 Washington Street, Hanover, MA 02339; 781/826-2306.

MERRIMACK RIVER VALLEY

You'll find no emergency animal hospitals in the towns in this chapter. For emergencies, we recommend the Tufts University School of Veterinary Medicine in North Grafton in the Sudbury River Valley.

SUDBURY RIVER VALLEY

Tufts University School of Veterinary Medicine: This emergency animal clinic is open 24 hours a day year-round. 200 Westboro Road, North Grafton, MA 01536; 508/639-5395.

CHARLES RIVER VALLEY

Animal Emergency Center: This emergency animal clinic is open 24 hours a day year-round. 595 West Center Street, West Bridgewater, MA 02379; 508/580-2515.

Parks and Hiking Trails

DEPARTMENT OF CONSERVATION AND RECREATION'S DIVISION OF URBAN PARKS AND RECREATION

Many Boston-area parks are part of the Metropolitan Parks System, which is run by the Department of Conservation and Recreation's Division of Urban Parks and Recreation (DCR). Dating back to 1893, and formerly known as

the Metropolitan District Commission, this park system was actually the first formal city-park program in the country. Charles Eliot, its visionary founder, created a master plan for maintaining and preserving Boston public spaces; many of his theories guide the DCR to this day. The Boston Parks and Recreation Department, which manages the day-to-day operations of many parks featured in this book, is a branch of the commission.

The DCR administers 16,000 acres, encompassing 34 towns and cities in the Greater Boston area. Its land includes city parks, wildlife reservations, historic monuments, 25 miles of beaches, and other recreation areas. All DCR parks require dogs to be leashed. For more information, contact the commission at 617/727-9547.

LAND CONSERVATION GROUPS

Both private and public organizations within the Commonwealth serve to preserve our precious lands. Most towns have a conservation commission that is designed to protect the community's natural resources, including public water supplies and forests. These commissions help by designating public lands with special open-space zonings that prevent their destruction and by purchasing plots of land and setting them aside for nonharmful recreation.

Private organizations such as the Trustees of Reservations are independent of local governments and rely on memberships and donations of land and money to reach their environmental goals of land and water protection. These organizations have saved thousands and thousands of acres from development and misuse.

Here are some ways for you to ensure that governments and conservation groups continue to work toward providing open spaces for you and your dog:

- Voice your opinion and participate in state and local government discussions on conservation issues.
- Become a member of one or more land conservation associations.
- Let these organizations know that as a member you want to be able to enjoy the parks with your dog. In some areas, these are the last leash-free parks available to us. Make sure the conservation commissions know how much you cherish this freedom. If you don't tell them, they won't know.
- Be very respectful of fragile public lands. Our continued enjoyment of them is a privilege.

The following organizations administer lands that are featured throughout *The Dog Lover's Companion to Boston.*

ESSEX COUNTY GREENBELT ASSOCIATION

This wonderful conservation group has one simple goal: to save land. For almost 30 years, the Essex County Greenbelt Association's efforts have led to the preservation of more than 4,000 acres in the Essex County region. All of these lands have been preserved for the public's use, which includes you and your dog. Your four-footed friend should be especially happy to accompany you to these properties, as (hooray!) there are no leash laws there. Please respect that other people use these areas and pick up after your pet.

We've listed the parks that we feel make for great doggy experiences. Some of the areas we haven't covered include delicate wildlife refuges and bird sanctuaries, marshes and swamps, and some spaces that are just too small to be much fun for your dog. If you'd like maps of all their parks, write for the Passport to the Essex County Greenbelt. And let us know if you feel we have left out any worthwhile lands.

The Essex County Greenbelt Association relies on the support of volunteers and donations. If you would like to become a member or learn more about this organization, contact the group's headquarters at: Cox Reservation, 82 Eastern Avenue, Essex, MA 01929; 978/768-7241; website: www.ecga.org.

THE TRUSTEES OF RESERVATIONS

Founded more than a century ago by Boston Parks founder Charles Eliot, this preservation organization set out to preserve a "museum of the Massachusetts landscape." All of its lands have been given in trust by families, organizations, and cities for future generations to enjoy. In all, the Trustees of Reservations manages more than 75 properties on nearly 18,000 acres throughout the Commonwealth.

Many of the properties are private estates that, while spectacularly beautiful, may not welcome your big, four-footed friend. We have listed the reservations where we think you'll have the best outdoor experience with your dog. Some are wild, untamed places, while others are manicured and cultivated. But all of those featured in the book are to be enjoyed and respected by you and your dog. All reservations are open from dawn to dusk and require dogs to be leashed.

To become a member of this preservation organization or receive a book detailing all of the reservations located throughout Massachusetts, contact: Membership Office, The Trustees of Reservations, 572 Essex Street, Beverly, MA 01915-1530; 978/921-1944; website: www.thetrustees.org.

Other private, nonprofit land conservation groups are listed in the introductions to the specific chapters where their lands appear. For information on the

Wildlands Trust of Southeastern Massachusetts, see the South Shore chapter. You will find a detailed description of the Sudbury Valley Trustees in the Sudbury River Valley chapter. The Andover Village Improvement Society (AVIS) is featured in the Andover section of the Merrimack River Valley chapter.

EXTENDED HIKING TRAILS

The Greater Boston area boasts several trails that cross town and county lines to provide extended hikes for you and your canine companion.

Bay Circuit Trail: The Bay Circuit Trail has been "in the works" since 1929, when it was first proposed as an extension to Boston's Emerald Necklace. The bad news is that this proposed 200-mile long trail, linking parks and reservations between Plum Island on the North Shore and Kingston Bay on the South Shore, has experienced many delays. The good news is that almost 150 miles have been completed - the most recent in 2006 when 15 miles between Hanson and Pembroke were completed. A new bike trail between Acton and Lowell is scheduled to break ground in late 2006. Dogs and hikers are welcome on the portions that have been completed.

The trail runs through towns listed in the North Shore, South Shore, Merrimack River Valley, Sudbury River Valley, and Charles River Valley chapters. We also note specific parks that include the Bay Circuit Trail in individual listings. For more information, contact the Bay Circuit Alliance, 3 Railroad Street, Andover, MA 01810; 978/470-1982; website: www.baycircuit.org.

Merrimack River Trail: Rolling along—and at times across—the Merrimack River, this trail leads from the New Hampshire border to Newburyport on the Atlantic Ocean. The route switches back and forth from the south side to the north side of the river; in some areas, it traverses both shorelines, and in other sections the trail is incomplete. Whether you and your dog head out for a big riverside excursion or a quick trip to the water's edge, the Merrimack is always impressive.

Towns that access the trail and the river are featured in the North Shore and Merrimack River Valley chapters. The Merrimack River Watershed Council, which manages the trail, is involved in preserving the river and the green spaces along it. It also publishes a trail guidebook. For details, contact the council at 694 Main Street, West Newbury, MA 01985; 978/681-5777; website: www.merrimack.org.

Two other notable trails cover lands in *The Dog Lover's Companion to Boston*. The Minuteman Bike Trail is described in the West of the Hub chapter, and the Warner Trail is detailed in the Charles River Valley chapter.

Travel Tidbits—
Useful Contact Information

BOSTON: THE OLDE TOWNE

Angell Memorial Animal Hospital/Massachusetts Society for the Prevention of Cruelty to Animals: Open 24 hours, this fully equipped hospital is the place to go in an emergency. The staff is knowledgeable and kind, and they'll help you stay calm if your dog needs emergency treatment. It's administered by the Massachusetts Society for the Prevention of Cruelty to Animals. 350 South Huntington Avenue, Boston, MA 02130. Emergencies, 617/522-7282; appointments, 617/522-6005; office, 617/522-7400; website: angell.org.

Department of Conservation: 20 Somerset Street, Boston, MA 02108. Main office, 617/727-5250; Boston Department of Parks and Recreation, 617/635-4505.

Greater Boston Convention & Visitors Bureau: For information regarding hours and special events in Boston, contact the bureau. Prudential Tower, P.O. Box 990468, Boston, MA 02199; 617/536-4100 or 800/888-5515 (outside Massachusetts).

Massachusetts Bay Transportation Authority: Customer Service Department, Transportation Building, 10 Park Plaza, Boston, MA 02116; 617/722-5215.

Massachusetts Department of Environment Management: Division of

Forests and Parks, Greater Boston Regional Headquarters, 100 Cambridge Street, 19th floor, Boston, MA 02202; 617/727-3180.

The Trustees of Reservations: Greater Boston Regional Office, Bradley Reservation, 2468B Washington Street, Canton, MA 02021; 617/821-2977.

NORTH OF THE HUB

Department of Conservation: North Region, 1 Woodland Road, Stoneham, MA 02180; 781/662-5230.

Friends of the Fells: P.O. Box 560057, West Medford, MA 02156; 781/627-7402.

Massachusetts Department of Environment Management: Division of Forests and Parks, Greater Boston Regional Headquarters, 100 Cambridge Street, 19th floor, Boston, MA 02202; 617/727-3180.

The Trustees of Reservations: Greater Boston Regional Office, Bradley Reservation, 2468B Washington Street, Canton, MA 02021; 781/821-2977.

WEST OF THE HUB

Department of Conservation: North Region, 1 Woodland Road, Stoneham, MA 02180; 781/662-5230.

Massachusetts Department of Environment Management: Division of Forests and Parks, Greater Boston Regional Headquarters, 100 Cambridge Street, 19th floor, Boston, MA 02202; 617/727-3180.

The Trustees of Reservations: Greater Boston Regional Office, Bradley Reservation, 2468B Washington Street, Canton, MA 02021; 781/821-2977.

SOUTH OF THE HUB

Department of Conservation: South Region, 695 Hillside Street, Milton, MA 02186; 617/698-1802.

Massachusetts Department of Environment Management: Division of Forests and Parks, Greater Boston Regional Headquarters, 100 Cambridge Street, 19th floor, Boston, MA 02202; 617/727-3180.

The Trustees of Reservations: Greater Boston Regional Office, Bradley Reservation, 2468B Washington Street, Canton, MA 02021; 781/821-2977.

NORTH SHORE

Essex County Greenbelt Association: 82 Eastern Avenue, Essex, MA 01929; 978/768-7241.

Massachusetts Department of Environment Management: Division of Forests and Parks, Greater Boston Regional Headquarters, 100 Cambridge Street, 19th floor, Boston, MA 02202; 617/727-3180.

The Trustees of Reservations: Northeast Regional Office, Castle Hill, P.O. Box 563, Ipswich, MA 01938; 978/356-4351.

SOUTH SHORE

Massachusetts Department of Environment Management: Division of Forests and Parks, Region 1 Headquarters, P.O. Box 66, South Carver, MA 02366; 508/866-2580.

The Trustees of Reservations: Greater Boston Regional Office, Bradley Reservation, 2468B Washington Street, Canton, MA 02021; 781/821-2977.

Wildlands Trust of Southeastern Massachusetts (Plymouth County Wildlands Trust): P.O. Box 2282, Duxbury, MA 02331; 781/934-9018.

MERRIMACK RIVER VALLEY

Essex County Greenbelt Association: 82 Eastern Avenue, Essex, MA 01929; 978/768-7241.

Massachusetts Department of Environment Management: Division of Forests and Parks, Greater Boston Regional Headquarters, 100 Cambridge Street, 19th floor, Boston, MA 02202; 617/727-3180.

The Trustees of Reservations: Greater Boston Regional Office, Bradley Reservation, 2468B Washington Street, Canton, MA 02021; 781/821-2977.

SUDBURY RIVER VALLEY

Massachusetts Department of Environment Management: Division of Forests and Parks, Greater Boston Regional Headquarters, 100 Cambridge Street, 19th floor, Boston, MA 02202; 617/727-3180.

Sudbury Valley Trustees: P.O. Box 7, Wayland, MA 01778; 508/443-6300.

The Trustees of Reservations: Central Regional Office, Doyle Reservation, 325 Lindell Avenue, Leominster, MA 01453; 978/840-4446.

CHARLES RIVER VALLEY

Massachusetts Department of Environment Management: Division of Forests and Parks, Region 1 Headquarters, P.O. Box 66, South Carver, MA 02366; 508/866-2580.

The Trustees of Reservations: Greater Boston Regional Office, Bradley Reservation, 2468B Washington Street, Canton, MA 02021; 781/821-2977.

INDEXES

Accommodations Index

Restaurant Index

General Index

UVWXYZ

Acknowledgments

The authors would like to thank the dog constables, conservation commissioners, parks and recreation directors, and town clerks and officials who proved to be indispensable in the writing of this book. More than half of the parks listed herein are located on conservation lands not detailed on most public maps, so we especially appreciate the hard work of the conservation commissioners and the many volunteers who made the maps, tended the trails, and answered our endless questions about these beautiful parks.

We are particularly grateful to Barbara Castleman of the Massachusetts Society for the Prevention of Cruelty to Animals and Ted Clarke of the Animal Rescue League for their assistance in helping us find the information we needed and directing us to the people who could answer our questions.

Special thanks to Maria Goodavage, who graciously contributed material to the introduction.

Keeping Current

Be a Travel Hound. If we've missed your favorite park, beach, café, hotel, or pooch permissible activity, please let us know. You'll help countless dogs get more enjoyment out of life in the Boston area. We welcome your comments about *The Dog Lover's Companion to Boston.* Please write to Avalon Travel Publishing, 1400 65th Street, Suite 250, Emeryville, CA 94608, or send us an email at atpfeedback@avalonpub.com. Visit our website at www.dogloverscompanion.com.

ALSO FROM
AVALON TRAVEL PUBLISHING

AVAILABLE AT BOOKSTORES AND THROUGH ONLINE BOOKSELLERS

Rick Steves®

More Savvy. More Surprising.
More Fun.

As the #1 authority on European travel, Rick gives you the inside information on what to visit, where to stay, and how to get there—economically and hassle-free.

www.ricksteves.com

MOON

With expert writers delivering a mix of honest insight, first-rate strategic advice, and an essential dose of humor, Moon Guidebooks ensure that travelers and adventurers have an uncommon experience—and a few new stories to tell.

www.moon.com

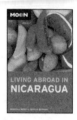

ROAD TRIP USA
OPEN ROAD. ENDLESS POSSIBILITIES.

See what the interstates have left behind. **ROAD TRIP USA** takes you off the beaten path, onto classic blacktop, and into the soul of America.

www.roadtripusa.com

The Dog Lover's Companion

The Inside Scoop on Where to Take Your Dog

A special breed of guidebook for travelers and residents who don't want to leave their canine pals behind.

www.dogloverscompanion.com

www.travelmatters.com